PERICLES

THE GARLAND
SHAKESPEARE BIBLIOGRAPHIES
(General Editor: William Godshalk)
Number 13

GARLAND REFERENCE LIBRARY
OF THE HUMANITIES
Volume 424

The Garland
Shakespeare Bibliographies
William Godshalk, *General Editor*

Number 1:
King Lear
   compiled by Larry S. Champion

Number 2:
Four Plays Ascribed to Shakespeare
Edward III
Sir Thomas More
Cardenio
The Two Noble Kinsmen
   compiled by G. Harold Metz

Number 3:
Cymbeline
   compiled by Henry E. Jacobs

Number 4:
Henry V
   compiled by Joseph Candido
   and Charles R. Forker

Number 5:
King Henry VI
Parts 1, 2, and 3
   compiled by Judith Hinchcliffe

Number 6:
Love's Labor's Lost
   compiled by Nancy Lenz Harvey
   and Anna Kirwan Carey

Number 7:
Hamlet in the 1950s
   compiled by Randal F. Robinson

Number 8:
As You Like It
   compiled by Jay L. Halio
   and Barbara C. Millard

Number 9:
Merchant of Venice
   compiled by Thomas Wheeler

Number 10:
Timon of Athens
   compiled by John J. Ruszkiewicz

Number 11:
Richard III
   compiled by James A. Moore

Number 12:
A Midsummer Night's Dream
   compiled by D. Allen Carroll
   and Gary Jay Williams

Number 13:
Pericles
   compiled by Nancy C. Michael

PERICLES
An Annotated Bibliography

Nancy C. Michael

GARLAND PUBLISHING, INC. • NEW YORK & LONDON
1987

Library of Congress Cataloging-in-Publication Data

Michael, Nancy C., 1942–
Pericles, An Annotated Bibliography.

(The Garland Shakespeare Bibliographies; no. 13)
(Garland Reference Library of the Humanities; v. 424)
Includes index.
1. Shakespeare, William, 1564–1616.   Pericles—
Bibliography.   I. Title.   II. Series.   III. Series:
Garland Reference Library of the Humanities; vol. 424.

Z8812.P47M5   1987   [PR2830]   016.8223′3   87-17295
ISBN 0-8240-9113-2 (alk. paper)

Printed on acid-free, 250-year-life paper
Manufactured in the United States of America

Dedicated to the memory of
Henry E. Jacobs
1946–1986

CONTENTS

Preface, *William Godshalk*   ix

Introduction   xi

    I. CRITICISM   3

    II. SOURCES, ANALOGUES, AND BACKGROUND   113

    III. DATING   133

    IV. AUTHORSHIP AND TEXTUAL STUDIES   135

    V. BIBLIOGRAPHIES AND CONCORDANCES   169

    VI. EDITIONS   173

    VII. STAGE HISTORY & RECORDED PERFORMANCES   197

    VIII. ADAPTATIONS, INFLUENCES, SYNOPSES, AND EXCERPTS   239

Index   247

PREFACE

In 1978 Lawrence Davidow, then Acquisitions Editor at Garland Publishing, invited me to edit a series of annotated bibliographies surveying Shakespeare scholarship published from 1940 until the present. Major contributions published before that period would also be included. We planned that each bibliography would be as comprehensive as possible, fully annotated, cross-referenced, and thoroughly indexed. Each would be divided into major sections that indicate the dominant critical and scholarly concerns of the play being discussed; these large divisions would be subdivided if such subdivision might be useful to the reader. The general format would thus have to remain flexible so that the form of each bibliography could reflect its contents. Although the authors would be presented with copies of our "Tentative Guidelines," we rejected a rigorous conformity to a style sheet in favor of humane, scholarly decisions based on individual perceptions and requirements. We desired a fairly uniform series of high quality, but we did not want to stifle creative initiative.

We emphasized that we wished complete surveys of current knowledge and critical opinion presented in such a way that the reader could retrieve that information rapidly and easily. To help the reader sift through large quantities of material, each bibliography would contain an Introduction that would trace briefly the history of recent criticism and research, as well as indicate new areas to be explored, if such areas had become apparent during the author's work on the project. Finally, the Introduction would make clear any special decisions made or procedures followed by the author in compiling and ordering his or her bibliography.

These were our plans, which now come to fruition in the individual bibliographies of the plays. We wish to thank all those who made this series possible, especially Ralph Carlson, Pam Chergotis, and Julia Johnson. Perhaps, however, our greatest thanks must go to the authors themselves, who, during the frequent meetings of the Garland Shakespeare Authors, came to act as a board of editors. Many of the most difficult questions confronting the series were raised and answered at those meetings. And, of course, we must acknowledge with thanks the hard work that went into the compiling, reading, and writing done by our authors.

October 9, 1980   W. L. GODSHALK
                                                  University of Cincinnati
                                                  General Editor

INTRODUCTION

New to the stage in 1606 or 1608, *Pericles* pleased
audiences as much as had *Richard 3*, *Romeo and Juliet*, and
Hamlet. As the six quarto editions published between 1609
and 1635 and contemporary allusions attest, its popularity
continued until 1642 when the theatres were closed. At the
Restoration in 1660, *Pericles* was the first performed of
Shakespeare's plays. However, when Shakespeare's plays
became the objects of stage revision and closet analysis in
the eighteenth century, *Pericles* lost its popularity and its
place in the canon as well, becoming by the end of the
century one of the least known and performed of Shakespeare's
plays, as it remains today. Consequently, the writings on
Pericles assembled would fill no more than a short library
shelf or two. Moreover, the critics, poets, and scholars who
have written about the play have done so chiefly from motives
that more concern Shakespeare than *Pericles*. Without
Shakespeare's name the play would attract next to no one.
   William Shakespeare's name, however, has always been a
part of *Pericles*. The name appears on the title pages of the
six quartos, each subsequent quarto derived from the first
quarto of 1609 (referred to hereafter as the Quarto).
Because it is the only substantive text and of poor quality,
the Quarto lies at the heart of the *Pericles* problem.
Despite the title page attributions and for reasons
unexplained, Hemings and Condell did not include the play in
the First Folio (1623). The corruptions of the Quarto and
the exclusion of *Pericles* from the Folio, of course, bring
the authorship in question. Indeed, *Pericles* did not enter a
Folio until the second issue of the Third Folio (1664), where
it was included along with six spurious attributions:
Locrine, *Sir John Oldcastle*, *Thomas Lord Cromwell*, *The London
Prodigal*, *The Puritan*, and *A Yorkshire Tragedy*. The play
also appeared in the Fourth Folio (1635) and in Nicholas
Rowe's three editions (1709; 1719), but Pope, Johnson, and
Capell, among others, left *Pericles* out of their editions
because they thought Shakespeare wrote little of it. Edmond
Malone included *Pericles* as a work partly by Shakespeare in

his 1780 Supplement to Steevens' 1778 edition of
Shakespeare's plays. In commenting on the mangled Quarto
text, he says that the fault rests more with the printer than
the poet (item 390).

Nineteenth-century scholars in the new science of
bibliography attempted to identify Shakespearean passages
with metrical tests involving patterns of grammar, prosody,
and diction and the identification and comparison of parallel
passages. Nicolaus Delius, F. G. Fleay, and Elimar Klebs
variously assigned parts of the play to lesser dramatists
Heywood, Rowley, and Wilkins (items 391-92, 339). George
Wilkins is most often proposed either as the original author
or as Shakespeare's major collaborator. Further complicating
the authorship question is Wilkins' "true History of the
Play," a novel entitled *The Painfull Aduentures of Pericles
Prince of Tyre*, published in 1608, the same year
Shakespeare's company entered *Pericles* in the Stationers'
Register and a year before the Quarto appeared (item 353).
In the mid-1970s, one hundred years after the initial
authorship tests of Delius, Fleay, and Klebs, literary
investigators began using computers to determine whether or
not one author wrote all of *Pericles*. Those conducting
computerized word-frequency tests, called stylometric
analysis, include A.Q. Morton (items 466, 481), G. Harold
Metz (items 469, 484), and M.W.A. Smith (items 473, 475-77,
482-83).

Questions of text and authorship continue to engage
twentieth-century critics, poets, scholars, and stage
directors, most of whom consider *Pericles* Shakespeare's work
either entirely or in part. No one thinks it a major play,
however splendid some of the poetry. Thus, *Pericles* remains
a minor work fraught with major problems of author and text.
Scholar and critics interested in the problems as well as the
play concentrate on the Quarto. In 1909 A. W. Pollard
labelled the Quarto "bad" (item 394), and in 1930 E. K.
Chambers spoke of it as the corrupt product of mixed
authorship (item 399). But since the 1940s Hardin Craig and
Kenneth Muir have separately argued that the Quarto is
"good," the result of Shakespeare's revision of a lost play
by Wilkins, and that the Quarto and *The Painfull Aduentures*
contain evidence of an *Ur-Pericles* (items 11, 364, 407-8,
427, 508, 559; 63, 185, 272, 348, 353, 360, 383, 426). Sina
Spiker, Philip Edwards, and Nancy Michael contend that
Wilkins wrote none of *Pericles*; instead, they suggest that
Wilkins concocted the "History of the Play" illegally to cash
in on the popularity of *Pericles*, supplementing his spotty
memory of a stage performance with passages from Laurence
Twine's *Patterne of Painefull Adventures*, which happens to be

one of the two major sources for the play (Spiker, 1933, item
400; Edwards, 1952, item 413; Michael, 1977, item 463).
  Working exclusively from bibliographic-textual evidence,
Philip Edwards advanced a new theory in 1952 (item 413).
Arguing foremost that the Quarto is indeed "bad," he proposed
that the textual irregularities result from two reporters,
one responsible for acts 1-2, another for acts 3-5, and that
three compositors in two printing shops compounded the
errors. Edwards' evidence of reportorial and compositional
corruption suggests that Shakespeare alone wrote *Pericles*.
Craig and Muir, however, disagree that the Quarto is "bad"
and consider the evidence for two reporters insufficient to
explain stylistic differences between acts 1-2 and acts 3-5.
For New Cambridge editor J. C. Maxwell, who agreed with
Edwards that the Quarto is "bad," *Pericles* remained
nevertheless a play of mixed authorship (item 513). S.
Musgrove argued in a 1978 analysis that the first half of the
Quarto derives from Shakespeare's foul papers and the second
half from reported copy (item 467). Like Craig and Muir,
Musgrove thinks that Wilkins wrote the original part of
Pericles (acts 1-2) and that Shakespeare later revised
Wilkins' half and added acts 3-5. In 1982, F. D. Hoeniger,
editor of the Arden *Pericles* (item 528), departed from his
earlier textual studies (items 425, 528) to argue that
differences between acts 1-2 and acts 3-5 reflect Gower's
narrative style versus Shakespeare's dramatic style (item
472). *Pericles* is now for Hoeniger a unique theatrical
experiment by Shakespeare alone (items 457, 472).
  The problems of text and authorship, far from solution,
may actually be incapable of solution, according to Edwards,
given the corrupt Quarto. Yet some scholars remain convinced
that the problems of *Pericles* are either irrelevant, as does
A. L. Rowse (item 567), or fabricated, as does J. P. Cutts
(items 116-17, 376, 424, 428). James O. Wood often argues
that the Quarto is correct and represents Shakespeare's
partial revision of his own early play (items 432, 436-37,
441, 450-51, 455, 464, 471).
  Fortunately, not all matters of *Pericles* are as difficult
of solution as the problem of the Quarto text. The play is
easily dated, if not precisely, thanks to external evidence.
Mention of a performance in *The Calendar of State Papers*
indicates that *Pericles* may have been staged as early as 1606
and no later than 1608, the year it was entered in the
Stationers' Register and George Wilkins published *The
Painfull Aduentures* (item 387).
  Along with textual investigations, source studies provide
an approach to the play. One of scores of versions of the
Apollonius of Tyre legend, *Pericles* has two major sources,

book 8 of John Gower's *Confessio Amantis* (1393) and Laurence Twine's *Patterne of Painefull Adventures* (c. 1594; 1607). The *Confessio* is the main source, as the plot of the play, numerous paraphrased passages, and the eight Gower choruses attest. The three brothel scenes in act 4 and smaller touches throughout the play show Twine's lesser influence. H. Dugdale Sykes argued in 1919 that Wilkins' *Painfull Aduentures* is the chief source for *Pericles* (item 395), but it is now generally agreed that Wilkins based his novel on the play. Kenneth Muir and Hardin Craig have suggested that an *Ur-Pericles* served as a source for *Pericles*, but no external evidence supports their claims (Muir, items 185, 348, 353, 360, 383, 426; Craig, items 407, 427, 508). Bertrand Evans' proposal in 1955 that Wilkins' novel and *Pericles* may stem from a lost narrative poem also lacks external evidence (item 354). The chief sources for *Pericles* remain Gower's *Confessio Amantis* and Twine's *Patterne of Painefull Adventures*.

Other sources are the first three books of Sidney's *Arcadia* (1590) and declamation 53 from Lazarus Piot's 1596 translation of *The Orator* by Alexander Silvayn (A. van den Busche). Each work has been argued as source and analogue. With its shipwrecks, separations, and knightly adventures, Sidney's story of Pyrocles is similar to that of Pericles. Silvayn's narrative, which resembles parts of Marina's and Thaisa's stories in acts 3-5, tells of a woman abducted by pirates and sold to a brothel where she kills an assailant; later she is tried, acquitted, and eventually becomes an abbess. Some scholars have proposed 2 Maccabees 9 as the source of the Gower Chorus's gruesome description of the deaths of Antiochus and his daughter; others have proposed Plutarch's *Moralia*. Various emblem books have been cited as the sources of the knights' devices and mottos in act 2. Percy Simpson considers Plautus' *Rudens* an analogue to acts 3-5 (item 356), and Peggy Ann Knapp suggests the Orpheus myth as a *Pericles* analogue (item 377).

The names and dispositions of the characters have received attention in source and analogue studies as well. In 1895 Samuel Singer proposed that the Prince's name may be a variation of Sidney's Pyrocles (item 337), but according to J.M. Tompkins, both name and character derive from Plutarch's Pericles of Athens (item 351). For Thelma N. Greenfield, the Prince is Plutarch's riddle-solving scholar but without his namesake's patience (item 367). Kenneth Muir thinks that Shakespeare may have taken the name Marina from Cortes' interpreter, an Indian girl sold into slavery by her mother before achieving high station among the Spanish adventurers (item 361). And according to A. F. Potts, Satyrane, tamed by

Una in Spenser's *Faerie Queene* (1.6), may have influenced the
portrayal of Lysimachus in act 4 (item 362).
    Pericles criticism before the latter part of the
nineteenth century is almost as scarce as stage productions.
The earliest mention of the play, in the anonymous *Pimlyco or
Runne Red-Cap* (1609), attests to its one-time popularity:

> Amazde I stood, to see a Crowd
> of *Ciuill Throats* stretched out so lowd;
> (As at a New-play) all the Roomes
> Did swarme with *Gentiles* mix'd with *Groomes*,
> So that I truly thought all These
> Came to see *Shore* or *Pericles*.

The earliest critical comment, that of Ben Jonson in "Ode to
Himself," has proved harshest:

> No doubt some mouldy tale
>   Like *Pericles*; and stale
> As the Shrivues crusts, and nasty as his fish--
>   scraps, out [of] euery dish,
> Throwne forth, and rak't into the common tub,
>   May keep vp the *Play-club*. . . .

The vituperation signals Jonson's outrage that his own
comedy, *The New Inn* (1629), failed to please London
audiences. Almost everyone has liked *Pericles* better than
Jonson did; nevertheless, many subsequent critics express a
sense that the text, or the art of the play, or both, are
flawed. Dryden wrote in his prologue to Davenant's *Circe*
(1677):

> Shakespear's own Muse his *Pericles* first bore,
> The Prince of Tyre was elder than the *Moore*:
> 'Tis miracle to see a first good Play
> All Hawthorns do not bloom on Xmas-day. . . .

He does not say why he thought Shakespeare wrote *Pericles*
"first," thus before *Titus Andronicus*. In such case,
however, "the *Moore*" is more likely Aaron than Othello.
Perhaps the remark is based on something Davenant told him
about Shakespeare, or perhaps it reflects Dryden's own
assessment of the play.
    By 1738 dramatist George Lillo, who adapted *Pericles* into
Marina for a Covent Garden audience (item 791), expressed in
his prologue the general eighteenth-century editorial opinion that
Pericles is not good enough to be Shakespeare's alone:

        We dare not charge the whole unequal play
        Of Pericles on him; yet let us say,
        As gold though mix'd with baser matter shines,
        So do his bright unimitable lines
        Throughout those rude wild scenes distinguish'd
           stand,
        And shew he touch'd them with no sparing hand.

Coleridge, too, in the nineteenth century, thought *Pericles* a
partial revision by Shakespeare of someone else's play (item
1). The paucity of stage productions and critical commentary
from the eighteenth century until the middle of the
nineteenth century, as well as the gist of what little was
said, indicate a widespread perception lasting over 250 years
of *Pericles* as a peripheral play of doubtful authorship.
     Biographical approaches to Shakespeare in the second half
of the nineteenth century and concomitant attempts to put the
canon into chronological order led to the twentieth-century
critical practice of categorizing Shakespeare's plays in
homogeneous clusters. Thus *Pericles*, heretofore treated
separately as a work of contested authorship, became one of
Shakespeare's "last plays," comedies written according to
Edward Dowden in *Shakspere: A Critical Study of His Mind and
Art* (1875) in the "serene wisdom" of Shakespeare's final
years. Dowden scarcely mentioned *Pericles*, but he began the
fashion of grouping *Pericles* (1609), *Cymbeline* (1610), *The
Winter's Tale* (1611), and *The Tempest* (1612), with *Henry 8*
(1613) and *The Two Noble Kinsmen* (1613) adjunctive, as the
"last plays." As the initial play in the group, *Pericles* has
received considerably more critical and theatrical attention
than either *Henry 8* or *The Two Noble Kinsmen*, both known
collaborations in good texts and the former a Folio play.
While few objected to Dowden's grouping, Lytton Strachey
disvalued it. In his essay "Shakespeare's Final Period"
(1904), this son of Victorian eminence and iconoclast to
fathers and their household gods declared that Shakespeare
was bored with everything except poetry when he wrote the
"miserable archaic fragment" *Pericles* (item 4). Thus, rather
than upending the impressionistic technique of his elders,
Strachey expressed the opposite opinion.
     As well as aesthetics, the new social sciences of the
nineteenth century influenced Shakespeare studies. The
interest in myth and ritual occasioned by the archaeological
and psychological excavations of Heinrich Schliemann and
Sigmund Freud in the nineteenth century and by Lord Carnarvon
and Sir James George Frazer in the twentieth affected
biographic and literary criticism as profoundly as
descriptive bibliography affected textual analysis. The

generation of critics writing between the two world wars
interpreted the plays as chapters in Shakespeare's spiritual
biography. The "last plays" too were read symbolically.
Influential interpretations in the 1930s with chapters on
Pericles include G. Wilson Knight's *The Shakespearian Tempest*
(item 6) and D. G. James's *Skepticism and Poetry* (item 7).
Knight and James interpreted the last plays, from Christian
and secular viewpoints respectively, as high points in the
spiritual allegory Shakespeare carried out in his plays. For
Knight, Shakespeare's parable in the last plays, the journey
from tempest to harmony, succeeds as revealed Christian
truth. For James, the myth of finding what is lost fails
because it remains secular. In *Shakespeare's Last Plays*
(1938), E. M. W. Tillyard opposed spiritual interpretation
with aesthetics, countering that in Shakespeare's plays the
evolving theme of tragic art (that of prosperity,
destruction, and regeneration) which culminates in *Cymbeline*,
The Winter's Tale, and *The Tempest*, mirrors life itself, not
Shakespeare's merely. Tillyard left *Pericles* out of his
study, cautioning others that themes discovered in such a
flawed play might exist outside Shakespeare's control (item
8).
　　Thematic readers of the last plays from the 1940s to the
present, who, despite Tillyard, more often than not included
Pericles in their interpretations, continued to base their
patterns of discovery on religion and aesthetics. In *The
Crown of Life* (1947), Knight treated *Cymbeline*, *The Winter's
Tale*, *The Tempest*, and *Henry 8*, with *Pericles* the precursor,
as poetic parables, again interpreting the imagery of
voyages, tempests, and shipwrecks as Christian emblems of
birth, death, and resurrection (item 14). In 1954 Derek
Traversi published an equally influential reading,
Shakespeare: The Last Phase, in which he said that paired
images of birth and death and of tempest and calm in the last
plays translate the families separated and reunited to a
higher world (item 34). Traversi and most interpreters of
the last plays think *Pericles* important as the forerunner of
greater plays. For Traversi in particular, the imperfections
of the play show the pains Shakespeare took to shape from
another's inferior and idiosyncratic work the pattern of
separation, suffering, and reunion refined in subsequent
plays.
　　In 1958, four years after Traversi published his book,
Philip Edwards spoke against symbolic interpretations in his
assessment of critical trends, "Shakespeare's Romances:
1900-57" (item 48), calling it "a disservice to Shakespeare
to pretend that one is adding to his profundity by
discovering that his plots are symbolic vehicles for ideas

and perceptions which are, for the most part, banal, trite
and colourless" (p. 11). Nevertheless, the majority of
critics of *Pericles*, *Cymbeline*, *The Winter's Tale*, and *The
Tempest* continue to discover themes, usually variations on
the birth, death, and rebirth cycle favored by spiritual and
aesthetic interpreters. History, philosophy, anthropology,
psychoanalysis, and sociology provide the models with which
to trace paradigms of James's court, Platonism, rites of
passage, father-daughter relationships, and metapoetry.
Pericles interpreters have abstracted numerous themes from
the setting, plot, and characters, including court-versus-
country, sin, banishment, faith, feasting, incest, harmony,
grace, forgiveness, resurrection, and Shakespeare's self-
conscious artistry.

The largest branch of thematics, character analysis,
often interprets *Pericles* through its father and daughter.
Pericles and Marina are examined as patterns of patience,
although the opposite is sometimes argued of the Prince.
Those who find the play spiritual analyze either the degree
of Pericles' sainthood or his sinfulness. Thematic criticism
abstracts Pericles, who sometimes remains impassive and other
times rages, into one extreme or another--patient or
impatient, saint or sinner, passive or active. Readings of
Marina are more consistent. Most critics consider her the
forerunner and counterpart to the progression of youthful
heroines in the other three romances: Imogen, Perdita, and
Miranda. Whether she is treated alone or in conjunction with
other heroines, interpretive critics abstract her into
personified virtue, the badge of which is her innocent and
militant chastity, either of which or both may be emphasized.

Marina, it should also be remembered, has drawn literary
artists as well as literary critics into her charmed circle.
Lillo recreated her as the title character of his adaptation
(item 791), and T. S. Eliot made her the informing spirit of
his lyric, "Marina" (item 796). Whereas Lillo's play
concerns Marina's defense of her virtue, Eliot's poem is
haunted by the daughter long lost to her wandering father.
Pericles and Marina's relationship as father and daughter
remains for literary critics the more popular subject of
interpretation, whether the approach is spiritual, aesthetic,
or psychoanalytical.

But if most critics of the last plays have found
thematics too rich a field of investigation to abandon as
Edwards urged, another of Edwards' suggestions did not go
unheeded. Impressed by John F. Danby's *Poets on Fortune's
Hill* (1952), a study of the influence of Sidney on
Shakespeare's plays from *King Lear* to *The Tempest* (item 25),
Edwards championed approaching the last plays as part of the

romance tradition. Against interpretations which seek
profoundity in abstraction, Edwards advocated studies
grounded in the genre of romance which take up dramatic
structure and audience response.

Considerations of *Pericles*, *Cymbeline*, *The Winter's Tale*,
and *The Tempest* as part of the romance tradition began at the
zenith of historical linguistics. Early studies of the many
versions of the Apollonius legend, including *Pericles*, are
those of Samuel Singer in 1895 (item 337), Albert Henry Smyth
in 1898 (item 338), and Elimar Klebs in 1899 (item 339).
Labelling and interpreting *Pericles*, *Cymbeline*, *The Winter's
Tale*, and *The Tempest* as Shakespeare's "late romances" began
some fifty years later. Three years before Danby published
his study of Sidneian romance and Shakespeare, E. C. Pettet,
in *Shakespeare and the Romance Tradition* (1949), defined the
four plays as romances by virtue of their extravagant plots;
the machinations involving disguise, mistaken identity, and
charms; the radical shifts of scene; the flat characters; and
the providential outlook (item 349). The plays became "the
four romances."

Regarding *Pericles* as part of the romance tradition has
offered critics several sorts of romances for comparison:
Greek romance, Latin romance, the medieval miracle play, and
Renaissance tragicomedy. For instance, in *Shakespeare and
the Greek Romance* (1970), Carol Gesner considers the
influence of Greek romance on Shakespeare's plays, especially
Pericles, *Cymbeline*, *The Winter's Tale*, and *The Tempest* (item
370). With regard to *Pericles*, Ben Edwin Perry argues in
Ancient Romance (1967) that the Apollonius legend is Latin,
not Greek (item 368). F. D. Hoeniger in the Introduction to
the Arden *Pericles* (1963) and Howard Felperin in his essay,
"Shakespeare's Miracle Play" (1967), and his book, *The
Shakespearean Romance* (1972), treat *Pericles* as a secular
miracle play (Hoeniger, item 528; Felperin, items 111, 155).
In *Shakespeare's Tragicomic Vision* (1972), Joan Hartwig
examines the relationship between dramatic structure and
audience response in the final six plays (item 158).

Such studies focus on Shakespeare the dramatist rather
than Shakespeare the man. The plays remain a progression as
in studies of the "last plays" but one that suggests growing
craftmanship rather than ripening spirituality or aesthetics.
The shift attempts to combine poetic analysis with dramatic
analysis. For instance, John Arthos in "*Pericles, Prince of
Tyre*: A Study in the Dramatic Use of Romantic Narrative" and
David Young in *The Heart's Forest* compare action with
language in *Pericles* (Arthos, 1953, item 28; Young, 1972,
item 163). Each concludes that the play is more narrative
than dramatic, despite the heightened language and scenes in

acts 3-5. For Arthos, the pictorial style of *Pericles*
constitutes a unified structure. The achievement for Young
remains crude; nevertheless, he says that if one considers
Pericles as the first of the four romances, its simplicities
emerge as the hallmarks of a dramatic experiment rather than
a full-fledged Shakespearean romance. Other studies
concentrate on staging. In *The Elizabethan Dumb Show* (1964,
trans. 1966), Dieter Mehl includes *Pericles* in his discussion
of Shakespeare's choruses and dumb shows as legacies of
classical tragedy (item 105); in *The Shakespeare Inset*
(1965), Frances Berry discusses stage space as a distancing
device in *Pericles* (item 91). For Northrop Frye, in *A
Natural Perspective* (1965), the pervasive music, linear and
symmetrical episodes, and far-fetched characters of *Pericles*
are characteristic of opera (item 93).

Scholars interested in the balance of art in the romances
proclaim the visual and musical components of drama as rivals
to the power of the word. In a 1981 dissertation, Joseph
Michael Hackett discusses the effect of music, dance, the
masque, and the court milieu on Shakespeare's last plays,
especially *Cymbeline* (item 293); J. M. Nosworthy, of many,
considers aural effects in a 1958 essay, "Music and Its
Function in the Romances of Shakespeare" (item 51); and
Frederick O. Waage, in "'Be Stone no More': Italian
Cinquecento Art and Shakespeare's Last Plays" (1980),
concentrates on the graphic and plastic arts (item 287).
Perhaps the final inversion belongs to those who say that the
romances celebrate art per se, whether sophisticated art, as
does Norman Rabkin in *Shakespeare and the Common
Understanding*, or, in the case of *Pericles*, folk art, as
Phyllis Gorfain argues in "Puzzle and Artifice: The Riddle as
Metapoetry in *Pericles*" (Rabkin, 1967, item 113; Gorfain,
1976, item 219).

Pericles interpreters who prefer apparent to coded form
often use dramatic theory as a method of analysis. Students
of stage romance have learned from the major anatomists of
Shakespearean romance such as Pettet and Frye that the chief
ingredients of romance--compounded adventures, one-
dimensional characters, and numerous exotic settings--
produce detached and diffused episodes that end in a sudden
cohesion. In such studies the centrifugal drift of *Pericles*
is seen as the structural given of dramatized romance rather
than a flaccid deviation from Shakespeare's centripedal
tragedies and romantic comedies. In "The Structure of the
Last Plays" (1958), Clifford Leech pointed out that the
Quarto has no act divisions, later editors (beginning with
the Third Folio) having imposed the obligatory five-act
structure on an open-ended construction (item 49).

Because dramatic romance is not centered on a single character, place, or plot, unity often depends on the chorus. Ancient Gower, who appears eight times as chorus in *Pericles*, narrates "his" play. N.W. Gilroy-Scott and Walter F. Eggers argue from different historical bases that ancient Gower's naivety heightens the irony inherent in the tale-telling of the presenter who unfolds more than he comprehends. In "John Gower's Reputation: Literary Allusions from the Early Fifteenth Century to the Time of *Pericles*" (1971), Gilroy-Scott accounts for two levels of irony in *Pericles* by linking the deliberate quaintness of Gower's medieval costume and language to the mild contempt in which Renaissance writers held John Gower as a moral authority (item 374). In "'Bring Forth a Miracle': Presentation in Shakespeare's Romances" (1979), Eggers explains Gower's role in *Pericles* as a refinement of the stage convention popular since the 1580s of the authorial presenter (Skelton in the Robin Hood plays, Guicciardini in *The Devil's Charter*). Naive Gower is for Eggers a dramatized version of the author and his problems in bringing fiction to life (item 265). For Richard Paul Knowles in "'Wishes Fall Out as They're Will'd: Artist, Audience, and *Pericles*'s Gower" (1983), the Gower choruses engage the audience in both the moral and creative process of *Pericles* (item 319). According to Knowles, Gower is a linking, not a distancing device. Indeed, in "Shakespeare's Gower and Gower's Shakespeare: The Larger Debt of *Pericles*" (1985), Richard Hillman contrasts studies of distanced Gower choruses with the most recent approaches, such as his own, which consider Gower as Shakespeare's method of approach to the audience in *Pericles* (item 329).

Antique and ubiquitous Gower in his role as guide to a remote time and scattered cities is not always appreciated by those unaccustomed or ill-disposed to the loose structures of medieval drama and narrative romance. Stage adapters bent on tightening and unifying the plot have removed the Gower choruses altogether as did George Lillo in 1738 and Samuel Phelps in 1854, curtailed them as Nugent Monck did in 1947, or adapted them into choruses for grouped and individual characters as Laird Williamson did in 1985.

Whether directly or indirectly, literary scholarship and criticism influence stage productions as much as stage performances influence the men and women who study and write about literature. To date, only a few studies treat *Pericles* in terms of actual rather than theoretical staging. One of these is Betty Jane Wylie's "Play-Doctoring the Text of *Pericles*" (1973), which mentions the textual changes, several of them additions from Wilkins' *Painfull Aduentures*, that Jean Gascon made in his 1971 production at Stratford, Ontario

xxii *Pericles*

(item 701). Most of the writing on *Pericles* in performance
are stage histories and theatre reviews, the latter numerous
and indicative of the many times *Pericles* has been acted in
the twentieth century. Of the several stage histories, the
most comprehensive, C. B. Young's essay in the New Cambridge
edition, discusses productions, chiefly British, from the
seventeenth century to 1954 (item 661). The play text is
available in both modern emended editions and facsimile
editions of the Quarto. Stage and text offer new ways to
measure the vitality of *Pericles* as literature.

The annotated bibliography that follows covers
discussions of *Pericles* written between 1940 and 1985.
Influential essays before 1940 also appear. The eight
categories of items—criticism; sources, analogues, and
background; dating; authorship and textual studies;
bibliographies and concordances; editions; stage history and
recorded performances; and adaptations, influences, synopses,
and excerpts—follow the arrangement of Larry S. Champion's
King Lear: An Annotated Bibliography, No. 1 in the Garland
Shakespeare Bibliographies series. Items are arranged
chronologically within each group. The chief sources for the
listings are MHRA, *PMLA*, *Shakespeare Quarterly*, and
Shakespeare Jahrbuch (Heidelberg and Weimar). An Index
concludes the volume.

For their generous assistance and patience, I owe thanks
to Tammy R. Dickerson, who typed the manuscript, to Martha B.
Irby, Head of Interlibrary Loan, Mitchell Memorial Library,
Mississippi State University, and to Joseph E. Milosh, Head
of the Department of English, Mississippi State University.

Pericles

I. CRITICISM

1. Coleridge, Samuel Taylor. [1810.] *Coleridge's
   Shakespearean Criticism.* Edited by Thomas Middleton
   Raysor. Vol. 2. Cambridge: Harvard University
   Press, 1930, p. 209.

   Henry Crabb Robinson noted on 23 December 1810 that
   Coleridge thought *Pericles* a Shakespeare revision.
   Beginning someone else's play in indifference,
   Shakespeare finished by writing almost all of the last
   two acts.

2. Swinburne, Algernon Charles. *A Study of Shakespeare.*
   London: Chatto and Windus, 1880, pp. 206-12.

   The realistic prose of the brothel scenes is prurient
   to the prudish. The poetry surrounding these scenes
   (Dionyza's maternal jealousy, Marina's lament over her
   nurse's grave, the storm scene, in especial) are
   matchless. Choruses excepted, acts 3-5 belong to
   Shakespeare at his ripest. In act 5, Shakespeare's
   image of "Patience gazing on kings' graves, and smiling
   Extremity out of act" (5.1.136-37) transcends the
   simpler image of "patience on a monument smiling at
   grief" in *Twelfth Night.* Shakespeare touched acts 1-2
   with only a cursory hand, adding, for instance, the
   blind mole speech in act 2.

3. Brandes, George. "Pericles--Collaboration with Wilkins
   and Rowley--Shakespeare and Corneille." *William
   Shakespeare: A Critical Study.* Vol. 2. New York:
   Macmillan, 1898, pp. 275-95.

   Pericles belongs to Shakespeare only in part and as
   such is not a play so much as a partially dramatized
   epic poem. It is likely that Wilkins and Rowley
   collaborated on the play before turning it over to
   Shakespeare, who added poetry to the sections he liked,
   touching little before the storm scene that opens act
   3. The brothel scenes in act 4 reflect Shakespeare's
   dark mood of 1608, the same mood that produced
   Coriolanus and *Timon of Athens.* Yet *Pericles* is as

well the prelude to Shakespeare's later, happier plays,
especially *The Tempest*. As poem and biography,
Pericles is a "remarkable fragment" (p. 295).

4. Strachey, G. Lytton. "Shakespeare's Final Period."
   Independent Review, 3 (1904): 405-18. Reprint.
   Books and Characters: French and English. London:
   Chatto and Windus; New York: Harcourt, Brace, 1922,
   pp. 49-69.

   Shakespeare wrote his final plays in boredom rather
   than serenity. *Pericles* is a "miserable archaic
   fragment" (*Review*, p. 415; *Books*, p. 65) completed by a
   Shakespeare uninterested in anything but "poetry and
   poetical dreams" (*Review*, p. 414; *Books*, p. 64).

5. Swinburne, Algernon Charles. *Shakespeare*. London:
   Oxford University Press, 1909, pp. 48-49.

   The brothel scenes are bold and realistic.
   Shakespeare revised *Pericles* in his final period from
   an earlier, inferior play. Simple and sublime *Pericles*
   can be compared only to Shakespeare's greatest works.

6. Knight, G. Wilson. *The Shakespearian Tempest, with a
   Chart of Shakespeare's Dramatic Universe*. 1932.
   Reprint. London: Methuen, 1953, pp. 218-92.

   In Shakespeare's last, symbolic plays, tempest and
   music imagery are the plot. In *Pericles*, which has the
   same imagery of storms, music, and jewels as the other
   last plays, only the poetry matters. The last plays,
   journeys from disorder to harmony, simplify
   Shakespeare's spiritual universe into patterns that
   display the value of love and resolve problems into
   forms of birth and death.

7. James, David G. "The Failure of the Ballad Makers."
   *Scepticism and Poetry: An Essay on the Poetic
   Imagination*. London: Allen and Unwin, 1937; rpt. New
   York: Barnes and Noble, 1960, pp. 205-41.

   Unlike Wordsworth, who resorted to Christianity for
   poetic sustenance in his last years, Shakespeare
   created a private myth in his last plays of finding
   what is lost. The myth encompasses bringing the dead
   to life, recovering a lost royalty, and seeking the
   lost by a royal person. In its simplicity and single-

mindedness, *Pericles* contains the most perfect
expression of the theme of lost and found royalty. The
love interest in the other three plays lessens the
significance of the royalty myth, but in *Pericles*
kingship, not love, dominates. Shakespeare represents
human tragedy in the romances with scenes of human
helplessness; yet evil sometimes helps deliver
characters from evil, as when Boult releases Marina
from the brothel. The theme of finding the lost
represents Shakespeare's awareness that man has lost
his soul through his own evil. In *Pericles* evil is
located, not in the Prince, but in those associated
with him, such as Cleon and Dionyza. The good are
recovered in each romance by either a royal person or a
child of royal birth. Thaisa's unique death possesses
religious significance, but the myth of resurrection
fails in *Pericles*. After Thaisa is resurrected, she
makes no attempt to find *Pericles*; it would have ruined
the plot. Instead, this "more than usually silly
mortal . . . is stored away in a temple" (p. 233). The
resurrection myth fails in the last plays because they
are secular and therefore contain mortal embodiments of
spiritual concepts. *The Tempest* is Shakespeare's last,
failed attempt to convey his spiritual vision. The
play records the creator-poet's dissolution of his
imagined universe.

8. Tillyard, E.M.W. *Shakespeare's Last Plays*. 1938.
   Reprint. London: Chatto and Windus, 1951, pp. 22-25.

   Only acts 3-5 belong to Shakespeare, and except for
   some of the verse, they are not of much account. The
   careless construction of the play makes it risky to
   base symbolic interpretations of the romances on
   Pericles as have G. Wilson Knight (see item 6) and D.G.
   James (see item 7). An incident in *Pericles*, which
   Shakespeare came to perhaps by accident, may not mean
   the same thing when repeated in a later play.

9. Bacon, Wallace Alger. "Shakespeare's Dramatic
   Romances." Ph.D. dissertation, University of
   Michigan, 1940. (not seen)

10. Spencer, Hazelton. "His Dramatic Romances: *Pericles,
    Prince of Tyre*." *The Art and Life of William
    Shakespeare*. 1940. Reprint. New York: Barnes and
    Noble, 1970, pp. 356-61.

Except for acts 1-2, *Pericles* is good theatre.

11. Craig, Hardin. "Shakespeare's Development as a
     Dramatist in the Light of His Experience." *Studies*
     in Philology, 39 (1942): 226-38.

     Pericles, among other plays discussed in this
     article, is an example of the continuing effect on
     Shakespeare of his own dramatic experience. The play
     has characteristics that mark it as entirely his.
     Probably Shakespeare's first tragicomedy, *Pericles*
     contains characters and situations found in *Cymbeline*,
     The Winter's Tale, and *The Tempest*. Like the three
     later plays, *Pericles* belongs to the world of Greek
     romance. The power of the poetry in some passages can
     only be Shakespeare's. But the strongest argument for
     Shakespeare's sole authorship is the similarity between
     Pericles and Prospero; Pericles seems an earlier
     version of Prospero in a rather bad play.

12. Armstrong, Edward A. *Shakespeare's Imagination: A*
     Study of the Psychology of Association and
     Inspiration. 1946. Reprint. Lincoln: University of
     Nebraska Press, 1963, pp. 44-47, 213, 218.

     Armstrong mentions four images from *Pericles* and
     their associations for Shakespeare: drones and kings
     (2.1.51), darkness and love-making (4.6.32), violets
     and breath (4.1.16), and violets and death (4.1.14).

13. Smith, Grover. "The Tennis-Ball of Fortune." *Notes*
     and Queries, 190 (1946): 202-03.

     Renaissance literature contains several tennis
     metaphors. One occurs in *Pericles* at 2.1.63-65.

14. Knight, G. Wilson. *The Crown of Life: Essays in*
     Interpretation of Shakespeare's Final Plays. 1947.
     Reprint. New York: Barnes and Noble, 1966.

     Pericles, *Cymbeline*, *The Winter's Tale*, *The Tempest*,
     and *Henry 8* are secular versions of man's journey from
     pain and despair to acceptance and joy. Having
     recently become an apostolic Christian, Shakespeare
     turned from realistic plays, such as *Twelfth Night* and
     King Lear, to write poetic parables. Beginning with
     Pericles, the last plays, which resemble morality
     plays, contain images of voyages, tempests, and

shipwrecks. The first two acts resemble "a parable of
human fortune" (p. 52) in which a young man of immature
fantasies meets disillusionment by realizing evil;
later, after performing charitable deeds, he is
temporarily rebuffed by fortune but through humility
finally wins a wife worthy of love. In the last three
acts, Shakespeare moves beyond the morality verse and
lessons of acts 1-2 into pure vision. The story and
its meaning matter less than the poetry. Shakespeare's
poetry of voyages, tempests, and shipwrecks evokes the
Christian vision of birth, death, and resurrection.
Pericles marks Shakespeare's step into parable, but the
plays from *The Comedy of Errors* to *Antony and Cleopatra*
show his inclination. The emphasis in *Pericles* is on
artistry: processions, dumb shows, monuments, dancing,
Marina's embroidery, etc. The price of such a
ritualistic play is Pericles' passivity; the character
remains unrealized as a man. Regardless of
particulars, all of *Pericles* belongs to Shakespeare.

15. Sitwell, Edith. *"Pericles."* *A Notebook on William
    Shakespeare.* 1948. Reprint. London: Macmillan,
    1965, pp. 208-11.

    Verse that is both masterful and halting fills
    Pericles. The uneven quality of the poetry remains a
    puzzle.

16. Drew, Elizabeth. "Ariel Poems." *T.S. Eliot: The
    Design of His Poetry.* New York: Scribner's, 1949,
    pp. 118-31.

    An analysis of "Marina" contains the following
    passage by Eliot on *Pericles* from his unpublished
    lecture, "Shakespeare as Poet and Dramatist" (see items
    19, 44, 139), given at Edinburgh University in 1937:
    "To my mind the finest of all the 'recognition scenes'
    is Act V:i of that very great play *Pericles.* It is a
    perfect example of the 'ultra-dramatic,' a dramatic
    action of beings who are more than human. . . [Drew's
    ellipsis]. It is the speech of creatures who are more
    than human, or rather, seen in a light more than that
    of day" (p. 127).

17. Spencer, Theodore. "Shakespeare's Last Plays."
    Shakespeare and the Nature of Man. 2nd ed. rev. New
    York: Macmillan, 1949, pp. 184-87.

Acts 3-5 of *Pericles*, the only part Shakespeare
wrote, differ entirely from *Timon of Athens*, the last
play of Shakespeare's tragic period. Evil is indeed in
the background, but all is finally redeemed. *Pericles*
and the plays that follow invert the tragic world; the
appearance may be evil, but the reality is good.

18.   Stauffer, Donald A. "A World of Images." *Shakespeare's
      World of Images: The Development of His Moral Ideas*.
      New York: Norton, 1949, pp. 266-323.

Pericles is the poor text of a play written entirely
by Shakespeare. Its extraordinary events are spiritual
miracles. Instead of presenting believable characters,
Shakespeare developed abstract ideas (obedience,
patience, healing, etc.) and supporting images.
Pericles is another book of *The Faerie Queene*; it is
King Lear as a romance. "It is a miracle play. . . .
It is a piece of music" (p. 270). Shakespeare replaced
causal relationships in *Pericles* with miraculous
revelations, "smiling hypotheses" (p. 275).

19.   Eliot, T.S. "Shakespeares Verskunst." *Der Monat*, 20
      May 1950, pp. 198-207.

An analysis of the poetry in Shakespeare's most
outstanding plays, the essay closes with a
consideration of the four romances (pp. 206-07).
Emotional reality is more important in the last plays
than everyday reality. The outer world becomes a dream
world in these plays of dream and vision. The verse is
richly musical and beyond the understanding of most
theatre audiences then or now. There is no more
beautiful scene in Shakespeare than the recognition
scene between Pericles and Marina in act 5 of *Pericles*.
Their duet is as perfect as that of Romeo and Juliet.
In the last plays Shakespeare took drama back to its
religious origins.

20.   Ellis-Fermor, Una. "Die Spätwerke grosser Dramatiker."
      Translated by E. Meierl. *Deutsche
      Vierteljahrsschrift für Literaturwissenschaft and
      Geistesgeschichte*, 24 (1950): 423-39.

The last plays of Aeschylus, Sophocles, Euripedes,
Ibsen, and Shakespeare possess a harmony signifying the
dramatists' eventual recognition and acceptance of a
universal power for good that lies beyond evil. This

ultimate state of knowing and belief is epitomized in
the scene in which Pericles recognizes his daughter and
hears the music of the spheres (5.1). In Shakespeare,
such assurance does not belong exclusively to the four
romances; the movement toward recognition and
acceptance exists in his earlier dramas as well. The
four romances, which are entirely similar, concern
reconciliation and self-recognition. Their reborn
heroes submit to the idea of divine guidance.

21. Leech, Clifford. *"Timon* and After." *Shakespeare's
     Tragedies, and Other Studies in Seventeenth Century
     Drama.* London: Chatto and Windus, 1950, pp. 126-32.

     Pericles is "a botched affair" (p. 127). Undecided
     about how to proceed after *Timon* and needing a rest,
     Shakespeare finished someone else's partially written
     dramatic romance. *Pericles* has black and white
     characters as does *Timon.* In the brothel scene,
     Marina, like Timon, is a reviler. As the forerunner of
     Shakespeare's other romances, *Pericles* is important.
     To Shakespeare's audience it was popular but probably
     less impressive than other Shakespeare plays.

22. Megaw, Robert N.E. "Shakespeare's Last Plays: An
     Inquiry into the Artistic Form of *Pericles,
     Cymbeline, The Winter's Tale,* and *The Tempest.*"
     Ph.D. dissertation, University of Chicago, 1950.
     (not seen)

23. Wincor, Richard. "Shakespeare's Festival Plays."
     Shakespeare Quarterly, 1 (1950): 219-40.

     Toward the end of his life Shakespeare chose to write
     a series of plays that may be compared with ancient
     festival plays celebrating the return of spring.
     Although spring's return was a theme in Shakespeare's
     plays from the first, the theme dominates the last
     plays. Ritual deaths and recoveries, such as those of
     Thaisa and Marina, are the most important
     characteristics of festival drama. Cerimon is the
     doctor with divine powers in festival rituals.
     Pericles is an example of "Nature veneration" (p. 229).

24. Goddard, Harold C. *"Pericles." The Meaning of
     Shakespeare.* Chicago: University of Chicago Press,
     1951, pp. 627-29.

Shakespeare probably wrote none of acts 1-2 and most
of acts 3-4, paying frequent attention to father-
daughter relationships.

25. Danby, John F. "Sidney and the Late Shakespearian
     Romance." *Elizabethan and Jacobean Poets: Studies in
     Sidney, Shakespeare, Beaumont and Fletcher* (original
     title, *Poets on Fortune's Hill*). London: Faber and
     Faber, 1952, pp. 74-107. Reprint. *"Pericles,
     Arcadia,* and the Scheme of Romance." *Shakespeare's
     Later Comedies: An Anthology of Modern Criticism.*
     Edited by D.J. Palmer. Harmondsworth: Penguin,
     1971, pp. 175-95.

     Pericles and Shakespeare's other romances belong to
     the moral world of Sidney's *Arcadia,* not to the worlds
     of anthropological criticism and Christian allegory.
     Pericles has the plots and moral concerns of Sidneian
     romance, even though Shakespeare did not write both
     parts. Acts 1-2, which serve as a prologue to the
     Shakespearean section, lack a guiding consciousness
     either in the central character or the dramatist
     capable of giving them coherence and moral
     significance. An audience finds only moral precepts in
     acts 1-2; Shakespeare stages moral occasions in the
     arresting and emotional scenes of acts 3-5. Pericles
     develops a personality and a moral consciousness in act
     3. The excitement and individuality of the last three
     acts show Shakespeare's interest in patience, the
     inward theme of romance.

26. Harbage, Alfred. *Shakespeare and the Rival Traditions.*
     New York: Macmillan, 1952, pp. 193-94, 197, 198-99,
     200, and 357.

     The brothel scenes in act 4 of *Pericles* are grim and
     the humor largely unconscious. Shakespeare treats
     Lysimachus ambiguously. In Twine's *Patterne of
     Painefull Adventures* he is an outright patron of the
     brothel, and his counterpart in Gower's *Confessio
     Amantis* has no connection with the brothel.

27. Nicoll, Allardyce. *Shakespeare.* Home Study Books.
     1952; rpt. London: Methuen, 1961, pp. 157-61.

     Shakespeare probably wrote most of *Pericles.* The
     peculiar Gower choruses seek to extend the action in
     time, make certain the audience remembers the play is a

fiction, and keep the scenes remote. Nevertheless, for
all their vitality and realism, neither the fishermen
scenes in act 2 nor the brothel scenes in act 4 are
remote. Evil and cruelty pervade *Pericles*, whether in
the shape of the incestuous Antiochus or the storms at
sea. Their opposites, virtuous humans such as Marina
and a universe of miracles, evoke wonder. In all,
Pericles is distant and dreamlike, and the characters
seem visionary. Perhaps Shakespeare contrived the very
artlessness of some parts of the play, including
Gower's archaic choruses.

28. Arthos, John. "*Pericles, Prince of Tyre*: A Study in
    the Dramatic Use of Romantic Narrative." *Shakespeare
    Quarterly*, 4 (1953): 257-70. Reprint. "*Pericles,
    Prince of Tyre*." *The Art of Shakespeare*. 1964.
    Reprint. New York: Barnes and Noble, 1965, pp.
    136-58. The reprint has a slightly altered
    introduction and an added conclusion.

    The structural coherence of the scenes, dumb shows,
    and prologues argues the unity of *Pericles*. In spite
    of the shift in act 3 to heightened language and
    scenes, the last three acts continue the narrative from
    acts 1-2, sometimes returning to their narrative style.
    Pericles gives its audience more pictures than drama,
    each picture contributing to the supreme image of
    Pericles awakened by Marina to the music of the
    spheres.

29. Bland, D.S. "The Heroine and the Sea: An Aspect of
    Shakespeare's Late Plays." *Essays in Criticism*, 3
    (1953): 39-44.

    Shakespeare included tragedy in the romances as a
    necessary prelude to regeneration. The plot is an
    agent of rebirth. Because the actions of heroes have
    political implications, Shakespeare chose heroines to
    symbolize resurrection. Standing too close to the
    tragic center of their respective plays, Imogen and
    Marina fail as figures of rebirth. Perdita and Miranda
    are successful because each is the completely innocent
    agent of rebirth, having been removed from the tragic
    center as an infant.

30. Fluchère, Henri. *Shakespeare*. Translated by Guy
    Hamilton. London: Longmans, Green, 1953, pp. 264-68.

The symbolic last plays depict the restoration of
order and the triumph of good. Shakespeare wrote the
final three acts of an unfinished *Pericles*. The three
Shakespearean acts are a genial and masterful
improbability. The most attractive symbols in the last
plays, "of fertility, resurrection, joy of life" (p.
265), are the youthful heroines, Marina, Imogen,
Perdita, and Miranda. Regeneration for the old in
these plays comes from their acceptance of the young.

31.   Spalding, Kenneth J. *The Philosophy of Shakespeare*.
      New York: Philosophical Library, 1953, pp. 171-78.

      Acts 1-3 of *Pericles* as well as all of *Cymbeline* and
      The Winter's Tale involve the same evils that appear in
      Shakespeare's tragedies. Ultimately, however, heaven
      will defeat the Titans. The evils in *Pericles* are envy
      and lust. In act 4 angelic Marina overcomes the
      lustful inmates of the brothel.

32.   Hoeniger, F. David. "The Function of Structure and
      Imagery in Shakespeare's Last Plays." Ph.D.
      dissertation, University of London, 1954. (not seen)
      Abstract. *Shakespeare Newsletter*, 5 (1955): 42.

      Pericles and *Cymbeline* are partially failed
      experiments in a new hybrid dramatic form, part miracle
      play and part Alexandrian romance.

33.   Oppel, Horst. "Shakespeares Tragödien und Romanzen:
      Kontinuität oder Umbruch?" *Akademie der
      Wissenschaften und der Literatur*. Abhandlungen der
      Klasse der Literatur, no. 2 (1954). Wiesbaden:
      Akademie der Wissenschaften und der Literatur in
      Mainz, 1954, pp. 17-62.

      Without Shakespeare's tragedies there would be no
      romances. The recognitions and reconciliations in
      Pericles give the play its importance as the first of
      the romances.

34.   Traversi, Derek. "*Pericles, Prince of Tyre*."
      Shakespeare: The Last Phase. 1954. Reprint.
      Stanford: Stanford University Press, 1965, pp. 19-42.

      The four late plays continue Shakespeare's experiment
      with dramatic form. The romances, which deal with the
      separation and reunion of families, are non-realistic,

symbolic plays in which the symbolism is neither
biographical nor allegorical. Because plot is an
extension of poetry in these plays, the symbolism
evolves from the poetry. Shakespeare's attempt to
unify an imperfect theme forms the chief interest of
Pericles, not the question of authorship. The play
enumerates a symbolic pilgrimage toward a chivalrous
ideal of love up to Pericles' marriage to Thaisa. In
act 3 the bare allegorical structure established in the
first two acts gains spiritual significance. Thaisa's
death and Marina's birth in a sea storm form the
turning point (3.1). With its pattern of birth, death,
tempest, and subsequent calm, the scene initiates the
main symbolic contrasts which Shakespeare was to
present in his succeeding plays. The poetry in
Thaisa's resurrection scene has a deliberately
supernatural quality. The realism of the brothel
scenes in act 4 is a fault, but they are a necessary
stage in the plot. In act 5 Shakespeare returned to
symbolism; Pericles' awakening is a moral rebirth. At
the end of the play Pericles, Marina, and Thaisa
represent humanity transformed by spiritual
enlightenment. A shorter version of this essay appears
in Traversi's *Approach to Shakespeare*. See item 125.

35. Feldman, A. Bronson. "Imaginary Incest: A Study of
    Shakespeare's *Pericles*." *American Imago*, 12 (1955):
    117-55.

    The article interprets *Pericles* according to the life
    of the Earl of Oxford, Edward de Vere (1550-1604), the
    man who wrote Shakespeare's plays.

36. Fischer, Walther. "Shakespeares Späte Romanzen:
    Vortrag gehalten auf der Tagung der Deutschen
    Shakespeare-Gesellschaft in Weimar, am 4. June 1954."
    Shakespeare Jahrbuch (Weimar), 91 (1955): 7-24.

    Christian interpreters of Shakespeare who find a
    transcendent optimism in the late romances are wrong.
    The late romances belong to the ancient tradition of
    folk tales which express the enduring human perplexity
    over what is and what only seems to be. The shadowy
    world of appearance and reality that Shakespeare dealt
    with in *The Comedy of Errors*, *A Midsummer Night's
    Dream*, *Macbeth*, and *Hamlet* remains a part of the late
    romances. As one of the late romances, *Pericles*
    possesses folktale elements, such as the incest between

Antiochus and his daughter, Marina's murderous
stepmother, Dionyza, and Marina herself, the saint in
the bordello. Grace in this play is not a free and
undeserved boon. As Gower says in the epilogue, reward
comes to the deserving after suffering.

37. Herrick, Marvin T. "English Tragicomedy before
     Beaumont and Fletcher." *Tragicomedy: Its Origin and
     Development in Italy, France, and England.* Illinois
     Studies in Language and Literature, vol. 39. Urbana:
     University of Illinois Press, 1955, pp. 215-60.

     Tragical-comical-historical *Pericles* resembles the
     Graeco-Roman tragicomedies of France. The play is one
     of the first romantic tragicomedies popular in England
     during the seventeenth century.

38. Parker, M.D.H. "Shadow and Substance: Nature and
     Grace." *The Slave of Life: A Study of Shakespeare
     and the Idea of Justice.* London: Chatto and Windus,
     1955, pp. 175-95.

     The four romances are expressions of religious
     orthodoxy. *Pericles* illustrates providence and grace,
     the theme of the Gower choruses. Pericles represents
     faith and patience; Cerimon stands for knowledge and
     charity; Marina figures the grace of *stella maris*.
     Like the later romances, *Pericles* contains
     Shakespeare's final theme, redemption. In the
     tragedies redemption is moral and mortal; in the last
     plays it is metaphysical.

39. Pettet, E.C. "Dangerous Sea and Unvalued Jewels: Some
     Notes on Shakespeare's Consciousness of the Sea."
     English, 10 (1955): 215-20.

     This essay concerns Shakespeare's fascination with
     undersea riches. *Pericles* contains the images of sea
     floors, shipwrecks, and treasures found throughout
     Shakespeare's work.

40. Traversi, Derek A. "Shakespeare: The Last Plays." *New
     Pelican Guide to English Literature, 2: The Age of
     Shakespeare.* Edited by Boris Ford. 1955. Reprint.
     Harmondsworth and New York: Penguin, 1982, pp.
     357-83.

In the *Pericles* section of the essay (pp. 357-61),
Traversi says that Shakespeare's unknown co-author was
responsible for the Gower choruses. The use of themes
as well as the differences in the verse distinguish
acts 3-5 above acts 1-2. The rather allegorical themes
of separation and reunion, the suffering king, and the
magical princess mark *Pericles* as the first of
Shakespeare's romances.

41. Guidi, Augusto. "In Margine a uno Studio dei Drammi
    Romanzeschi di Shakespeare" [In Introduction to a
    Study of Shakespeare's Dramatic Romances].
    Letteratura, 4, no. 24 (1956): 3-10. Reprint.
    L'Ultimo Shakespeare. Guide di Cultura
    Contemporanea. Padova: Liviana, 1958, pp. 1-13.
    (not seen)

    Archetypal characters and symbolic plots make the
    romances a group. Episodic *Pericles* and *Cymbeline* are
    experimental plays in which Shakespeare moves from the
    closed structure of the problem comedies to the open
    structure of romance. *Pericles* and *Cymbeline* resemble
    medieval drama with their fables of reconciliation and
    regeneration and in their emphasis on narrative,
    lyrical mood, and music and dance rather than
    individuated characters.

42. Guidi, Augusto. "L'Ultimo Shakespeare" [The Late
    Shakespeare]. *English Miscellany*, 7 (1956): 9-18.
    (not seen)

    The romances of Shakespeare show his own evolution
    from custom in the early comedies, to history in the
    chronicle plays, to human problems in the tragedies, to
    man's spiritual destiny in the romances. The romances
    contain Shakespeare's orthodox resolution within
    Catholicism and the New Testament. Horizontal
    structure in the tragedies is replaced by the vertical,
    Gothic structure of the romances in which allegorical
    characters resemble the figures of medieval drama. As
    such, they move from a purgatorial existence to a
    vision of an earthly paradise. Shakespeare's romances
    deny Jacobean realities in the vigor of their
    orthodoxy.

43. Brunner, Karl. *William Shakespeare*. Tübingen: Max
     Niemeyer, 1957, pp. 173-75.

     The essay presents a brief history of *Pericles* and
     summarizes the plot.

44. Eliot, T.S. "Preface" (1956). *On Poetry and Poets*.
     New York: Farrar, Straus, Giroux, Noonday Press,
     1957, pp. xi-xii.

     Eliot chose not to publish two Edinburgh lectures,
     "The Development of Shakespeare's Verse," which contain
     comments on *Pericles*, because he thought them badly
     written and in need of revision. See items 16, 19,
     139.

45. Guidi, Augusto. "Le fasi del *Pericles*." *Studi in
     onore di Pietro Silva*. Edited by the Facolta di
     Magistero, Rome University. Florence: F. Le Monnier
     (Tip. Ariani), 1957, pp. 107-17. Reprint. *L'ultimo
     Shakespeare*. Guide di Cultura Contemporanea.
     Padova: Liviana, 1958, pp. 15-32. (not seen)

46. Lüthi, Max. "*Pericles*." *Shakespeares Dramen*. Berlin:
     De Gruyter, 1957, pp. 276-83.

     Pericles most likely is Shakespeare's revision of
     someone else's work. The play, which emphasizes fairy-
     tale ideality, resembles many of Shakespeare's
     preceding dramas.

47. Chujo, Kazuo. "The Development of Structural Devices
     in Shakespeare's Tragicomedies." *Studies in English
     Grammar and Linguistics: A Miscellany in Honour of
     Takanobu Otsuka*. Edited by Kazuo Araki et al.
     Tokyo: Kenkyusha, 1958, pp. 301-16.

     Pericles is beset with structural problems, beginning
     with a faulty opening in which three different themes
     are introduced in two acts (the danger posed by
     Antiochus, the famine at Tharsus, and the courtship of
     Thaisa); consequently, the play is episodic and
     diffuse. The rapid shifts from scene to scene and the
     alternation of tragic and comic scenes represent a new
     unifying technique whereby tragic potential is reduced
     to an appropriate mood for tragicomedy. In *Pericles*
     and the other romances, the union between a harsh
     tragic world and a gentler pastoral world allows the

happy ending of tragicomedy to evolve naturally.

48. Edwards, Philip. "Shakespeare's Romances: 1900-1957."
     Shakespeare Survey, 11 (1958): 1-18.

     Literary critics have interpreted the romances,
     including *Pericles* and *Henry 8*, according to
     biographical speculations, studies of the Jacobean
     theatre, mythology and symbolism, and the conventions
     of romance. Perhaps enough has been said for the time
     about the profundity of the romances; instead,
     something more might be said about the structure of
     romance and audience response.

49. Leech, Clifford. "The Structure of the Last Plays."
     Shakespeare Survey, 11 (1958): 19-30.

     The cyclical pattern of the last plays suggests the
     repetitiveness rather than the uniqueness of
     experience. Shakespeare's pattern of cycle and crisis
     is contained within the five-act structure popular at
     the time. In the third and fourth folios, act 3 of
     Pericles begins at the 3.3 of modern editions, act 4
     begins at 4.2, and act 5 at 5.1.241 (the vision of
     Diana). There are no act divisions in the Quarto;
     instead, a solid line follows the scene of Pericles'
     arrival at Tharsus and another underscores the
     conclusion of the Pentapolis scenes. These lines
     correspond to the ends of acts 1 and 2 in modern
     editions. Although there are no printer's lines in the
     last three acts, the action falls into three
     distinct phases. *Pericles* editors have imposed the
     traditional five-act structure on an episodic
     narrative. The ending of *Pericles* suggests the
     conclusion of a phase instead of a final action. As an
     open-ended story of cycles leading to crises, *Pericles*
     marks a new departure for Shakespeare. The article
     discusses *Cymbeline, The Winter's Tale, the Tempest*,
     and *Henry 8*, also.

50. Nicoll, Allardyce. "Shakespeare and the Court Masque."
     Shakespeare Jahrbuch (Heidelberg), 94 (1958): 51-62.

     The masque influenced Shakespeare's poetic
     imagination rather than his staging. With their
     narrative choruses, *Pericles* and *The Winter's Tale* are
     not like masques.

51. Nosworthy, J.M. "Music and Its Function in the
     Romances of Shakespeare." *Shakespeare Survey*, 11
     (1958): 60-69.

     Music was an act of faith, not a diversion, to the
     Elizabethans. The romances are musically the richest
     of Shakespeare's plays. The five instances of music in
     Pericles include instrumentals to open the action
     (1.1.11) and accompaniment for the knights' dance
     (2.3.98), the knights and ladies' dance (2.3.107),
     Marina's song (5.1.80), and the theophany (5.1.234).
     Some of the original dances for the romances may be in
     the British Museum (Add. MS. 10444). The music in
     Pericles and *Cymbeline*, which shows the influence of
     the masque on these plays, is unexceptional. Omission
     would make little difference.

52. Levitsky, Ruth Mickelson. "Shakespeare's Treatment of
     the Virtue of Patience." Ph.D. dissertation,
     Missouri, 1957. *Dissertation Abstracts*, 19 (1959):
     2940.

     Shakespeare treated heroes in adversity differently
     at various stages in his career. Christian patience
     and forgiveness are the acceptable modes in the
     romances: conscience punishes sinners; repentance ends
     punishment; prayer counters evil.

53. Melchiori, Giorgio. "Note sul problema di *Pericles*."
     English Miscellany, 10 (1959): 135-55. (not seen)

54. Simpson, Robert Ritchie. *Shakespeare and Medicine*.
     Edinburgh: Livingstone, 1959.

     Simpson cites two nobles, contemporaries of
     Shakespeare's who practiced medicine, as precedents for
     Shakespeare's making Cerimon a lord of Ephesus, quotes
     passages on pregnancy and venereal diseases in
     Pericles, and includes a list of medical references in
     the play.

55. Dobrée, Bonamy. "The Last Plays." *The Living
     Shakespeare*. Edited by Robert Gittings. 1960.
     Reprint. New York: Barnes and Noble, 1967, pp.
     140-54.

The romances are a group of plays written at the end
of Shakespeare's career with similar themes and moving
poetry.

56. Evans, Bertrand. "A Lasting Storm: The Planetary
    Romances." *Shakespeare's Comedies.* 1960. Reprint.
    Oxford: Clarendon, 1969, pp. 220-315.

    Shakespeare denies the audiences of the romances the
    information that all is well. This is especially true
    in *Pericles,* where the tenuously linked events in acts
    1-2 fail to reveal dramatic ironies to the audience.
    Throughout the play scenes with unmistakable dramatic
    potential are given to Gower for narrative exposition
    and dumb show. Gower maintains until the epilogue that
    Pericles is in the hands of an indifferent fortune; the
    Prince thinks himself beset with a malevolent deity.
    The audience does not learn until an attendant lord
    tells Cerimon that an enormous wave has washed a body
    ashore (3.2) that neither is true; instead, a
    benevolent providence controls the seas and the
    fortunes of Pericles and his family. Only the absolute
    Marina directly assists providence by opposing and
    overcoming her adversaries. *Pericles,* a play based on
    a lost narrative poem, is too narrative a drama.
    Shakespeare the dramatizer did not gain the upperhand
    of Gower the narrator until after the opening chorus in
    act 4. See item 354.

57. Maitra, Sitangshu. *Shakespeare's Comic Idea.*
    Calcutta: Mukhopadhyay, 1960, p. 88.

    The four romances are folklore reaffirmations of
    forgiveness, charity, and spiritual renewal.

58. Melchiori, Barbara. "'Still Harping on My Daughter.'"
    English Miscellany, 11 (1960): 59-74.

    The essay examines father-daughter relationships in
    the last plays. In *Pericles,* Simonides is the foil to
    Antiochus and Pericles, fathers whose relationships to
    their daughters are unnatural, Antiochus' explicitly
    so, Pericles' by implication only.

59. Alexander, Peter. "The Final Period: *Pericles.*"
    Shakespeare's Life and Art. New York: New York
    University Press, 1961, pp. 221-22.

The Quarto is "good." Heminge and Condell left
Pericles out of the Folio because Shakespeare wrote
only part of the play. In the Shakespeare fragment,
Pericles and Marina are companion portraits to Prospero
and Miranda.

60. Howarth, Herbert. "Shakespeare's Gentleness."
    Shakespeare Survey, 14 (1961): 90-97. Reprint. *The
    Tiger's Heart: Essays on Shakespeare*. London: Chatto
    and Windus; New York: Oxford University Press, 1970,
    pp. 1-23.

    The essay concerns gentleness as characteristic of
    both Shakespeare and his style. Shakespeare's
    gentleness involves social status as well as natural
    virtue. Howarth discusses *Pericles* briefly in treating
    the recognition scene between Pericles and Marina. In
    his awareness "of the partnership of folly and merit,"
    Shakespeare "startlingly uses violence and tenderness
    in the last scenes of *Pericles* and *Cymbeline*" (p. 96).
    The *Pericles* text makes it seem that Shakespeare could
    not make up his mind whether to follow the original
    story in having the father slap his daughter before
    recognizing her or to refine the story. The something
    that glows on Marina's cheek, then, may be her
    instinct; and instead of slapping Marina, Pericles may
    only shake her and shove her away. The scene is
    tender, but its dramatic impact is defused.

61. Kiefer, Harry Christian. "Elizabethan Attitudes Toward
    Music in Shakespeare's Plays." Ph.D. dissertation,
    Columbia University, 1961. *Dissertation Abstracts*,
    22 (1961): 1177A-78A.

    The section on Boethius' *musica humana* explains
    Marina, Imogen, and Perdita as harmonious characters
    who serve as the sources of harmony in others.

62. Long, John H. *"Pericles." Shakespeare's Use of Music,
    Vol. II: The Final Comedies*. 1961. Reprint. New
    York: Da Capo, 1977, pp. 35-49.

    Music in *Pericles* follows characteristic Renaissance
    patterns: it symbolizes the distinction of
    metaphysical truth from phenomenal semblance,
    represents social harmonies, such as friendship and
    marriage, remedies despondence, and revives the dead.
    For the entrance of Antiochus' daughter and her

presentation to Pericles (1.1), "a broken consort of
strings and woodwinds" (p. 38) might have been used to
suggest her sensuality and perversion. At Simonides'
friendly and harmonious court (2.3), the knights' dance
was likely a martial almain played with drum and fife.
Afterward, Pericles and Thaisa may have danced a solo
galliard. To produce "The rough and Wofull Musick"
which Cerimon commands to help Thaisa revive (3.2), a
gamba viol would have been appropriate (see item 327).
It is likely that the Quarto contains no lyrics for
Marina's song to Pericles (5.1) because Shakespeare
used the song in Twine. Later in this scene hidden
recorders, instruments associated with celestial music,
may have played a solemn measure to represent the music
of the spheres and accompany Diana's entrance. No
music is indicated for the dumb shows because Gower
speaks during them. Throughout the play music
accompanies Pericles' increasing ability to distinguish
between the appearances of the mortal world and the
reality of the divine world.

63. Muir, Kenneth. "Shakespeare." *Last Periods of
    Shakespeare, Racine, Ibsen*. Detroit: Wayne State
    University Press, 1961, pp. 29-60.

    Pericles, the first play of Shakespeare's last
    period, exists only in a "bad" quarto. The differences
    between acts 1-2 and acts 3-5 may be either reportorial
    (see item 413) or authorial. If they are authorial,
    did Shakespeare write acts 3-5 and an unknown
    collaborator contribute acts 1-2, or did Shakespeare
    revise the last three acts of an older play, leaving
    acts 1-2 relatively unchanged? George Wilkins' novel,
    The Painfull Aduentures, which is based on a play of
    Pericles and contains blank-verse fossils not in
    Shakespeare's style, provides the evidence for an
    Ur-Pericles. Whatever the case, the adventures of
    Pericles in acts 1-2 serve as a mere prologue to the
    story of the separation and reunion of him and his
    family in acts 3-5. There is no attempt to make
    plausible this episodic play. But perhaps the
    corruptions in the Quarto have blurred some of
    Shakespeare's intentions. The characters in *Pericles*
    and the other last plays are uninteresting as human
    representatives; instead, they are "symbolic puppets"
    (p. 35). Fate manipulates the characters in *Pericles*
    toward a joyful outcome for the Prince and his family.
    Pericles' misfortunes are accidental; his fortunes are

providential. Shakespeare eliminated accidents from
the subsequent plays and attached the workings of
providence to sin and forgiveness. The essay continues
with discussions of *Cymbeline, The Winter's Tale,* and
The Tempest.

64. Tachibana, Tadae. "Eliot no Shakespeare" [Eliot's
     Shakespeare]. *Bungeikenkyu* (Meiji-daigaku,
     Bungeikeukyu-kai), no. 8 (March 1961): 1-15. (not
     seen)

65. Barton, Anne [Righter]. "From Resemblance to Identity:
     The Final Plays." *Shakespeare and the Idea of the
     Play.* 1962. Reprint. Westport, Conn.: Greenwood,
     1977, pp. 192-94.

     The theatrical language in *Pericles,* the first of
     Shakespeare's plays to depart from the biting realism
     of the tragedies, has a remote, unbitter quality. At
     the end of the play illusion and dreams prove
     substantial and replace "reality."

66. Leech, Clifford. *The John Fletcher Plays.* Cambridge:
     Harvard University Press, 1962. Reprint. London:
     Chatto and Windus, 1972.

     Although A.H. Thorndike recognized in *The Influence
     of Beaumont and Fletcher on Shakspere* (1901) that
     Pericles predates Beaumont and Fletcher's
     tragicomedies, he exaggerated the differences between
     Pericles and Shakespeare's other romances. In theme
     and detail *Pericles* resembles the later romances. The
     differences in *Pericles* include its loose, episodic
     narrative, unelaborated denouement, formal manner, and
     blameless protagonist. See item 340.

67. Marsh, Derick R.C. *The Recurring Miracle: A Study of
     "Cymbeline" and the Last Plays.* 1962. Reprint.
     Lincoln: University of Nebraska Press, 1969.

     Precursor to Shakespeare's greater romances, *Pericles*
     is only partly by Shakespeare. The play concerns
     "suffering and redemption" (p. 13) and shares with the
     other romances the theme of loss and recovery and the
     examination of the struggle of good and evil. Chastity
     and purity are the virtues of central concern, but they
     are not elaborated because of the simple, allegorical
     structure of the play. *Pericles* comes alive in act 3

when the Prince speaks out in the storm. Here
Shakespeare introduces both the cycle of life and death
prominent in the last plays and the "central problem":
"what value can attach to a life where everything
passes away?" (p. 17). *Pericles* never resolves or
explores the problem; rather, it suggests that life is
a mixture of opposites: "love and violence, pleasure
and pain, gain and loss" (p. 18). The scene of
Thaisa's recovery by Cerimon foreshadows the final
scene of *The Winter's Tale*. Of special note is the
jewel imagery. The scene contains some of
Shakespeare's greatest poetry, although the effect is
diminished by its weak context. Thaisa's sudden,
guiltless death, her immediate resurrection, and her
disappearance into fourteen-year seclusion at Ephesus
are the silly hallmarks of *Pericles*. The brothel
scenes were probably not meant to be funny. The Bawd
is vital, but Marina is too cold and her triumph too
easy. She is a lifeless symbol of chastity compared to
Imogen. The recognition scene between Pericles and
Marina (5.1) is as great as the storm scene in act 3.
Pericles' address to Helicanus, the poetic and thematic
high point of the play, points toward its successors.
By comparison the rest of the play is trite and
unsatisfying. *Pericles* is important only as "a source"
(p. 23) for *Cymbeline*, *The Winter's Tale*, and *The
Tempest*.

68. Matthews, Honor. *Character and Symbol in Shakespeare's
    Plays: A Study of Certain Christian and Pre-
    Christian Elements in Their Structure and Imagery*.
    Cambridge: At the University Press, 1962, pp.
    179-208.

    Sin, judgment, and redemption are characteristic of
Shakespeare's plays. Shakespeare associates sin "with
hubris and the breach of degree" (p. 179). Pericles
breaches degree. As Prince he leaves Helicanus to rule
Tyre; as a father he leaves Marina to the care of Cleon
and Dionyza. When Pericles and Thaisa are reunited, he
returns to his proper place as a ruler. Shakespeare
combined natural magic with Christianity in the last
plays. Thus, Marina first appears carrying spring
flowers in her arms. She shares her sea birth with
Venus. Redemption in these plays belongs to sinner and
innocent alike. Hermione, mother of Perdita in *The
Winter's Tale*, and Thaisa, mother of Marina in
Pericles, suffer for their husbands' sins; each is

finally reunited with her husband and daughter. When
Pericles recognizes Marina at Mytilene, he becomes
reconciled to himself and accordingly hears the music
of the spheres.

69. Bender, Robert Morton. "Such Noble Scenes: The
    Function of Spectacle in Shakespeare's Last Plays."
    Ph.D. dissertation, University of Michigan, 1963.
    Dissertation Abstracts, 24 (1963): 2472A.

    Between 1599 and 1613 a vogue for stage spectacle
    existed that included both the delicate pastorals of
    the private theatres and the hearty plays performed on
    the public stage. With its simplified plot and
    characters and its emphatic music, dance, costuming,
    and spectacle, *Pericles* is a thoroughly visual play,
    Shakespeare's first experiment in spectacle drama.

70. Durrett, Carlos William. "Shakespeare's Final
    Comedies: The Christian Patterns." Ph.D.
    dissertation, Vanderbilt University, 1962.
    Dissertation Abstracts, 23 (1963): 3886.

    Pericles, *Cymbeline*, *The Winter's Tale*, and *The
    Tempest* are comedies in the medieval sense, each play
    offering a variation on the Christian pattern of sin,
    punishment, remorse, repentance, and redemption.
    Pericles does not sin; he finds sin. Suffering makes
    him aware of evil and gives him a new understanding of
    good.

71. Guidi, Augusto. "L'Ultima fase di Shakespeare" [The
    Last Phase of Shakespeare]. *Cultura e Scuola* (Rome),
    no. 7 (1963): 85-91.

    Guidi surveys critical approaches to the last plays
    and discusses reasons for grouping these plays (romance
    and pastoral motifs, narrative structures, complex
    plots, stereotyped characters).

72. Kermode, Frank. "*Pericles*." *William Shakespeare: The
    Final Plays*. Writers and Their Work, no. 155. 1963.
    Reprint. Harlow, Essex: Longman Group, 1973, pp.
    10-17.

    Shakespeare wrote the better part of *Pericles*,
    beginning with act 3. The last three acts demonstrate
    his interest in restoring harmony. The theme of

separation and reunion in *Pericles* is prototypical of the other romances. The book includes a bibliography of editions and critical studies (pp. 55-56).

73. Pafford, J.H.P., ed. "Introduction." *The Winter's Tale*. New Arden Shakespeare. London: Methuen, 1963, pp. xliv-l.

> *The Winter's Tale* and *Pericles* are similar in plot and the theme of jealousy. In *Pericles*, however, the Prince is no sinner, as Leontes is, nor is he responsible for the separations. All four romances center on parents and children; but in *The Winter's Tale* and *Pericles*, the older generations have renewed lives before them. In both plays the older generations suffer, as does a young heroine in danger, and the sea threatens young and old alike. Fairytale, folklore, and music combine in a rhythm that moves toward harmony in each of Shakespeare's romances, including *Cymbeline* and *Henry 8*.

74. Rowse, A.L. *William Shakespeare: A Biography*. London: MacMillan, 1963, pp. 415-20.

> The plague years 1608-1609 separate Shakespeare's tragedies from the romances. Perhaps E.K. Chambers was right to conjecture that Shakespeare attempted *Timon of Athens* early in 1608 and suffered a nervous breakdown thereafter. Perhaps he came to write his part of *Pericles*, acts 3-5, in a religious frame of mind. Shakespeare seems to have revised parts of acts 1-2. The themes and atmosphere of *Pericles* are Shakespearean throughout. Such visions of reunion, reconciliation, and forgiveness belong to Shakespeare's final period of writing. The romances are withdrawn and enigmatic like Beethoven's final quartets. Like *The Tempest*, *Pericles* is composed of sea and music. With their language of disease, the brothel scenes suggests the Jacobean age, characteristic Shakespeare images, and *Timon*.

75. Srinivasa, K.R. Iyengar. "Shakespeare's Last Plays." *Literary Criterion* (Mysore), 6, no. 1 (1963): 121-30. Reprint. *Shakespeare Came to India*. Edited by C.D. Narasimhaiah. Bombay: Popular Prakashan Press, 1964, pp. 47-56.

> Srinivasa points out common characteristics in the four romances and reviews criticism which analyzes the

late romances as Shakespeare's final artistic
statement.

76. Alexander, Peter. "*Pericles.*" *Alexander's
    Introductions to Shakespeare.* London: Collins; New
    York: Norton, 1964, pp. 174-76.

    Dual authorship for *Pericles*, the simplest solution
    to the authorship problem, agrees with the external
    evidence. The themes and poetry of act 3-5 are
    entirely Shakespeare's. The loss and restoration theme
    is a part of *The Winter's Tale* and *The Tempest* as well.
    George Wilkins seems too unfamiliar with *Pericles* in
    his *Painfull Aduentures* (1608) to have been the other
    author.

77. Anaya Valdepeña, Gabriel. "!¿Qué nunca hizo
    Shakespeare un drama en el que el matrimonio fuera el
    tema?!" *Impacto* (Mexico), 4 March 1964, p. 42. (not
    seen)

    The article concerns conjugal love in Shakespeare,
    especially *Pericles*.

78. Eastman, Arthur M. and G.B. Harrison. *Shakespeare's
    Critics from Jonson to Auden: A Medley of Judgments.*
    Ann Arbor: University of Michigan Press, 1964.

    Pericles is mentioned in commentaries by Northrop
    Frye (p. 119) and E.K. Chambers (pp. 138-39).

79. Empson, William. "Hunt the Symbol." *Times Literary
    Supplement*, 23 April 1964, pp. 339-41.

    Locators of religious symbolism in the last plays,
    including G. Wilson Knight in *The Crown of Life* (see
    item 14) and Derek A. Traversi in *Shakespeare: The Last
    Phase* (see item 34) exaggerate. While there is much
    religious or mythical feeling in the last plays, it is
    not a credo. Shakespeare was tired of writing
    tragedies when he chose *Pericles*, a bad play by someone
    else, as easy work; he continued the same story in the
    other romances. Passages from the brothel scenes in
    act 4 of *Pericles* contain false sentiment that may
    denote "a new mood of Puritanism" (p. 340).

80. Falconer, Alexander Frederick. *Shakespeare and the
    Sea.* London: Constable, 1964.

The trappings of Pericles' ship riding at anchor in the Mytilene harbor (5.1) as well as the approach of Lysimachus by barge, his boarding by rope ladder, his formal challenge, and its acceptance by Helicanus show Shakespeare's familiarity with the sea. Thaisa's consignment to the sea (3.1) may have been marked by a cannon volley. *Pericles* is mentioned also in sections on storms, ships' officers, ordinary seamen, parts of a ship, fishermen, and blessings for those born at sea.

81. Garcia Lora, José. "Pericles y Apolonio." *La Palabra y el Hombre* (Veracruz), 32 (1964): 597-611. (not seen)

82. Leech, Clifford. "Shakespeare's Greeks." *Stratford Papers on Shakespeare 1963.* Edited by B.W. Jackson. New York: Drama Book Specialists, 1964, pp. 1-20.

   Among Shakespeare's Greek plays—*The Comedy of Errors, A Midsummer Night's Dream, Troilus and Cressida, Timon of Athens,* and *The Winter's Tale*—*Pericles* is the most loosely structured, simply charactered, and variously localized. Discussion centers on *Troilus and Cressida* and *Timon of Athens.*

83. Martin, Walther. "Die Bedeutung der Romanzen Shakespeares für unsere Zeit." *Shakespeare Jubiläum 1964.* Weimar: Hermann Böhlaus Nachfolger, 1964, pp. 121-43.

   In determining what the four romances have to say to us today, the casual reader or spectator may conclude from the bewildering number of opinions put forward over the years that Shakespeare had no viewpoint. However, the message of the four romances is the eventual victory of harmony over disharmony.

84. Mashita, Yasutoshi. *"Pericles." Eigoseinen,* 110 (1964): 344-45. (Japanese—not seen)

85. Mashita, Yasutoshi. *"Pericles." Rising Generation,* May 1964, pp. 88-89. (Japanese—not seen)

86. Mehl, Dieter. *Die Pantomime im Drama der Shakespearezeit.* Heidelberg: Quelle and Meyer, 1964.

   See item 105.

87. Milward, Peter. "The Last Plays." *An Introduction to*
     Shakespeare's Plays. 1964. Reprint. Folcroft, Pa.:
     Folcroft, 1970, pp. 132-55.

     In the last plays, which concern forgiveness and
     reconciliation between two generations, tragedy is
     finally overcome. Shakespeare was little concerned
     with unity or characterization in these plays.
     Instead, he wished to present in new dramatic form his
     triumphant vision of life. *Pericles*, the first play to
     express the new vision, is flawed and only partially
     Shakespeare's. Acts 1-2, seemingly part of an old
     play, have no value in themselves, but acts 3-5,
     beginning with the sea storm, contain Shakespeare's
     revision of the old play.

88. Rajasekharaiah, T.R. "The Transcendent Vision (A Note
     on Shakespeare's Last Plays)." *Journal of the*
     Karnatak University (Dharwar). 8 (1964): 99-112.
     (not seen)

89. Speaight, Robert. "Christian Significance of
     Shakespeare's Later Plays: The Forgotten Fact." *The*
     Critic: A Magazine of Christian Culture, 22
     (February-March 1964): 15-19.

     Shakespeare's later plays are theophanies arising
     from myth. Shakespeare took over someone else's flawed
     Pericles at act 3 because of its Christian themes of
     innocence triumphant, guilt repentant, and
     resurrection. The ceremony of the last plays,
     including the dumbshows and Thaisa's recovery in
     Pericles, are natural to religion as well as theatre.
     With its stereotype characters, *The Tempest* moves
     toward masque and is the greatest mystery play. *The*
     Winter's Tale is as counterpointed as *The Tempest* is
     unified. The scenes of the Delphan oracle in *The*
     Winter's Tale and in Diana's temple at Ephesus in
     Pericles resound with Christian harmonics. The themes
     and scenes of the romantic comedies echo in the
     romances even as the tempests in *Pericles* prefigure
     those in *The Winter's Tale* and *The Tempest*. What Dante
     achieved with allegory, Shakespeare achieved less
     explicitly in his later plays.

90. Srinivasa, K.R. Iyengar. *Shakespeare: His World and*
     His Art. New York and Bombay: Asia Publishing House,
     1964, pp. 565-73.

Pericles is enough Shakespeare's play to be part of the canon. This story of an Ulysses spans a lifetime with Gower to link the loose episodes for the audience. In *Pericles* life is a journey and a battle. Even though the play is botched in its first two acts, Shakespeare's attempt at a new version is undeniable. Wandering and suffering Pericles comes to patience and faith. The reward of evil is death. Cerimon represents higher knowledge. Marina is grace personified and the symbol of resurrection.

91. Berry, Francis. "Word and Picture in the Final Plays." *The Shakespeare Inset: Word and Picture.* London: Routledge and Kegan Paul, 1965, pp. 144–65. Reprint. *Later Shakespeare.* Stratford-upon-Avon Studies 8. Edited by John R. Brown and Bernard Harris. London: Edward Arnold, 1966; New York: St. Martin's, 1967, pp. 80-101.

Stage space creates temporal distance in *Pericles*. Speaking his prologue downstage, Gower describes upstage events more distant in time than himself. After Gower has relegated his story to the distant past and the audience has seen the episode prefigured in dumb show, the characters move forward, into the present, to act out the story. After each action Gower reappears, returning the audience to time long past. The spatial and temporal manipulation in *Pericles* is Shakespeare's attempt to merge stories combining two generations and two genres, tragedy and romance, into one play.

92. Bowers, J.L. "The Romances." Shakespeare at 400: A Series of Public Lectures Given in May and June 1964 by Members of the Department of English (Literature) on the Occasion of the Four-Hundredth Anniversary of William Shakespeare's Birth. Edited by R.G. Howarth et al. Mimeographed. Capetown: Editorial Board of the University of Cape Town, 1965, pp. 42-63.

The romances are tragicomedies which have aroused different critical opinions. *Pericles* and *The Winter's Tale* follow the medieval pattern of sin, judgment, and redemption softened by faith in nature and love. Pulled from the natural hierarchy of princely duty by his escape from Antiochus, Pericles loses both kingdom and family before Marina, his child from the sea,

restores them.   The dramatic distancing in *Pericles* is
the result of limited dramatic tension.

93. Frye, Northrop. *A Natural Perspective: The Development
     of Shakespearean Comedy and Romance*. New York:
     Columbia University Press, 1965.

     The four lectures in the book examine the general
     characteristics of Shakespeare's comedies and dramatic
     romances. No play is given sustained attention.
     Chapter 1 defines romance; chapter 2 explains the
     characteristics of romance; chapter 3 explores
     structure, and chapter 4 considers the cyclical
     movement of the romance. The most extensive comments
     on *Pericles* occur in chapter 1. *Pericles* is one of the
     first operas. The role of music in *Pericles*
     corresponds to that of magic in *The Tempest*. *Pericles*
     influenced Eliot's "Waste Land," in which the
     dislocations of narrative structure serve as the
     organizing principle. The symmetrical design of
     Pericles, the unbelievable actions of the characters,
     and the simplicity of the plot belong to an art form
     that demands uncritical acceptance from the audience.

94. Hunter, Robert Grams.   "The Romance and the Comedy of
     Forgiveness." *Shakespeare and the Comedy of
     Forgiveness*. New York: Columbia University Press,
     1965, pp. 132-41.

     A play clearly in the medieval romance tradition,
     Pericles shows the influence of the melodramatic,
     "Fortune-my-foe" theatrical romances, perhaps because
     the play is not entirely Shakespeare's. In *Cymbeline*,
     Measure for Measure, *The Winter's Tale*, and *The
     Tempest*, Shakespeare "imposes . . . a meaningful
     pattern of sin, repentance, and forgiveness" on the
     "disordered series of thrilling adventures" (p. 141)
     that make up plays such as *Pericles*.

95. Russell, Patricia Howard. "Shakespeare and the
     Dramatic Romance." Ph.D. Dissertation, University of
     Toronto, 1965. *Dissertation Abstracts*, 26 (1965):
     2728.

     Shakespeare was indebted to the dramatic romances of
     the 1580s, to court entertainments, and to the plays of
     Lyly and Greene. *Pericles* matches an old tale with
     spectacle derived from the masque. Beaumont and

Fletcher's extravagantly plotted plays differ from
Cymbeline, The Winter's Tale, and *The Tempest,* plays
that combine versimilitude with artificiality.

96. Thorne, William Barry. "The Influence of Folk-Drama on
     Shakespearian Comedy." Ph.D. dissertation,
     University of Wisconsin-Madison, 1965. *Dissertation*
     Abstracts, 25 (1965): 6603-04.

     Thorne studies Shakespeare's use of elements of
     English folk drama in eight of Shakespeare's plays.
     These elements include the mummers' play, the Maying
     theme, the "flight to the woods," misrule, and the
     resurrection motif. The early comedies—*The Taming of*
     the Shrew, The Two Gentlemen of Verona, Love's Labor's
     Lost, and *A Midsummer Night's Dream*—show the
     development of a structural opposition between a normal
     world and a green world. *Much Ado about Nothing,* a
     transitional play, contains a structural use of the
     rebirth motif, a folk theme hinted at in the early
     comedies and central to *Pericles, Cymbeline,* and *A*
     Winter's Tale. Thus, Shakespeare's late plays contain
     sophistications of themes present in the early
     comedies. Throughout his career, Shakespeare used folk
     themes increasingly, along with classical or literary
     tales. Shakespeare's polar structure presents an
     artificial world for the main action that provides a
     perspective from which to evaluate the reality to which
     the characters return in the end.

97. Van Domelen, John Emory. "G. Wilson Knight and the
     Last Plays of Shakespeare." Ph.D. dissertation,
     Michigan State University, 1964. *Dissertation*
     Abstracts, 25 (1965): 5288.

     In his "spatial" approach to *Pericles, Cymbeline, The*
     Winter's Tale, The Tempest, and *Henry 8,* Knight finds
     mythic patterns and gives the plays metaphysical
     interpretations. All Knight's critical work reflects
     his Shakespearean theories. Knight does not
     Christianize Shakespeare; he approaches him as a
     romantic.

98. Brown, John Russell. "Laughter in the Last Plays."
     Later Shakespeare. Stratford-upon-Avon Studies 8.
     Edited by John Russell Brown and Bernard Harris.
     1966. Reprint. New York: St. Martin's Press, 1967,
     p. 120.

Pericles, of which Shakespeare probably wrote only a
portion, has the least comedy among the romances. The
brothel scenes in act 4, led by Boult as clown,
contrast the on-going narrative of the play.

99. Collier, Lewis Arlen. "The Redemptive Element of the
     Natural Setting in Shakespeare's Tragedies and Late
     Romances." Ph.D. dissertation, University of
     Washington, 1966. *Dissertation Abstracts*, 27 (1966):
     1781A.

     The natural settings of *Hamlet* and *King Lear* are in
     contrast to those of *Timon of Athens*, *Pericles*,
     Cymbeline, *The Winter's Tale*, and *The Tempest*.
     Shakespeare's plays with the most natural settings
     contain the themes of purgation and redemption.
     Boethian philosophy informs the sea settings in
     Pericles.

100. Felperin, Howard Michael. "Shakespeare's Romances: The
     Aesthetics of Maturity." Ph.D. dissertation, Harvard
     University, 1966. (not seen)

101. Hiraiwa, Norio. "Ben Jonson to *Pericles* no Emblem"
     [Ben Jonson and the Emblem in *Pericles*]. *Shiron*
     (Shiron-Donin-kai, Sendai), no. 8 (March 1966):
     113-15. (not seen)

102. Ingram, R.W. "Musical Pauses and the Vision Scenes in
     Shakespeare's Last Plays." *Pacific Coast Studies in
     Shakespeare*. Edited by Waldo F. McNeir and Thelma N.
     Greenfield. Eugene: University of Oregon Books,
     1966, pp. 234-47.

     Shakespeare used musical interludes in his plays to
     keep emotion alive. The musical pause in *Pericles*--
     the vision scene (5.1.241-49)--duplicates Pericles and
     Marina's reunion. The vision scene in *Pericles* is the
     first and simplest in the romances.

103. Kaul, Mythili. "The Court and the Country: A Study of
     Shakespeare's Last Plays." Ph.D. dissertation, Yale
     University, 1965. *Dissertation Abstracts*, 26 (1966):
     4662.

     The theme of court versus country dominates
     Shakespeare's four romances. Three background chapters
     survey criticism of the last plays, the romance

tradition, and the opposition between court and country
in the writing of Shakespeare and his contemporaries.
Individual essays on the romances demonstrate their
"remarkable plot-coherence and dramatic unity."

104. Kohl, Norbert. "Das Wortspiel in der Shakespeareschen
     Komödie, Studien zur Interdependez von Verbalem and
     Aktionalem Spiel in den Frühen Komödien und in den
     Späten Stücken." Ph.D. dissertation, Cologne, 1966.
     (not seen)

105. Mehl, Dieter. *The Elizabethan Dumb Show: The History
     of a Dramatic Convention*. Cambridge: Harvard
     University Press, 1966, pp. 105, 156-59, 183. First
     published as *Die Pantomime im Drama der
     Shakespearezeit*. Heidelberg: Quelle and Meyer, 1964.

     The skillful dumb shows in *Pericles* regularly link
     otherwise isolated episodes and introduce new events
     concisely. In separating acts with dumb shows,
     Shakespeare followed the tradition of the formal dumb
     shows in classical tragedies. However, in *Pericles*
     these formal pantomimes fit rather than contrast the
     tone and episodic sequence of the play; the emphasis is
     on the strange rather than the probable. The choruses,
     dialogue, scenes, and dumb shows create the loosely-
     woven enchantment of *Pericles*.

106. Mirek, Roman. "Sylwetki osobowosciowe postaci
     Szekspirowskich tragedii: *Troilus i Kresyda,
     Koriolan, Tymon Atenczyk, Perykles, Tytus Andronikus,
     Cymbelin, Romeo i Julia*." *Przeglad Lekarski*, 23
     (1966): 477-80. (not seen)

     The article contains personality sketches of
     characters in Shakespeare's tragedies.

107. Mohan, Laxmikant. *Shakespeare's Men and Women: A
     Psychological Interpretation. Vol. II: The Kings from
     the Historicals*. Hyderabad: Folk Theatre Books,
     1966. (not seen)

     This volume offers psychological analyses of the
     royal characters in the history plays and *Pericles*.

108. Nelson, Thomas Allen. "Shakespeare's Comic Theory: A
     Study of Symbolic Action and Character in the
     Dramatic Romances." Ph.D. dissertation, Tulane

University, 1966. *Dissertation Abstracts*, 27
(1966): 1343A. Reprint. *Shakespeare's Comic Theory:
A Study of Art and Artifice in the Last Plays*. The
Hague: Mouton, 1972.

This dissertation compares the characters, actions,
and themes in the romances with those in other
Shakespeare plays.

109. Salingar, L.G. "Time and Art in Shakespeare's
      Romances." *Renaissance Drama*, 9 (1966): 3-35.

The fifth section of this eight-part essay concerns
the dramatic construction of *Pericles*. Shakespeare had
to make believable in performance the passage of many
years in *Pericles*. To do so he avoided character
development and distanced his audience with a fable
resembling a miracle play presented by ancient Gower.
Unlike Shakespeare's later, somewhat more modern heroes
of romance, Pericles is the passive receiver of divine
providence. In the romances that follow *Pericles*,
Shakespeare attempted to synthesize medieval and
Renaissance stagecraft.

110. Auberlen, Eckhard. "Die Rolle des Unwahrscheinlichen
      in den Romanzen Shakespeares." Ph.D. dissertation,
      Frankfurt, 1967. (not seen)

111. Felperin, Howard. "Shakespeare's Miracle Play."
      Shakespeare Quarterly, 18 (1967): 363-74.

The shift from more naturalistic plays to a
deliberately archaic and allegorical play denotes
Shakespeare's acceptance around 1607 of a more
spiritual vision of life. Shakespeare used Gower with
his archaic language and moralizing approach to prepare
the audience of *Pericles* for a parable. The equation
of incest and essential sin in the first scene is
treated similarly in *Duk Moraud*. Pericles is an
Everyman; the play is an allegory. When Everyman-
Pericles washes ashore at Pentapolis, he is treated to
a feast emblematic of life itself and enjoys the
secular blessings of love and marriage. In act 3 the
allegorical method changes. Pericles' experiences
become increasingly more personal; through oblique
suggestion Shakespeare relates them to universal
experience. The pain of loss suffered by Pericles and
Thaisa moves them toward medieval asceticism. Act 4

belongs to Marina; her abduction by Valdes' pirates is
comparable to Prosperpina's capture by Dis.
Shakespeare continues the myth in the Mytilene
underworld where Marina, unlike Prosperpina, remains
absolute. Shakespeare's heroine belongs to the
tradition of virtuous heroines which includes St.
Agnes, Virginia, Grissill, Desdemona, and Cordelia. In
act 5 a religious vision emerges. Shakespeare stresses
endurance and submission to the gods over his sources.
Pericles' rapture in the recognition scene (5.1) is a
secular treatment of the salvation scene that ends
numerous miracle plays. Mortal union in *Pericles* is an
analogue for reunion in the afterworld. Shakespeare
had used escatalogical metaphors in his earlier plays,
but in *Pericles* the metaphors become real. In the
plays after *Pericles*, Shakespeare returned to a more
naturalistic world, his vision of life having become
increasingly more complex. See item 155.

112. Kirsch, Arthur C. *"Cymbeline* and Coterie Dramaturgy."
     ELH, 34 (1967): 285-306. Reprint, *Shakespeare's
     Later Comedies: An Anthology of Modern Criticism*.
     Edited by D.J. Palmer. Harmondsworth: Penguin, 1971,
     pp. 264-87.

     In arguing *Cymbeline, The Winter's Tale*, and *The
     Tempest* as plays written for the private theatre,
     Kirsch says that *Pericles* is "[t]he one intractable
     stumbing block" (p.305). Even if *Pericles*, a play
     indisputably written for the public stage, initiated
     the last plays, Shakespeare's later involvement with
     Blackfriars affected the plays written after *Pericles*.
     Like *Troilus and Cressida, Pericles* itself shows the
     influence of coterie theatre in the Antioch scenes,
     which deal with incest, and the brothel scenes.
     Neither the sexual aspect of *Pericles* nor its
     distancing features--its pageantry and ancient narrator
     Gower--stem from earlier public plays such as *The Rare
     Triumphs of Love and Fortune* and *Mucedorus*.

113. Rabkin, Norman. "The Great Globe Itself." *Shakespeare
     and the Common Understanding*. London: Collier; New
     York: Macmillan, 1967, pp. 192-237.

     The last romances concern art, although the first two
     plays, *Pericles* and *Cymbeline*, fail to celebrate
     artistic technique fully. *Pericles* treats art only
     tangentially. The Prince has no inner life; he is a

passive hero. Seldom is the language of the play
vital. The naive and artificial Gower choruses
emphasize the distance between his flat and lengthy
narrative and the transforming power of the stage. In
crude form *Pericles* contains the final focus of
Shakespeare's complementary vision: "the paradoxical
simultaneity of the convincing illusion created by art
and the paltry, often claptrap materials that make
illusion possible" (p. 200).

114.   Silverman, John Michael. "Formal Solutions: Structure
       in Shakespearean Romance." Ph.D. dissertation,
       University of Washington, 1966. *Dissertation
       Abstracts International*, 27 (1967): 3018A-19A.

       Shakespeare's last plays avoid resolution. In
       Pericles there is a tension between "form and disorder"
       exemplified by the disparity between the antiquarian
       demands Gower makes on his story and the story which
       the audience sees.

115.   Smith, Hallett. "Shakespeare's Last Plays: Facts and
       Problems." *Shakespeare Research Opportunities*, 3
       (1967): 9-16.

       There is room for studies of the following: the last
       plays and the theatres for which they were written, the
       relationship between the romances and the early
       comedies, and the dating and authorship of particular
       plays, including *Pericles*. Future critical analyses
       should avoid misusing myth and theology.

116.   Cutts, John P. "*Pericles*: 'Downright Violence.'" *Rich
       and Strange: A Study of Shakespeare's Last Plays*.
       [Pullman:] Washington State University Press, 1968, pp.
       4-23.

       The last plays are not romances; they are something
       "rich and strange" beyond tragedy where sin is either
       killed or locked away. All characters in the last
       plays are guilty of sin; each hides behind a mask of
       what he thinks he is. Pericles sins in having desired
       Antiochus' daughter, and Thaisa sins by breaking her
       vow to Diana. The recognition scenes bring expiation.
       The Quarto is not corrupt; scenes in the Quarto are
       correct as they stand.

117. Cutts, John P. "Pericles' 'Downright Violence.'"
    Shakespeare Studies, 4 (1968): 275-93.

    With minor differences this essay appears in *Rich and
    Strange: A Study of Shakespeare's Last Plays*. See item
    116.

118. Edwards, Philip. "Last Plays." *Shakespeare and the
    Confines of Art*. London: Methuen, 1968, pp. 139-59.

    Shakespeare wrote a play of *Pericles* for which only a
    maimed text, the work of two reporters, remains (see
    item 413). As an old tale *Pericles* asks to be
    disbelieved. The play deals with moments, not the
    relationship between the moments. The strongest links
    between *Pericles* and the other romances is virgin
    Marina's defeat of the brothel crew and the reunion
    between father and daughter.

119. Hartwig, Helen Joan. "Shakespeare's Tragicomic
    Vision." Ph.D. dissertation, Washington University,
    1967. *Dissertation Abstracts International*, 28
    (1968): 4129A-30A.

    This dissertation is an earlier version of an
    identically titled book. See item 158.

120. Jachmann, Jochen. "Ein nützliches Denkmal für Gower.
    Der alte englische Dichter, die Elisabethaner und das
    Pericles Schauspiel." *Prisma* (Bochum), 14 (1968):
    160-62. (not seen)

121. Barber, C.L. "'Thou That Beget'st Him That Did Thee
    Beget': Transformation in *Pericles* and *The Winter's
    Tale*." *Shakespeare Survey*, 22 (1969): 59-67.

    This essay traces themes of transformed incest and
    homosexuality in *Pericles* and *The Winter's Tale*. The
    climactic scenes in the romances represent
    transformations during which the main characters regard
    one another in a central tableau while the other
    characters describe and eulogize them. The effect is
    to move these distinctive humans toward deity. Whereas
    in festive comedy sexuality is freed from familial
    restraint, in the romances family ties are freed "from
    the threat of sexual degradation" (p. 61). During the
    recognition scene in *Pericles* (5.1), which is filled
    with sea imagery, when Pericles recognizes Marina as

his daughter, he also sees in her an image of his wife.
Shakespeare joined sea imagery with that of
childbearing during the storm scene at the beginning of
act 3. In *King Lear* Sheakespeare contrasts Goneril and
Regan's sexual greed with Cordelia's gentle,
sacrificial nature. He deals overtly with incest and
sexual jealousy in *Pericles*. Early in the play
Pericles escapes entanglement with Antiochus and his
daughter; later Dionyza, the stepmother of Marina,
tries to kill her. In *Pericles* Marina gains self-
knowledge as a regenerated Thaisa. In *The Winter's
Tale* Shakespeare dramatizes Perdita's sexual awakening.
The final recognition scene in *Pericles* is
anticlimactic because it is foreknown; Pericles' has
already recovered Thaisa symbolically in Marina.
Pericles contains the motif of transformed incest; *The
Winter's Tale* contains that of transformed
homosexuality.

122.   Dunn, Catherine M. "The Function of Music in
       Shakespeare's Romances." *Shakespeare Quarterly*, 20
       (1969): 391-405.

       Boethius divided music into three branches: *musica
       mundana, musica humana,* and *musica instrumentalis*.
       Musica mundana refers to universal harmony; *musica
       humana* is the harmony of reason maintained between the
       body and the soul; and *musica instrumentalis* is applied
       music. *Pericles* contains examples of *musica humana* and
       musica mundana. Instances of *musica humana*, such as
       Pericles' reference to Antiochus' daughter as "a fair
       viol" and the musical terms used by Lysimachus to
       describe Pericles' madness, concern temperament, the
       harmonious or disharmonious tuning of character. There
       are also references to music as therapy; namely,
       Simonides' call for dancing to remedy Pericles'
       melancholy, Cerimon's appeal to music as a restorative
       for Thaisa, and Lysimachus' request that Marina sing to
       the distempered Pericles. Marina's song introduces
       musica mundana, the music of the spheres, which
       Pericles hears on waking from his trance. By placing
       this single instance of *musica mundana* at the dramatic
       high point of the play, Shakespeare suggests a
       Neoplatonic answer to mankind's problems. The
       exclamation, "I am wild in my beholding" (5.1.224),
       does not refer to Pericles' unkempt appearance; rather,
       it indicates a state of musical rapture which
       culminates in Pericles' hearing the music of the

spheres and seeing a vision of Diana. The number of
musical references and occasions in *Pericles*
demonstrates its Neoplatonic foundations.

123. Harder, Harry R. "A Critical Study of Shakespeare's
     Last Plays." Ph.D. dissertation, Bowling Green State
     University, 1969. *Dissertation Abstracts
     International*, 30 (1969): 2485A.

     Realism unites Shakespeare's four romances. *Pericles*
     is the most romantic and least realistic of the four
     plays. Its lack of realism results from Shakespeare's
     having written only the second half of the play.
     Cymbeline is less like the other romances, especially
     Pericles, than critics have thought. *The Winter's Tale*
     resembles *Pericles* in plot, but it has fully developed,
     believable characters. With believable characters and
     a hopeful but mature outlook, *The Tempest* is the high
     point of Shakespeare's career.

124. Stuart, Betty Kantor. "Principles of Structure in
     Shakespeare's Last Plays." Ph.D. dissertation,
     University of California-Berkeley, 1968.
     Dissertation Abstracts International, 29 (1969):
     4470A-71A.

     The structure of *Pericles*, *Cymbeline*, *The Winter's
     Tale*, *The Tempest*, and *Henry 8* is circular. Life and
     death merge constantly. Even though the plays differ,
     their theme is the same. To understand the
     significance of a particular action, one must know the
     entire play. The imagery in *Pericles*, especially the
     references to Jonah, signals Pericles' unwitting sin in
     act 1, the audience's initial ignorance of his guilt,
     and his eventual salvation through Marina.

125. Traversi, Derek A. *"Pericles: Prince of Tyre."* An
     Approach to Shakespeare. 3rd ed. rev. Garden City,
     N.Y.: Doubleday, 1969, pp. 560-70, and vol. 2 of 2
     vol. ed., Doubleday, Anchor, 1969, pp. 264-75.

     The chapter is a revision of a longer essay in
     Shakespeare: The Last Phase (see item 34). Some parts
     offer slightly altered opinions; other parts appear
     verbatim in the earlier essay, including the erroneous
     betrothal of Marina to Cerimon in the final sentence.
     Pericles and *Cymbeline* are plays of poetic symbolism
     which presage Shakespeare's greater artistic successes,

The Winter's Tale and *The Tempest*. In *Pericles*
Shakespeare attempted to unify an imperfect theme in a
play not entirely his. Acts 1-2 contain a series of
events that show Pericles' moral growth, beginning with
his false dream of love for Antiochus' daughter and
ending with his marriage to Thaisa. Shakespeare gave
the story a tragic turn in act 3 with a sea strom and
Thaisa's seeming death. The true play begins here and
introduces the symbolism of Shakespeare's romances:
death and birth, storm and calm, old and new. Act 3
contains resurrection images; namely, the jewel imagery
symbolizing Thaisa's transformation from death to life.
Act 4 lacks the depth and artistry of act 3, but the
poetry in act 5 equals that of act 3. In the
recognition scene (5.1) a transfigured Marina brings
Pericles to new life. The recognition scene at Ephesus
(5.3) celebrates final spiritual awakening.

126.   Ueno, Yoshiko. *"Pericles." A Shakespeare Handbook*.
       Edited by Jiro Ozu. Tokyo: Nanundo, 1969, pp.
       469-75. (Japanese--not seen)

127.   Babula, William. "Shakespeare's Romances and Early
       English Tragicomic Patterns." Ph.D. dissertation,
       University of California-Berkeley, 1969.
       Dissertation Abstracts International, 31 (1970):
       726A.

       Medieval drama and Renaissance tragicomedy, tragedy,
       and dramatic romance possess a dual structure which
       represents a worldly view of life and a belief in
       providence. Tragicomedy uses historical examples of
       divine justice; dramatic romance emphasizes the artist
       as the instrument of providence. Each of Shakespeare's
       romances has a dual structure and perspective, and in
       each romance artifice helps reconcile the worldly with
       the divine. Shakespeare used artificiality and
       audience manipulation increasingly in the romances to
       achieve a tragicomic solution acceptable to the
       audience. By combining with the providential viewpoint
       a secular view of life as random and meaningless, he
       extended the limits of tragicomedy. See item 196.

128.   Garber, Marjorie Beth. "The Size of Dreaming: Uses of
       Dream in Shakespeare." Ph.D. dissertation, Yale
       University, 1969. *Dissertation Abstracts
       International*, 31 (1970): 1227A.

The last part of the dissertation concerns the four romances, plays in which dream blends with reality. Metamorphoses and transformations move the characters into dream states from which they wake with heightened knowledge. Containing various symbols and myths of life as a cyclical journey of growth and renewal, the last plays are deliberately non-naturalistic. Art is the transforming, renewing agent; the dream state is the necessary place of transfiguration and renewal. See item 180.

129. Halperin, Richard. "The Final Vision of William Shakespeare." Ph.D. dissertation, City University of New York, 1969. *Dissertation Abstracts International*, 31 (1970): 358A.

   Pericles, Cymbeline, The Winter's Tale, and *The Tempest* contain Shakespeare's final statement on humanity. With *Pericles* Shakespeare began a new dramatic form that finally established certain themes ("man and woman, father and daughter, king and subject, friend and friend, youth and age, wit and bluntness, willfulness and meekness, birth-death-rebirth, magnanimity") present in his earlier plays. The evolution of these themes accompanied the development of Shakespeare's dramatic consciousness. Shakespeare maintains an authorial presence in his final plays.

130. Heckscher, William S. "Shakespeare in His Relationship to the Visual Arts: A Study in Paradox." *Research Opportunities in Renaissance Drama*, 13-14 (1970-1971): 5-71.

   Shakespeare alluded to actual art works vaguely; the art works of his imagination he described in detail. The first of two sections in this essay concerned with *Pericles* (p. 9) links the *impresa* Shakespeare was commissioned to design for a tournament on 24 March 1613 with his 1608 *impresa* in *Pericles* (2.2) for the five knights. Heckscher also discusses (pp. 24, 36-56) Pericles' oblique allusion to "Patience gazing on kings' graves" (5.1.136) as an icon with which his audience would have been familiar. The image in the play represents Pericles' enoblement through long suffering. The play is itself a treatise on patience. Shakespeare probably had in mind an actual gazing statue such as those attached to royal tombs, an example of which is the fourteenth-century Fortitudo-

Patientia statue that forms a part of the royal tomb at
St. Denis.

131. Konishi, Eirin. "Shijin no Shakespeare Hihyo--T.S.
      Eliot no Shakespeare-kan" [Shakespeare as Seen by a
      Poet--T.S. Eliot on Shakespeare]. *Kiyo* (Kyoyobu,
      Ehime Daigaku), no. 2 (Feb. 1970): 53-78. (not seen)

132. Kuhnert, Reinhard. "Studien zu Christlichen Gestalten
      in Shakespeares Romanzen: Eine Untersuchung im Lichte
      der Theologie der Shakespeare-Zeit." Ph.D.
      dissertation, Hamburg, 1970. (not seen)

133. Miyauchi, Bunshichi. "Shakespeare's Romances."
      Volcano (Kagoshima University), 6 (1970): 22-33.
      (Japanese--not seen)

      Instead of learning generosity and selflessness, the
      aged heroes of the romances remain self-centered in
      their regard for political power. Pericles and Leontes
      stay self-centered throughout *Pericles* and *The Winter's
      Tale* and assume political power in the end. Prospero
      gives up generosity to reassume his dukedom. Cymbeline
      alone becomes generous and forgiving. Thankfully he
      admits his mistakes and sacrifices to the gods.

134. Barton, Anne. "Shakespeare and the Limits of
      Language." *Shakespeare Survey*, 24 (1971): 19-30.

      Barton discusses *Richard 2*, *1 and 2 Henry 4*, *Love's
      Labor's Lost*, *King Lear*, *Coriolanus*, *Pericles*, and *The
      Tempest*, plays in which Shakespeare in especial dealt
      with the inadequacies and distortions of language. She
      says of the romances that they are no less skeptical of
      language than the tragedies. In making her point,
      Barton turns to *Pericles*, whose Marina remains in her
      own uncomprehending and private world until the
      "[w]ords and eyes" (p. 30) of father and daughter meet
      in the recognition scene. Communication in this play
      has at last been restored. But in *The Tempest*, the
      barriers between characters stay in place,
      foreshadowing the breakdown of language depicted in
      modern drama. Perhaps *The Tempest* was the last of
      Shakespeare's plays because Shakespeare had reached an
      impasse in his study of the power of words.

135. Brockbank, J.P. "*Pericles* and the Dream of
      Immortality." *Shakespeare Survey*, 24 (1971): 105-16.

Pericles is a metaphor for seeing through and beyond
death. The sea is Shakespeare's comprehensive
metaphor. Clarence's speech on drowning in *Richard 3*
heralds Shakespeare's use of sea imagery in *Pericles*
and *The Tempest*. Shakespeare probably rewrote *Pericles*
from an older play. The deliberately artless Gower
choruses are proper for retelling an old story. Like
Rowley's Chatterton, Shakespeare's Gower, the
unaffected representative of a past age, is meant to be
remembered with nostalgia. The spectacle of *Pericles*
reminds the audience constantly that the ancient story
being staged is art, not reality.

136. Cox, Clyde Perry, Jr. "Music as a Unifying Element in
     Shakespeare's Romances." Ph.D. dissertation,
     University of Michigan, 1970. *Dissertation Abstracts
     International*, 31 (1971): 6545A.

     This dissertation analyzes the romances according to
     the attitude of Shakespeare's original audience to
     music. Because of the perceptiveness of Renaissance
     audiences to music and musical allusions, Shakespeare
     made musical elements a part of the structure and
     characterization of the romances.

137. Hunt, Maurice Arthur. "Ways of Knowing in
     Shakespeare's Late Plays." Ph.D. dissertation,
     University of California-Berkeley, 1971.
     Dissertation Abstracts International, 31 (1971):
     6612A.

     The dissertation defines knowing by examining
     Bassanio's and Hamlet's ideas on the subject and by
     comparing them to those of the average man described by
     Sir John Davies and Robert Burton. There are three
     moments of knowing in the late romances: the first is
     imperfect or incomplete; the second reveals a new way;
     and the third forms a dream or vision. In *Pericles*,
     when the Prince meets Antiochus and his daughter, he
     depends only on his ears and eyes (1.1.91-108). Over
     the course of the play he learns to use all his
     faculties and achieves reunion with his family.

138. Kawachi, Yoshiko. "Shakespeare and the Blackfriars
     Theatre." *Bulletin* (Kyoritsu Junior Women's
     College), no. 14 (1971): 97-117. (not seen)

     This essay is a study of *Pericles*.

139. Knight, G. Wilson. "T.S. Eliot and *Pericles*."
      *Neglected Powers: Essays on Nineteenth and Twentieth
      Century Literature*. New York: Barnes and Noble,
      1971, pp. 489-90.

      T.S. Eliot gave a two-part lecture on *Pericles* and
      the late romances, "Shakespeare as Poet and Dramatist,"
      at Edinburgh University in 1937 and Bristol University
      in 1941; the lecture was adapted for presentation in
      Germany in 1949. A German version by Eliot was
      published in 1950 (see item 19). In the 31 lines
      quoted from the lecture, Eliot says that the "'musical'
      and 'ultra-dramatic' patterns" (p. 489) in Shakespeare
      grow more insistent after *Hamlet*. See items 16, 44.

140. Lawrence, Harold Whitney. "'To Sing a Song That Old
      Was Sung': *Pericles* and *Apollonius of Tyre*, the Play
      and the Tradition." Ph.D. dissertation, Texas
      Christian University, 1970. *Dissertation Abstracts
      International*, 31 (1971): 6062A-63A.

      The moral lessons in the Apollonius story provide a
      means of assessing the worth of *Pericles* for its
      seventeenth-century audience. Both the *Confessio
      Amantis*, chief source for the play, and *Pericles*
      contain the moral lessons of Boethius' *Consolation of
      Philosophy*, King Alfred's *Prefaces*, and medieval
      literature and sermons generally. Shakespeare brought
      the lessons of self-discipline and virtue home to the
      Jacobeans by stressing the value of chaste love.

141. Nicholl, James Robert. "The Development of
      Shakespeare's Artistry: Irony in the Comedies and
      Romances." Ph.D. dissertation, University of Texas,
      1970. *Dissertation Abstracts International*, 31
      (1971): 6019A-20A.

      Irony may be divided into verbal irony, irony of
      action, and irony of manner. Although the culmination
      of Shakespeare's balanced use of irony occurs in
      Twelfth Night, the dark comedies and the romances
      contain clever and original irony.

142. Rabkin, Norman. "The Holy Sinner and the Confidence
      Man: Illusion in Shakespeare's Romances." *Four
      Essays on Romance*. Edited by Herschel Baker.

Cambridge: Harvard University Press, 1971, pp.
33-53.

A comparison between Thomas Mann's late novels, *The
Holy Sinner* and *The Confessions of Felix Krull,
Confidence Man*, initiates a new approach to the late
romances. Grigorss, Mann's holy sinner, resembles
Pericles, Leontes, and Prospero. Felix Krull and
Autolycus are cosmic confidence men. With their
emphases on story-telling and storytellers,
Shakespeare's romances and Mann's late novels celebrate
God's artfully providential nature.

143.   Ratsi, I. "Problema tragikomedii i poslednie p'esy
       Shekspira" [The Problem of Tragicomedy in
       Shakespeare's Last Plays]. *Teatr* (Moscow), no. 2
       (1971): 105-13. (not seen)

       Because of the ambiguities and contradictions
       inherent in the genre, Shakespeare's tragicomedies have
       proved unpopular in Russia. *Pericles*, for instance,
       has never been staged. The tragicomedies result from
       Shakespeare's crisis in humanism during which he
       abandoned the classical distinction between tragedy and
       comedy. Nature no longer redeems man as it did in the
       comedies; the broad vision and integration of the
       tragedies is gone as well; and the characters are
       static. Yet Shakespeare's tragicomedies are superior
       to those of tricksters Beaumont and Fletcher. Action
       in Shakespeare can be at once both tragic and comic.

144.   Schwartz, Hans-Günther. "Lenz and Shakespeare."
       Shakespeare Jahrbuch (Heidelberg), 107 (1971): 85-96.

       As a disciple of Goethe and participant in the Sturm-
       und-Drang movement, J.M.R. Lenz venerated the
       naturalness of Shakespeare above the artificiality of
       the French classicists. Nevertheless, he insisted that
       Shakespeare's plays have a formal structure. In *Das
       Hochburger Schloss*, Lenz used the recognition scene in
       Pericles, as well as scenes in other Shakespeare plays,
       to demonstrate Shakespeare's compositional art in
       preparing for and executing evocative scenes.
       Shakespeare readies the audience for the high emotion
       of the recognition scene (5.1) by telling Marina's
       story in act 4. Unlike most Shakespeare critics in his
       own day, Lenz did not consider *Pericles* an inferior and

un-Shakespearean play. He thought the movement of the
play entirely Shakespearean.

145. Semon, Kenneth Jeffrey. "Fantasy and Wonder:
      Shakespeare's Last Plays." Ph.D. dissertation,
      Washington University, 1971. *Dissertation Abstracts
      International*, 32 (1971): 2653A.

      The dissertation examines interpretations of the
      concept of wonder in Italian poetic theory and
      discusses wonder in the four romances. The fantasy
      world of these plays provides a context for perceiving
      wonders beyond the "realities" of the primary world.
      See items 190, 191.

146. Solberg, Susan Riley. "The Design of *Pericles*." Ph.D.
      dissertation, Columbia University, 1968.
      Dissertation Abstracts International, 32 (1971):
      401A.

      A single author unified *Pericles*, regardless of
      whether or not he wrote the entire play. The
      popularity of *Pericles*, a more sophisticated play than
      earlier Renaissance tragicomedies, may result as much
      from its unifed theme and plot as from its
      dramatization of a well-known romance.

147. Stratton, John David. "The Dramatic Structures of the
      Plays in the King's Men's Repertory, 1604-1608."
      Ph.D. dissertation, University of Nebraska, 1971.
      Dissertation Abstracts International, 32 (1971):
      2711A.

      The seventeen plays performed by the King's Men
      between 1604 and 1608 involve either plots of
      rejection, which interest the audience in the
      characters, or plots of manipulation, which interest
      the audience in incidents.

148. Stuckas, Regine. "'Vue indirecte' in Shakespeares
      Sp</i>ten Dramen." Master's thesis, Mainz, 1971. (not
      seen)

149. Thorne, W.B. "*Pericles* and the 'Incest-Fertility'
      Opposition." *Shakespeare Quarterly*, 22 (1971):
      43-56.

Shakespeare's early comedies treat the influence of
fertility on immediate events in the lives of young and
old; *Pericles* and the other late romances concern its
influence on a man's entire lifetime and that of his
children. Shakespeare refined from medieval folk-drama
and festival plays the stock comic plot of the young
suitor who outwits age and authority by changing the
opposition between father and suitor to an incestuous
father-daughter relationship. Antiochus' daughter, who
on the surface seems exemplary of fertility, is really
the incestuous representative of winter and death.
Pericles' reaction to her is important to him as an
individual and as a ruler. Tainted by his desire for
her, Pericles spends the rest of the play in atonement;
by plunging into disorder, he finally establishes a new
order. The spring-fertility theme triumphs over the
winter-incest theme. The generalized folk patterns in
Pericles are more specific in *Cymbeline*, *The Winter's
Tale*, and *The Tempest*. In *Pericles* and *The Winter's
Tale* the maturation of the ruler is dramatized; in
Cymbeline and *The Tempest* the youth of Cymbeline and
Prospero is described in retrospect. In the late
plays, which are remarkably similar to Shakespeare's
early comedies, the young appear as the old reborn;
both stages in the continuum are desirable.

150. Weinstock, Horst. "Loyal Service in Shakespeare's
Mature Plays." *Studia Neophilologica*, 43 (1971):
446-73.

Leonine (pp. 457, 460) and Helicanus (p. 471) figure
in this essay on Shakespeare's absorption with
obedience in the plays written after 1600.

151. Wigod, Sheldon William. "The Lasting Storm of
Pericles." Ph.D. dissertation, Wayne State
University, 1971. *Dissertation Abstracts
International*, 31 (1971): 3525A.

The theory of doubtful authorship is incorrect and
responsible for the dearth of aesthetic criticism of
Pericles. The allegorical settings display Pericles,
not as an innocent victim, but as "the first of the
fallen father figures" in the late romances.

152. Zacharias, Peter James. "An Analysis of the Motif of
Death and Revival in the Tragicomedies of
Shakespeare, Daniel, and Fletcher." Ph.D.

dissertation, Michigan State University, 1970.
Dissertation Abstracts International, 31 (1971):
6028A-29A.

The image of the dying knight reborn in the four
romances patterns Shakespeare's inquiry into the nature
of a perfect ruler.

153. Colman, Elizabeth Lee. "The Sense of Sounds: An
      Investigation of Verbal Music in Shakespeare's Late
      Plays." Ph.D. dissertation, George Washington
      University, 1972. *Dissertation Abstracts
      International*, 33 (1972): 270A.

Verbal music, "the consecutive flow of sound of the
drama in performance" (p. 227), is made up of music,
sound effects and silence, song, rhymed and blank
verse, and prose. Even though sense in the four
romances is more important than sound, verbal music
reinforces word meaning.

154. Eggers, Walter Frederick, Jr. *"Pericles* and
      Shakespearean Romance." Ph.D. dissertation,
      University of North Carolina, 1971. *Dissertation
      Abstracts International*, 32 (1972): 5179A.

This dissertation offers an analysis of *Pericles* as
performed at the Globe and compares it with other
dramatic romances. An experiment by Shakespeare in the
style of the popular stage romances of the day,
Pericles helps define the popularity of his later
dramatic romances.

155. Felperin, Howard. "This Great Miracle: *Pericles.*"
      Shakespearean Romance. Princeton: Princeton
      University Press, 1972, pp. 143-76.

The archaic Gower choruses and the highly moralized
adventures of Pericles are analogous to medieval
religious romance. Pericles' trials in acts 1-2 are
those of a public man; the private man is tested in
acts 3-5. Marina is another of the popular saintly
maidens, such as Virginia, Grissill, Desdemona, and
Cordelia; Pericles has much in common with St. Eustace
and the Red Cross Knight. In shifting from relatively
naturalistic drama to dramatic parables, Shakespeare
exchanged kinds of verisimilitude. In making *Pericles*
into a revived saint's legend, Shakespeare revived a

dramatic tradition he had seen in his youth and
appreciated for its special perception of reality. See
item 111.

156. Greer, Richard Allen. "Adaptations of the Greek
Romances in the English Renaissance as Reflections of
the Debate Between Fortune and Virtue." Ph.D.
dissertation, Harvard University, 1972. (not seen)

157. Gibson, Richard Joseph. "*All's Well That Ends Well,
Measure for Measure*, and *Pericles*: Experiments in
Comic Resolution." Ph.D. dissertation, University of
North Carolina, 1971. *Dissertation Abstracts
International*, 32 (1972): 6974A.

Distinct from either Shakespeare's romantic comedies
or the romances, *All's Well That Ends Well, Measure for
Measure*, and *Pericles* are experiments. *All's Well*
differs from the earlier comedies in undercutting and
parodying the heroine. *Measure for Measure* differs
from them by dealing with brotherly love and offering a
new basis for justice and marriage in love. *Pericles*
is different from the early comedies, *All's Well*, and
Measure for Measure. Characters in *Pericles* suffer
without sin, but their suffering is not gratuitous and
belongs to an harmonious order. The results of these
three experiments formed the later romances.

158. Hartwig, Joan. "*Pericles*: The Old and the New."
Shakespeare's Tragicomic Vision. Baton Rouge:
Louisiana State University Press, 1972, pp. 34-60.

In the final plays, which mingle the immediacy of
tragedy with the distance of comedy, Shakespeare's
emphasis on artifice calls the audience's attention to
the double awareness of their response: they are
involved yet distanced. Holding both awarenesses
simultaneously, the audience has a sense of mastering
illusion. In the tragicomedies Shakespeare gives the
audience a vision of reality that affirms divine
control. Like that of *Cymbeline, The Winter's Tale,
The Tempest, Henry 8*, and *The Two Noble Kinsmen*, the
artifice in *Pericles* encourages the audience to accept
the reality of miracles. The devices of the play--the
Gower choruses, the dumb shows, the tournament, the
music, and the dances--keep the story distinct from
real life and substitute stasis for dramatic
development. The audience sees a play of individual

pictures as in a museum. Acts 1-2 form a cycle of loss
and restoration. By contrast, acts 3-5 repeat the
cycle but focus on Marina to create wonder in Pericles
and the audience alike. At the end of the play, the
potential for restoration extends to the audience. An
appended chapter, "The Authorship of *Pericles*" (pp.
181-83), argues that the stylistic differences between
acts 1-2 and acts 3-5 may be considered an artistic
experiment without discounting either collaboration
theories or Edwards' argument for two reporters (see
item 413).

159.   Jacquot, Jean. "The Last Plays and the Masque."
       *Shakespeare 1971: Proceedings of the World
       Shakespeare Congress, Vancouver, August 1971*. Edited
       by Clifford Leech and J.M.R. Margeson. Toronto:
       Toronto University Press, 1972, pp. 156-73.

       Scenery, introduced from Italy around 1608 for use in
       court entertainments, influenced Shakespeare's
       romances. In *Pericles* both the lavish word pictures
       and Gower's appeals to the audience to use its
       imagination show the influence of court entertainments.
       The richly trimmed sable banners on Pericles' ship
       described by Gower may actually have been stage props
       in the recognition scene at Mytilene (5.1). *Pericles*
       was no doubt chosen for performance at Whitehall in
       1619 because of its frequent use of spectacle.

160.   Rose, Mark. *Shakespearean Design*. Cambridge: Belknap
       Press of the Harvard University Press, 1972.

       In this book on Shakespeare's dramatic structure,
       Rose discusses *Pericles* and *Cymbeline* briefly in his
       last chapter, "The Later Plays" (pp. 151-74). The two
       plays are deliberately artless of structure, especially
       the naive *Pericles* with its ancient plot from Greek
       romance, its episodic scenes that take place here and
       there about the Mediterranean, and its presenter Gower,
       who comments frequently on the dramatic action and
       introduces the dumb shows. The loose structure of
       Pericles and *Cymbeline*, harking back to *Clyomon and
       Clamydes*, signals Shakespeare's search for more
       technical freedom and an initial exploration of art as
       a theme. The seeming artlessness of *Pericles* and
       Cymbeline, however, make them less successful than the
       artful *Winter's Tale* and *Tempest*. Without design,

Pericles and *Cymbeline* lack the richness of
Shakespeare's art.

161. Roux, Susan. "Les personnages dans le *Conte d'hiver* et
      dans *Péricles.*" *Revue d'Histoire du Théâtre*, 24
      (1972): 269–80.

      The mixture of realism and fantasy in the two plays
      lends their characters ambivalence. They have the
      value of types without the loss of individuality. The
      characters' universe is ruled by moral, social, and
      logical laws but depends above all on the logic of
      narrative structure, which allows for occasionally
      contradictory behavior. In *Pericles*, the Prince,
      Marina, Cerimon, the fishermen, and the brothel inmates
      depict the diversity of human nature; the other
      characters are types presented for their effect on
      Pericles and Marina. The characters in *Pericles* and
      The Winter's Tale belong to a logical system which
      appears concrete and can be communicated to the
      audience.

162. Smith, Hallett. *Shakespeare's Romances: A Study of
      Some Ways of the Imagination.* San Marino: Huntington
      Library, 1972.

      Discussion of *Pericles* appears in five chapters. The
      first chapter concerns the Apollonius myth as the
      romance most influential on Shakespeare. Chapter 4
      contains a discussion of the theme of patience in *King
      Lear* and *Pericles*; Shakespeare's granddaughter,
      Elizabeth, was the inspiration for the heroines of the
      late romances. Chapter 6 compares the father-and-
      daughter relationship in *Pericles* with the husband-and-
      wife relationship in *The Winter's Tale*. "Landscape
      language," most of which in *Pericles* occurs in acts
      3–5, is the subject of chapter 8. Mentioned also in
      this chapter are the differences between the choruses
      in acts 1–2 and acts 3–5. The ninth chapter, on the
      evolution of language into music in the last plays,
      discusses the reunion of Pericles and Marina as a
      musical high point.

163. Young, David P. "The Argument of Time: *The Winter's
      Tale.*" *The Heart's Forest: A Study of Shakespeare's
      Pastoral Plays.* New Haven: Yale University Press,
      1972, pp. 104–45.

Pericles, the simplest and crudest of the romances, may be an experiment in turning a slightly altered older narrative romance into a stage play. Shakespeare became preoccupied in the late romances with the ancient and fabulous tales he only mentioned in *Richard 2*, *Twelfth Night*, and *Hamlet*. With deliberately chosen words and a meter from long ago, Gower evokes a double consciousness in the *Pericles* audience by showing them wonderful events from a sophisticated distance.

164.   Arakawa, Mitsuo. "Pastoral to Shakespeare's Romances" [Pastoral and Shakespeare's Romances]. *Ronshu* (Tohokugakuin Daigaku), no. 60 (Sept. 1973): 49–66. (not seen)

165.   Bluestone, Stephen Edward. "William Shakespeare and the Circles of the Imagination: A Study of the Art of *Pericles*, *Cymbeline*, *The Winter's Tale*, and *The Tempest*." Ph.D. dissertation, University of Michigan, 1972. *Dissertation Abstracts International*, 33 (1973): 6301A.

During the revival of tragicomedy in the early seventeenth century, Shakespeare chose to present "modern" artifice rather than plain tales. He jested with romance. Gower chiefly creates this effect in *Pericles*. Shakespeare's romances revel in displaying the "instrumentality" and limitations of art. Marina is a creature whom fourteenth-century Gower could never have created.

166.   Evans, Gareth L. "A Flawed Masterpiece: *Pericles*." *Shakespeare V: 1606–1616*. Writers and Critics Series. Edinburgh: Oliver and Boyd, 1973, pp. 38–46.

An actor's instinct goes against assigning acts 1–2 of *Pericles* to Shakespeare. The play is eminently playable because of its spectacle, musical words, and music. Especially powerful on the stage are the realistic brothel scenes and the ceremonial recognition scenes.

167.   Glazier, Phyllis Gorfain. "Folklorist Devices and Formal Structure in Shakespearean Drama." Ph.D. dissertation, University of California-Berkeley, 1973. *Dissertation Abstracts International*, 34 (1973): 3341A–42A.

This dissertation examines riddles, proverbs, games,
folklore plots, and dramatic devices, such as the play-
within-the-play, double plots, choruses, and prologues,
in Shakespeare's plays, especially *The Merchant of
Venice*, *King Lear*, *Macbeth*, and *Pericles*. The riddles,
prologues, dumb shows, and games in *Pericles* form "a
rite of passage for the audience." Puzzled by the
archaic style and loose structure of the play, the
audience finds itself tested by the play as the
characters are tested in the play. The dumb shows and
choruses study art "metapoetically": the riddles,
tests, and the incest theme show the related concerns
of art, recreation, and procreation. See items 219,
238.

168. Homan, Sidney R. "*The Tempest* and Shakespeare's Last
Plays: The Aesthetic Dimensions." *Shakespeare
Quarterly*, 24 (1973): 69-76.

Shakespeare reveals a divided attitude toward art in
his four romances. In *Pericles* the division is
expressed in a simple dichotomy. On one side Marina
serves the arts, which represent man's accord with
nature; similarly, Cerimon's art has healing power.
The other side of art is its deceptiveness and seeming
lack of integrity; hence, Gower must ask the audience
to piece out and believe in his imperfect story. The
only subtle treatment of art in the play is the
equation of art with a dream, or dream vision, in the
recognition scene (5.1.163-64).

169. Hoy, Cyrus. "Jacobean Tragedy and the Mannerist
Style." *Shakespeare Survey*, 26 (1973): 49-67.

In the concluding section of the essay, Hoy says that
Jacobean tragicomedy with its various levels of reality
and modes of vision is mannerism epitomized.
Shakespeare's tragicomedies attempt to "sanctify human
suffering" (p. 64). In *Pericles* and *Cymbeline*, Diana
and Jupiter, in their respective plays, appear above
scenes of desolation. The epiphanies in these two
plays are crude but effective; in *The Winter's Tale* and
The Tempest, the human and the spiritual are
increasingly less divided. The difference between
Shakespeare's tragicomedies and those of Beaumont and
Fletcher is the difference between mannerism at its
apogee and the baroque.

170. Leonard, Nancy Scott. "Romance as Recovery: A Study of Shakespeare's *Pericles*." Ph.D. dissertation, Indiana University, 1973. *Dissertation Abstracts International*, 33 (1973): 4352A.

Pericles is a sophisticated romance with a coherent plot that improves on its episodic sources. The metaphor of loss and recovery unifies the play. Much can be learned from *Pericles* about the romance tradition and the use that Elizabethan dramatists made of prose sources and stage spectacle. Shakespeare used the conventions of Greek, medieval, and Renaissance romance to dramatize human destiny. The uneven style of the play is the work of reporters (see item 413), not the author. *Pericles* is by Shakespeare entirely. Even though indebted to both his major sources, Gower's *Confessio Amantis* and Twine's *Patterne of Painefull Adventures*, Shakespeare conformed unusually closely to Gower's version of the Apollonius legend. Out of Gower's traditional episodic story, Shakespeare achieved a "figurative unity" by working the conventional romance themes of quest, fortune, and adversity into a providential scheme.

171. McIntosh, William A. "Musical Design in *Pericles*." *English Language Notes*, 11 (1973): 100-06.

Almost all important events in *Pericles* involve music and are linked to Boethius' three cosmic parallels in *De Institutione Musica*: *musica instrumentalis*, *humana*, and *mundana*. The contrasting characters whom Pericles meets in Antioch and Pentapolis express the ambiguous connotations of *musica instrumentalis*. Music helps define Antiochus and his daughter as negative characters and Simonides and his daughter as positive. Cerimon's call for music in his treatment of Thaisa and in Marina's song to Pericles demonstrate the healing power of *musica humana*. Following Marina's song, Pericles hears the music of the spheres, *musica mundana*.

172. Peterson, Douglas L. "*Pericles*: The World as 'a Lasting Storm.'" *Time, Tide, and Tempest: A Study of Shakespeare's Romances*. San Marino: Huntington Library, 1973, pp. 71-107.

Pericles, Shakespeare's play entirely, is an emblem of the four tempestuous events in the Prince's life:

(1) Antiochus' threat which sends Pericles to sea, (2)
the storm that shipwrecks him at Pentapolis, (3) the
sea storm during which Marina is born and Thaisa
seemingly dies, and (4) the scene at Tharsus when Cleon
and Dionysa tell Pericles that Marina is dead. The
play is a series of talking pictures with Gower serving
as the audience's moral guide. A foreknowledge of
events is essential to the audience of a play which
deals with the difference between the illusory
phenomenal world and transcendent reality. Knowing the
truth already, the audience watches Pericles hold firm
in his four trials. Pericles is a free and active
agent in a play unified by a series of correspondences
between past and present (Antioch-Pentapolis,
Antiochus-Simonides, Antiochus' daughter-Thaisa, the
fishermen-Cerimon, Thaisa-Marina, etc.). Episodic
Pericles forms "the Wheele of Time" (p. 81) emblem.
Pericles is Shakespeare's pattern of constancy, the
opposite of Timon, who believes only what his senses
tell him. The other romances are less didactic than
Pericles, but all celebrate the constancy of love.

173. Peterson, Douglas L. "Tempest-Tossed Barks and Their
Helmsmen in Several of Shakespeare's Plays."
Costerus, 9 (1973): 79-107.

Metaphors of tempest-tossed ships with unfailing
helmsmen in sixteenth-century poetry represent
constancy or patience. Shakespeare used the
ship-in-storm metaphor in many of his plays; *Pericles*
and *The Tempest* seem especially to depend on it.
Pericles personifies constancy. Like Shakespeare's
other comedies, *Pericles* demonstrates the limitations
on man's freedom which time, place, and circumstances
impose; nevertheless, providence gives men occasions
for self-knowledge and patient faith.

174. Sider, John Wm. "The Serious Elements of Shakespeare's
Comedies." *Shakespeare Quarterly*, 24 (1973): 1-11.

Over his career Shakespeare moved from light to
serious comedy. All his comedies contain serious
elements, but in the comedies before *The Merchant of
Venice* Shakespeare used serious circumstances for
humorous or sentimental purposes without engaging the
audience's deeper emotions. With *The Merchant of
Venice* Shakespeare began to treat serious themes
seriously, yet he handled them imperfectly. Swift

denouements and conventional comic endings sweep
serious matters aside in the plays between *Merchant* and
Measure for Measure. Shakespeare gave longer
denouements to his later, serious comedies--*Pericles*,
Cymbeline, *The Winter's Tale*, and *The Tempest*. These
plays combine the characters and plots of tragedy with
the accidents, good and bad, of comedy. The emotional
effect created by the union is unlike that of tragedy
or comedy. The audience sees that a man can come to
happiness in spite of adversity. In *Pericles* the
Prince's passivity, considering his circumstances, is a
virtue. Faith in divine justice brings Pericles and
his family to joy. The play rewards the intellect and
the emotions. The earnest lack of humor in *Pericles*,
except for the brothel scenes, contributes to the joy
of the reunions in act 5.

175. Sinnott, Bethany Strong. "The Father-Daughter Theme in
      Shakespeare's Plays." Ph.D. dissertation, University
      of North Carolina, 1972. *Dissertation Abstracts
      International*, 34 (1973): 339A.

      Shakespeare used the father-daughter theme most
      consistently in *Pericles*, *Cymbeline*, *The Winter's Tale*,
      and *The Tempest*, and he used it in ways that are joyful
      and creative. In these plays fathers and daughters who
      are unified in wisdom and virtue become redeemers and
      conciliators. The theme in *Pericles* is less
      significant than it is in either *King Lear* or the late
      romances. As in the early comedies, the theme in
      Pericles often has more structural than thematic use.
      The reunion of Pericles and Marina has more to do with
      plot than with character development. In celebrating a
      new life and a new order, *Pericles* marks the way to the
      other, more polished romances.

176. Wickham, Glynne. "From Tragedy to Tragi-comedy: *King
      Lear* as Prologue." *Shakespeare Survey*, 26 (1973):
      33-48. Reprint. "Von der Tragödie zur Tragikomödie:
      König Lear als Prolog." Translated by V.R. Scheiber.
      Shakespeare Jahrbuch (Weimar), 100 (1974): 7-33.

      Homage to James I and his court life behind
      Shakespeare's shift from tragedies to tragicomedies.
      The plays written from 1608 and 1613, from *Pericles*
      through *The Two Noble Kinsmen*, are political allegories
      celebrating the fortunate and hopeful events of James's
      first decade as monarch. *Pericles*, for instance,

reworked from an old play by George Wilkins, reflects James's reunion with his daughter Elizabeth, who came to London in 1608 after seclusion in the country. Pericles' hardships represent James's troubles before the succession, the family's escape from assassination in the Gunpowder Plot, and the reunification of the British Isles under the Stuarts and of James, his wife, and daughter at Whitehall. Helicanus represents Sir Francis Bacon. The marriage of Marina and Lysimachus signifies the union of Scotland and England.

177. Colman, E.A.M. "The Language of Sexual Revulsion." *The Dramatic Use of Bawdy in Shakespeare*. London: Longman, 1974, pp. 139-40.

The simplicity of the brothel scenes in act 4 heightens the tension between Marina's purity and the threats of the down-and-out brothel crew. The idealism of these scenes is at the farthest remove from the casual indecencies in Shakespeare's early comedies.

178. Empric, Julienne Helen. "Levels of Illusion: A Study of Shakespeare's Internal Shows." Ph.D. dissertation, University of Notre Dame, 1974. *Dissertation Abstracts International*, 35 (1974): 2936A-37A.

The internal shows, plays within the plays, in Shakespeare's comedies and romances demonstrate the nature and function of illusion. Internal shows are few, simple, and straightforward in the early comedies. Those in the "transvestite plays" are slightly more complex. The internal plays of the middle comedies mingle illusion and reality, thereby necessitating a confrontation between the two. The death show, introduced in these plays, elicits in the highest degree "credibility, recognition and transformation in the internal audience." In the romances the internal shows amplify the death show. By means of the theophanies near the end of each play, the audience knows that the entire play is itself an internal show in a larger divine scheme and participates in the emotions of loss and recovery that make up the resurrection following the death show.

179. Gajdusek, R.E. "Death, Incest, and the Triple Bond in the Later Plays of Shakespeare." *American Imago*, 31 (1974): 109-58.

Confronting his own approaching death, Shakespeare
held a dialogue with the fates in his last plays and,
like Paris, chose Aphrodite, death disguised as love.
Coriolanus, Pericles, The Winter's Tale, and *The
Tempest*, all of which focus on the child as successor
to the father, demonstrate Shakespeare's shift in his
later years from plays of heroic idealism to anti-
heroic, dialectical plays. *Pericles* is fixed on death.
Pericles acknowledges from the first his thralldom to
death, and Gower, Shakespeare's surrogate, has been
resurrected from death to serve as chorus (art as
redeemer). Incest causes the deathspell which
threatens Shakespeare and Pericles. Antiochus'
daughter, the simultaneous reality of the female as
child, maiden, and woman, is the Triple Goddess,
elemental destroyer "of idealistic masculine
consciousness" (p. 120). Marina is the transforming
goddess Sophia, who effects Pericles' metaphoric rescue
from death. Father and daughter, male and female, at
last become one. *Pericles* is one of Shakespeare's most
religious plays; it delineates the process of mastering
the death goddess by transcending death through art.
In Pericles and Marina's recognition scene (5.1), the
sex roles are reversed. The daughter gives metaphoric
rebirth to the father; Pericles is saved from real
incest by artificial incest. The play is the dramatic
equivalent for Pericles and Shakespeare alike of the
victory of the Apollonian Christian trinity over the
Dioynsian triple goddess.

180.   Garber, Marjorie B. "The Truth of Your Own Seeming:
        Romance and the Uses of Dream." *Dream in
        Shakespeare: From Metaphor to Metamorphosis*. New
        Haven: Yale University Press, 1974, pp. 139-214.

Characters and symbols in the romances are universal
rather than particular; dreaming moves through metaphor
into metamorphosis. In *Pericles* neither the word
"dream" nor dream motifs, with the possible exception
of Antiochus' riddle (1.1), appear in acts 1-2, the
non-Shakespearean section of the play. Dream metaphors
begin with act 3, where the tone of the play shifts
radically. For all the structural and poetic
shortcomings of *Pericles*, the play possesses phrases,
such as Marina's description of her birthplace, "not of
any shores" (5.1.106), and Thaisa's question to
Pericles, "Did you not name a tempest, / A birth and

death?" (5.3.33-34), which transform the play into universal myth.

181. Grodal, Torben Kragh. "Hieraki, aegteskab og social forandring i Shakpespeare's *Som man behager* [*As You Like It*] *Storem* og *Pericles*." *Poetik*, 22 (1974): 45-74. (Danish--not seen)

182. Ino, Mikio. "A Note on Shakespeare's Final Mode." *Albion* (Kyoto University), 20 (1974): 1-16.

   Pericles is mere stage entertainment. *Cymbeline*, by contrast, with its more delicate and subtle wording, is a deeper, less theatrical work.

183. Ishikawa, Minoru K. "Shakespeare's Romances--Illusion and Reality." *Hiyoshi-Kiyoh* (1974): 41-47. (not seen)

   This essay mainly concerns the dramatic structure of *Pericles*. The romances affirm Shakespeare's belief in divine providence during his later years.

184. Leggatt, Alexander. *Shakespeare's Comedy of Love*. London: Methuen, 1974, pp. 259-60.

   Because of their "total vision of order" (p. 259), Shakespeare's final plays are comedies. The order and the fantastic plots make the late comedies seem artificial. *Pericles* and *Cymbeline*, the earliest, are the farthest removed from tragedy. Behind the moral pattern of *Pericles* is comedic wish fulfillment. In *Cymbeline* wish fulfillment dominates. In both plays, the fantastic is reality.

185. Muir, Kenneth. "Theophanies in the Last Plays." *Shakespeare's Late Plays: Essays in Honor of Charles Crow*. Edited by Richard C. Tobias and Paul G. Zolbrod. Athens: Ohio University Press, 1974, pp. 32-43.

   No gods appear in Shakespeare's plays before 1607. In *Pericles* the Prince and his family rely on Diana, their dependence stemming from a vow to Diana made in Thaisa's name by King Simonides. Neptune is important to Pericles; unlike Diana, the sea god makes no on-stage appearance. Theophanies in *Pericles* and the other late romances embody divine providence.

186. Neiditz, Minerva Heller. "Banishment: Separation and
      Loss in the Later Plays of Shakespeare." Ph.D.
      dissertation, University of Connecticut, 1974.
      Dissertation Abstracts International, 35 (1974):
      2235A.

      This dissertation explores the relationship between
      the banishment theme and the psychology of infantile
      "wishes and fears" in Shakespeare's plays from the
      Henriad through *The Tempest*. The section on the late
      romances concerns the ascendance of Jupiter in
      Cymbeline and Apollo in *The Winter's Tale* over dark
      Ephesian Diana in *Pericles*. Mythic figures in these
      plays represent psychic awareness; the banishment of
      female power concerns supremacy.

187. Panaitescu, V. "Pericle de Shakespeare." *Romania
      literara* (Bucarest), 7, no. 17 (1974): 24. (not
      seen)

188. Perez Gallego, Candido. *Dramatica de Shakespeare*.
      Saragossa, Spain: Ediciones del Portico, 1974. (not
      seen)

      The first part of the book concerns *Henry 4*, *Hamlet*,
      Troilus and Cressida, *King Lear*, and *Pericles*.

189. Schiffhorst, Gerald Joseph. "Art and Design in
      Pericles: A Study in Shakespearean Experimentation."
      Ph.D. dissertation, Washington University, 1973.
      Dissertation Abstracts International, 34 (1974):
      5928A.

      Pericles is a sophisticated experiment using artifice
      to construct tragicomedy. Diffuse episodic scenes in
      the medieval manner replace unified dramatic scenes.
      Ancient Gower, not the plot, unifies the play. The
      characters' stylized action and speech and the Gower
      choruses keep the audience removed enough from the
      action to perceive the artist's control over seemingly
      tragic events. Pericles cannot fully comprehend the
      meaning of what he has endured, but the audience
      understands that his reunion with his family is a
      rebirth and that providence is possible. *Pericles*
      marks Shakespeare's first attempt to use fabulous
      stories to give qualified assurance of divine
      providence.

190. Semon, Kenneth J. "Fantasy and Wonder in Shakespeare's Last Plays." *Shakespeare Quarterly*, 25 (1974): 89-102.

The sense of wonder in Shakespeare's four tragicomedies makes the irrational believable. In *Pericles* Gower makes certain that the audience knows his tale is old and fantastic. Until the storm scene in act 3, the play is like a fairy tale. The realistic world of cause and effect appears for an instant when Pericles asks why Thaisa has been taken from him, but there is no answer. Through his suffering Pericles learns to embrace the gods and know that they are good. All things are possible in such a world. Ephesus in particular represents the divine order.

191. Semon, Kenneth J. "*Pericles*: An Order Beyond Reason." *Essays in Literature* (Western Illinois University), 1 (1974): 17-27.

The sense of wonder inspired by *Pericles* results from the tension between Gower's mundane understanding of the miraculous actions he presents and the audience's deeper understanding. Gower tries but cannot assign suitable morals to such random happenings. Causal events occur in tragedy; incalculable events take place in *Pericles*. Even though Pericles initially questions what happens to him, he finds joy by accepting his suffering. Gower's rationality prevents his sense of wonder. (Perhaps Shakespeare took over the Gower choruses from an earlier version of the play.) Only Marina never believes in the false idea of order that rationalism encourages, and even rational Gower seems aware of her as a creature of wonder. Fantastic, wonder-inspiring events occur constantly in *Pericles*.

192. Tanaka, Susumu. "Shakespeare no Romance Geki ni okeru 'Toki' no Seikaku" [The Nature of Time in Shakespearean Romances]. *Studies in English Language and Literature* (Fukuoka, Japan), no. 24 (1974): 41-61. (not seen)

The journal provides a summary in English of the article (pp. 156-57). The romances differ from the tragedies in that tragic events are softened by the passage of time and harmony eventually restored.

193.   Welsh, Andrew. "Heritage in *Pericles*." *Shakespeare's
       Late Plays: Essays in Honor of Charles Crow*. Edited
       by Richard C. Tobias and Paul G. Zolbrod. Athens:
       Ohio University Press, 1974, pp. 89-113.

       Heritage is a scattered theme throughout *Pericles* and
       the central theme of Pericles and Marina's reunion
       (5.1). Four sorts of heritages appear in the play.
       Three stem from the Apollonius story, namely, "the
       telling of the tale, the riddles, [and] the tradition
       of capital sins" (p. 108). The fourth heritage, the
       devices carried by the knights at Simonides' court,
       comes from emblem books. As the teller of the tale,
       Gower, too, is an emblem.

194.   Wheeler, Richard P. "The King and the Physician's
       Daughter: *All's Well That Ends Well* and the Late
       Romances." *Comparative Drama*, 8 (1974-75): 311-27.

       This essay examines the so-called difficulties of
       All's Well That Ends Well by comparing it with the late
       romances. As in the festive comedies, the main plot of
       All's Well moves toward marriage, but the strong bond
       between the King of France and Helena, "father and
       daughter," aligns the play with the romances. The
       incest theme in *All's Well* may be compared to that of
       the romances, *Pericles* containing the simplest example.

195.   Aoyama, Seiko. "*King Lear* and Beyond." *Kiyo* (Kyoritsu
       Woman's Junior College), 19 (1975): 13-27.
       (Japanese--not seen)

196.   Babula, William. "*Pericles*." "*Wishes Fall Out as
       They're Willed": Shakespeare and the Tragicomic
       Archetype*. Elizabethan and Renaissance Studies, 48.
       Salzburg: Institut für Englische Sprache und
       Literatur, Universität Salzburg, 1975, pp. 113-33.

       All's Well That Ends Well, Measure for Measure, and
       Pericles contain the providential view of life found in
       mystery and morality plays and in later secular
       tragicomedy and romance as well. Providence is aligned
       with nature, time, and the Christian god in *All's Well*
       and *Measure for Measure*; Shakespeare links providence
       with art and the classical gods in *Pericles*. Although
       Pericles believes in chance, the artificial Gower
       choruses assure the audience that events are divinely
       guided.

197. Beneke, Jürgen. *Metaphorik im Drama: Dargestellt an Shakespeares "Pericles" und "Cymbeline."* Studien zur Englischen Literatur, 13. Bonn: Bouvier, 1975.

Because neither *Pericles* nor *Cymbeline* has received considerable critical attention and because verbal and representational metaphors in the late romances are particularly closely knit, these earliest two of Shakespeare's four romances serve to demonstrate the intimate structural connection between word and scene in drama. The first chapter defines dramatic metaphor, or imagery; the second chapter reviews criticism of the romances, ending with an assessment of the authorship problem in *Pericles*. Even though the question is unresolved, the imagery throughout the play is Shakespearean. Chapter three examines metaphor in *Pericles*. Image patterns in the play underlie themes of disintegration and regeneration in Pericles, his family, the state, and society; the nature of nobility; appearance versus reality; and the problem of worth. The fourth chapter treats metaphor in *Cymbeline*.

198. Cornett, Patricia Ann Laping. "The Parted Eye: Tragicomic Perception in Shakespeare's Last Plays." Ph.D. dissertation, University of Michigan, 1975. *Dissertation Abstracts International*, 36 (1975): 3726A.

Shakespeare attempted to blend tragedy and comedy into a simultaneous union in *Pericles, Cymbeline, The Winter's Tale,* and *The Tempest.* To express his tragicomic view of the world and provoke a new and similar response in his audience, Shakespeare exposed "the limitations of traditional stage conventions" and demanded "an open, dynamic response." *The Winter's Tale* more fully expresses Shakespeare's tragicomic perception than *Pericles* or *Cymbeline*. *The Tempest* offers a more personal approach to the insights in *The Winter's Tale.*

199. Eggers, Walter F., Jr. "Shakespeare's Gower and the Role of the Authorial Presenter." *Philological Quarterly,* 54 (1975): 434-43.

This essay identifies the authorial presenter as a popular and special stage convention dating from the 1580s and compares Gower, the most fully developed of the type, with forerunners and contemporary examples,

such as Lydgate in *2 The Seven Deadly Sins* (c. 1585),
Skelton in Chettle and Munday's Robin Hood plays (c.
1598), and Guicciardini in *The Devil's Charter* (1607),
to see what Renaissance audiences would have expected
of Gower and to understand his special achievement.
Authorial presenters in Elizabethan and Jacobean drama
served not only as narrators but also called attention
to the play as a play and moralized about the plot.
The antiquity of the presenters gave their moralizings
authority. The effect of Gower's story of Pericles is
different from its purpose. Acknowledging that his old
story cannot be told faithfully in a modern drama,
Gower requests from his audience a double kind of
patience in waiting for the unfolding of the moral
lessons and in bearing with the discrepancies between
his story and its dramatization. In the epilogue Gower
blesses the audience for their patience; the drama
meanwhile has been ocular proof that his words on the
rewards of virtue are correct. The epilogue is an
inadequate gloss of the wonders presented in act 5.
The final complexity is Shakespeare's use of Gower as
an ironic presenter, one whose story is more
significant than he knows. An authorial presenter is a
dramatist's image of himself and his problems in
turning fiction into drama; he also serves to distance
an audience from the illusion of the play.

200. Flower, Annette C. "Disguise and Identity in *Pericles,
      Prince of Tyre.*" *Shakespeare Quarterly,* 26 (1975):
      30-41.

      The "mouldiness" of *Pericles* is a deliberate means of
transforming fantasy into archetypes of reality. By
having Gower tell his own tale, Shakespeare emphasized
storytelling. The most important elements in this play
of transformed reality are the disguises of Pericles,
Thaisa, and Marina. Each of Pericles' roles helps the
Prince adjust to life. From Antiochus and his daughter
Pericles learns the relationship between hypocrisy and
disguise. When he returns to Tyre, he changes roles
with Helicanus. By the time he arrives at Pentapolis,
the Prince has become a "mere man." Like Pericles,
Simonides and Thaisa disguise their true feelings, yet
all three are adept at looking for worth below the
surface. Shakespeare subordinates Pericles to Thaisa
in act 3 and to Marina in act 4; his role is that of
sufferer. In act 5, dressed in a Job-like disguise,
Pericles is restored to himself when he recognizes his

daughter. At the end of the play he is father,
husband, and king. Thaisa's disguise as a nun is less
important than her disguise as a corpse. Rejecting the
world when she thinks she has lost her husband and
daughter, Thaisa becomes Pericles' passive feminine
counterpart. Pericles' active, and therefore real,
counterpart is Marina. As Pericles did with Antiochus
and his daughter, Marina learns the baseness of the
seemingly princely Cleon and Dionyza. In the brothel
Marina displays a militant chastity unlike her
mother's. Lysimachus finally recognizes Marina's worth
just as Simonides did that of Pericles. In the
recognition scene (5.1), Pericles accepts his daughter
as flesh and blood restored to him by the gods.

201. Fox, Jonathan Roy. "The Trial of Merit in
     Shakespeare's Last Plays." Ph.D. dissertation,
     University of Washington, 1974. *Dissertation
     Abstracts International*, 35 (1975): 4517A.

     Shakespeare unified his four romances through the
     trial of merit. The sins of Prospero, Leontes,
     Cymbeline, and Posthumous bring on their trials, but
     Pericles, hero of Shakespeare's archetypal romance, is
     not such a certain sinner. Even though he risks his
     life in pursuit of a tainted goal in Antioch, Diana
     always protects him, as the theophany in act 5 shows.
     After *Pericles*, Shakespeare's emphasis changed from a
     trial to tests.

202. Hikichi, Masatoshi. "Shakespeare's Romances and Greek
     Romance." *English Literature* (Waseda University), 42
     (1975): 106-20. (Japanese--not seen)

203. Il'in, M.V. *Nekotorye problemy tvorceskoyo metoda
     poslednich p'es Sekspira* [Some Problems in the
     Construction of Shakespeare's Last Plays]. Ph.D.
     dissertation, Moscow: MGU, 1975. (not seen)

204. Il'in, M.V. "Some Peculiarities of Style in *Pericles*."
     Georgian Shakespeareana, vol. 4. Papers Read at the
     Shakespeare Symposium, Tbilisi, 8-13 October 1972.
     Edited by N. Kiasashvili. Tbilisi: Tbilisi
     University Press, 1975, pp. 101-11. (Russian--not
     seen)

205. Mauch, Russell C., II. "The Testing Concept in
     Shakespearean Comedy." Ph.D. dissertation,

University of Massachusetts, 1975. *Dissertation Abstracts International*, 36 (1975): 907A.

In Shakespeare's comedies, characters test feelings, emotions, or formal relationships with an action. Such tests help define the characters and the dimensions of their comic world. The romances include the threat of death in their tests and equate action with intention. The limitations of the characters suggest to the audience their own limitations.

206. Millman, Lawrence. "Rider Haggard and the Male Novel. What is *Pericles*? Beckett Gags." Ph.D. dissertation, Rutgers University, 1974. *Dissertation Abstracts International*, 35 (1975): 6675A.

Dissimilarities between acts 1-2 and acts 3-5 do not represent the work of different dramatists. *Pericles* is Shakespeare's play in two parts instead of five acts. The parts, or plays, resemble a disjointed Elizabethan plot and subplot. Each plot concerns royal persons, Pericles and Marina, whose reunion integrates the halves.

207. Price, Roger Carson. "Pauline Perils: A Religious Reading of *Pericles, Prince of Tyre*." Ph.D. dissertation, University of California-Berkeley, 1975. *Dissertation Abstracts International*, 35 (1975): 7266A-67A.

Pericles is a secular sermon illustrating in 63 "visual compositions" the wisdom of John 3.3: "[E]xcept a man be borne againe, he can not se the kingdom of God" (1560 Geneva). The Levantine setting, the eternal time scheme, and the plot contain religious correspondences. An emblematic staging of *Pericles* could have been achieved at the Globe with minimal editing, doubled parts, and symbolic colors, masks, costumes, and stage devices.

208. Rush, Felix. "The Hybrid Rose: A Study of Shakespearean Comedy." Ph.D. dissertation, Harvard University, 1975. (not seen)

209. Sanderson, James L. "Patience in *The Comedy of Errors*." *Texas Studies in Literature and Language*, 16 (1975): 603-18.

This essay includes discussion of the theme of
patience in *Pericles*. Because of the patience of
Pericles and his family, good eventually emerges from
evil. Shakespeare, who used the Apollonius story from
Gower's *Confessio Amantis* as a source for *The Comedy of
Errors* and *Pericles*, seems to have introduced the theme
into both plays, for patience is treated in none of the
sources. *The Comedy of Errors* and *Pericles*, an early
and a late study of patience, exemplify the unity of
Shakespeare's art.

210. Ueno, Yoshiko. "Romance-geki ni yosete" [On Romance
Plays]. *Shakespeare News*, 14, no. 2 (1975): n.p.
(not seen)

211. Barratt, Harold S. "The Rose Distilled: Virginity,
Fertility and Marriage in Shakespeare." Ph.D.
dissertation, University of Western Ontario, 1975.
Dissertation Abstracts International, 36 (1976):
5309A.

Shakespeare's interest in the theme of virginity
reached its height in *All's Well That Ends Well*,
Measure for Measure, and the final romances.
Premarital virginity, the state of disciplined
sexuality, represented for Shakespeare the spiritual
and physical fertility fulfilled in marriage; fallen
man is redeemed by marriage to a female who is morally
and sexually pure. In *Pericles*, as in the succeeding
romances, female virginity is a mystique. Marina seems
supernatural. Her beauty, charm, and skill as a
needlewoman and musician are repeated in Imogen,
Perdita, and Miranda. In acts 1-2 Shakespeare
contrasts the cannibalism and sterility of Antiochus'
union with his daughter and the famine in Tharsus with
the fertility of Pericles' marriage to the chaste
Thaisa. As potential fertility, virginity is tested in
the romances. Thus, in the second half of *Pericles*,
Marina, like Shakespeare's other romantic virgins, is
almost raped. Good is tested by evil and endures. The
reward of virtue in Shakespeare is marriage; his
heroines reject celibacy. The final scene of *Pericles*,
in which Thaisa and Pericles are reunited and Marina
and Lysimachus betrothed, takes place at the Temple of
Diana in Ephesus. Directed by divine providence, the
heroines of Shakespearean romance redeem men.

212. Becker, Marvin B. "A Historian's View of Another
      Pericles." *Modern Quarterly Review,* 15 (1976):
      197-211.

      Love is the major theme of the play. Pericles'
      odyssey takes him from the vision of sinful, private
      eros he witnesses at the court of Antiochus to a
      religious state of perfection. The Prince is "the
      beleaguered saint" (p. 204) of a Renaissance miracle
      play. Even though *Pericles* emblemizes suffering
      through the use of music and uses intentionally
      artificial verse, it contains frequent reminders of
      social reality, such as the fishermen and brothel
      scenes. Shakespeare makes actual events inseparable
      from ritual meanings in the play.

213. Cabas, Victor Nicholas, Jr. "The Broken Staff: A
      Generic Study of the Problem of Authority in *Beowulf,*
      The Tempest, and *Moby Dick.*" Ph.D. dissertation,
      State University of New York-Buffalo, 1975.
      Dissertation Abstracts International, 36 (1976):
      6654A.

      This dissertation explores the relationship between
      the artist and his surrogate in an epic, a drama, and a
      novel. The chapter on Shakespeare includes readings of
      *Richard 3, Othello, A Midsummer Night's Dream, Measure
      for Measure, Pericles,* and *The Tempest.*

214. Carpenter, Nan Cooke. "Shakespeare and Music:
      Unexplored Areas." *Renaissance Drama,* 7 (1976):
      243-55.

      A study might be made of the relationship between
      Shakespeare's ideas on music and neo-Platonic
      pneumatology.

215. Collings, R.L.E. "The Antiphonal Structure of
      Shakespeare's *Pericles*: A Stylistic Analysis." Ph.D.
      dissertation, University of Manchester, 1976. (not
      seen)

216. Dutz, Ingold.. *Shakespeares "Pericles" and "Cymbeline"
      in der Bildkunst.* Ph.D. dissertation, Marburg, 1976.
      Europäische Hochschulschriften, Reihe
      XIV-Angelsächsische Sprache and Literatur, 34. Bern:
      Herbert Lang; Frankfurt: Peter Lang, 1976.

This dissertation considers the influence that
illustrations of *Pericles* and *Cymbeline* have had on
understanding the two plays. The study covers the work
of three centuries of English, French, and German
artists, including J.H. Füssli and Gordon Browne, in
the Shakespeare-Bildarchivs, der Akademie der
Wissenschaften und der Literatur, Mainz.

217. Ford, Jane M. "The Father/Daughter/Suitor Triangle in
Shakespeare, Dickens, James, Conrad, and Joyce."
Ph.D. dissertation, State University of New York-
Buffalo, 1975. *Dissertation Abstracts International*,
36 (1976): 4507A.

The incest theme, which concerns the artistic
process, involves a missing mother, a ripe daughter, an
exile, and a resolution of a father's rejection or
acceptance of his daughter's suitor. *Pericles* contains
most of the plots used by later writers, including
incest, a suitor chosen by a father, a mother's
attempted destruction of a daughter, the daughter's
exploitation by her father, or, the daughter's final
acceptance of a suitor at her parents' reunion. *The
Winter's Tale* expands this plot; *The Tempest* condenses
it.

218. Frye, Northrop. "Romance as Masque." *Spiritus Mundi:
Essays on Literature, Myth, and Society.*
Bloomington: Indiana University Press, 1976, pp.
148-78.

Shakespeare's romances, from *Pericles* through *The Two
Noble Kinsmen*, resemble the masque, in which spectacle
counts more than plot. The main theme of the romances
is the reintegration of the older, mature generation.
Reintegration constitutes resurrection, not rebirth.
As in the masque the movement from death to
resurrection in the romances is vertical, up the chain
of being. Music represents the higher world. The
ending in the romances reveals something beyond social
integration; it envisions a reconciliation with nature
that individualizes characters against nature as Adam
and Eve were in Eden.

219. Gorfain, Phyllis. "Puzzle and Artifice: The Riddle as
Metapoetry in *Pericles*." *Shakespeare Survey*, 29
(1976): 11-20.

The ordering principle in *Pericles* is analogical
rather than causal. The recurring analogues involve a
timeless, circular pattern of separation, loss, and
recovery. In folk custom, marriage riddles such as
that of Antiochus and his daughter are ritual
representations of the tension between old and new
blood ties. The Gower choruses and dumb shows are
self-conscious art, deliberately crude representatives
of reality. The plot is ritual performed in three
stages: separation ending in symbolic death,
suspension, and rebirth. The self-conscious choruses,
the clumsy dumb shows, and the ritual plot are the
structural devices of metatheatre; riddle is a metaphor
of metaphor.

220. Hikichi, Masatoshi. "Shakespeare's Romances and Greek
     Romance." *Eibungaku* (Waseda University), 44 (1976):
     1-17. (Japanese--not seen)

221. Hoeniger, F. David. "Shakespeare's Romances Since
     1958: A Retrospect." *Shakespeare Survey*, 29 (1976):
     1-10.

     Covering criticism of Shakespeare's romances
     published between 1958 and 1975, this essay follows
     Philip Edwards' evaluation of criticism published
     between 1900 and 1957 (see item 48). *Pericles* is
     mentioned in conjunction with studies of music,
     cyclical structure, staging, and stage productions.

222. Marsh, Derick R.C. "The Romances." *Passion Lends Them
     Power: A Study of Shakespeare's Love Tragedies*.
     Manchester: Manchester University Press; New York:
     Barnes and Noble, 1976, pp. 201-33.

     The chapter concentrates on *Cymbeline* and *The
     Winter's Tale* in considering Shakespeare's treatment of
     love in *Romeo and Juliet*, *Othello*, *Anthony and
     Cleopatra*, *Troilus and Cressida*, and the romances.
     There is little in the plot or theme of *Pericles* to
     link the play directly with the love tragedies.

223. McMahan, C.E. "Psychosomatic Concepts in the Works of
     Shakespeare." *Journal of the History of the
     Behavioral Sciences*, 12 (1976): 275-82.

     The three psychosomatic ideas expressed in
     Shakespeare's plays--emotion affects heartbeat, outside

events can cause human disorders, and chronic repression of emotions causes disease—reveal Shakespeare's predualistic understanding of human nature. In *Pericles*, for instance, the threat of shipwreck causes Thaisa's death in childbirth.

224. Mincoff, Marco. "Predgovor" [Preface]. *Tragekomedii*. Sofia: Narodna Kultura, 1976, pp. 5-33. (not seen)

225. Mowat, Barbara A. "The Romances as Open Form Drama." *The Dramaturgy of Shakespeare's Romances*. Athens: University of Georgia Press, 1976, pp. 95-110.

The formal patterns and themes of the later romances belong to *Pericles* also. The play, its problems of authorship notwithstanding, profoundly influenced Shakespeare in writing *Cymbeline*, *The Winter's Tale*, and *The Tempest*.

226. Plummer, Denis Lee. "Generative Poesis: The Book and Child Metaphor in Renaissance Poetry." Ph.D. dissertation, University of Washington, 1975. *Dissertation Abstracts International*, 37 (1976): 990A-91A.

Generative poesis refers to the creation of children and poetry as man's protection against time. The poet locates himself within the book and child metaphor by creating characters who are pregnant with a book or a child. This theory is applied to *The Old Wives Tale*, *A Midsummer Night's Dream*, *Pericles*, and *Paradise Lost*.

227. Ranald, Margaret. *Women in Shakespeare's Last Plays*. Cassette Curriculum: Women's Studies. Deland, Fla.: Everett/Edwards, 1976.

Shakespeare's four dramatic romances, plays in a more symbolic and cerebral mode than before, use a presentational method. The chaste heroines of the romances teach the heroes virtue without denying their sexuality. In these plays chaste marriage is the ultimate human condition, a joyful acceptance of life that brings earthly immortality. Optimistic *Pericles*, probably not entirely Shakespeare's, which ushered in the new dramatic style, contains all the characteristics of that style. The opposite of misanthropic *Timon of Athens*, *Pericles* treats women affirmatively. The evil women in the play, Antiochus'

daughter, Dionyza, and the Bawd, represent disasters to
Pericles and Marina rather than distinctive characters.
Marina, the first springtime virgin of the romances,
possesses the curative and redemptive powers of
chastity. This symbolic gift from the sea, like
Botticelli's Venus, restores Pericles to harmony and
brings him a nearly Platonic vision. For all her
militant chastity, however, Marina remains
"marriageable flesh and blood." *Pericles* combines the
romance tradition of fruitful marriage with the
Platonic vision of the beautiful, the sacrament of love
beyond passion. Pericles is not repentant; he is
rewarded with redemptive love after suffering,
receiving a vision of heaven that is mirrored in
harmonious marriage.

228. Sekiya, T. "Shakespeare's Last Plays and Beaumont and
      Fletcher." *Eibungaku Ronshu*, 1 (1976): 69-91.
      (Japanese--not seen)

229. Wells, Henry W. and H.H. Anniah Gowda. *"Pericles* as a
      Folk Play." *Shakespeare Turned East: A Study in
      Comparison of Shakespeare's Last Plays with Some
      Classical Plays of India.* Prasaranga: University of
      Mysore, 1976, pp. 49-61.

      Pericles is similar to *Rathnavali* and *Priyadarsika*,
      two Indian plays from the A.D. 600s. Shakespeare moves
      in Eastern fashion from unlikely events to final
      equipoise and peace in *Pericles*, which is half-Asian
      because of its origin in Greek romance.

230. Yoshimatsu, Sachiko. "The Religiously Devoted Women in
      Shakespeare's Plays." *Tokyo University Studies in
      English*, 11 (1976): 81-118. (not seen)

      This essay concerns *The Comedy of Errors, Pericles,*
      and *Measure for Measure.*

231. Andretta, Richard A. "Copiousness in Shakespeare's
      Romances: *Pericles, Cymbeline, The Winter's Tale,* and
      The Tempest." Ph.D. dissertation, New York
      University, 1977. *Dissertation Abstracts
      International*, 38 (1977): 3507A.

      The Renaissance fondness for copiousness made
      romances popular in Shakespeare's day. By transforming
      his earlier work, literary convention, and folklore and

by using abundant illusion and disguise, symbols, and
various structures and themes, Shakespeare achieved a
copiousness in his late romances which suggests an
inclusive but harmonious universe. Unlike tragedy,
which deals with a central conflict, romance depends on
the numerous conflicts that form the hero's quest for
an ideal. Copiousness is an outstanding characteristic
of romance.

232. Brownlow, Frank. W. *"Pericles, Prince of Tyre."* Two
     Shakespearean Sequences: "Henry VI" to "Richard II"
     and "Pericles" to "Timon of Athens." London:
     Macmillan; Pittsburgh: University of Pittsburgh
     Press, 1977, pp. 117-33.

Even though *Pericles* may be a collaboration, it has a
unified tone and theme. Perhaps Shakespeare provided
the unifying parts and his collaborator added final
touches. The text is corrupt, but questions of
authorship are not important to interpretation, except
for the Gower choruses. Critics and editors have paid
attention to Gower only to remark on the crudity of his
function as a device for turning narrative into drama.
Gower frames the action and distances the audience from
the play. The closeness of Gower and his story of
Pericles to the medieval Gower and his Apollonius may
mean that *Pericles* belongs to the tradition of Celtic
storytellers and their salutary tales handed down
verbatim. If so, *Pericles* may be an experiment in
returning drama to narrative form. *Pericles* is a
larger, more typical story than *King Lear*. The typical
in *Pericles* "is marvellous, and appearances are
riddles" (p. 127). Marina is the good and the
beautiful. Her reunion with Pericles seems more than a
meeting between a father and a daughter long lost. When
Pericles hears the music of the spheres, inaudible to
the audience but accepted by them as real, the audience
witnesses a miracle. *Pericles* moves toward essential,
original truth.

233. Cook, Ann Jennalie. "The Mode of Marriage in
     Shakespeare's England." *Southern Humanities Review*,
     11 (1977): 126-32.

Early marriages were uncommon in Elizabethan England.
The extreme youth of Marina (14), Perdita (16), and
Miranda (14) reflects Shakespeare's sources, the
quality of fantasy in the late romances, and

Shakespeare's dramatic purpose. Each heroine's youth
emphasizes her innocence and the threat to her
innocence. The extremely youthful heroines of the
romances seem more a part of their families.

234. Deese, Ethel Helen. "Shakespeare's Comedies of
      Renascence." Ph.D. dissertation, University of
      California-Riverside, 1977. *Dissertation Abstracts
      International*, 38 (1977): 2137A-38A.

      In *Much Ado About Nothing, All's Well That Ends Well,
      Pericles, Cymbeline*, and *The Winter's Tale*, the plot
      motif of the heroine who is reported dead suggests a
      renascence theme. The plays contain the following
      correspondences: the heroine disappears because the
      hero errs; while the heroine is presumed dead, moral
      confusion and barrenness grip the hero and society; the
      heroine's return in act 5 coincides with the hero's
      repentance or renewal of love. *Pericles* has two
      heroines, both of whom return from apparent death.
      Thaisa and Marina share the role of redeemer, Marina
      becoming Pericles' spiritual mother.

235. Dunbar, Mary Judith. "*Pericles*: A Study of Dramatic
      Construction." Ph.D. dissertation, Stanford
      University, 1976. *Dissertation Abstracts
      International*, 37 (1977): 7760A.

      The structure of *Pericles* is both coherent and
      dramatically effective. The dissertation reviews
      critical assessments of the structure of the play and
      examines romance conventions. *Pericles* departs
      considerably from its narrative sources to reveal a
      vision of universal coherence.

236. Frey, Charles. "Teaching Shakespeare's Romances."
      College Literature, 4 (1977): 252-56.

      After demonstrating to students that the grouping of
      these plays and the dating of all Shakespeare's plays
      are modern considerations, the instructor compares the
      journey motif in the romances with other romances,
      ancient and modern. Plot is approached by comparing
      the family relationships and emphasizing that each play
      deals with the dilemma of a ruler left without male
      heirs and threatened by enemies. In considering
      individual plays, students find the repetitive devices
      of poetry and staging that characterize the play.

Pericles, for instance, has images of eating, hunger,
and appetite which blend with the contrasting scenes of
famine and plenty, loss and restoration, profanity and
holiness. The three dumb shows that precede sea storms
are countered by scenes in which music restores.
Students are asked to consider the contemporary
significance of the romances, such as their holistic
and ecological interest and their colonial
implications. To focus on the romances as stage plays,
students learn and present principal speeches and
scenes.

237. Garber, Marjorie. "Coming of Age in Shakespeare."
      Yale Review, 66 (1977): 517-33.

      This essay studies patterns of sexual maturation in
      two kinds of Shakespearean characters: those of moral
      strength, such as Hermia, Juliet, and Cordelia, who
      leave peers or kin to find self-knowledge in fruitful
      marriage, and weaklings, such as Cressida, Ophelia, and
      Coriolanus, who choose to remain in childlike
      subjugation to parents. Among the romances, *Pericles*
      contains the most striking examples of Shakespeare's
      parallels between "filial choice and moral strength"
      (p. 532).

238. Gorfain, Phyllis. "Remarks Toward a Folklorist
      Approach to Literature: Riddles in Shakespearean
      Drama." *Southern Folklore Quarterly,* 40 (1977):
      143-57.

      This survey of riddling patterns in Shakespeare's
      plays contains a paragraph on *Pericles.* By failing to
      answer the riddle at Antiochus' court, Pericles
      temporarily forfeits his princely power and identity.
      Even though he understands the explicit references to
      incest, Pericles refuses to name Antiochus' sin to his
      face. Unanswered riddles lead to successive episodes
      of dramatic instability; after Pericles leaves Antioch,
      he, and later his family, continues to suffer shifts of
      fortune.

239. Link, L.T. "Limitations of Shakespeare: The Child,
      General, Villain, and Romance Plays." *Kiyo* (Aoyama
      Gakuin University), 18 (1977): 41-51. (not seen)

      The essay explores the role of children in the last
      plays.

240. Mickov, Georgi. "Tragikomediite i romansite na
      Sekspir." *Literaturen front* (Sophia), 4 August 1977,
      p. 7. (not seen)

241. Mowat, Barbara A. "Images of Women in Shakespeare's
      Plays." *Southern Humanities Review*, 11 (1977):
      145-57.

      Women in Shakespeare function as humans, as myths,
      and, illusively, as Shakespeare himself perceived them.
      Each of these images is superimposed on the others.
      Mowat deals with the second image, "woman as she
      sometimes appears to the Shakespearian male" (p. 146).
      In the romances the virtuous young heroines are chaste
      ideals; the evil females are grotesques.

242. Nagata, Yoshiko. *Shakespeare's Underthought in the
      Later Plays*. Renaissance Monographs 4. Tokyo:
      Renaissance Institute, Sophia University, 1977.

      Part 2 of this monograph examines the four romances
      according to the doctrine of providence. Evil in
      Pericles is rather simply and boringly presented.
      Pericles and his family are sinless. Shakespeare
      emphasizes the theme of patience through Pericles.
      Physician Cerimon, almost a supernatural agent,
      cooperates with divine providence. The unexpected
      happiness of Pericles and his family at the end of the
      play is the work of the gods. Pericles is reconciled
      with divinity as well as his family. The fortune
      mentioned by Gower in the epilogue is not fate as
      presented in the Greek tragedies; it is a trial
      arranged by heaven to lead men to joy.

243. Nakabayhashi, Kenji. "Language in Shakespeare's Later
      Plays." *Gakuen* (Showa Woman's College), April 1977,
      pp. 1-27. (not seen)

244. Niki, Hisae. "Low Comedy as a Structural Element in
      Pericles." *Tsuda Review* (Tsuda College), 22 (1977):
      29-44.

      The realistic comic episodes in *Pericles*, the
      fishermen scene (2.1) and the brothel scenes (4.2,
      4-6), interrupt the narrative flow of the play. The
      fishermen scenes contain philosophy and sympathy as
      well as humor. Shakespeare moved the brothel scenes
      inside, elaborated on them, and made them funny. The

play explores four types of relationships: the incest
of Antiochus and his daughter, which infects Pericles;
the ideal father and daughter relationship between
Simonides and Thaisa, to which Pericles seems
indifferent; the perverted relationship of Cleon and
Dionyza and their daughter; and the happy family
relationship which Pericles and Marina finally recover.
By exchanging the somber mood induced by fantastic evil
in the previous scenes for a social evil that can be
laughed at in the brothel scenes, Shakespeare prepares
the audience to experience the happiness appropriate to
Pericles and Marina's reunion.

245. Ratsky, I. "Shakespeare's Last Plays and the Romance
     Tradition." *Shakespeare Readings 1976.* Edited by A.
     Anikst. Moscow: "Nauka," 1977, pp. 104-39.
     (Russian--not seen)

     The essay concerns folk and literary traditions in
     Shakespeare's romances.

246. Rohrsen, Peter. *Die Preisrede auf die Geliebte in
     Shakespeares Komödien und Romanzen.* Ph.D.
     dissertation, Göttingen, 1977. Schriftenreihe d.
     Deutschen Shakespeare-Gesellschaft West, N.F., vol.
     14. Heidelberg: Quelle and Meyer, 1977. (not seen)

247. Schanzer, Ernest. *Construction in Shakespeare.* New
     York: Jeffrey Norton, 1977. (not heard)

     Schanzer analyzes the two-part structure of *Timon of
     Athens, Coriolanus, Pericles,* and *The Winter's Tale* in
     this 1965 recording (27 minutes).

248. Csetneki, Gábor. "Shakespeare Periclesének
     dramaturgiai problémái [Dramaturgical Problems in
     Shakespeare's *Pericles*]." *Szinháztudományi Szemle,* 2
     (1978): 21-29. (Hungarian--not seen)

249. Dean, John. "Constant Wanderings and Longed-For
     Returns: Odyssean Themes in Shakespearean Romance."
     Mosaic, 12 (1978): 47-60.

     This essay compares Shakespeare's romances and *The
     Odyssey* as Mediterranean romances, *The Tempest*
     receiving particular attention. Unlike Shakespeare's
     other romance heroes, Pericles, a flat and passive

character, is victimized by shameless women before
finding virtuous women whom he loses and recovers. The
play concerns Pericles' sorrows as well as the creative
and destructive effects of women on men. Pericles is
the first of Shakespeare's Odyssean heroes who turns
reaction to action.

250. Doyle, Charles Clay. "Below the Belt: Hamlet's Crude
     Insult." *Maledicta*, 2 (1978): 177-81.

     In this article about *Hamlet*, Doyle mentions
     Pericles' sexual reference to Antiochus' daughter as "a
     fair viol" misplayed (1.1.81-85).

251. Frey, Charles. "Shakespeare's Imperiled and Chastening
     Daughters of Romance." *South Atlantic Bulletin*, 43,
     no. 4 (1978): 125-40. Reprint. "'O Sacred, Shadowy,
     Cold, and Constant Queen': Shakespeare's Imperiled
     and Chastening Daughters of Romance." *The Woman's
     Part: Feminist Criticism of Shakespeare*. Edited by
     Carolyn Ruth Swift Lenz, Gayle Greene, and Carol
     Thomas Neely. Urbana: University of Illinois Press,
     1980, pp. 295-313.

     In the four romances, where the relationship between
     father and daughter is central, the daughter travels
     away from the father, returning to teach him
     forgiveness and give pardon. In this way, patterns of
     patriarchal domination and incestuous self-seeking are
     broken by movements away from the center which lead
     eventually to harmonious reunion. The virginal
     daughters win husbands through their own adventures,
     such as Marina's triumph over the brothel crew,
     returning to extend the family in fresh bloodlines.
     The essay also considers the women in *Henry 8*, *The Two
     Noble Kinsmen*, and *Cardenio*.

252. Gira, Catherine R. "Shakespeare's Venus Figures and
     Renaissance Tradition." *Studies in Iconography*, 4
     (1978): 95-114.

     Often Renaissance writers portrayed Venus as a
     wanton. By contrast, Shakespeare's less conventional
     Venus figures possess a winning vitality and charm in
     the midst of wantonness. The ideal Venuses of
     Shakespeare combine the best attributes of the goddess.
     Marina, for instance, displays characteristics of two
     goddesses: like Venus she was born at sea; in the

Mytilene brothel she remains faithful to Diana.
Lysimachus is drawn to the chaste sensuality of this
Venus-Diana, who stands in marked contrast to
Antiochus' depraved Venus of a daughter.

253. Heims, Neil Stephen. "Fathers and Daughters in the
      Plays of Shakespeare." Ph.D. dissertation, City
      University of New York, 1978. *Dissertation Abstracts
      International,* 39 (1978): 2954.

      The father-daughter relationship in Shakespeare has
      incestuous undertones generally representing cupidity.
      The plays examined are *King Lear, Timon of Athens,* and
      the four romances, particularly *The Tempest.*

254. Hillman, Richard Wright. "Mortality and Immortality in
      Shakespeare's Later Tragedies and Romances." Ph.D.
      dissertation, University of Toronto, 1976.
      Dissertation Abstracts International, 39 (1978):
      2290A-91A.

      The main characters' instinct for immortality works
      against a rational awareness of mortality in
      Shakespeare's major tragedies and late romances. In
      Pericles, Cymbeline, and *The Winter's Tale,* spiritual
      freedom from death replaces tragedy. Even though
      Prospero has gained true immortality (represented by
      Ariel), a tragic strain, the futility of rebelling
      against death, appears in *The Tempest.*

255. Hoeniger, F. David. "Anticipations of Shakespeare's
      Romances in His Earlier Work." *Shakespeare: Pattern
      of Excelling Nature.* Shakespeare Criticism in Honor
      of America's Bicentennial from the International
      Shakespeare Association Congress, Washington, D. C.,
      April, 1976. Edited by David Bevington and Jay L.
      Halio. Newark: University of Delaware Press; London:
      Association of University Presses, 1978, pp. 258-62.

      This essay is a seminar report. Essays and
      bibliographies having been submitted in advance,
      seminar members discussed the submissions, including an
      essay by Richard Van Fossen on parallels in *The Comedy
      of Errors, Pericles,* and *The Tempest.* Eastern Kentucky
      University has a tape of the seminar.

256. Hoy, Cyrus. "Fathers and Daughters in Shakespeare's
      Romances." *Shakespeare's Romances Reconsidered.*

Edited by Carol McGinnis Kay and Henry E. Jacobs.
Lincoln: University of Nebraska Press, 1978, pp.
77-90.

The romances are quests to replace "the shrill
mistress-wife-mother figures" (p. 84) of the late
tragedies with ideals of femininity that free the
imagination from guilty passion.

257. Khan, Maqbool H. "The Design of Wonder in *Pericles*."
      Aligarh Journal of English Studies, 3 (1978): 80-106.

Pericles foreshadows the benevolent manipulations in
Cymbeline, *The Winter's Tale*, and *The Tempest*. The
Gower choruses, an embarrassing reminder that in
Pericles narration replaces much direct presentation,
make the events in the story remote and stylized.
Pericles comes to know of sin and death at Antiochus'
court. A significant theme in the play is the contrast
between Antiochus and Pericles as fathers. The journey
that the Prince undertakes following his return to Tyre
is one of atonement. At the beginning of act 3 there
is a shift from the presentation of Pericles as an
ideal king to one that denotes a spiritual interest in
Pericles as a man. Pericles' patience is not an
ethical virtue; it stands for the perception of
redemption in time. Likewise, Marina's chastity,
embodiment of the soul's integrity, is the focus of
Shakespeare's work. When Pericles is reunited with
Marina and hears the music of the spheres, Shakespeare
evokes a kind of wonder that is beyond theatrics.

258. McIver, Bruce. "'Upon Such Sacrifices': *King Lear* and
      the Late Comedies." *Shakespeare Newsletter*, 28
      (1978): 15.

King Lear and the romances reveal by means of a
father-daughter relationship a changeless spiritual
world. These plays, and especially *The Tempest*, affirm
man's goodness and demonstrate the ability of art to
improve human nature by infusing it with the divine.
The essay is an abstract of McIver's Ph.D. dissertation
(University of California-Santa Barbara).

259. Nakabayhashi, Kenji. "The Effects of Run-on Verse in
      Shakespeare's Later Plays." *Gakuen* (Showa Woman's
      College), 460 (1978): 1-24. (Japanese--not seen)

260. Naumann, Walter. *"Pericles."* *Die Dramen Shakespeares.*
Darmstadt: Wissenschaftliche Buchgesellschaft, 1978,
pp. 474–84.

> *Pericles* is the story of a perfect hero who bears all
> in a universe that he is powerless to control.

261. Schiffhorst, Gerald J. "Some Prolegomena for the Study
of Patience, 1480–1680." *The Triumph of Patience:*
Medieval and Renaissance Studies. Edited by Gerald
J. Schiffhorst. Orlando: University Presses of
Florida, 1978, pp. 1–64.

> Patience in Shakespeare is "calm dispassion rather
> than quiet perseverance" (p. 8). Cordelia, Desdemona,
> and Marina show signs of Stoic, Christian, and heroic
> forebearance. Patience is an important theme in
> *Hamlet, King Lear,* and in particular *Pericles,* whose
> pre-Christian Prince displays a modified Christian
> version based on the Apollonius source story. Pericles
> accepts the divine will rather than despairing.
> Learning from the sea around him, he gradually accepts
> the birth-to-death cycle of life. He is the
> traditional patient hero who chooses to accept the
> workings of divine providence. His faith is active,
> and in the end he is rewarded for enduring.
> Shakespeare emblemized patience as a smiling, seated
> female figure, as in *Pericles* (5.1.134–39) and *Twelfth*
> *Night* (2.4.109–14).

262. Wada, Yuichi. *Sheikusupia Sakuhin Kenkyu* [A Study of
Shakespeare's Works]. Tokyo: Eiho-sha, 1978. (not
seen)

263. Weisz, Carole Lynn. "Shakespeare: Growth or
Deterioration." Ph.D. dissertation, Purdue
University, 1977. *Dissertation Abstracts*
International, 38 (1978): 4800A.

> Weisz traces the maturation of Shakespeare's psyche
> in the comedies from *Love's Labor's Lost* through *The*
> *Tempest.* Chapter 1 presents a broad analysis of the 14
> comedies under discussion. Chapter 2 finds the early
> comedies "oral, immature, and situational," while
> chapter 3 deals with the maturer male-female
> relationships in the middle comedies. Chapter 4
> explores Shakespeare's later "catharsis of hate,

jealousy, and violence" in the romances that allowed
for expiation finally in *The Tempest*.

264. Dean, John. *Restless Wanderers: Shakespeare and the
     Pattern of Romance*. Elizabethan and Renaissance
     Studies, 86. Salzburg Studies in English Literature.
     Salzburg: Institut für Anglistik and Amerikanistik,
     Universität Salzburg, 1979.

The book includes discussion of *Pericles* in chapters
6-9. Gower's *Confessio Amantis* was the positive and
pervasive source for the play; Shakespeare used
matter-of-fact Twine little. Shakespeare departed from
Gower and Twine in using the theme of regeneration and
recovery, the sea as a metaphor for fortune, the Gower
choruses, the dumb shows, and music. However, he did
not break away from the techniques of narrative romance
until *Cymbeline*. The uncertainty of natural forces
gives *Pericles* its structure, the Gower choruses
serving as guides for the audience. *Pericles* is the
first Shakespearean play to extend its action over such
a long period of time. In the first part of *Pericles*,
Shakespeare compares the depraved love of Antiochus and
his daughter with the healthy relationship between
Simonides and his daughter, Thaisa. The second part of
the play, centered on Marina in act 4, compares the
true love exemplified by Marina, Thaisa, Cerimon, and
the reformed Lysimachus with the false love sold in the
Mytilene brothel. The virtuous characters in *Pericles*,
types rather than individuals, are constants amid the
inconstant world of the play. Love eventually rescues
storm-tossed Pericles. The goddess Diana represents
the spiritual love that guides Pericles and his family
safely through the diseased and disordered world of
Priapus.

265. Eggers, Walter F., Jr. "'Bring Forth a Wonder':
     Presentation in Shakespeare's Romances." *Texas
     Studies in Literature and Language*, 21 (1979):
     455-77.

Wonders in the romantic comedies take place off stage
and are reported in the past tense; but in the four
romances Shakespeare put wonders on stage, risking the
audience's credulity to engage their sense of wonder.
As the first of Shakespeare's dramatic romances,
Pericles seems a deliberate experiment in the
techniques of dramatic presentation and the effects of

wonder on an audience. The Globe's deep stage and
large discovery space are important staging elements in
Pericles and offer a firm basis for analysis. From his
downstage position, Gower is able to emphasize the
wonder of the upstage action. Other characters also
present their scenes; for instance, Antiochus acts as a
downstage chorus for his distanced and nameless
daughter. The audience thereby identifies with
Pericles and shares his wonder at the spectacle of
Antioch. Thaisa is also presented formally, by
Simonides (2.2) and by Cerimon (3.2); Marina, who is
never alone on stage, is always on display. The
wonders culminate for the audience in the two act 5
reunions, both of which are presentations: Pericles to
Marina, Marina and Thaisa to Pericles. At the reunion
of Pericles and Marina, the music of the spheres
belongs only to Pericles and the audience; Diana
appears to the audience alone. The theatricality of
her appearance seems designed to awaken in the audience
the same sense of discovery that has been awakened in
Pericles. Both reunions take place before an on-stage
audience and a theatre audience. The reactions of the
audience on stage express the wonder of the theatre
audience. The mundane didactic epilogue reveals
Gower's failure to understand that his story presented
is even more wonderful than his story told. The essay
also examines presentational techniques in *Cymbeline*,
The Winter's Tale, and *The Tempest*, particularly the
presenter-characters, such as Iachimo, Paulina, and
Prospero, and the epiphanic final scenes which stir
wonder and a new understanding in the audience.

266. Gilbert, Miriam. "'This Wide Gap of Time':
Storytelling and Audience Response in the Romances."
Iowa State Journal of Research, 53 (1979): 235-41.

The essay considers the problem of long time spans in
the late romances. The solution in *Pericles* is Gower,
a narrator who remains outside the story. Like
Pericles, *The Tempest* is a highly narrated play; the
audience is asked to watch these plays, not to become
emotionally involved. The occasionally narrated
Cymbeline and *The Winter Tale* are plays of jealousy.
Emotions in these plays engage the audience.
Shakespeare manipulated the amount of narration to deal
with time problems and control audience involvement.

267. Harding, D.W. "Shakespeare's Final View of Women."
      Times Literary Supplement, 30 Nov. 1979, pp. 59-61.

      Shakespeare presented destructive women in *Macbeth*,
      Antony and Cleopatra, and *Coriolanus*. *Timon of Athens*
      is almost womanless, but Shakespeare hints in it at the
      benignity of women. In the four succeeding plays,
      Pericles, *Cymbeline*, *The Winter's Tale*, and *The
      Tempest*, Shakespeare emphasized the benign aspects of
      women as symbolized by girls. Shakespeare's young
      heroines of romance seem self-created, as if
      motherless. When Marina and Perdita do finally meet
      their mothers, the reunion is formal and contained.
      Emotional reunions are with the fathers. These
      heroines are not associated with the more sinister and
      rigorous aspects of womanhood. Perhaps it was the
      story of incest at Antiochus's court that interested
      Shakespeare in the *Pericles* fragment. By retaining the
      story of Antiochus' incest with his daughter,
      Shakespeare has the audience consider and dismiss the
      possibility of incest for Pericles. The escape from
      Antioch marks the end of the threat of incest in
      Pericles' life and in Shakespeare's later plays as
      well. The emotional focus in *Pericles* is Marina's
      resurrection of her father; Pericles recognizes his
      wife in the daughter. By reviving her father Marina
      prepares him for his restoration to his wife. The
      union between Pericles and Thaisa, a woman in her early
      thirties, promises a return to a sexual life for
      Pericles, not merely a return to public
      responsibilities. The essay continues with readings of
      Cymbeline, *The Winter's Tale*, and *The Tempest*. In the
      first three plays continuity of the ruling line depends
      on the daughter; for instance, in *Pericles* Thaisa and
      Marina give thrones to their husbands (Pentapolis to
      Pericles and Tyre to Lysimachus). Because of the
      importance of the father-daughter relationship,
      Lysimachus serves merely to round off the play.
      Perhaps Shakespeare wrote of strong father and daughter
      relationships in the four romances to flatter James 1,
      who succeeded through the female line, or because
      Shakespeare's oldest daughter was married in 1607 and
      bore his granddaughter in 1608. Perhaps he was trying
      to understand why Lear demanded of Cordelia as he did.
      This article is the text of "Fathers and Daughters in
      Shakespeare's Last Plays," the 1979 Arthur Skemp
      Memorial Lecture, delivered at the University of
      Bristol.

268. Hasegawa, Mitsuaki. "Dramatic Structure of
     Shakespeare's Last Plays." *Kiyo* (Kyoto Kyoiku
     College), Series A, no. 55 (1979): 95-139.

     The first part of the essay concerns *Pericles* (pp.
     95-105). Cerimon and Marina are divine instruments.
     Fortune rules Pericles before he has a family;
     afterward, providence takes over. Perhaps the
     sufferings of Pericles in the early part of the play
     result from his hubris. Gower's epilogue attests to
     the actuality of divine intervention in the play.

269. Hasegawa, Mitsuaki. "Essays on *Pericles* and
     Cymbeline." *Kiyo* (Bulletin of the Kyoto University
     of Education). Series A, no. 54 (1979): 49-76.

     The first part of the essay concerns *Pericles* (pp.
     49-62). As a passive escapist, Pericles does not
     represent enduring humanity. Marina is the human
     instrument of the gods. The fishermen (2.1) are
     touchingly human.

270. Ichikawa, Mariko. "Dramaturgy of the Romances—On the
     Distance between Drama and the Audience." *Leo* (Tokyo
     Gakugei University), 8 (1979): 53-65. (not seen)

271. Knowles, Richard Paul. "Imaginative Engagement in the
     Last Plays of Shakespeare." Ph.D. dissertation,
     University of Toronto, 1977. *Dissertation Abstracts
     International*, 39 (1979): 4276A-77A.

     The devices which engage audience attention and
     belief in the romances include direct address, used by
     Gower, Time, and Prospero, induction scenes involving
     ancient stories that awaken faith, comic characters in
     supporting roles, and music, masque, and spectacle.
     The most important devices are the presiding deities,
     the artist figures who engage the audience
     imaginatively. Depending less than *Pericles* and
     Cymbeline on such presiding figures, *The Winter's Tale*
     and *The Tempest* emphasize the artist within the play.
     In *The Tempest* Shakespeare makes the audience feel the
     artist's struggle to impose order. Prospero eventually
     turns his powers over to the audience and sets them
     free to operate on their own, as he does Ariel.

272. Muir, Kenneth. "Tragi-comedies: *Pericles*."
      Shakespeare's Comic Sequence. Liverpool: Liverpool
      University Press, 1979, pp. 151-56.

      Even though a loosely connected series of accidents
      form the plot of *Pericles*, the play is sophisticated.
      The Gower choruses, with their suggestively medieval
      flavor, link the episodes by means of a naive,
      moralizing commentary meant to ease the audience into
      an unsophisticated acceptance of the story. The
      simplified plot and characters are sometimes
      inconsistent; for instance, Lysimachus visits the
      Mytilene brothel but pleads innocence (4.6). Perhaps
      Shakespeare realized the inconsistency too late to
      change the portrait. Shakespeare's mature style is
      evident for the first time in the scene of Pericles and
      Marina's reunion (5.1); Pericles' powerful image of
      Marina as an emblematic Patience (11. 134-38) embodies
      the main theme of the play, restoration after suffering
      and grief. Yet the play fails to satisfy; Shakespeare
      was not entirely successful in reshaping his original;
      Pericles' misfortunes are mere accidents and the
      characters mere emblems. In the later plays sin and
      repentance replace an arbitrary providence.

273. Schütze, Johannes. "Shakespeares *Pericles*: Gedanken zu
      einem umstrittenen Drama." *Jahrbuch der Wittheit zu
      Bremen*, 23 (1979): 113-33.

      The first three sections of this nine-part essay
      consist of a plot summary, an examination of sources,
      and a discussion of the characteristics of
      Shakespeare's romances. The fourth section looks at
      the relationship between the romances and the earlier
      plays and discusses Shakespeare's fascination with
      young heroines in the late romances. Part 5, a history
      of English productions of *Pericles* to 1974, also
      contains citations for several German, Australian,
      American, and Canadian productions. The next three
      sections include a summary of the controversy over
      questions of authorship and text. Section 8 reviews
      James O. Wood's evidence that Shakespeare wrote acts
      1-2 early in his career, revising and completing the
      play around 1608 (see items 375, 432, 436, 437, 441,
      450, 451, 455, 464, 471). Part 9 concludes that the
      evidence favors *Pericles* as Shakespeare's play
      entirely.

274. Takahashi, Shozo. "Women in the Last Plays." *Hoskusei Ronshu* (Hoskusei Gakuen University), 17 (1979): 59-96. (Japanese--not seen)

275. Takayama, Hiroko. "Love and Paganism in *Pericles*." *Musashino Eibei Bungaku* (Musashino Women's College), 12 (1979): 45-59. (Japanese--not seen)

276. Tanner, Tony. *Adultery in the Novel: Contract and Transgression*. Baltimore and London: Johns Hopkins University Press, 1979, pp. 39-40.

In the introductory chapter to a study of transgression, particularly adultery, in the bourgeois novel, Tanner examines Shakespeare's "growing horror" (p. 39), manifested in the middle and late plays, especially *King Lear, Pericles, Cymbeline,* and *The Winter's Tale,* at the social collapse that occurs when the word given as bond breaks down. In its connection of incest with a riddle and a famine, *Pericles* is closer than *Hamlet* in feeling to Sophocles' *Oedipus Rex.* Pericles' refusal to speak of Antiochus' incest (1.1) is itself a sort of linguistic incest in which the tongue wishes to stay in its womb, the mouth, in the presence of the actual incest between a father-king, the law-giver, and his daughter.

277. Yamagishi, Masayuki. "Shakespeare's Last Plays Toward *The Tempest*." *Gakujutsu Zasshi* (Shiga Kenritsu Junior College), 20 (1979): 116-21.

Shakespeare's sense of time, dream, and vision, always rooted in the Elizabethan age, is especially strong in the last plays. As old tales, allegories of time gone by, these four plays remind the audience of its own past and the brevity of life.

278. Ewbank, Inga-Stina. "'My Name Is Marina': The Language of Recognition." *Shakespeare's Styles: Essays in Honour of Kenneth Muir.* Edited by Philip Edwards, Inga-Stina Ewbank, and G.K. Hunter. Cambridge: At the University Press, 1980, pp. 111-30.

In the reunion of Pericles and Marina (5.1.118-42, 91-214), Shakespeare attempted to put into words "the wonder of recognition" (p. 112). The sense of wonder that is a part of recognition is often dramatized by silence, inarticulate sounds, spectacle, or music;

wonder put into words normally distances the speaker
from what he describes. Shakespeare used each of these
methods in his plays. In *Pericles*, however, he used a
different method. To effect Pericles and Marina's
discovery of one another, he gave Marina words simple
and direct enough to generate the meaning and the
emotion of Pericles' deliverance. The literal, even
naturalistic, language of the encounter between father
and daughter individualizes them and makes their
reunion particular. Such simple, characterizing
language makes adventures strange and renders metaphors
literal. In this sense Shakespeare successfully
combined the far-fetched events of a romance plot with
a particularity of characterization unusual for
romance. *Pericles* is more like *King Lear* than the
romantic comedies. In both plays a daughter brings her
father from madness; "the language of recognition" (p.
122) spoken at their reunions belongs to them as
individuals rather than to larger thematic patterns.
In the tragedies recognition moves from particular
knowledge to a general application of knowledge. The
process is reversed in the romances, for Shakespeare
had discovered in the recognition scene in *Pericles* the
possibility for making plot, character, and language
one. Because recognition knows beyond the limits of
understanding, the scene suggests an acceptance of the
impossible.

279. Hasegawa, Mitsuaki. *Shakespeare no Romances Geki*
     [Shakespeare's Romances]. Satsuki, 1980.
     (Japanese--not seen)

280. Kahn, Coppélia. "The Providential Tempest and the
     Shakespearean Family." *Representing Shakespeare: New
     Psychoanalytic Essays*. Edited by Murray M. Schwartz
     and Coppélia Kahn. Baltimore: Johns Hopkins
     University Press, 1980, pp. 217-43.

     The essay examines the thematic quest for "masculine
     selfhood" in *The Comedy of Errors*, *Twelfth Night*,
     Pericles, *The Winter's Tale*, and *The Tempest*, romances
     about journeys through time and space that suggest an
     individual's emergence from the family into independent
     manhood. "The providential tempest," which generates
     the action in these plays, represents the often
     violent, confusing, and terrifying changes a person
     experiences in achieving independence. In *The Comedy
     of Errors* and *Twelfth Night*, twins depict an early

stage of selfhood, the narcissistic mourning for
parents that heralds the shift to heterosexual love.
Pericles, *The Winter's Tale*, and *The Tempest* concern a
later stage in which fathers fight externalized battles
to accept themselves as fathers instead of sons; they
must realize their dependence on but difference from
women. *Pericles*, *The Winter's Tale*, and *The Tempest*
are more Oedipal than *The Comedy of Errors* and *Twelfth
Night*. The twins in the latter two plays are doubles
of the mother. The daughters in the former three plays
are doubles of their fathers. In *The Tempest*
Shakespeare uses revenge and the renunciation of
revenge to end a father's struggle against time and
children, the embodiments of time. In *Pericles* the
Prince's double, Marina, removes him from the Oedipal
family he discovered at Antioch and gives him a second
birth as a father. Through Marina Pericles stops
denying the mortality implicit in his fatherhood. The
reunion of father and daughter opposes the incestuous
father and daughter Pericles meets at the first of the
play. Marina's purity counteracts the threat of
incestuous sexuality and brings Pericles to his
rightful wife and place in the world.

281. Kawakami, Akiko. "Music in *Pericles* and *The Tempest*."
     Bungaku-Shigaku (Seishin Women's University), 2
     (1980): 100-06. (not seen)

282. Nakamura, Yasuo. "A Study of *Pericles*--The Meaning of
     Suffering and Submission of Pericles." *Kyoyobu Kiyo*
     (Ehime University), 13 (1980): 1-34. (Japanese--not
     seen)

283. Sacks, Elizabeth. "'Beyond Beyond': The Last Plays."
     Shakespeare's Images of Pregnancy. New York: St.
     Martin's, 1980, pp. 87-104.

     The pregnancy imagery in the last plays, emblematic
     of Shakespeare's fondness for feminine metaphors,
     supports the theme of generation. Shakespeare was
     concerned with external action in these plays; thus,
     his generational images are the drama. The language of
     birth in the last plays prefigures the conclusions of
     these plays. Three fertility images--ships, flowers,
     and gold--show as well as the direction of the late
     plays.

284. Schotz, Myra Glazer. "The Great Unwritten Story:
      Mothers and Daughters in Shakespeare." *The Lost
      Tradition: Mothers and Daughters in Literature*.
      Edited by Cathy N. Davidson and E.M. Broner. New
      York: Frederick Ungar, 1980, pp. 44-54.

      Although uneven, poorly written, and probably a
      collaboration, *Pericles* is important as the
      transitional play between the misogynistic *King Lear*
      and the most "maternal" of Shakespeare's plays, *The
      Winter's Tale*, the play in which the mother most
      contains the daughter. In *Pericles* the sexually
      threatening female is separated into two characters,
      Thaisa and Marina, a mother and daughter. Fear of
      incest haunts Pericles, but the plot helps him avoid
      committing the sin he recognized in Antiochus and his
      daughter. He marries Thaisa, who seems to die
      delivering Marina but revives with the help of a male,
      Cerimon, and vows celibacy. The daughter's sexuality
      is later threatened by her foster mother; Marina must
      also defend her virginity in a brothel. A sexually
      purified mother and daughter rejoin the father; it is
      Pericles, the male, who finds them. At the end of the
      play Pericles contains Thaisa, and Marina is given a
      sexless marriage to her mother's deliverer, Cerimon
      [sic].

285. Silva, Naoe Takei da. "The World of Shakespeare's Last
      Plays." *Poetry and Drama in the English
      Renaissance--in Honour of Professor Jiro Ozu*. Edited
      by Koshi Nakanori and Tamaizumi Yasuo. Tokyo:
      Kinokuniya Shoten, 1980, pp. 33-59. (not seen)

286. Vaughn, Jack A. *Shakespeare's Comedies*. Literature
      and Life Series. New York: Frederick Ungar, 1980,
      pp. 174-84.

      In *Pericles*, Shakespeare experimented with the ideas
      he developed fully in *Cymbeline*, *The Winter's Tale*, and
      The Tempest. Acts 3-5 belong to Shakespeare; acts 1-2
      do not. The Gower choruses are part of the fairy-tale
      atmosphere of this childlike play with its episodic and
      improbable plot. At the center of the play is
      Pericles' marriage to Thaisa, his loss of her and
      Marina, and their reunion after fourteen years.
      Pericles is a biography of the Prince of Tyre in the
      Homeric tradition. As a passive sufferer, Pericles is
      a unique Shakespeare hero. Act 4 centers on the more

Criticism

Criticism   91

active Marina. The realistic prose and the humor of
the brothel scenes (4.2, 5-6) are in marked contrast to
the fantasy world of acts 1-3. The sea and its storms
abound in this play in which external forces dominate.
The reunion scene between Pericles and Marina (5.1)
contains the themes of the other three late romances:
restored families, recovered royalty, time as healer,
and the triumph of patience. Pericles is in fact
patience personified. The sublimity of act 5 redeems
all the play, yet the lean stage history of *Pericles*
betokens the superiority of *Cymbeline*, *The Winter's
Tale*, and *The Tempest*.

287. Waage, Frederick O. "'Be Stone No More': Italian
      Cinquecento Art and Shakespeare's Last Plays."
      Bucknell Review, 25, no. 1 (1980): 56-87.

      Shakespeare used the aesthetics of Renaissance visual
art in the four romances to show art's redeeming power.
These plays possess characteristics which many
mistakenly think awkward or medieval; instead,
"apotheoses and spatial anachronism" (p. 64) are
conventions in sixteenth-century Italian art. As a
portrait of a hero, *Pericles* does not depend on plot.
The credibility of the theophanies in *Pericles* and the
other romances rely on those in the work of Tintoretto
and Giulio Romano. The aesthetic distance maintained
by Gower intensifies emotion in the audience.
Shakespeare structured the romances according to the
Platonic scale, which represents the human ascent to
theophany and the godly descent to aid humans. Marina
is an artist whose Platonic music transforms nature.

288. Wheeler, Richard P. "'Since First We Were Dissevered':
      Trust and Autonomy in Shakespearean Tragedy and
      Romance." *Representing Shakespeare: New
      Psychoanalytic Essays*. Edited by Murray M. Schwartz
      and Coppelia Kahn. Baltimore: Johns Hopkins
      University Press, 1980, pp. 150-69.

      Shakespeare's tragedies and romances represent the
poles of self-fulfillment: the need for trust and the
need for autonomy. *Hamlet*, *Othello*, *King Lear*, and
Antony and Cleopatra concern trust and merger; *Troilus
and Cressida*, *Macbeth*, *Timon of Athens*, and *Coriolanus*
involve autonomy and isolation. In the later plays,
these patterns are balanced, even in experimental
Pericles and *Cymbeline*. Shakespeare's late romances

concern destruction survived. *Pericles* and *The Winter's Tale* belong to the plays of trust and merger. *Cymbeline* and *The Tempest* are plays of autonomy and isolation. Hermione's reappearance at the end of *The Winter's Tale* is a sacred moment, as is Diana's appearance in *Pericles*. In *Cymbeline* and *The Tempest*, restoration is qualified by loss and separation. *The Winter's Tale* and *The Tempest* culminate the series of plays that deal with Shakespeare's and his audience's divided identities. *The Winter's Tale* moves from male and female divided to the restoration of Leontes to himself and Hermoine to him. At the end of *The Tempest*, Prospero, who has willed himself autonomous, appeals for the audience's applause to "save him from isolation and despair" (p. 166). Wheeler altered this essay slightly from a chapter in his book, *Shakespeare's Development and the Problem Comedies* (1981). See item 301.

289.   Yamagishi, Masayuki. "The Road to *The Tempest*." *Essays Presented to Professors Yasuo Suga and Kazuso Ogoshi*. Kyoto: Apollon-sha, 1980, pp. 186-98. (Japanese—not seen)

290.   Barber, Vivian Ann Greene. "Medieval Drama and Romance: The Native Roots of Shakespearean Tragicomedy." Ph.D. dissertation, University of Texas, 1981. *Dissertation Abstracts International*, 42 (1981): 1156A.

       Shakespeare's tragicomedies differ from other contemporary tragicomedies because Shakespeare based his plays on medieval drama and romances, not on Italian tragicomedy. Medieval tragicomedy produced the tragicomic hero, a man who sins, repents, expiates his sin through exile or isolation, and is forgiven and reconciled. The dissertation examines tragicomedy in medieval drama and romance and in Spenser's *Faerie Queene* before turning to Shakespeare. Shakespeare changed his source in *Pericles* to achieve tragicomedy, emphasizing the hero's encounter with sin and the acts of providence over fortune.

291.   Bosworth, Denise Mary. "'Fail Not Our Feast': The Dramatic Significance of Shakespeare's Repasts." Ph.D. dissertation, University of Oregon, 1981. *Dissertation Abstracts International*, 42 (1981): 701A.

Criticism — 93

    This dissertation examines the feasts in *The Comedy of Errors*, *The Taming of the Shrew*, *Titus Andronicus*, *Macbeth*, *Antony and Cleopatra*, *Pericles*, *The Winter's Tale*, and *The Tempest*. In the romances feasting reveals the mutability of human relationships and the existence of a larger order that makes change acceptable. The food and feasts in Shakespeare's plays correspond to the themes and ideas in successive plays and demonstrate Shakespeare's belief that physical nourishment is not enough.

292. Caldwell, Ellen Marie. "Theatrical Self-Consciousness in Shakespeare's Romances." Ph.D. dissertation, University of California-Los Angeles, 1981. *Dissertation Abstracts International*, 41 (1981): 3588A.

    The dissertation studies audience response and Shakespeare's self-consciousness as a creator of themes in the romances. Shakespeare reveals an ambiguous attitude toward drama in his portraits of artists: Marina in *Pericles*, Jachimo in *Cymbeline*, Autolycus in *The Winter's Tale*, and Prospero in *The Tempest*. Audiences of the romances find that the power of art to entertain, instruct, and heal may be the delusion of a selfish artist and adjust their delight accordingly. Castiglione's *Courtier* and Montaigne's *Essays*, works with dramatic personalities, anticipate *Pericles* and *The Winter's Tale*, plays with characters and plots that make statements about the relationship between theatrical metaphor and dramatic art. In Erasmus' *Praise of Folly* and More's *Utopia*, the authors take playful attitudes toward their audiences. These works influenced Shakespeare's satire concerning the limits of fiction in *Cymbeline* and *The Tempest*. Shakespeare detached his audience critically from an art that reveals its artifice and limits, using "emblematic motifs" in *Pericles* to initiate the same critical skills in the audience that the characters have. The romances do not celebrate creative imagination; instead, Shakespeare used them to judge drama skeptically and to induce critical distance in his audience.

293. Hackett, Michael Joseph, III. "*Cymbeline* and the Late Plays: Shakespeare's Use of Dramatic Structure." Ph.D. dissertation, Stanford University, 1981.

Dissertation Abstracts International, 42 (1981):
2141A.

Cymbeline criticism tends to separate symbolic from
dramatic action. Non-verbal aspects of the romances,
such as music and dance, the masque, and the milieu of
the court of James 1 are as important as the words, as
The Winter's Tale and *The Tempest* in particular
demonstrate. Placed in their proper critical and
aesthetic context, *Pericles* and *Cymbeline*, plays that
are thought to have muddled structures, reveal clearly
formulated structures instead.

294. Kahn, Coppélia. "The Providential Tempest and the
      Shakespearean Family." *Man's Estate: Masculine
      Identity in Shakespeare*. Berkeley: University of
      California Press, 1981, pp. 193-225.

      This final chapter appeared first in *Representing
      Shakespeare: New Psychoanalytic Essays* (1980), edited
      by Murray Schwarz and Coppélia Kahn (item 280).

295. Kai, Hiromi. "J.W. Mackail's 'Note on Shakespeare's
      Romances.'" *Kiyo* (Musashino Women's College), 16
      (1981): 31-38. (Japanese--not seen)

      The essay is an introduction to and partial
      translation of Mackail's "Note."

296. Keyes, Laura Catherine. "Silence in Shakespeare."
      Ph.D. dissertation, State University of New York-
      Buffalo, 1981. *Dissertation Absracts International*,
      42 (1981): 1647A.

      Silences in Shakespeare's plays have textual and
      subtextual meanings. Dumbness may indicate
      powerlessness, passivity, threat, betrayal, refusal of
      love, or denial of humanity. Shakespeare's women are
      often the quiet ones, Shakespeare equating silence with
      chastity. In the romances silence stands for the
      healing power of mute time and answers the problems
      that are unsolved in the tragedies.

297. Maguin, Jean-Marie. "Stratégie de l'emblème et
      stratégie du théâtre: De quelques interludes de
      l'image et du langage dans la production du sens."
      Emblèmes et devises du temps de la Renaissance.

Edited by M.T. Jones-Davies. Paris: Jean Touzot,
1981, pp. 107-19.

Perhaps language became pure code when it lost its
figurative values, as represented in pictographs.
Language as it is codified in drama moves toward a
rhetoric of gesture. Phonetic language and figurative
language are the twin halves of a single entity.
Commemorative sculpture, coins, medallions, illustrated
manuscripts and books, paintings, tapestries, armor,
ensigns, emblems, etc., are sources for examining the
relationship between word and picture. The spectacle
of theatre and opera expresses the dynamic of the
configuration. Renaissance drama offers a rich area
for the study of the halves of language. In
particular, the development of the emblem book in
sixteenth-century Europe coincides with the spread of
poetic drama. In a discussion of the dumb show in
Elizabethan drama, Maguin speaks of *Pericles* briefly.
The two dumb shows at the beginning of acts 2 and 3 are
narrative recapitulations that compress the action and
place it within the discourse of the play. These
narrative dumb shows are related only distantly to the
emblem. They stand in contrast to the symbolic, or
emblematic, style of the procession of knights at
Simonides' court (2.2). Whether the procession is a
masque or a pantomime is not essential. Important is
that the appearance of the first five champions takes
meaning from the symbols on their shields. Pericles,
the sixth knight, carries no shield and wears rusty
armor. He himself is an emblem. Accordingly, the
disguised prince carries a dried branch, green only at
the top, and a motto, *"In hac spe vivo"* (1. 43). The
rusty armor, which suggests negligence, reveals itself
later as symbolic of combative ardor. This mannered
and hermetic personified emblem means that the habit
does not make the monk. Thus, the two sorts of
pantomimes in *Pericles* are narrative and symbolic.

298. Rabkin, Norman. "Both/And: Nature and Illusion in the
     Romances." *Shakespeare and the Problem of Meaning*.
     Chicago: University of Chicago Press, 1981, pp.
     118-40.

Rabkin discusses Thomas Mann's late novels, *The Holy
Sinner*, *The Confessions of Felix Krull*, *Confidence Man*,
and *The Black Swan* as analogues to Shakespeare's
romances, in particular *Cymbeline*, *The Winter's Tale*,

and *The Tempest*. These late romances by Mann and
Shakespeare accept in peace the intransigence of
reality. Rabkin revised and expanded this chapter from
a 1971 essay in *Four Essays on Romance*, edited by
Herschel Baker (see item 142).

299.   Takahashi, Yasunari. "Women in Shakespeare." *Tsurumi
       Review* (Tsurumi University), 11 (1981): 46-59.
       (Japanese--not seen)

       In Shakespeare's comedies the women, who are superior
to the men, unify polarities. In the tragedies the
women often strain their virtue. In the romances the
daughters redeem the heroes.

300.   Uphaus, Robert W. *Beyond Tragedy: Structure and
       Experience in Shakespeare's Romances*. Lexington:
       University Press of Kentucky, 1981.

       Shakespeare wrote of a world beyond tragedy in his
romances from *Pericles* through *Henry 8*. Indicative of
this transcendent world is the chronological position
of these five plays, written after *Macbeth*, *King Lear*,
and *Anthony and Cleopatra*, and their conclusions that
betoken a "second chance or fresh start" (p. 5) instead
of death. The characters of romance are collective
representatives rather than individuals; accordingly,
time loses its exactitude. In the romances, providence
replaces fate and fortune and brings an assured
benevolence that defies probability. In their
transcendence of the tragic world, Shakespeare's
romances challenge the audience's perceptions of art
and life. *Pericles* is "a magnificent outline" (p. 34)
of romance conventions. It is a "skeleton" romance, a
"first draft" (p. 34), containing the basic conventions
of romance without variations. *Pericles* is a moral
fable with types, not individuals, for characters.
Patient Pericles, like Gower and Marina, pays no
attention to time; he remains patient and rides out his
storm. The plot is that of a moral fable which tells
of a providential universe of reunion and life beyond
the storms that bring separation and stand for death.
The hieratic language and emblematic characters of
Pericles suggest an experience that transcends
humanness.

301.   Wheeler, Richard P. "'Since First We Were Dissevered':
       Trust and Autonomy in Shakespeare's Development."

Shakespeare's Development and the Problem Comedies:
Turn and Counter-Turn. Berkeley: University of
California Press, 1981, pp. 154-221.

See item 288.

302. White, R.S. *Shakespeare and the Romance Ending.*
Newcastle upon Tyne: Tyneside Free Press, 1981.

This essay on the relationship between romantic
comedy and dramatic romance concentrates on
Shakespeare's romance ending, which contains finality
within timelessness, tragedy within comedy. White
discusses *Pericles* (pp. 77-90) as Shakespeare's single
narrative romance; as such, it is romance pure and
simple, without the sophistications of wit and irony.
After taking over someone else's play at act 3,
Shakespeare heightened the poetry and pace of the story
and broadened its significance. With Gower as a
narrator both stilted in his art and familiar in his
manner toward the audience, Shakespeare succeeds in
creating specific events which the audience perceives
within the timeless flow of romance. At the end of
Pericles, individual family members are reconciled with
their past.

303. Blue, William R. "Calderón and Shakespeare: The
Romances." *Calderón de la Barca at the Tercentenary:
Comparative Views.* Edited by Wendell M. Aycock and
Sydney P. Cravens. Lubbock: Texas Tech Press, 1982,
pp. 89-102.

In proposing Calderón's *comedias novelescas* as
romances, Blue examines theme, character, and structure
in Shakespeare's four romances. *Pericles* is an example
of the episodic structure of romance. Each episode of
Pericles is an adventure, a trial of the hero, a man of
abiding love.

304. Boose, Lynda E. "The Father and the Bride in
Shakespeare." *PMLA,* 97 (1982): 325-47.

Twenty-one of Shakespeare's plays and one narrative
poem depict the relationship between father and
daughter in underlying rituals, most frequently the
marriage ceremony. As a rite of passage, the marriage
ceremony in Shakespeare's time, as in our own, involved
"separation, transition, and reincorporation" (p. 325).

The ritual preeminently concerns the bride's separation
from the father; later occurs the consummation which
results in a new family. Shakespeare's early comedies
use the Roman dramatic pattern of the father as a
blocking figure who must be outsmarted by the younger
male. The mature comedies, the tragedies, and the
romances concentrate on "the problems of bonds, filial
obedience, and parental possessiveness" (p. 326) as
reflected by the parts taken by father and daughter in
the ceremony of marriage. In *Pericles* the ritual
substructure involves a riddle and caskets. Antiochus'
story (1.1) mirrors the recognition scene between
Pericles and Marina (5.1). The events in Antioch,
involving a father, a bride, and a groom, parody the
wedding ceremony. The remainder of the play is "a
flight from incest" (p. 339). Because of what he has
seen in Antioch, Pericles resists responding sexually
to his own daughter when he discovers her in Mytilene.
Long before, Pericles had made Antiochus' choice
symbolically when he coffined and threw overboard his
seemingly dead wife. After years of wandering, the
Prince frees his daughter from the brothel, an image of
his own desires, and faces his dark secret. At last
Pericles can rightly begin his family by recovering
Thaisa, the wifely treasure he had thrown away in a
coffin.

305.   Cohen, Walter. "Shakespeare and Calderón in an Age of
        Transition." *Genre*, 15, no. 1-2 (1982): 123-37.

        During final and embattled moments of national unity,
Shakespeare and Calderón wrote plays which synthesize
popular and learned traditions. Shakespeare wrote
these plays between 1608 and 1614 and Calderón his
plays beginning in the 1630s. The amalgam plays or
romances include for Shakespeare *Pericles*, *Cymbeline*,
The Winter's Tale, and *The Tempest* and for Calderón *La
vida es sueno* (Life Is a Dream, 1635), *Hado y divisa de
Leonido y Marfisa* (Destiny and Device of Leonido and
Marfisa, 1680), and *En la vida todo es verdad y todo
mentira* (In Life Everything Is Truth and Everything
Falsehood, 1659). All seven plays are structurally
kin, each occurring in an absolutist turning point: for
England the approaching Civil War and for Spain the
serious defeats to the imperial crown following the
Thirty Years' War. Romance adds the dimension of a
utopia to tragedy by extending beyond "the contemporary
failure of the aristocracy" (p. 129). The dramatist of

romance creates plausible versions of national unity, a utopian synthesis in Shakespeare's case between the aristocracy and the rural lower classes such as Perdita in *The Winter's Tale* represents. Whereas Spanish drama, including that of Calderón, remained concerned with eastern Europe, England and Shakespeare looked westward to the New World for their imperial vision of national unity. *The Tempest*, Shakespeare's fullest utopian vision and romance, proposes for absolutism a synthesis of "feudal communism and bourgeois science" (p. 135).

306. Flenberg, Nona. "Marina in *Pericles*: Exchange Values and the Act of Moral Discourse." *Iowa State Journal of Research*, 57, no. 2 (1982): 153-61.

Francis Bacon's essay "Of Truth" (1625) differentiates between the truth of everyday business transactions and higher moral truth. Similarly, Marina, the embodiment of truth in *Pericles*, survives and triumphs by the virtue of her words over base marketplace values. In the brothel scenes, she offers moral discourse as a commodity instead of her body, and in her strength of virtue she is accepted. The greatest test of her active truth comes in the encounter between Marina and the ailing stranger in the Mytilene harbor where Marina's eloquence reveals the long-lost daughter to her father and Prince Pericles to himself. Gower's words likewise lift the audience over the course of play from the mundane world of business to a vision of charity.

307. Kaul, Mythili. "References to Food and Feeding in *Pericles*." *Notes and Queries*, 29 (1982): 124-26.

The many images of food and feeding in *Pericles* are ambivalent. Images of unnatural feeding (Antiochus and his daughter, the famine in Tharsus, the sexual appetites of the brothel customers, the fisherman's description of the big fish eating the little fish) suggest perverted social relationships. Yet nurture images in the play also suggest natural relationships.

308. Knowles, Richard Paul. "'The More Delay'd, Delighted': Theophanies in the Last Plays." *Shakespeare Studies*, 15 (1982): 269-80.

Influenced by the earlier miracle plays and dramatic
romances, the late romances are like no other of
Shakespeare's plays in their depiction of lesser heroes
and heroines dependent on powerful and providential
gods. In the four romances theophanies make known the
benevolent power of the gods in men's lives and the
artistic control of the dramatist over the play world
as well. In *Pericles*, for instance, Diana's appearance
in act 3, scene 1, ends Fortuna's seeming caprices,
encouraging the audience to expect a happy end. Diana
represents also the power of art in bringing order from
chaos. By *The Tempest*, Shakespeare had shifted his
attention from the providential gods to the artist
whose pleasures and rigors the audience shares.

309.   Meszaros, Patricia K. *"Pericles*: Shakespeare's Divine
       Musical Comedy." *Shakespeare and the Arts: A
       Collection of Essays for the Ohio Shakespeare
       Conference, 1981, Wright State University, Dayton,
       Ohio*. Edited by Cecile Williamson Cary and Henry S.
       Limouze. Washington, D.C.: University Presses of
       America, 1982, pp. 3-20.

       The pattern of harmony (of ritual, words, poetry,
       dance, and music) which counteracts at every turn the
       irrational evil and chaos in *Pericles* promise Pericles
       and audience alike a final victory. Although Pericles
       alone hears the music of the spheres, the occasion
       serves to reassure prince and audience that a greater
       miracle, Pericles' reunion with Thaisa at Ephesus, is
       yet to come. The anticlimax following that reunion
       shows the audience that Pericles' life is a continuum
       of which they have seen a portion.

310.   Musaki, Tsuneo. "On the Mode of Shakespeare's Last
       Plays: Suspension of Conflicts." *Shakespearean
       Comedy*. The Shakespeare Society of Japan. Tokyo:
       Kenkyu-sha, 1982, pp. 153-68. (Japanese--not seen)

311.   Pinciss, G.M. "The Savage Man in Spenser, Shakespeare,
       and Renaissance English Drama." *The Elizabethan
       Theatre VIII*. Papers Given at the Eighth
       International Conference on Elizabethan Theatre Held
       at the University of Waterloo, Ontario, in July 1979.
       Edited by G.R. Hibbard. Port Credit, Ontario: P.D.
       Meany, 1982, pp. 69-89.

The convention of the savage man represents at one extreme the "soft" primitivism of Hesiod, Locke, Rousseau, and Levi-Strauss and at the other that of Machiavelli, Hobbes, Vico, and Freud. In *Pericles,* the Prince in his melancholia and depression has some of characteristics of the latter sort. The descriptions of his unkempt appearance after losing his family as well as his violent behavior, including the powerful slap on Marina's face, are supplemented by those in Wilkins' *Painfull Adventures.* Because Pericles has known the evil of men, the loss of his family, and the indifference of nature, in his catatonic state he is less than human. But his destiny is a fortunate one. The sorrow that rendered him brutish is the measure of the intensity of his joy at recovering his wife and daughter. Pericles is reborn in his reunion with Marina. His desire to change his tattered and dirty garb on rediscovering his daughter and himself at Mytilene signals his exchange of wildness for rationality. As a play with a "savage man," *Pericles* is closely related to *King Lear* before it and the romances that followed.

312.   Taylor, Michael. "'Here Is a Thing too Young for Such a Place': Innocence in *Pericles.*" *Ariel: A Review of International English Literature,* 13, no. 3 (1982): 3-19.

Like other of Shakespeare's villains, including Lady Macbeth, Dionyza is naively evil in her reductive equation of innocence with stupidity. She is more than a fairy-tale monster, however. This creature of casual horror belongs to the three-act section of *Pericles* written by Shakespeare. As such, she is a creation of Shakespeare's mature artistry. Perhaps Shakespeare took his idea of simplistic evil from the dramatist who wrote the opening scene, in which Pericles encounters the melodramatic incest of Antiochus and his daughter. In contrast to Dionyza's naive evil is the morally educated Marina of militant chastity. In the first two acts, written as they were by someone other than Shakespeare, Thaisa in her spirited wooing of Pericles is a pale version of Marina. Whoever wrote acts 1-2 intended to contrast naive good and naive evil; Shakespeare in acts 3-5 reworked the theme to display the manifest integrity of innocent good and the horror of uncomprehending evil. Both Pericles' and Thaisa's innocence retreats into asceticism, but their

daughter's is forthright and evangelical in the brothel
scenes and in her recovery of Pericles. Innocence in
The Winter's Tale continues with boldness the process
of reawakening; the manner in *Cymbeline* and *The Tempest*
is more ambiguous.

313. Thorne, W.B. "The Cycle of Sin in Shakespeare's Last
      Plays." *Upstart Crow*, 4 (fall 1982): 86-93.

      Pericles, Cymbeline, The Winter's Tale, and *The
      Tempest* explore spiritual regeneration in sequence,
      from sin and guilt to penance and reconciliation.
      Having developed this pattern in the histories and
      tragedies, Shakespeare formalized it in the late plays,
      which are tragicomedies. Each play takes up one or
      more of the sequences leading to rebirth in recounting
      the protagonist's spiritual journey. The audience
      witnesses the youth and maturity of Pericles and
      Leontes. The mature Cymbeline and Prospero speak of
      their youth. The emphasis in *Cymbeline*, unlike the
      other three plays, is on the king's children. All four
      plays focus on suffering as penance and offspring as
      the chief means of spiritual rebirth. Evil exists
      outside of Shakespeare's tragicomic protagonists. As
      in the Fisher King legend, evil once created
      encompasses the kingdom, and the protagonist becomes a
      scapegoat. In Shakespeare's tragicomedies the evil is
      sexual. The incest theme in *Pericles* parallels the
      theme of adultery in *Cymbeline* and *The Winter's Tale*.
      The Tempest hints of sexual evil in Caliban's designs
      on Miranda. The children in each play help cure the
      tainted protagonist and his nation. Unlike the
      comedies, which deal with rebellious young love, the
      four tragicomedies concern mature kingship in its
      ritual significance. In these plays an isolated and
      maimed king is cured and restored to the harmony of the
      community by a daughter's fertility.

314. Tomita, Soko. "Antiochus's Evil in *Pericles*." *Senzoku
      Ronso* (Senzoku Women's College), 11 (1982): 1-17.
      (not seen)

      The essay concerns Shakespeare's unique handling of
      evil within the romance tradition.

315. Ueno, Yoshiko. "Romance Plays." *Eigo Seinen* (Tokyo),
      128, no. 1 (1982): 60-61. (Japanese—not seen)

Ueno discusses the characters in the romances.

316. Bates, Paul A. "Elements of Folk Literature and
      Humanism in *Pericles*." *Shakespeare Jahrbuch*
      (Weimar), 119 (1983): 112-14.

      Gower tells a moral folk tale and should be costumed
      as a spokesman for the art of the past. *Pericles* is,
      after all, an optimistic, humanistic drama describing
      in popular good sense the struggle between good and
      evil. Shakespeare's farfetched romance contains truths
      appropriate to today. Bates's article is the result of
      a conversation between him and director Heinz-Uwe Haus,
      preparatory to Haus's March 1978 staging of *Pericles* in
      Weimar.

317. Dunbar, Mary Judith. "'To the Judgement of Your Eye':
      Iconography and the Theatrical Art of *Pericles*."
      Shakespeare, Man of the Theatre. Proceedings of the
      Second Congress of the International Shakespeare
      Association, 1981. Edited by Kenneth Muir, Jay L.
      Halio, and D.J. Palmer. Newark: University of
      Delaware Press; London and Toronto: Associated
      University Presses, 1983, pp. 86-97.

      In *Pericles*, verbal and presentational imagery
      analogous to the visual arts depict the moral vision
      behind the play. Thus, the death's heads at Antioch
      are stage properties that display the link between lust
      and death in a deceiving court (1.1). At Pentapolis,
      Antioch's opposite, shipwrecked Pericles, emblemizes
      the sufferer as one tossed about by fortune. Soon,
      however, fortune in the shape of a simple fisherman
      clothes the naked prince. At the tournament, Pericles,
      who has no shield, presents Thaisa with a live branch
      (most likely), green at the top (2.2.42). The device
      symbolizes Pericles' rejuvenation after Antioch and
      shipwreck. In the dumbshow in the Mytilene harbor,
      Pericles personifies grief; Gower's metaphors describe
      the inner tempest (4.4.29-31). The most powerful image
      of suffering is Pericles dumb with grief (5.1). In
      this scene Helicanus' words emblemize suffering. When
      Pericles identifies Marina verbally with Patience, her
      position, apart from Pericles after he shoves her away,
      figures his words: "thou dost look / Like Patience
      gazing on kings' graves, and smiling / Extremity out of
      act" (5.1.137-39). Visual symbols in the romances

arouse wonder and suggest the form of divine providence
behind events.

318. Ewbank, Inga-Stina. "The Word in the Theatre."
      Shakespeare, Man of the Theatre. Proceedings of the
      Second Congress of the International Shakespeare
      Association, 1981. Edited by Kenneth Muir, Jay L.
      Halio, and D.J. Palmer. Newark: University of
      Delaware Press; London and Toronto: Associated
      University Presses, 1983, pp. 55-75.

      Ewbank includes in her semiotic approach to
      Shakespeare a comparison between Pericles' metaphor of
      recognition to Marina, "Thou that beget'st him that did
      thee beget" (5.1.195), and Torvald Helmer's image of
      Nora reborn in his forgiveness of her as his double
      property of wife and child (*A Doll's House*, act 3).
      Shakespeare's line produces a "theatrical moment" (p.
      63) in which the past and future of the family are met
      in the present. In Ibsen, by contrast, there is no
      mutual recovery, only self-discovery.

319. Knowles, Richard Paul. "'Wishes Fall Out as They're
      Will'd': Artist, Audience, and *Pericles's* Gower."
      English Studies in Canada, 9, no. 1 (March 1983):
      14-24.

      The Gower choruses are not distancing devices;
      rather, they link audience and stage to share moral
      instruction and the creative process. In all
      Renaissance drama, only the Gower choruses ask for
      imaginative assistance. The others, including the
      Chorus in *Henry 5*, are distancing figures who call for
      judgement. Unlike the *Henry 5* Chorus, Gower is an
      individual who speaks for the dramatist and himself,
      the narrator. The Chorus in *Henry 5* speaks for the
      acting company. The *Henry 5* Chorus solicits
      acceptance; Gower asks for belief. The narrative
      distance in *Pericles* has nothing to do with critical
      detachment. Gower's audience serves in imagination as
      gods, as Fortuna herself, and as storyteller in the
      outcome of the plot. Thus, in *Pericles* the audience's
      will is linked with narrative structure. Gower is wish
      fulfillment personified. The Epilogue, however, is
      grating in the theatre because it reduces myth to the
      level of event by explaining the miraculous and the
      magical. The technique of lifting the audience from

mere acceptance of to a level of participation in the
creative process succeeds in the later romances.

320. Pukstas, Daniel Joseph. "Camel, Weasel, Whale:
     Shakespeare's Riddles." Ph.D. dissertation, Syracuse
     University, 1982. *Dissertation Abstracts*
     International, 43 (1983): 3326A-27A.

     The dissertation points out that riddles were an
     important part of Elizabethan life, that the riddles in
     Shakespeare's plays contribute significantly to the
     dramatic technique, and that a knowledge of riddling in
     Shakespeare enhances critical awareness of the plays
     and Shakespeare. The first chapter provides background
     on the human impulse to riddle and discusses
     definitions of the riddle in terms of Shakespeare and
     his times. Chapter 2 concerns the dramatic function of
     riddling in Shakespeare. In chapter 3 Pukstas looks at
     the riddles in *The Merchant of Venice*, *Othello*, and
     Pericles; the fourth chapter examines riddles in the
     history plays.

321. Tristram, Philippa. "Strange Images of Death." *Leeds*
     Studies in English, 14 (1983): 196-211.

     The images of death in Shakespeare are medieval,
     appearing most often and explicably in *Pericles*,
     Shakespeare's most medieval play. Acts 1-2 are not
     inferior to acts 3-5; they represent an antique past
     essential to an understanding of acts 3-5. It is not
     surprising that toward the end of his life as a writer,
     Shakespeare wrote or took over from someone else a play
     about death and transcendence. The medieval images in
     Pericles are those of death, purgation, and
     resurrection. The first scene of the play, set at
     Antiochus' incestuous court, opens with images of
     death. The failed suitors' heads on poles recall
     medieval legends of the living who encounter the dead.
     Pericles' meeting with Antiochus and his daughter
     implicates him in the original sin of their incest.
     The rest of the play chronicles his journey toward
     redemption. Thus, *Pericles* forms a circle, from
     Antiochus' daughter's riddle of death (1.1.63-69) to
     Marina's life-giving riddle (5.1.199), turning on
     thesis and antithesis: riddle and counter-riddle,
     appearance and reality, the moods of Fortune and the
     sea versus providential Diana, the lost and the found.
     The Mary Magdalene legend of the barren queen made

fruitful who delivers at sea and dies, found in the
Digby MS play and in Caxton's translation of *The Golden
Legend*, may be sources for *Pericles*, especially the
latter. The jewel and alchemy images of Cerimon's
resurrection of Thaisa after her burial at sea may mean
that Shakespeare knew the medieval *Pearl*, a work that
extols the immortalizing power of art. Even though
Gower is no Prospero of magic, he rises from ashes long
enough to tell his tale, thus paralleling the scenes of
temporal resurrection in *Pericles*.

322.   Fabiny, Tibor. "'Veritas Filia Temporis': The
       Iconography of Time and Truth in Shakespeare."
       *Shakespeare and the Emblem: Studies in Renaissance
       Iconography and Icongraphy*. Edited by Tibor Fabiny.
       Acta Universitatis Szegediensis de Attila Jozsef
       Nominatae: Papers in English and American Studies,
       vol. 3. Szeged, Hungary: Department of English,
       Attila Jozsef University, 1984, pp. 215-71.

       Renaissance emblems of time and truth uphold the
       Biblical, or linear, concept of time. Emblems
       representing truth as the daughter of time, *veritas
       filia temporis*, express the Christian relationship
       between time and revealed truth. Shakespeare wrote his
       romances at a time when emblems were being revised,
       especially in the masque. Words emblemizing truth as
       the daughter of time abound in Shakespeare's poetry and
       dramas. In the romances, the emblem is a structural
       device linking the four plays. In the romances, plays
       written near the end of Shakespeare's career as
       dramatist, time is a redeemer. Likewise, the sea
       represents providence instead of chaos. The young
       females of the romances resemble daughter truth. Like
       the other three romances, *Pericles* concerns the loss
       and rebirth of truth. Marina represents truth and
       chastity. In the reunion at Mytilene, Pericles
       recognizes her as truth before he knows she is his
       daughter (5.1.23-25). Time as prophecy is represented
       in the play by Diana. Recognition of truth in the
       fullness of time comes twice in *Pericles* and is
       emblemized by music: at Cerimon's recovery of Thaisa
       from death music plays (3.2.88-92), and Pericles hears
       the music of the spheres on recognizing Marina
       (5.1.230). Shakespeare's romances are not romantic
       idylls. Rather, they demonstrate that reconciliation
       can come from tragic experience.

323.   Hoeniger, F.D.   "Musical Cures of Melancholy and Mania
       in Shakespeare." *Mirror Up to Shakespeare: Essays in
       Honour of G.R. Hibbard.* Edited by J.C. Gray.
       Toronto: University of Toronto Press, 1984, pp.
       55-67.

       The recoveries by Lear and Pericles to music in their
       respective plays indicate that Shakespeare was familiar
       with the use of music in the treatment of severe
       depression and madness. Richard's rejection of music
       as maddening, in *Richard 2* (5.5.61-65), demonstrates
       that Shakespeare also knew the counter theory as well.
       Both on-going traditions date from antiquity.

324.   Kataoka, Arika.   "*Pericles*: A Quest of Purity." *Eigo
       Eibungaku Ronschu* [Studies in English Language and
       Literature] (Seinan Gakuin University), 24, no. 3
       (1984): 19-41. (Japanese—not seen)

       This structural study of *Pericles* concerns sin.

325.   Leggatt, Alexander.   "*Macbeth* and the Last Plays."
       *Mirror Up to Shakespeare: Essays in Honour of G.R.
       Hibbard.* Edited by J.C. Gray. Toronto: University
       of Toronto Press, 1984, pp. 189-207.

       From time to time a narrative voice is heard in the
       last plays in which a narrative pattern of loss,
       wandering, and reunion dominates. For instance, Gower
       with his simple, regular rhythms is the voice of the
       story in *Pericles*. Similar are "some of Ariel's
       speeches . . . and Prospero's epilogue" (p. 192).
       Revelatory of the inner narrative of these plays are
       the ceremonies, visions, and spectacles, such as the
       banqueting in *Pericles* and Diana's appearance at
       Pericles' reunion with Marina. The guiding narrative
       presence in the last plays and the large-scale stage
       devices suggest a pervasive divine order. *Macbeth*,
       too, possesses an ideal of order, but in *Macbeth* order
       is violated by hero and dramatist alike. Visions that
       should assure the audience of an over-arching order are
       twisted and perverted instead, for at the center of the
       play is Macbeth's agony, not the salvation of Scotland.
       The audience remains close to Macbeth and removed from
       the larger story. Whereas the romances end in
       community, *Macbeth* ends with "the solitary figure who
       wins at last an integrity of his own" (p. 206). A dual
       play of a villain confounded and a community restored,

Macbeth is told by means of the masque, romance, and
folk-tale devices of Shakespeare's last plays. The
spectacles and rituals of both *Macbeth* and the last
plays are in *Macbeth* the outward trappings of the inner
play: the tale of a villain who is more than his
villainy. Even though *Macbeth* does not parody the
romances, Shakespeare broke the romance form with
Macbeth before he used it in his last plays.

326. McNeir, Waldo. "Shakespeare's Epilogues." *CEA*
     [College English Association] *Critic*, 47, no. 1-2
     (1984): 7-16.

     Thirteen of Shakespeare's plays contain formal
     epilogues; other of the plays have implied epilogues.
     Four formal epilogues occur in the plays before 1600;
     the plays after 1600 have nine. Epilogues attached to
     tragedies often look to the future; those in the
     histories are occasional. Epilogues in the comedies
     promise the restoration of order. In *Pericles*,
     medieval Gower is both the presenter and a major
     character. In the Epilogue, Gower rounds out the plot
     with didactic comments on the action of the play and
     informs the audience concerning events forgotten or
     left out in the sweep of action.

327. Ungerer, Gustav. "The Viol da Gamba as a Sexual
     Metaphor in Elizabethan Music and Literature."
     Renaissance and Reformation, 8 (1984): 79-90.

     In a discussion of the history of the Renaissance
     joke concerning amateur musicians playing the viol in a
     sexually suggestive position, Ungerer mentions a
     reference to the viol in *Pericles*. In the scene at
     Antiochus' court, Pericles tells Antiochus's daughter
     that she is a viol misplayed (1.1.82-87).

328. Dickey, Stephen John. "Character in Shakespeare's
     Romances." Ph.D. dissertation, Harvard University,
     1984. *Dissertation Abstracts International*, 45
     (1985): 2109A.

     The dissertation explores characterization in the
     four romances in terms of Shakespeare's accommodation
     of psychological motivation to the improbabilities of
     romance. Readings, mainly ironic, demonstrate that the
     self-conscious protagonists of the romances create
     overly-simplified moral and emotional roles for

themselves that cannot survive their complex dramatic
worlds.

329. Hillman, Richard. "Shakespeare's Gower and Gower's
     Shakespeare: The Larger Debt of *Pericles*."
     Shakespeare Quarterly, 36 (1985): 427-37.

     The Gower who once embarrassed *Pericles* critics with
     his seemingly distanced antiquity is now perceived as a
     stage presence warmer and more engaging than the other
     characters in the play. The unique figure of Gower in
     Pericles is both a sophisticated chorus and "the most
     sustained literary allusion . . . in Shakespeare" (p.
     428). From John Gower's *Confessio Amantis* Shakespeare
     took not only the Apollonius story but also the love
     themes in the *Confessio* at large to explore
     spirituality and self-realization. The departures in
     Pericles from the Apollonius story link the play to
     Shakespeare's other romances and align it with the
     central plot of the *Confessio*, Amans' "psychic journey
     . . . toward self-discovery" (p. 430). The motifs of
     suffering and redemption in *Pericles* also come from the
     Confessio. Gower acts in *Pericles* as the audience's
     guarantor of the suffering prince's salvation; thus
     fortune in *Pericles* is providential. The characters in
     Pericles are more engaging than those in the Apollonius
     story; they extend harmony beyond themselves in their
     reunions. Apollonius suffers pain, but Pericles
     endures a spiritual death. The Gower of *Pericles*
     stresses the moral force of unselfishness. Similarly,
     in the *Confessio* the renewed Amans-Gower emerges
     selfless. Comparison between Amans-Gower and Pericles
     makes it clear that Pericles did not bring his
     sufferings on himself. Nevertheless, the moral
     universe of *Pericles* poses a problem in that it begins
     arbitrarily hostile only to end in purposeful
     benevolence. Both Amans and Pericles wake eventually
     to accept the power of death. Pericles' journey toward
     a new selfhood and toward transcending death by
     accepting its power begins in Antiochus' court. The
     miracle of the resurrected Gower as Chorus who assures
     the audience from the first of Pericles' eventual
     triumph over death indicates Gower's own hope for
     himself as moral singer.

330. Lief, Madelon Jean. "The Evolution of Shakespeare's
     Tragicomic Vision." Ph.D. dissertation, Indiana

University, 1984. *Dissertation Abstracts
International*, 45 (1985): 2533A-34A.

Instead of treating *Pericles* as an imperfect
forerunner of *The Tempest*, Lief explains Shakespeare's
move from the simple, providential world of *Pericles* to
the complexities and turbulence of Athens in *The Two
Noble Kinsmen*. The romances show Shakespeare's growing
skeptical vision.

331. Browning, Andrew Holt. "*King Lear* and the Development
of Shakespeare's Romances." Ph.D. dissertation,
University of Virginia, 1985. *Dissertation Abstracts
International*, 46 (1986): 3038A-39A.

In combining history and tragedy with elements of
romantic comedy (Fool, disguises, double plot, exile to
the wild), *King Lear* is central to an understanding of
Shakespeare's shift from tragedy to romance. The
diction of *Lear* (nature, kind, forgiveness, blame,
monster, acknowledge, nothing, charity) involves as
well the concerns of the romances. *Lear* has its roots
in romance and morality plays. The link between human
kindness and natural order continues in *Pericles,
Cymbeline, The Winter's Tale,* and *The Tempest*. In
these four plays, Shakespeare developed the themes,
language, and structure of *King Lear* into the genre of
romance.

332. Noling, Kim Hunter. "The Self-Dramatizing Matron in
Shakespeare's Romances." Ph.D. dissertation, Cornell
University, 1985. *Dissertation Abstracts
International*, 46 (1986): 159A.

Shakespeare depicts family relations in his romances
from a male perspective. The maternal characters in
Pericles act out male desires. In *The Winter's Tale,*
Hermione initially acts out of her own will, but in the
statue scene at the end she represents a woman without
a self or will. In *Henry 8*, however, because she is
not primarily a mother, Katherine is a self-dramatizing
woman of will.

333. Nudd, Rosemary. "Coming to Life: The Four Last Plays
of Shakespeare as Beginning and End of Drama." Ph.D.
dissertation, Vanderbilt University, 1985.
Dissertation Abstracts International, 46 (1986):
2301A.

With increasing artistry in *Pericles, Cymbeline, The
Winter's Tale,* and *The Tempest,* Shakespeare used ritual
and theatrical illusion to bring his characters and
audience in a cycle that passes through death into
renewed life. As characters who return from seeming
deaths, Marina, Imogen, Hermione, and Prospero are thus
models whereby the audience perceives reality through
theatrical illusion.

334. Shaw, Gary Howard. "Gracing Monsters: A Study of
     Shakespeare's Last Plays." Ph.D. dissertation,
     University of Virginia, 1984. *Dissertation Abstracts
     International,* 46 (1986): 2702A.

The style, action, and staging of *Pericles,
Cymbeline, The Winter's Tale,* and *The Tempest* show
Shakespeare's commitment to the form of romance. Each
of the four dramatized tales focuses on psychological
monsters, parables, and landscapes, the most troubling
of which concerns human sexuality and mortality.
Chapter one of the dissertation links patterns of
dreaming and wish fulfillment with romance form. The
succeeding four chapters each focus on one of the
romances. *Pericles* concerns the Prince's ambivalence
toward the objects of his love and his attitude toward
sex and death. The play strongly affirms life at its
conclusion. *Cymbeline* is a tale of collective
psychology that entwines sex, affirmation of life,
nationalism, and community. In *The Winter's Tale,*
natural cycles are related to individual psychological
and sexual pressures. The final chapter on *The Tempest*
explores the balance and tension between the individual
and society, guilt and freedom.

See also items 340, 349, 351, 353-54, 356-57, 360, 362-64,
366-67, 369-70, 372, 377-78, 381, 383, 393, 409-10, 412, 414,
424, 426, 429, 434-35, 441, 443, 446, 449-50, 457-58, 461,
470-72, 478, 485, 487, 490-91, 493-96, 500-01, 503-04,
507-09, 513-14, 516, 518-20, 523-24, 527-28, 530, 533, 538,
542, 551, 554, 558-61, 564-67, 570-72, 575-76, 649, 660, 676,
685, 711, 713, 720, 724, 732-33, 735, 737, 758, 760, 794,
800, 804, 807, 810, 812, 815-16.

II.   SOURCES, ANALOGUES, AND BACKGROUND

335.   Mommsen, Tycho, ed. *Pericles Prince of Tyre. A Novel by George Wilkins, Printed in 1608, and Founded upon Shakespeare's Play.* Oldenburg: Gerhard Stalling, 1857.

This reprint of Wilkins' *Painfull Aduentures*, from the copy in the Zürich Stadtbibliothek, includes Mommsen's Introduction, Collier's Preface, and Wilkins' novel. Mommsen says that Wilkins' concocted *The Painfull Aduentures* from Shakespeare's play and Twine's *Patterne of Painefull Adventures*. The origin of the Pericles story is Latin, not Greek, and the Prince is not Pericles of Athens. The Preface by Collier contains a letter he sent to the *Athenaeum* in 1834 describing a fragment of *The Painfull Aduentures* in his possession (now lost). Collier, too, says Wilkins based his novel on the play and used its language, having taken notes at a performance. Lost portions of Shakespeare's *Pericles* can be recovered from *The Painfull Aduentures*. See item 353.

336.   Green, Henry. "Some Direct References in the *Pericles* to Books of Emblems, Some of Their Devices Described, and of Their Mottos Quoted." *Shakespeare and the Emblem Writers; An Exposition of Their Similarities of Thought and Expression. Preceded by a View of Emblem-Literature Down to A.D. 1616.* Research and Source Work Series 103. 1870. Reprint. New York: Burt Franklin, [n.d.], pp. 156-86.

Versions of the five knights' devices--an Ethiopian reaching for the sun, an armed knight conquered by a lady, a wreath of chivalry, an inverted torch that burns, and a hand extended from clouds to offer gold

tried on a touchstone--and their mottos (2.2) occur in
sixteenth-century French, Italian, and English emblem
books. There are no models for Pericles' device, a
withered branch green at the top and motto, *"In hac spe
vivo."* Device and motto may be compared to several
period emblems that illustrate hope and resurrection
motifs. Either the sixth emblem is original or its
source unlocated. The following chapter, on moral and
aesthetic emblems, mentions two other emblematic images
in *Pericles*: the "thread of life" (1.2.107) and "That
monster, Envy" (4ch.12).

337. Singer, Samuel. *Apollonius von Tyrus: Untersuchungen
      über das Fortleben des Antiken Romans in Spätern
      Zeiten*. Halle: Max Niemeyer, 1895.

      This book describes many versions of the Apollonius
      legend--in Danish, Anglo-Saxon, English, Latin, Dutch,
      Hungarian, Swedish, Russian, Polish, German,
      Scandanavian, neo-Latin, and Greek--including *Pericles*
      and Wilkins' *Painfull Aduentures*. Shakespeare derived
      Pericles, his name for Apollonius, from Pyrocles in
      Sidney's *Arcadia*.

338. Smyth, Albert Henry. *Shakespeare's Pericles and
      Apollonius of Tyre: A Study in Comparative
      Literature*. 1898. Reprint. New York: AMS, 1972.

      The book contains nineteen sections, the first four
      concerning the Apollonius story and its history. The
      following eleven sections offer discussions of the
      European variants, including the eight English
      versions: an Anglo-Saxon romance, an early English
      metrical translation, Gower's *Confessio Amantis* (1483),
      Copland's translation from the French (1510), Twine's
      Patterne of Painefull Adventures (1579), Shakespeare's
      Pericles (1609), Wilkins' *Painfull Aduentures* (1608),
      and Lillo's *Marina* (1738). Section sixteen concerns
      Pericles and is followed by two sections on the
      continued integrity of the story and related versions.
      The text of the Apollonius story from the *Gesta
      Romanorum* takes up the final section.

339. Klebs, Elimar. *Die Erzählung von Apollonius aus Tyrus:
      Eine Geschichtliche Untersuchung über Ihre
      Lateinische Urform und Ihre Späteren Bearbeitungen*.
      Berlin: Georg Reimer, 1899.

This history of the Apollonius legend and description
of extant versions has a chapter on the transmission of
the story in medieval manuscripts dating from the tenth
century and chapters on Spanish, French, Italian,
Greek, English, and German versions. The chapter on
the English versions includes discussions of Gower's
Confessio Amantis, Twine's *Patterne of Painefull
Adventures*, *Pericles*, Wilkins' *Painfull Aduentures*, and
Lillo's *Marina*.

340. Thorndike, Ashley H. "Appendix. *Pericles*." The
      Influence of Beaumont and Fletcher on Shakspere.
      1901. Reprint. New York: AMS, 1966, pp. 171-76.

Accepting the hypotheses that *Pericles* contains three
distinct styles of authorship, that Shakespeare had no
hand in acts 1-2, and that only the Marina story is by
Shakespeare, Thorndike argues that *Pericles* bears
little relationship to *Cymbeline*, *The Winter's Tale*,
and *The Tempest*. *Pericles* lacks the inventiveness, the
emphases on love stories, and the pastoral elements in
Shakespeare's other romances. Its undramatic plot,
consisting mainly of narrative interpolation and dumb
shows, flatly presented episodes, and a casually worked
out denouement, stands in contrast to the romances of
Shakespeare and Beaumont and Fletcher. The undramatic,
old-fashioned plot suggests that *Pericles* was written
earlier than 1608. In her purity and trials of virtue,
Marina, the only important character in *Pericles*,
resembles Isabella in *Measure for Measure* more than
Imogen, Perdita, Miranda, and Beaumont and Fletcher's
romance heroines, all of whom celebrate sentimental
love. Shakespeare's romances were influenced by the
innovative romances of Beaumont and Fletcher, such as
Philaster, staged about 1608, not by *Pericles*, which
harks back to older, more narrative dramatic romances.

341. Garrett, Robert Max. "Gower in *Pericles*." *Shakespeare
      Jahrbuch*, 48 (1912): 13-20.

This essay examines the reputation of John Gower in
Shakespeare's day, describes Gower's tomb at St.
Savior's Church, Bankside, and quotes from Elizabethan
literary critics, including Puttenham, Peacham, and
Jonson, on Gower's poetry. The deliberate antiquities
of the Gower choruses in *Pericles* are carefully planned
experiments, unique among Shakespeare's plays.

342. Singer, Samuel. "Apollonius von Tyrus." *Aufsätze und
      Vorträge*. Tübingen: J.C.B. Mohr (Paul Siebeck),
      1912, pp. 79-103.

      The essay reviews numerous errors in A.H. Smyth's
      book on versions of the Apollonius legend (see item
      338) and adds that the hero of the ancient story was
      not always called Apollonius (pp. 101-02). In the
      French version, in the Vienna Bibliothek, Apollonius
      calls himself *Perillie* at the court of King
      Archistrates (Simonides in *Pericles*).

343. Greene, Guy Shepard. *George Wilkins*. An Abstract of a
      Thesis Presented to the Graduate School of Cornell
      University for the Degree of Doctor of Philosophy.
      February 1926.

      Chapter 1 gives an account of the life of George
      Wilkins, possibly the son of the poet George Wilkins,
      who died in 1603 and lies buried in Shoreditch. Son
      Wilkins may also be the "victualler" who testified in
      the Belott-Mountjoy lawsuit (1612). Chapter 2
      summarizes evidence that this second Wilkins wrote acts
      1-2 of *Pericles* alone and collaborated with Shakespeare
      for acts 3-5. Wilkins' *Painfull Aduentures* predates
      Pericles. The remaining eight chapters concern
      Wilkins' authorship of other plays and a tract.

344. Goepp, Philip H., II. "The Narrative Material of
      Apollonius of Tyre." *ELH*, 5 (1938): 150-72.

      The story motifs show that the Latin *Apollonius of
      Tyre* is a traditional rather than an original story.

345. Dawkins, R.M. "Modern Greek Oral Versions of
      Apollonios of Tyre." *Modern Language Review*, 37
      (1942): 169-84.

      This essay traces the Westernizing of the ancient
      Greek narrative of Apollonius of Tyre before turning to
      several modern oral versions that mark the return of
      the legend to Greece. The longest and most artistic of
      the modern versions is based on a Venetian version and
      adapted to the dialect and customs of the village of
      Asphendiou in Kos.

346. Haight, Elizabeth Hazelton. "*Apollonius of Tyre* and
      Shakespeare's *Pericles, Prince of Tyre*." *More Essays*

on *Greek Romances*. New York: Longmans, Green, 1945,
pp. 142-89.

The chapter discusses the Greek background of the
Apollonius story, recounts the anonymous fifth- or
sixth-century Latin version, compares Shakespeare's
Pericles with its sources, and reviews Shakespeare's
changes in names and plot. *Pericles* remains true to
its classical origins.

347.   Elton, William. "*Pericles*: A New Source or Analogue."
       Journal of English and Germanic Philology, 48 (1949):
       138-39.

Lazarus Piot's 1596 translation of *The Orator* by
Alexander van den Busche is a possible source for
Pericles. The 95th of Busche's hundred tales may be a
source for *The Merchant of Venice*; the 53rd tale, "Of
her who having killed a man being in the stewes claimed
for her chastity and innocence to be an abbesse,"
corresponds to the brothel scenes in act 4 of *Pericles*.

348.   Muir, Kenneth. "The Problem of *Pericles*." *English
       Studies*, 30 (1949): 65-83.

This essay counters three theories concerning the
relationship between George Wilkins' novel, *The
Painfull Aduentures* (1608), and Shakespeare's *Pericles*
(1609): that the novel was based on the play; that the
play was based on the novel; that Wilkins wrote a play
based on his own novel, Shakespeare later revising the
last three acts. Instead, the essay argues that
Wilkins' novel and Shakespeare's play are based on a
lost play by Wilkins. Blank-verse fossils in the
novel, for which there are no corresponding passages in
the Quarto, show that Wilkins' novel derives from an
Ur-Pericles, a cruder version of the play than the
Quarto. Echoes of Shakespeare's play in the novel
suggest that Wilkins may have seen Shakespeare's
revisions or that Wilkins or the printer corrected the
novel after seeing Shakespeare's play performed.
Wilkins may have written the *Ur-Pericles*, as H. Dugdale
Sykes has said, but the novel did not serve as its
source (see item 395). The Quarto cannot be based on
Wilkins' *Painfull Aduentures*, but the printers may have
used the novel to correct the Quarto. Since
Shakespeare's play was based on Wilkins' *Ur-Pericles*,

Gower and Twine probably influenced Shakespeare
indirectly through the *Ur-Pericles*.

349. Pettet, E.C. "The Romances." *Shakespeare and the
      Romance Tradition*. 1949. Reprint. London: Methuen,
      1970, pp. 161-99.

      Several characteristics mark *Pericles*, *Cymbeline*, *The
      Winter's Tale*, and *The Tempest* as romances. They are
      based on romance sources; each play is characterized by
      extravagance instead of realism and by disguises,
      mistaken identity, and enchantments; each play contains
      changes of scene, one-dimensional characters, and a
      comedic spirit of providence. The wider time frame and
      looser structure distinguish the romances from
      Shakespeare's romantic comedies. Strong but theatrical
      emotions keep the audience remote. Destructive evil
      diffused by lyrical passages and the theme of
      reconciliation are also characteristic. The diminished
      and transformed emphasis on love stories, the sharply
      decreased humor, and the increased meditative and
      contemplative verse further distinguish them from the
      romantic comedies. Shakespeare returned to romantic
      drama after the tragedies because the long-standing
      popularity of romance provided him with a genre he
      preferred and which promised immediate success on the
      stage.

350. Waith, Eugene. *"Pericles* and Seneca the Elder."
      Journal of English and Germanic Philology, 50 (1951):
      180-82.

      Although William Elton mentioned that *The Orator*
      (1596) is a translation of Alexander van den Bushe's
      Epitomes de cent histoires tragicques (see item 347),
      he did not notice that the declamation in Bushe is
      itself a translation, "Sacerdos Prostituta," a version
      of the ancient Apollonius story in Seneca the Elder's
      Controversia. *The Orator* therefore probably did not
      influence *Pericles* directly.

351. Tompkins, J.M.S. "Why *Pericles*?" *Review of English
      Studies*, n.s. 3 (1952): 315-24.

      Shakespeare chose to write *Pericles* for its spectacle
      and its protagonist, the most patient of his heroes.
      Apollonius is not a patient character in Gower's
      Confessio Amantis or Twine's *Patterne of Painefull*

Adventures. Wilkins' novel, *The Painfull Aduentures,*
which gives an account of the play, emphasizes
Pericles' gentleness and courtesy, especially at the
first of the novel, before Wilkins began to plagiarize.
The novel may reflect Burbage's stage performance.
Shakespeare got Pericles' name and his patience from
reading Plutarch's parallel lives of Pericles of Athens
and Fabius Maximus. Shakespeare had already used the
two preceding lives in Renaissance editions of
Plutarch, Coriolanus and Alcibiades, to create the two
impatient characters in *Coriolanus* and *Timon of Athens,*
respectively.

352.   Kane, Robert J. "A Passage in *Pericles.*" *MLN,* 68
       (1953): 483-84.

       Although Gower and Twine give similar accounts of the
       death of Antiochus and his daughter, neither source
       refers to the noisome condition of the bodies.
       Pericles' description to Helicanus of the loathsome
       corpses (2.4.9-12) may have been suggested by the
       account of Antiochus' fate in 2 Maccabees 9.
       Apollonius is the name of more than one person in
       several passages of 1 and 2 Maccabees.

353.   Wilkins, George. *The Painfull Aduentures of Pericles
       Prince of Tyre.* Edited by Kenneth Muir. Liverpool
       Reprints no. 8. 1953. Reprint. Liverpool:
       Liverpool University Press, 1967.

       The introduction discusses Wilkins' individual and
       collaborative writings, *The Painfull Aduentures,* and
       Pericles. Wilkins based *The Painfull Aduentures* on a
       play performed by Shakespeare's company, not
       necessarily *Pericles* as it stands in the Quarto. He
       used Twine's *Patterne of Painefull Adventures* to fill
       out the deficiencies in the play. The last three acts
       were not set from Shakespeare's "foul papers"; nor do
       reportorial differences account for the two distinctive
       styles in the play. Wilkins' novel and Shakespeare's
       play share the same original, an *Ur-Pericles,* which
       Wilkins and Heywood may have written. The text of *The
       Painfull Aduentures* is based on two extant copies
       of the novel, one in the British Museum and the other
       in the Zürich Stadtbibliothek. This edition includes
       three passages from Twine's prose narrative paraphrased
       especially closely by Wilkins, a brief discussion of
       the text, textual notes, and corrections.

354. Evans, Bertrand. "The Poem of *Pericles.*" *The Image of the Work: Essays in Criticism.* Ed. Benjamin H. Lehman et al. University of California Publications English Studies, 2. Berkeley and Los Angeles: University of California Press; London: Cambridge University Press, 1955, pp. 35–56.

Wilkins' novel and the Quarto may be based on a lost narrative poem in octosyllabic couplets that appeared sometime between 1579, when Twine published *The Patterne of Painefull Adventures*, and 1608, when Wilkins published his novel and the play was entered in Stationers' Register. The first four choruses seem to be independent fragments from a lost poem. Gower dominates acts 1–2; the lifeless characters merely illustrate what Gower speaks. The last four choruses seem to be Shakespeare's revisions of a poem. At the beginning of act 4, following Gower's last tetrameter chorus, Shakespeare finally succeeded in turning *Pericles* into a work that is more play than poem.

355. Goolden, P. "Antiochus's Riddle in Gower and Shakespeare." *Review of English Studies*, n.s. 6 (1955): 245–51.

The essay compares versions of the riddle which Pericles solves at Antiochus' court (1.1) from its earliest appearance in the medieval Latin *Apollonius of Tyre* to its altered form in *Pericles*. Gower used the corrupt version in Geoffrey of Viterbo's *Pantheon* for his *Confessio Amantis*. Whoever wrote act 1, scene 1, of *Pericles* saw that the riddle in Gower made little sense and clarified it by recasting the clues and making Antiochus' daughter the speaker.

356. Simpson, Percy. *Studies in Elizabethan Drama.* 1955. Reprint. New York: Folcroft, 1971, pp. 17–21.

Acts 3–5 of *Pericles* and Plautus' *Rudens* are similar.

357. Gesner, Carol. "The Greek Romance Materials in the Plays of Shakespeare." Ph.D. dissertation, Louisiana State University, 1956. *Dissertation Abstracts*, 16 (1956): 2162.

The elements of Greek romance were a strong but minor influence on many of Shakespeare's plays before

> *Pericles* and a major influence on *Pericles* and the
> other romances. See item 370.

358. Nathan, Norman. *"Pericles* and *Jonah."* *Notes and Queries,* n.s. 3 (1956): 10–11.

The Book of Jonah influenced *Pericles,* particularly 2.1.32–47, where there are three similarities between the two stories: the occurrence of a storm, the throwing overboard of a live body, and the protagonist's flight to Tharsus.

359. Raith, Josef. *Die Alt- und Mittelenglischen Apollonius-Bruchstücke: Mit dem Text der Historia Apollonii nach der englischen Handschriftengruppe*. Munich: Max Hueber, 1956.

The book includes three versions of the Apollonius story: the eleventh-century prose fragment in Old English from Corpus Christi College, Cambridge, the oldest known vernacular version; the fifteenth-century Middle English fragment in rhyme, from the Bodleian Library, Oxford; and the Latin version, *Historia Apollonius Regis Tyri,* found in numerous medieval manuscripts in England and Europe. A chapter on the history of the Apollonius story which recounts studies of the Apollonius legend and *Pericles* precedes the texts.

360. Muir, Kenneth. "Last Plays: *Pericles." Shakespeare's Sources: Comedies and Tragedies.* London: Methuen, 1957, pp. 225–31.

George Wilkins' *Painfull Aduentures* (1608) is based on an *Ur-Pericles.* Wilkins' novel resembles acts 1–2 of *Pericles* more closely than it does acts 3–5. This indicates that the last three acts were revised more heavily than the first two. Shakespeare based his play on an earlier version (perhaps by Heywood and Wilkins, perhaps by himself), revising extensively the last three acts but not acts 1–2. *Pericles* has three sources: Twine's *Patterne of Painefull Aduentures,* Gower's *Confessio Amantis,* and the *Ur-Pericles,* written perhaps by Shakespeare himself.

361. Muir, Kenneth. "A Mexican Marina." *English Studies,* 39 (1958): 74–75.

Cortes' Indian interpreter, Marina, who was stolen
and sold into slavery before rising to high estate, may
be the source for Shakepeare's Marina. Perhaps
Shakespeare read her story in a translation of Cortes'
adventures such as T. Nicholas' translation of
Francisco López de Gomara's *Historie of the Conquest of
the Weast India, now called new Spayne*, published in
1578 and 1596.

362.   Potts, Abbie Findlay. "Tutorial Action in the Last
       Plays." *Shakespeare and "The Faerie Queene."*
       Ithaca: Cornell University Press, 1958, pp. 218-21.

The scenes before Pericles' arrival at Simonides'
court (2.2) have no ethical significance; the
Pentapolis scenes carry the plot to its conclusion.
Marina's education wins her parents' escape from
chance. Lysimachus recognizes Marina's breeding and is
instrumental in bringing her to her parents.
Shakespeare may have been influenced by Satyrane in
book 1, canto 6, of *The Faerie Queene* in creating
Lysimachus. In book 1 the Red Crosse Knight escapes
from the House of Pride as Pericles escapes from
Antiochus. Later satyrs abduct Una, who saves herself
from harm by tutoring her captors. Satyrane meets Una
as Lysimachus meets Marina. She brings Pericles to
happiness; Una accompanies the Red Crosse Knight
through the House of Holiness. The brothel scenes in
Pericles are as much Shakespeare's creation as Una's
trial among the satyrs is Spenser's.

363.   Barker, Gerard D. "Themes and Variations in
       Shakespeare's *Pericles*." *English Studies*, 44 (1963):
       401-14. Reprint. *Shakespeare's Later Comedies: An
       Anthology of Modern Criticism*. Edited by D.J.
       Palmer. Harmondsworth: Penguin, 1971, pp. 196-215.

Similarities between *Pericles* and George Wilkins'
Painfull Aduentures which are not found in other
versions of the Apollonius story offer a way to
reconstruct the lost original and learn how Shakespeare
shaped it into *Pericles*. Kingship was the dominant
theme of the source play. Wilkins concentrated on the
theme in his novel, but kingship is prominent only in
acts 1-2 of *Pericles*. Patience dominates acts 3-5.
The shift of themes in *Pericles* is the work of
different authors. As Hardin Craig has said, *Pericles*
is Shakespeare's revision of someone else's play;

Shakespeare did not begin extensive revision until act
4 (see items 407, 427). In spite of the comparatively
slight attention Shakespeare gave to the first part of
Pericles, the play is unified. Unlike Wilkins and the
author of the *Ur-Pericles*, Shakespeare made Antiochus
the indirect cause of all Pericles' troubles. The
Prince's suffering and the theme of patience begin at
the outset of the play, not with Pericles' loss of wife
and daughter in act 3. Shakespeare transformed hero
Apollonius into a Job; thus, an older play about
kingship became a play about faith.

364. Craig, Hardin. "When Shakespeare Altered His Sources."
    Centennial Review, 8 (1964): 121-28.

Departures from the sources of *King Lear, Measure for
Measure, The Winter's Tale*, and *Pericles* indicate
Shakespeare's decision to tell the truth rather than
recount established tales. In *Pericles* (4.6),
Lysimachus changes from a good to a better character,
whereas in the *Ur-Pericles*, which Shakespeare must
surely have revised (see items 407, 427), a Hellenic
Lysimachus tries to save Marina from prostitution by
making her his mistress. Shakespeare's Lysimachus
becomes a moral paragon instead and marries Marina.

365. Nowottny, Winifred. "Shakespeare and *The Orator*."
    Bulletin de la faculté des Lettres de Strasbourg, no.
    14 (1965): 813-33.

Shakespeare hints at his debt to *Epitomes de cent
histoires tragicques* by Alexandre Sylvain (Alexander
van den Busche), translated as *The Orator* by Lazarus
Piot (1596), in seven plays, including *Pericles*.
Decalamation 53, which may be an analogue to *Pericles*,
concerns a nun, stolen and sold by pirates to a
brothel, who kills an assailant, is acquitted of
murder, and later becomes an abbess.

366. Bullough, Geoffrey, ed. "*Pericles, Prince of Tyre*."
    Narrative and Dramatic Sources of Shakespeare. Vol.
    6. London: Routledge and Kegan Paul; New York:
    Columbia University Press, 1966. pp. 349-564.

The *Pericles* section contains an introduction, the
texts of the sources and analogues, an appendix chapter
comparing *Pericles* and George Wilkins' novel, and a
bibliography. Included are the texts of the two

sources of *Pericles*, book 8 of John Gower's *Confessio
Amantis* (1554 ed.) and Twine's *Patterne of Painefull
Adventures* (c. 1594), and three analogues: sections
from the first three books of *The Countesse of
Pembrokes Arcadia* (1590) by Sir Philip Sidney, George
Wilkins' *Painfull Aduentues of Pericles Prince of Tyre*
(1608), and the 53rd declamation in Lazarus Piot's 1596
translation of *The Orator* by Alexander Silvayn (A. van
den Busche). The introduction opens with a textual and
critical history of the play. Wilkins prepared his
account of the play before Shakespeare revised it.
Because the novel is such a plagiarized piece of work,
Wilkins is unlikely to have written acts 1-2 of
Pericles. F. D. Hoeniger's argument for John Day is
convincing (see items 425, 528). *Pericles* is an
experimental play, the first of other, more proficient
dramatic romances. The appended chapter, "*Pericles* and
the Verse in Wilkins' *Painfull Aduentures*," is a
shorter version of a 1965 article (see item 430).

367. Greenfield, Thelma N. "A Re-Examination of the
      'Patient' Pericles." *Shakespeare Studies*, 3 (1967):
      51-61.

      Pericles is not a pattern of patience; he is a
scholar who uses his accomplishments to solve riddles,
escape dangers, and excel in the arts. After his
griefs have mastered his learning, he submits to the
gods without believing in their beneficence. Marina
is more an ideal of Christian patience than Pericles.
Refusing to blame the gods for her misfortunes, she
continues to rely on them. In the recognition scene
(5.1) it is Marina who personifies patience. Pericles
offers her more violence than supporters of a patient
Pericles are willing to concede, but Pericles does not
strike his daughter down as Apollonius does in Twine's
Patterne of Painefull Adventures. Although Pericles is
patterned after his namesake in Plutarch, as J.M.S.
Tompkins argues, he is not modelled after the patience
of the Prince of Athens (see item 351). It is
Plutarch's portrait of Pericles as a scholar and man of
natural wit that Shakespeare followed. Pericles is
comparable to Odysseus and Oedipus, adventurers and
riddle-solvers. In repeating her father's adventures
in her own and possessing his learning in the arts and
skill in solving riddles, Marina is Pericles' heir.

368. Perry, Ben Edwin. "The Latin Romance of *Apollonius of
      Tyre*." *The Ancient Romances: A Literary-Historical
      Account of Their Origins*. Berkeley and Los Angeles:
      University of California Press, 1967, pp. 294-324.

          Elimar Klebs (see item 339) and P.H. Goepp (see item
      344) are correct; the Apollonius romance is Latin, not
      Greek, in origin.

369. Scott, William O. "Another 'Heroical Devise' in
      Pericles." *Shakespeare Quarterly*, 20 (1969): 91-95.

          The essay compares Pericles' waking to music and his
      daughter (5.1.42-220) with the harsher versions in
      Gower and Twine. The scene in *Pericles*, with its
      emphasis on Marina's virtues and musical skills,
      suggests a providential interpretation. Shakespeare
      may have been influenced in writing the scene by an
      emblem from Paradin's *Heroical Devises* of a troubled
      man being roused from a profound sleep by harp music.
      The push Pericles gives Marina before he listens to her
      is closer to the spirit of Paradin's emblem than the
      slap in Gower or the kick in Twine. Shakespeare's
      scene depends on Paradin's emblem and the waking scene
      in *King Lear* in addition to the versions in Gower and
      Twine. Because emblems from Paradin are used in the
      tournament scene (2.2), it is possible that Shakespeare
      wrote it. There are other probable connections between
      Shakespeare and Paradin in *Pericles* (2.1.127-28) and *2
      Henry 4* (4.5).

370. Gesner, Carol. "Shakespeare's Greek Romances:
      Pericles, Prince of Tyre." *Shakespeare and the Greek
      Romance: A Study of Origins*. Lexington: University
      Press of Kentucky, 1970, pp. 84-90.

          Shakespeare's change of names to Pericles, Thaisa,
      and Marina from his sources lends an air of historicity
      to the ancient Apollonius legend and indicates
      Shakespeare's wide reading for the play. The Gower
      choruses adapted from the *Confessio Amantis* condense
      the Apollonius story while preserving its antique
      flavor and narrative drift. Pericles offers Marina no
      violence in the recognition scene (5.1), whereas
      Apollonius in the *Confessio* strikes his daughter. This
      difference marks Shakespeare's departure from "the ugly
      tradition" (p. 87) in which the hero of romance strikes
      the heroine on mistaking her identity. Shakespeare

also uses three fishermen instead of one and three
bawds instead of two. The additional characters make
the comedy more flexible and realistic. Shakespeare's
achievement in *Pericles* is different from his earlier
work and his use of sources. The changes infuse
Pericles with ceremony and ritual which give a sense of
miracle and wonder to the play.

371. Ostrowski, Witold. "Władca Tyru w Polsce i w Anglii"
      [The Polish and the English Versions of the History
      of the Prince of Tyre]. *Romans i Dramat: Angielsko-
      polskie studia renesansowe*. Warsaw: PAX, 1970, pp.
      116-55. (not seen)

372. White, Howard B. "The Blind Mole." *Copp'd Hills
      Towards Heaven: Shakespeare and the Classical Polity*.
      International Archives of the History of Ideas, 32.
      The Hague: Martinus Nijhoff, 1970, pp. 93-112.

      Pericles probably takes place at the time when
      Antioch rivaled Alexandria in power, some 600 years
      after Pericles of Athens lived. Shakespeare's Prince
      is the Christian Pericles. His voyages remind us of
      St. Paul's travels. Even though he solves Antiochus'
      riddle of incest, Pericles is like a blind mole when he
      leaves Antioch; he is not yet truly wise. In the
      course of the play, Pericles comes to reality and good
      statesmanship. Although he is essentially a private
      man, Pericles moves closer to his namesake by the end
      of the play.

373. Gearin-Tosh, Michael. "*Pericles*: The Death of
      Antiochus." *Notes and Queries*, n.s. 18 (1971):
      149-50.

      When Pericles describes to Helicanus the deaths of
      Antiochus and his daughter (2.4.10-14), he says that
      they were struck by lightning, their bodies stank, and
      no one would bury them. Sources for the passage are
      Gower, Twine, and, possibly, 2 Maccabees 9, but none
      contains all three details--death by lightning,
      stinking bodies, and refused burial. Shakespeare
      probably used Plutarch's *Moralia*, which contains an
      account of deaths from lightning, as an additional
      source. Johan. Kirchmannus' *De Funeribus Romanorum*
      also contains information on the subject.

374. Gilroy-Scott, N.W. "John Gower's Reputation: Literary
     Allusions from the Early Fifteenth Century to the
     Time of *Pericles.*" *Yearbook of English Studies*
     (Birmingham), 1 (1971): 30-47.

     Chaucer and Gower are the fathers of English
     literature. Early writers spoke admiringly of Chaucer;
     Gower was spoken of respectfully as a moral authority.
     Renaissance authors took a more derisive attitude
     toward Gower's solemnities. In *Pericles*, Gower's
     costume and language underscore his antiquity before a
     sophisticated, modern audience and suggest that his
     story should be appreciated as a quaint reversion to
     the days of medieval *exempla*. In act 3, where
     Shakespeare's influence begins, Gower's verse becomes
     freer and the imagery more concrete. The poetry in
     these acts resembles Chaucer's, and a more dynamic,
     less humble figure with a sly sense of humor takes
     over. Thus, even though the chorus in act 3, scene 2,
     and the epilogue return to the medieval temper of the
     choruses in acts 1-2, the diction remains fairly
     modern. Gower's influence on *Pericles* is indirect and
     pervasive.

375. Wood, James O. "A Touch of Melanchthon in
     Shakespeare." *Notes and Queries*, n.s. 18 (1971):
     150.

     In a 1969 note William O. Scott said that Shakespeare
     was probably indebted in writing the reunion scene at
     Mytilene (5.1) to an emblem in George Paradin's
     Heroical Devices that shows the power of music in
     restoring a comatose melancholic (see item 369). The
     name of the author, Philipp Melanchthon, from whom
     Paradin took his account did not appear in the
     translation which Shakespeare used.

376. Cutts, John P. "Pericles in Rusty Armour, and the
     Matachine Dance of the Competitive Knights at the
     Court of Simonides." *Yearbook of English Studies*, 4
     (1974): 49-51.

     Phalantus' defense of Artesia's beauty in book 1 of
     Sidney's old *Arcadia* may have influenced the tournament
     scene in act 2 of *Pericles*. In both contests five
     knights are defeated by a sixth disguised and meanly
     attired knight. Each knight in disguise wears old and
     rusted armor. Sidney describes the contest between the

poorly equipped knight (Pyrocles) and the black knight
(Musidorus) as "a matachin daunce to imitate fighting"
(p. 50). The dance which the knights perform following
the tournament in *Pericles* may also have been a sword
dance in armor. In book 2 of the new *Arcadia* Pamela
describes to Philoclea a sword dance she remembers
Musidorus' having performed. Sidney's imagery of the
tilt at the ring also is sexual. In *Pericles*,
Simonides makes suggestive remarks to the knights
following their dance. The tournament in Twine's
Patterne of Painefull Adventures involves tilting at a
ring and dancing in armor. The principal characters in
each tournament feel guilty because of their various
dissemblances.

377. Knapp, Peggy Ann. "The Orphic Vision of *Pericles*."
      Texas Studies in Literature and Language, 15 (1974):
      615-26.

      The lack of causality in *Pericles* hinders critical
      appreciation. Its narrative structure parallels the
      Orpheus myth. Music and the storm are the main
      metaphors of this play, which concerns the loss and
      recovery of harmony. More specifically, *Pericles*
      parallels the plot of the medieval romance *Sir Orfeo*;
      both stories tell of a good man who loses his happiness
      and harmony but has it restored through the power of
      music.

378. Comito, Terry. "Exile and Return in the Greek
      Romances." *Arion* (Boston University), n.s. 2 (1975):
      58-80.

      Perhaps Shakespeare gained from Greek romances the
      idea of blurring the beginning, middle, and end of his
      romances and the distinction between comedy and
      tragedy. Pericles moves about in a vast and doubtful
      world which reflects the new world as the Jacobeans saw
      it. The romances of Heliodorus, Chariton, Achilles
      Tatius, and Longus help define the romance sensibility
      appreciated by Shakespeare and his contemporaries.

379. Jackson, MacD. P. "North's Plutarch and the Name
      'Escanes' in Shakespeare's *Pericles*." *Notes and
      Queries*, n.s. 22 (1975): 173-74.

The name "Escanes," "Eschines" in Wilkins' *Painfull Aduentures*, comes from "Aeschines" in Plutarch's life of Pericles.

380. Kau, Joseph. "Daniel's Influence on an Image in *Pericles* and Sonnet 73: An *Impresa* of Destruction." *Shakespeare Quarterly*, 26 (1975): 51-53.

The device which Pericles carries in the knights' procession--a down-turned torch bearing the motto *"Qui me alit me extinguit"* (2.2.32-33)--is taken from Samuel Daniel's *Worthy Tract of Paulus Jovius* (1585), a translation of Bishop Paola Giovio's work on *imprese*, not from *A Choice of Emblems* (1586) by Geoffrey Whitney as Henry Green claimed (see item 336). Daniel's *impresa* also influenced the third quatrain of Sonnet 73.

381. Pickford, T.E. *"Apollonius of Tyre* as Greek Myth and Christian Mystery." *Neophilologus*, 59 (1975): 599-609.

The Apollonius of Tyre story was popular in the middle ages because the Greek myth and its hero were suitable to Christian interpretation.

382. Dean, John. *Shakespeare's Romances and Herodotus' "Histories."* Jacobean Drama Studies, 74. Salzburg: Institut für Englische Sprache and Literatur, Universität Salzburg, 1977, pp. 95-100.

Herodotus' *Histories*, which have romance characteristics, may have influenced Shakespeare's four romances. Shakespeare could have read the 1584 English translation.

383. Muir, Kenneth. *"Pericles." The Sources of Shakespeare's Plays*. London: Methuen, 1977, pp. 252-58.

When Shakespeare revised the *Ur-Pericles*, he made three changes: he had Thaisa sin against Diana by failing to keep a vow of chastity and expiate her sin by serving the goddess in Ephesus; he gave Marina eloquent speeches in the brothel scene; and he increased the sordidness and realism of the Mytilene brothel. Shakespeare departed from his sources,

including the *Ur-Pericles*, by having Pericles merely
shove Marina in the recognition scene (5.1).

384.   Levith, Murray J.   *What's in Shakespeare's Names*.
       Hamden, Conn.: Shoe String, Archon, 1978.

       Most of the names in *Pericles* are Latin and Greek
       derivatives, and many, including Pericles, come from
       Plutarch. The name Marina may be meant to recall St.
       Margaret, pearl of the sea.

385.   Ronan, Clifford J.   "The Onomastics of Shakespeare's
       Works with Classical Settings." *Literary Onomastics
       Studies*, 8 (1981): 47-69.

       This study of names in *Titus Andronicus* and *Pericles*
       comments on the name Pericles, "widely famous," with
       its echoes of "peril," the anachronistic Latin name
       Marina, additional sources for the name Lysimachus in
       Plutarch and the Geneva Bible, and the location of
       Pentapolis. Shakespeare's Pentapolis lies in Thrace,
       some 600 miles north of Ephesus, just as Tyre lies 600
       miles to the southeast of Ephesus. Perhaps the
       Thracian Pentapolis is the "farthest Greece" spoken of
       in *The Comedy of Errors* (1.1.132) and known by Tamora,
       Queen of the Goths, in *Titus Andronicus*.

386.   Woodbridge, L.T.   "Shakespeare's Use of Two Erasmian
       Colloquies." *Notes and Queries*, 30 (1983): 122-23.

       Woodbridge proposes that two colloquies of Erasmus,
       published by Nicholas Leigh in 1568 as *A modest meane
       to Mariage*, may have influenced *1 Henry 4*, *As You Like
       It*, *Othello*, and *Pericles*. The colloquy *Adolescentis
       et scorti*, entitled by Leigh "Of the young man and the
       euill disposed woman," concerning a man who converts a
       prostitute to honesty, may have influenced indirectly
       the brothel scenes in *Pericles*.

See also items 11, 23, 25-26, 32-33, 36-37, 41-43, 48, 54,
56, 60-63, 65-66, 70, 74, 86, 93-96, 99, 101, 103, 105, 109,
111-13, 115, 119-20, 122, 130, 132, 135, 140, 143, 149, 151,
155-60, 162, 165, 167, 170, 176, 193, 196, 199, 202, 209,
214, 219-21, 228-29, 231-32, 235, 238, 245, 249, 261, 264,
267, 273, 278, 286-87, 290, 292-93, 297, 303, 305-06, 308,
311, 316-17, 319-23, 327, 329, 331, 388, 399-400, 402, 406,
408-09, 411-13, 415, 418, 426, 430-33, 435, 444, 446-49, 457,
460, 463-64, 470-72, 478, 485, 490-91, 493-96, 498-500,

507-09, 513-14, 518-20, 527-28, 533, 538, 542, 551, 554,
559-61, 564-67, 570, 576, 701, 789, 795, 804, 806-07, 812.

III. DATING

387. Graves, T.S. "On the Date and Significance of
     Pericles." *Modern Philology*, 13, no. 9 (January
     1916): 177-88.

     Pericles may have been staged as early as 1606. An
     entry in *The Calendar of State Papers* recounts that
     "Giustinian went with the French ambassador and his
     wife to a play called *Pericles*, which cost Giustinian
     more than 20 crowns. He also took the Secretary of
     Florence." The performance mentioned took place as
     early as November or December of 1606 or early in 1607.
     Shakespeare's company was acting in London at the time,
     and Giustinian, the Venetian ambassador, had a special
     reason for entertaining the French ambassador and the
     Duke of Tuscany's agent with a performance of *Pericles*,
     for by the end of 1606 Giustinian was attempting to buy
     grain from England to relieve a famine in Venice and
     Tuscany. Knowing that *Pericles* contains the episode of
     the Prince's relief of Tharsus with a shipload of grain
     (1.4), Giustinian paid for a performance of the play in
     hopes that James 1 would hear of the performance, draw
     the proper analogies between himself and Pericles as a
     relieving prince, and aid the negotiations. The
     tournament scene (2.1), which is more fully developed
     in *Pericles* than in Wilkins or Twine, was meant to
     flatter James, who had recently made a bad showing in a
     tournament he had given for his brother-in-law, the
     King of Denmark.

388. Hastings, William T. "*Exit* George Wilkins?"
     Shakespeare Association Bulletin, 11 (1936): 67-83.

The character of *The Painfull Aduentures* (1608),
essentially a reissue of Twine's *Patterne of Painefull
Adventures*, makes it impossible that its author, George
Wilkins, wrote *Pericles*. Wilkins was too unfaithful to
the play to be its author. *Pericles* is totally unlike
either Wilkins' *Miseries of Inforst Marriage*, a
domestic tragedy that ends happily, or *The Travailes of
the Three English Brothers*, a contemporary, pseudo-
realistic play. Arguments based on grammatical and
stylistic peculiarities, versification statistics, and
parallel passages prove nothing. *Pericles* as
Shakespeare revised it was produced between 1606 and
1607; because of the popularity of the play, Twine's
Patterne was reissued in 1607; in 1608 an attempt to
bring out a pirated edition was thwarted by entry of
the play in Stationers' Register, and Wilkins' novel
was published instead; in 1609 a pirated quarto was
published.

389. McManaway, James G. "Recent Studies in Shakespeare's
      Chronology." *Shakespeare Survey*, 3 (1950): 30.

      The essay includes a paragraph reviewing dating and
      authorship problems in *Pericles*.

See also items 63, 66, 74, 115, 236, 340, 366, 383, 395-97,
399-400, 405, 411-12, 415, 446, 449, 468, 471, 491, 494-96,
507-09, 513, 518, 520, 527-28, 533, 538, 542, 551, 554,
559-61, 564-67, 570, 576, 807.

IV.   AUTHORSHIP AND TEXTUAL STUDIES

390.   Malone, Edmond.   *"Pericles, Prince of Tyre."*
       Supplement to the Edition of Shakespeare's Plays
       Published in 1778 by Samuel Johnson and George
       Steevens.   Vol. 2.   London: Bathhurst, 1780, pp.
       179-86.

       Unlike Steevens, who contends that Shakespeare
       embellished someone else's inferior play (pp. 159-79),
       Malone counters that the play is indeed Shakespeare's
       and that its irregularities and crudities may indicate,
       as Dryden suggested, that Shakespeare wrote *Pericles*
       early in his career.

391.   Delius, Nicholaus.   "Über Shakespeare's *Pericles,*
       Prince of Tyre."   Shakespeare Jahrbuch, 3 (1868):
       175-204.

       Acts 1-2, the Gower choruses up to act 4, and the
       epilogue are too lame to be Shakespeare's work.   Acts
       3-5 are Shakespeare's revision of a play by George
       Wilkins.   Stylistic and metrical parallels occur
       between Wilkins' play, *The Miseries of Inforst Marriage*
       (1608), and *Pericles.*

392.   Fleay, Frederick G.   "On the Play of *Pericles."*
       Transactions of the New Shakespeare Society, 4
       (1874): 195-209.   Reprint.   *Shakespeare Manual.*
       London: Macmillan, 1876, pp. 209-23.

       Metrical comparisons involving numbers of lines,
       rhymes, and endings show that Shakespeare did not write
       acts 1-2 of *Pericles.*   Neither did he write the
       uncharacteristic and unwholesome brothel scenes in act

4 nor the Gower choruses. Shakespeare wrote Marina's
story, minus Gower and the brothel scenes. George
Wilkins wrote acts 1-2, and William Rowley wrote the
Gower choruses and the brothel scenes.

393.   Furnivall, F.J. "Discussion on *Pericles.*"
        Transactions of the New Shakespeare Society, 4
        (1874): 252-54.

        In 1874 F.G. Fleay gathered what he considered
        Shakespeare's portion of *Pericles* into a three-act
        play, "The Birth and Life of Marina." In this note
        Furnivall seconds Fleay's judgment by invoking
        Tennyson's authority. He recalls a visit he made to
        Tennyson during which the poet read the sections in
        Pericles he thought Shakespeare wrote; namely, the
        scenes dealing with Marina's birth and recovery and
        Thaisa's recovery. Although Furnivall did not record
        the scene numbers of the sections which Tennyson read,
        he says that they correspond to those in Fleay's text.
        See item 392.

394.   Pollard, Alfred W. *Shakespeare's Folios and Quartos: A
        Study in the Bibliography of Shakespeare's Plays
        1594-1685.* 1909. Reprint. New York: Cooper Square,
        1970.

        Chapter 2 includes titlepage descriptions, the 1608
        Stationers' Register entry, the collation, head-title,
        and running-title of Q1 and Q4 (1619). Blount's is a
        "blocking" entry in Stationers' Register. Gosson's
        1609 quarto (Q1) was an unauthorized edition in "a
        scandalously bad text" (p. 78). Q1 was printed from
        the shorthand report of a performance. Extant copies
        of Q4 are discussed in chapter 4, which concerns the
        1619 Pavier-Jaggard quartos. The ninth and tenth
        chapters include remarks on editions of *Pericles*
        published after 1623 and descriptive title pages.

395.   Sykes, H. Dugdale. "Wilkins and Shakespeare's
        Pericles, Prince of Tyre." *Sidelights on
        Shakespeare: Being Studies of the Two Noble Kinsmen.
        Henry VIII. Arden of Feversham. A Yorkshire
        Tragedy. The Troublesome Reign of King John. Leir.
        Pericles Prince of Tyre.* 1919. Reprint. Folcroft,
        Pa.: Folcroft, 1972, pp. 143-203.

George Wilkins was the original and principal author
of *Pericles*. Shakespeare only revised portions of acts
3-5. Four characteristics of Wilkins' writing--
frequent omission of the relative pronoun in the
nominative case, excessive use of verbal antitheses,
especially in rhymed couplets, repeated words within a
line, and repeated rhymes--occur in *Pericles*, *The
Miseries of Inforst Marriage*, *The Travailes of the
Three English Brothers*, and *A Yorkshire Tragedy*, which
Wilkins also wrote. Wilkins' fuller treatment of the
Pericles story in his novel, *The Painfull Aduentures*
(1608), repeats the language of the play. Passages
from acts 1-2 of *Pericles* are echoed in Wilkins' other
works, especially *Miseries*. The play precedes the
novel. Wilkins wrote the choruses in acts 3-5;
Shakespeare revised the last three acts, leaving traces
of Wilkins' original version.

396. Chambers, Edmund K. *"Pericles." Shakespeare: A
      Survey*. London: Sidgwick and Jackson, 1925.
      Reprint. New York: Hill and Wang, 1958, pp. 277-85.

      Shakespeare did not write all of *Pericles*: acts 1-2
      are "tedious"; acts 3-5 are "magnificent" (p. 277). It
      is Victorian sentiment which assumes that Shakespeare
      did not write the brothel scenes in act 4; he wrote all
      of acts 3-5, except for the silly Gower choruses. Acts
      1-2 are not written in Shakespeare's early style;
      others may be right to think that George Wilkins wrote
      them. Shakespeare seems to have undergone a breakdown
      between writing *Timon of Athens* and *Pericles*. Perhaps
      when he returned to the theatre he picked up the
      inconsequential play Wilkins had begun and turned it
      into an idyll centered on Cerimon, another redeeming
      physician, as son-in-law John Hall may have been to him
      in 1607.

397. Cowl, Richard P. *The Authorship of "Pericles"; The
      Date of "The Life and Death of the Lord Cromwell."*
      London: Elkin Mathews and Marrot, [1928]. 8 pp.

      Pericles was influenced by the style of Shakespeare;
      it was not written by him. *Cymbeline, The Winter's
      Tale*, and *The Tempest* predate *Pericles*.

398. Oliphant, E.H.C. "How Not to Play the Game of
      Parallels." *Journal of English and Germanic
      Philology*, 28 (1929): 1-15.

Although H. Dugdale Sykes makes a convincing prima facie case for Wilkins' authorship of parts of *Pericles*, several of Sykes's parallels--omitted relative pronouns in the nominative, verbal antitheses, and word repetitions--are characteristics that Wilkins held in common with most Elizabethan dramatists. His strongest arguments involve Wilkins' repeated rhymes and assonance rhymes. See item 395.

399. Chambers, Edmund K. *"Pericles." William Shakespeare: A Study of Facts and Problems.* Vol. 1. 1930. Reprint. Oxford: Clarendon, 1966, pp. 518-28.

The chapter includes descriptions of Stationers' Register entries and quarto title pages and a brief bibliography. The Quarto is "extremely corrupt" (p. 520), the corruptions suggesting a shorthand report. The text is of mixed authorship. George Wilkins' novel. *The Painfull Adventures* (1608), was based on the play containing Shakespeare's contributions. Perhaps there was an earlier version of the play which Shakespeare and someone else revised, Wilkins putting the novel together from his memory of both versions. H. Dugdale Sykes's claim that Shakespeare revised a play written by Wilkins is mistaken (see item 395). The chapter also mentions the early versions of the Apollonius legend and the derivation of several of the characters' names in *Pericles*.

400. Spiker, Sina. "George Wilkins and the Authorship of *Pericles*." *Studies in Philology*, 30 (1933): 551-70.

Wilkins based his novel, *The Painfull Adventures* (1608), on the play much as it is found in the Quarto (1609). The novel clarifies passages in the Quarto, echoes wording in the Quarto, and uses stage language. Such phrasing could have been learned by Wilkins at performances of *Pericles*. Wilkins wrote his novel from memory, not a manuscript. Wilkins does not have an intimate enough knowledge of the play to have been its author, for the novel fails to clear up numerous corruptions in the Quarto, and Wilkins copied more than a third of Laurence Twine's *Patterne of Painefull Adventures* into his novel. Most of the borrowings from Twine pertain to the Gower choruses and acts 3-5 in the Quarto, with stage language and details added by Wilkins. The novel and the Quarto are accounts of the stage play of *Pericles*, but Wilkins did not write it.

401. Kirschbaum, Leo. "A Census of Bad Quartos." *Review of English Studies*, 14 (1938): 25.

   The corruptions in Shakespeare's "bad" quartos parallel those in the *Pericles* Quarto.

402. Dickson, George B. "The Identity of George Wilkins." *Shakespeare Association Bulletin*, 14 (1939): 195-208.

   By the seventeenth century Wilkinses were living in every English county, and men named George Wilkins were London residents. The George Wilkins who was a victualler in St. Sepulchre's Parish and the George Wilkins who gave a deposition with Shakespeare in the Belott-Mountjoy suit cannot be proved to be the same man. The rest of the article reviews conjectures concerning the identity of George Wilkins.

403. Ness, Frederic W. *The Use of Rhyme in Shakespeare's Plays*. Yale Studies in English, vol. 95. New Haven: Yale University Press, 1941. Reprint. [Hamden, Conn.:] Archon, 1969, pp. 40-44, 49.

   The gnomic speeches in *Timon of Athens* and in acts 1-2 of *Pericles* seem interpolated, as do the many speech-pause couplets ("Enough! no more! / 'T is not so sweet now as it was before") in *Timon*, *Pericles*, and *Cymbeline*. Those in *Pericles* are gnomic and not usually in keeping with the rest of the speech. As in other of Shakespeare's plays, speech-link rhyme, in which linking rhyme between characters emphasizes the second line, also occurs in *Pericles*.

404. Lloyd, Bertram. "'Portage' in *Pericles*." *Notes and Queries*, 182 (1942): 342-43.

   "[P]ortage" (3.1.34) should read "partage," meaning share.

405. Sisson, Charles J. "Shakespeare Quartos as Prompt-Copies with Some Account of Cholmeley's Players and a New Shakespeare Allusion." *Review of English Studies*, 18 (1942): 129-43.

   Traveling companies often used printed quartos as prompt copies. One such company was Sir Richard Cholmeley's Players, a recusant Catholic troup led by members of the Simpson family, shoemakers from Egton,

who traveled extensively in Yorkshire in 1609. Their
up-to-date repertory that year included a lost play of
Saint Christopher, Day, Wilkins, and Rowley's *Travailes
of the Three English Brothers*, and Shakespeare's *King
Lear* and *Pericles*. Both Shakespeare plays were
performed on successive nights at Candlemas, 1609-1610,
at Gowthwaite Hall, the seat of Sir John York, in
Nidderdale.

406. Munro, John. "Some Matters Shakespearian--III." *Times
Literary Supplement*, 11 October 1947, p. 528.

      This essay opposes H. Dugdale Sykes's theory that
George Wilkins' *Painfull Aduentures* was the source for
Pericles (see item 395). Passages from Wilkins'
Miseries of Inforst Marriage and *Three Miseries of
Barbary* which show Wilkins' tendency to write prose
containing verse-rhythms encourage the mistaken idea
that the play was based on the novel. Statements
contained in the titlepage and dedication suggest that
Wilkins was disgruntled at the time the novel was
printed. Perhaps Wilkins wrote a play called *Pericles*
which Shakespeare revised. With no right to the play
and disliking Shakespeare's changes, Wilkins wrote his
novel as the true history of the play.

407. Craig, Hardin. "*Pericles* and *The Painfull Adventures*."
Studies in Philology, 45 (1948): 600-05.

      The Quarto (1609) and Wilkins' *Painfull Aduentures*
(1608) are based on a stage performance of *Pericles*,
Wilkins having supplemented his novel with borrowings
from Laurence Twine's prose narrative, *The Patterne of
Painefull Adventures*. The one obvious divergence
between the Quarto and the novel occurs in the handling
of the brothel scenes and the character of Lysimachus.
The differences show that someone revised the play
after Wilkins wrote his novel. In Wilkins, Lysimachus
converts from sin to virtue. His motivation is
different in the Quarto: like the Duke in *Measure for
Measure*, he observes sin; he does not participate in
it. Extensive revision began with Leonine's attempt on
Marina's life in act 4, scene 1. Act 5 shows complete
revision. *Pericles* is not a "bad quarto"; it is a
careful and successful revision. The text seems worse
than it is because much of the verse was printed as
prose. This occurred because Shakespeare wrote most of
the verse revisions in prose form. The copy for the

Quarto was probably a crowded manuscript containing
Shakespeare's handwritten revisions.

408. Craig, Hardin. "*Pericles Prince of Tyre.*" *If by Your
      Art: Testament to Percival Hunt.* Edited by Agnes
      Lynch Starrett. [Pittsburgh:] University of
      Pittsburgh Press, 1948, pp. 1-14.

Once there must have been an earlier, more correct
version of *Pericles*. The Quarto is the acting version
for a company on tour. Wilkins' novel, *The Painfull
Aduentures* (1608), contains evidence of the more
perfect original. To the two main theories of
composition (that Shakespeare finished another man's
play; that Shakespeare finished his own play begun
early in his career), is added a third: that
Shakespeare wrote the play in an archaic style which he
gave up when he reached Marina's story.

409. Craig, Hardin. "Romance or Tragi-Comedy: *Pericles.*"
      An Interpretation of Shakespeare. New York: Citadel,
      1948, pp. 302-14.

The significance of *Pericles* lies in its being the
first of a new sort of play for Shakespeare, a play
that is exclusively a romance. Gower's *Confessio
Amantis* is the original source, but the play and
Wilkins' *Painfull Aduentures* depend jointly and
independently on Twine's *Patterne of Painefull
Adventures*. Thus, the Quarto does not represent the
original play that Wilkins recorded in his novel;
rather, it is a shortened corrupt version compiled and
used by a touring company. Speculation concerning who,
other than Shakespeare, wrote acts 1-2 has proved
nothing. Shakespeare himself wrote the doubtful areas:
the brothel scenes, the dumb shows, and the Gower
choruses. The awkward verse in acts 1-2 is a
deliberate, if unsuccessful, attempt to imitate Gower's
antique style; textual corruption, too, may be
responsible for clumsy lines; therefore, Shakespeare
should not be dismissed as the author of acts 1-2. The
first two acts possess a distant, fairy-tale quality,
whereas the characters in acts 3-5 have a direct
address. Pericles, Thaisa, Cerimon, Dionyza, and
Marina are comparable to Shakespearean characters past
and to come. The formality, spectacle, and remoteness
of *Pericles* were new to the original audience of the
play.

410. Muir, Kenneth. *"Pericles*, II.v." *Notes and Queries*
      193 (1948): 362.

      Unintentional omissions in the Quarto may have
      blurred Shakespeare's intentions. For instance,
      Shakespeare perhaps intended for Thaisa's misfortunes
      to result from Diana's wrath. Simonides tells Thaisa's
      suitors that his daughter has sworn by Diana not to
      marry for a year, but in a note to her father a few
      lines later Thaisa says that she intends to marry
      Pericles, and no more mention is made of the vow.
      Nevertheless, the goddess is mentioned several times
      later in the play and appears in act 5. Perhaps lines
      in 2.5 that explain Diana's role in the play and
      prevent the fortunes of Pericles and his family from
      seeming accidental are missing.

411. Parrott, Thomas Marc. *"Pericles*: The Play and the
      Novel." *Shakespeare Association Bulletin*, 23 (1948):
      105-13.

      Pericles predates Wilkins' *Painfull Aduentures*.
      Wilkins wrote none of the play. Wilkins did not call
      his novel "the true History" as a means of protesting
      the changes that Shakespeare made in Wilkins' original
      Pericles, as John Munro argues (see item 406).
      Sometime before Blunt's 1607 entry in Stationers'
      Register a play called *Pericles* became a success on the
      London stage; Blunt's copy may have been this
      Ur-Pericles, a dramatization of Twine's *Patterne of
      Painefull Adventures* by Heywood or someone else.
      Shakespeare revised the play. In 1608 Wilkins
      published his novel to capitalize on the stage success
      of Shakespeare's *Pericles*. Gosson published a corrupt,
      reported text of *Pericles* in 1609. Perhaps the
      performances at court in 1619 and the Globe in 1631
      used a cleaner, more complete prompt-copy now lost.

412. Parrott, Thomas Marc. "The Sunset." *Shakespearean
      Comedy*. New York: Oxford University Press, 1949, pp.
      368-75.

      Pericles is Shakespeare's hasty revision of a play on
      Apollonius of Tyre written about 1607 by an unknown
      dramatist, perhaps Heywood. Shakespeare became
      interested in his task at the beginning of act 3,
      although the brothel scenes in act 4 do not seem as
      heavily revised as the rest of acts 3-5.

413.   Edwards, Philip. "An Approach to the Problem of
       Pericles." *Shakespeare Survey*, 5 (1952): 25-49.

       Bibliographic-textual analysis of the nature and
       extent of the corruptions in the Quarto establishes it
       as a "bad" quarto and the work of two reporters, one
       for acts 1-2 and another for acts 3-5. If the theory
       of two reporters is correct and if they are the sole
       cause of the literary differences between acts 1-2 and
       acts 3-5, then Shakespeare alone wrote *Pericles*.
       Excluding the Gower choruses, over a third of the
       Quarto contains verse printed as prose, incorrectly
       divided lines, and prose printed as verse. Acts 1-2,
       however, contain only about ten per cent of the
       irregularities. The sharp division in the number of
       irregularities between acts 1-2 and acts 3-5 is the
       result of three compositors. Compositor x set the type
       for sheets A and C-E; compositors y and z each set half
       of sheets B and F-I. Where verse was written as verse,
       in the copy for acts 1-2, the compositors did a fair
       job. Acts 3-5 were set from crowded, untidy copy
       containing verse written as prose. The differences in
       the copy indicate the existence of two reporters, a
       mere versifier for acts 1-2, who reconstructed the play
       from memory or from notes of a more skillful writer's
       work, and a more accurate reporter for acts 3-5, who
       recorded the original but wrote the words down helter-
       skelter, sometimes as verse, sometimes as prose. The
       Quarto and George Wilkins' account of the stage play of
       Pericles, *The Painfull Aduentures*, often diverge
       because the Quarto is corrupt and because Wilkins was
       both lazy and careless in preparing his novel.
       Wilkins' "true History" of the play is a fraud; for
       much of the novel, especially toward the end, is copied
       from Twine's *Patterne of Painefull Adventures*. Because
       The Painfull Aduentures contains heavy doses of Twine
       and additions from Wilkins' imagination, it can only be
       used subjectively to correct the Quarto. An appendix
       on the compositors containing information on shifts in
       work load and a difference in one compositor's style
       demonstrates that type for the Quarto was probably set
       in two printing houses.

414.   Maurer, Oscar. "Swinburne vs. Furnivall: A Case Study
       in 'Aesthetic' vs. 'Scientific' Criticism."
       University of Texas Studies in English, 31 (1952):
       86-96.

The essay mentions Fleay's, Furnivall's and
Tennyson's similar judgments on which parts of *Pericles*
Shakespeare wrote. See items 392, 393.

415. Seiler, Grace Elizabeth. "Shakespeare's Part in
      Pericles." Ph.D. dissertation, University of
      Missouri, 1951. *Dissertation Abstracts*, 12 (1952):
      309-10.

      Pericles is the revision of a lost play. Which parts
      are Shakespeare's can be established by comparing the
      Quarto with its sources and with Wilkins' *Painfull
      Aduentures*, by examining the Quarto, and by discovering
      in it examples of Shakespeare's mature style.
      Comparisons of the Quarto with Wilkins' novel, Gower's
      Confessio Amantis, and Twine's *Patterne of Painefull
      Adventures* reveal much of the older play and indicate
      Shakespeare's revisions. Quarto errors (prose printed
      as verse, verse printed as prose, and wrongly divided
      verse) also reveal Shakespeare's revisions. The fewer
      errors in acts 1-2 suggest that Shakespeare wrote his
      revisions for these acts in the margins of the lost
      play. The large sections of verse printed as prose in
      acts 3-5, especially in act 4, indicate that
      Shakespeare must have revised the last three acts in
      haste, placing his revisions on separate sheets in
      unlined blank verse; passages in Shakespeare's mature
      style must have been written in correctly aligned blank
      verse. In making a better play out of an older one,
      Shakespeare refined the Apollonius story and its
      characters, particularly Pericles and Lysimachus.

416. Craig, Hardin. "Review of Shakespeare Scholarship in
      1952." *Shakespeare Quarterly*, 4 (1953): 122.

      Philip Edwards' major premise in "An Approach to the
      Problem of *Pericles*" (see item 413) is incorrect. The
      Quarto is not "bad." Henry Gosson printed *Pericles*
      from foul papers, Shakespeare's revision of an older
      play now lost.

417. McManaway, James G. "Textual Studies." *Shakespeare
      Survey*, 6 (1953): 163-72.

      This survey includes a generally favorable review of
      Edwards' "Approach to the Problem of *Pericles*" (see
      item 413). However, Edwards is wrong to conclude that
      Pericles was left out of the Folio for reasons of

copyright. He is also wrong to think that the type for
the Quarto was set in two shops. Since the work was
distributed among three compositors, they must all have
worked in one shop.

418. Edwards, Philip. Review of *The Painfull Aduentures of
      Pericles Prince of Tyre by George Wilkins*, edited by
      Kenneth Muir. *Review of English Studies*, n.s. 6
      (1955): 85-86.

Muir's reprint (see item 353) is valuable because
there are only two copies of the original and because
Tycho Mommsen's 1857 reprint is scarse (see item 335).
The Painfull Aduentures is shoddy but essential to the
study of *Pericles*. The main problem of the novel is to
explain the differences between it and *Pericles* apart
from those sections that Wilkins copied from Twine.
Muir says in the reprint and in a 1949 article (see
item 348) that the discrepancies indicate that Wilkins
based his novel on an *Ur-Pericles*, arguing that the
blank verse fossils in the novel, especially in the
brothel episode, are too primitive for Shakespeare and
resemble the verse in acts 1-2. Nevertheless, the
divergences are Wilkins' inventions and the fossils are
prosaic renderings of Shakespearean verse poorly
reported in the Quarto. Wilkins and the Quarto report
the same play by different methods. Had Wilkins
written an *Ur-Pericles*, he would have known Gower's
version of the story, yet he knew Gower only through
Pericles. It is Twine's version he copied.

419. Long, John H. "Laying the Ghosts in *Pericles*."
      Shakespeare Quarterly, 7 (1956): 39-42.

No ladies take part in the two dances at Simonides'
court (2.3), yet some editors since Edmond Malone's
1780 edition (see item 390) have included a stage
direction for a dance of knights and ladies. The two
dances are an almain, or soldier's dance, and a duet by
Pericles and Thaisa, the only female in the scene.

420. Sisson, Charles J. *"Pericles." New Readings in
      Shakespeare*. Vol. 2. Cambridge: At the University
      Press, 1956, pp. 286-300.

The essay includes notes on the name "Pericles," the
Quarto, and 49 emendations.

421. Greg. W.W. *The Editorial Problem in Shakespeare: A
      Survey of the Foundations of the Text.* 3rd ed. rev.
      Oxford: Clarendon, 1959, pp. 16-17, 19-21, 74, and
      170.

      Pericles has no more claim to inclusion in the canon
      than *The Two Noble Kinsmen.* Had the publisher of F3
      (1664) not included *Pericles,* neither would modern
      editors, the evidence of Shakespeare's authorship being
      solely internal. Most likely, Heminge and Condell
      omitted *Pericles* and *The Two Noble Kinsmen* because they
      were not substantially Shakespeare's but admitted *Henry
      8* to round out the English history series. Although
      Pollard included *Pericles* in his list of "bad" quartos,
      probably because of its irregular publication (see item
      394), the Quarto is far from the worst. *Pericles* also
      appears in an "Appendix of Stage Directions" at the end
      of the book.

422. Hulme, Hilda M. "Two Notes on the Interpretation of
      Shakespeare's Text." *Notes and Queries,* n.s. 7
      (1959): 354-55.

      The notes concern *Pericles* and *Timon of Athens.* The
      word "poup'd" in *Pericles* (4.2.25) has obscene
      connotations.

423. Biggins, D. *"Pericles,* IV.ii.25 (cciv.354)." *Notes
      and Queries,* n.s. 7 (1960): 237.

      The American slang word "pooped" follows its
      seventeenth-century English meaning in *Pericles.* See
      item 422.

424. Cutts, John P. "Pericles' 'Most Heauenly Musicke.'"
      Notes and Queries, n.s. 7 (1960): 172-74.

      The dialogue at 5.1.224-37 has puzzled editors and
      critics. After recognizing Marina, Pericles hears the
      music of the spheres, but out of Pericles' hearing
      Helicanus and Lysimachus confide that they cannot hear
      the music. Lysimachus then orders a pillow be brought
      to soften Pericles' sleep and urges all to leave. It
      is irrelevant that no music is mentioned in Wilkins'
      novel, for music is indicated in the Quarto. Pericles
      and the audience hear the music, but Helicanus and
      Lysimachus do not. It does not matter whether or not
      Marina hears it. The Cambridge editors incorrectly

shorten Lysimachus' line, "Musicke my Lord?   I heare,"
to "Musicke my Lord?" which gives "I heare" to
Pericles: "I heare Most heavenly Musicke" (see items
513, 536). The line as it stands in the Quarto fits
Lysimachus' previous remark, "It is not good to crosse
him, give him his way." The real questions in the
scene are why only Pericles hears the music of the
spheres and what his hearing it means. Pericles hears
the music when the seeming discord of his world is
resolved into harmony by his recovery of Marina. The
music of the spheres is also a necessary introduction
to the vision of Diana, which only the sleeping
Pericles and the audience see.

425. Hoeniger, F.D. "How Significant Are Textual Parallels?
      A New Author for *Pericles*?" *Shakespeare Quarterly*,
      11 (1960): 27-37.

      Textual parallels between *Pericles* and John Day's
      plays, some probably of mixed authorship, show that Day
      wrote act 2, scenes 1 and 3, of *Pericles*. He was fond
      of tragicomic plots and themes involving separated
      families who are finally reunited. If Day did write
      the two scenes, probably other scenes, especially in
      acts 1-2, were not written by Shakespeare. See items
      472, 528.

426. Muir, Kenneth. *Shakespeare as Collaborator*. New York:
      Barnes and Noble, 1960.

      The book contains two chapters about *Pericles*, one on
      the authorship question (pp. 56-76) and another on
      literary interpretation (pp. 77-97). The former
      chapter is a revision of a 1949 article (see item 348).
      The differences between acts 1-2 and acts 3-5 are not
      reportorial (see item 413). They are the result of two
      levels of revision used by Shakespeare in reworking an
      older play. An unknown dramatist wrote a play based on
      the Apollonius story. About 1607 Shakespeare revised
      the play, slightly in acts 1-2, considerably in acts
      3-5, changing characters' names in the process. After
      Shakespeare's play was performed, Wilkins, who knew the
      older version, wrote his novel, taking some of his
      departures from the original of Shakespeare's play.
      Sometime later the printer Gosson acquired a reported
      text of Shakespeare's play in which pirates had used
      Wilkins' novel to construct their copy. The second
      chapter repeats several of Muir's critical theories

that have appeared elsewhere: an *Ur-Pericles*, rather
than Gower's *Confessio Amantis* or Twine's *Patterne of
Painefull Adventures* is the chief source of *Pericles*
(see items 348, 353, 360, 383); Shakespeare may have
taken the name Marina from a history of Cortes'
conquest of Mexico (see item 361); Thaisa may have
spent her years as a votaress in Ephesus to expiate a
broken vow made in her name by Simonides, although the
corrupt text blurs Shakespeare's attempt to elevate the
events in his sources beyond mere happenstance (see
item 410). The concluding analysis comes from a 1959
lecture on Shakespeare's romances given at Wayne State
University and published in *Last Periods of
Shakespeare, Racine, Ibsen* (see item 63). Characters
in *Pericles* are deliberately simplified; Shakespeare's
imagination did not seize the play until the reunion of
Pericles and Marina (5.1).

427. Craig, Hardin. "Classification and Misclassification."
      A New Look at Shakespeare's Quartos. Stanford:
      Stanford University Press, 1961, pp. 17-26.

Wilkins' *Painfull Aduentures* (1608) is an accurate
witness of the original *Pericles* before Shakespeare
revised it. Wilkins wrote his novel from memory, using
Twine to supply missing information and for
embellishment. Some time after Wilkins wrote his novel
Shakespeare revised the older play. The Quarto (1609)
was printed from the prompt copy of the old play
containing Shakespeare's revisions in the margin or on
attached sheets. Shakespeare's most extensive
revisions occur in the last two acts. The brothel
scenes in the novel and the character of Lysimachus
reflect ethics cruder and older than those of
Shakespeare, whose motive in revising the brothel
scenes was to make Lysimachus a more suitable lover for
Marina. Act 5 has been completely revised. The Quarto
is "good," "the result of successful revision" (p. 25).
Pericles was not included in the Folio because the
prompt copy was misplaced at the time the material was
being sent to the printers.

428. Cutts, John P. "*Pericles* and *The Vision of Diana*."
      American Notes and Queries, 3 (1964): 21-22.

In the 1963 Arden *Pericles* (see item 528), F.D.
Hoeniger said of 5.1.237 that Daniel's masque, *The
Vision of the Twelve Goddesses* (1604), might offer a

clue to Diana's costume in *Pericles*. In quoting
Daniel's description of Diana, however, Hoeniger
conflated parts of Daniel's descriptions of Diana and
Prosperpina. [The 1969 University Paperback edition
contains a silent emendation.]

429. Habicht, Werner. "Thaisa und der Wal: Eine Anmerkung
      zum *Pericles*." *Anglia*, 82 (1964): 76-87.

The continuation of allusions to the Jonah story that
begin in the fishermen scene (2.1) is important in
interpreting *Pericles* and in deciding the authorship
question. In the storm scene, during Pericles' lament
for his dead Thaisa (3.1.57-64), the Prince uses whale
imagery suggesting both life and death, destruction and
creation, the devil and Christ. The sea in this scene
is compared to a grave. The imagery is repeated when
Pericles exclaims to his wife, "O come, be buried / A
second time within these arms" (5.3.43-44), in the
device of the false grave prepared for Marina
(4.3.42-50), and in Pericles' words of joy at
recovering Marina (5.1.191-94). The skillful use of
the ambivalent whale image in the fishermen scene and
the storm scene deepens the irony of these later scenes
largely because of the reference to the Biblical Jonah
and indicates that one man, Shakespeare, wrote all
these scenes. Just as God punished Jonah for
disobeying, Thaisa is punished for not keeping her vow
to Diana, as Kenneth Muir correctly points out (see
item 410). Likewise, both Jonah and Thaisa are
restored.

430. Bullough, Geoffrey. "*Pericles* and the Verse in
      Wilkins's *Painfull Aduentures*." *Bulletin de la
      faculté des Lettres de Strasbourg*, no. 14 (1965):
      799-812.

The essay assumes that the Quarto is independent of
Wilkins' novel, *The Painfull Aduentures of Pericles*,
and that the novel follows in part a stage production
of *Pericles*. Verse-fossils in the novel show that
Wilkins followed an older play. Shakespeare revised
the old play into *Pericles* as we have it in the Quarto,
making numerous cuts for dramatic economy.

431. Honigmann, E.A.J. "George Wilkins and *Pericles*." *The
      Stability of Shakespeare's Text*. London: Edward

Arnold; Lincoln: University of Nebraska Press, 1965, pp. 193-99.

George Wilkins wrote *The Historie of Justine* (1606), a Latin translation. Stylistic evidence from *Justine* strengthens the case for Wilkins as the author of acts 1-2 of *Pericles*. Both *Justine* and *Pericles* contain Antiochus the Great, a medieval setting, sensational events, and some names (Pericles and Lysimachus) not found in Gower or Twine. Wilkins wrote *Pericles*; Shakespeare rewrote it. Because Wilkins translated *Justine*, there may be a lost Latin source for *Pericles*.

432.　Wood, James O. "Humming Water." *Notes and Queries*, n.s. 13 (1966): 293-94.

The word "hum" (5.1.83) is further proof that Shakespeare wrote acts 3-5 of *Pericles*. As others have shown, Shakespeare placed images of sleep, death, riches, and music in association with the word "hum." A passage in Golding's Ovid which refers to humming surges and a seeming echo of the passage in *2 Henry 6* (3.1.97) indicate that "humming" in *Pericles* (3.1.64) is correct and Shakespeare's word.

433.　Lambin, Georges. "De Longues Notes sur de brefs passages Shakespeariens." *Etudes Anglaises*, 20 (1967): 58-68.

Section 3 contains notes on the city of Pentapolis, where Pericles meets Simonides and his daughter Thaisa in act 2 (pp. 62-66). Shakespeare took Pentapolis from Gower. The close adherence to the verities of time and place in *Pericles* casts doubt on the collaboration theory. The author of the play was a sailor who knew, perhaps at first hand, the places mentioned in the play. After all, he did not confuse the two different cities of Pentapolis, one Greek and the other Libyan (Cyrène). Thaisa's coffin floats only five hours in *Pericles*, a reasonable amount of time to reach Doric Pentapolis.

434.　Schiffhorst, Gerald J. "The Imagery of *Pericles* and What It Tells Us." *Ball State University Forum*, 8, no. 3 (1967): 61-70.

The imagery in *Pericles* is characteristic of Shakespeare. The presence of numerous images in acts

1-2 which reappear later in the play and the clusters
of sin and death images argue Shakespeare's involvement
in the first two acts. *Pericles* is Shakespeare's
revision of an earlier play, the heaviest revision
occurring in acts 3-5.

435. Wasson, John. "The Itinerant Scholar." *Shakespeare
      Newsletter*, 17 (1967): 37.

      This essay is a summary of a paper read during the
      Western Shakespeare Conference at Ashland, Oregon,
      August, 1967. The double plot of father and daughter
      in *Pericles* is new, but the imagery and set speeches
      are reminiscent of Shakespeare's earliest plays.
      Pericles is probably a partial revision of an early
      play.

436. Wood, James O. "Notes on *Pericles*, Acts I and II."
      Notes and Queries, n.s. 14 (1967): 142-43.

      The note points out two unnecessary emendations and
      two words in the Quarto which antedate *OED* citations.
      The word "Copt" (1.1.101) is Shakespeare's word choice.
      Paradin's *Heroical Devices* may be a minor source for
      Pericles.

437. Wood, James O. "*Pericles*, I.ii." *Notes and Queries*,
      n.s. 14 (1967): 141-42.

      Pericles' interview with Helicanus and the lords
      following his return from Antioch makes sense in the
      Quarto.

438. Bentley, Gerald Eades. "Eleven Shakespeare Quartos."
      Princeton University Library Chronicle, 30 (1969):
      69-76.

      The essay reports the gift to the Princeton library
      of a quarto of *Sir John Oldcastle* and ten quartos of
      Shakespeare's plays, including the Crawford-Hogan copy
      of Q4 of *Pericles*, the 1619 quarto printed for Thomas
      Pavier by Isaac Jaggard.

439. Lake, D.J. "Rhymes in *Pericles*." *Notes and Queries*,
      n.s. 16 (1969): 139-43.

      The assonance instead of true rhyme (sung-come,
      run-dum, Shippe-split) in *Pericles* and in the choruses

of Day, Rowley, and Wilkins' *Travailes of the Three
English Brothers* (1607), suggest that whoever wrote the
choruses for *Travailes* also wrote parts of *Pericles*.
Assonance in Shakespeare is rare; the most assonance in
Pericles occurs in acts 1-2. Because the same type of
assonance in *The Miseries of Inforst Marriage* exists in
Pericles and *Travailes*, George Wilkins must have
written part of *Pericles*.

440. Lake, D.J. "Wilkins and 'Pericles'--Vocabulary (1)."
      Notes and Queries, n.s. 16 (1969): 288-91.

      Because the words "yon" and "sin" are used frequently
and in the same manner in acts 1-2 of *Pericles*, in
Wilkins' *Miseries of Inforst Marriage*, and in the
supposed sections by Wilkins of *The Travailes of the
Three English Brothers*, Wilkins, or someone who wrote
like him, may have written part of *Pericles*. [In a
note published the following year (see item 442), Lake
says he no longer considers his evidence involving
"yon" a serious argument for Wilkins' authorship.]

441. Wood, James O. "The Running Image in *Pericles*."
      Shakespeare Studies, 5 (1969): 240-52.

      The sustained vegetation imagery in *Pericles* is
evidence that Shakespeare wrote all of the play,
although not at one time. The vegetation, sun-king,
and jewel imagery in acts 1-2 of *Pericles* occurs in
other Shakespeare plays, particularly the early history
plays. In the Henry 6 plays and acts 1-2 of *Pericles*,
the man-as-tree metaphor appears in rudimentary form.
Thereafter it is found only occasionally until it
reappears as a theme in *Macbeth*, which was written
about the time of *Pericles*. Tree imagery in acts 3-5
does not occur in scenes written in Shakespeare's
mature style, namely, the storm scene (3.1) and the
reunion of Pericles and Marina (5.1). Tree imagery is
associated with Pericles and flower imagery with
Marina. Shakespeare wrote *Pericles* early in his
career; later he revised the last three acts partially
and the first two acts barely.

442. Lake, D.J. "The *Pericles* Candidates--Heywood, Rowley,
      Wilkins." *Notes and Queries*, n.s. 17 (1970): 135-41.

      The note discounts Heywood and Rowley as authors of
parts of *Pericles* and credits Wilkins with *The Miseries*

of Inforst Marriage, acts 4-5 of *A Woman Never Vexed*,
portions of *The Travailes of the Three English
Brothers*, and *Pericles*.

443. Kahn, Coppélia Huber. "Structure and Meaning in
      Shakespeare's *Pericles*." Ph.D. dissertation,
      University of California-Berkeley, 1970.
      Dissertation Abstracts International, 31 (1971):
      3507A.

      This dissertation establishes *Pericles* as
      Shakespeare's work by redefining the structure of the
      play. Misunderstandings of *Pericles* arise when plot is
      considered instead of total structure. In *The Idea of
      a Theatre*, Francis Fergusson interprets Aristotle's
      definition of structure as a combination of action and
      praxis, the movement of thought embodied by action.
      Pericles unites character, plot, and poetry into an
      extended metaphor of tempest, death, and rebirth.
      Resurrected Gower, who represents this action
      literally, also demonstrates it by reducing the causal
      links in events to dumb shows while emphasizing the
      recurring patterns of tempest, death, and rebirth in
      the lives of the major characters. Both the supposed
      parts of the play follow this pattern to form a
      dialectic in which the futility of the mode of the
      experiential hero, represented by Pericles, is compared
      to Marina's superior pastoral mode of "chastity,
      patience, and withholding oneself from the world."

444. Warren, Michael J. "A Note on *Pericles*, Act II, Chorus
      17-20." *Shakespeare Quarterly*, 22 (1971): 90-92.

      Editors should explicate rather than emend the phrase
      "for though he striue." Gower uses "forthe," meaning
      "therefore" or "accordingly," five times in the
      Confessio Amantis, chief source for *Pericles*. "For
      though" may represent "forthi," Shakespeare's attempt
      to imitate Gower's style. Because "forthy" appears in
      Renaissance usage, "though" may represent a baffled
      printer's expansion of "thy." The verb "striue" may be
      the author's incorrectly formed preterite.

445. Andrews, John Frank. "The Pavier Quartos of 1619--
      Evidence for Two Compositors." Ph.D. dissertation,
      Vanderbilt University, 1971. *Dissertation Abstracts
      International*, 32 (1972): 6364A.

One of the conclusions in this dissertation is that
compositor f set up *Pericles* and the other quartos.

446. Michael, Nancy Carolyn. "Shakespeare's *Pericles*: The
      Play and Its Problems." Ph.D. dissertation, Tulane
      University, 1971. *Dissertation Abstracts
      International*, 32 (1972): 3959A.

      This dissertation examines the textual and authorial
      problems of the Quarto and offers a critical analysis.
      Textual and stylistic evidence indicates that one or
      more dramatists wrote acts 1-2 and that Shakespeare
      wrote acts 3-5. The narrative sources and Gower
      choruses provide additional evidence of a divided
      authorship (see item 470). Thematic differences exist
      between acts 1-2 and acts 3-5 as well. An appended
      chapter contains a stage history of *Pericles* to 1969.

447. Prior, Roger. "The Life of George Wilkins."
      Shakespeare Survey, 25 (1972): 137-51.

      The essay reports new evidence concerning the
      identity of George Wilkins, author of acts 1-2 of
      Pericles, in the Middlesex Sessions of the Greater
      London Record Office. George Wilkins, who wrote plays,
      pamphlets, and a novel between 1606 and 1608 and George
      Wilkins, an innkeeper in Cow Cross Street, mentioned in
      18 separate actions between 1610 and 1618, are the same
      man. This man may also be the 36-year-old victualler
      of the same name who gave evidence with Shakespeare in
      the Belott-Mountjoy suit of 1612. The evidence
      suggests that Wilkins gave up an apparently
      unsuccessful writing career to turn innkeeper (and
      possibly brothel owner) in a particularly unsavory
      section of St. Sepulchre's parish. Brothel and tavern
      scenes, ruined or degenerate protagonists, whores,
      thefts, and encounters with the law in Wilkins'
      Miseries of Inforst Marriage (1607) and Day's (and
      possibly Wilkins') *Law-Trickes* (1608), Wilkins' *The
      Painfull Aduentures* (1608), and *Pericles* (1609) look to
      Wilkins' career as an innkeeper after 1609. In other
      words, Wilkins' writings foretell the future. Wilkins
      was a self-destructive melancholic particularly given
      to acts of violence against women. Two indictments of
      George Wilkins of Cow Cross for abusing women call to
      mind kicking references in *Law-Trickes* and *Miseries*,
      the slapping scene in *The Painfull Aduentures*, and the
      similar incident in *Pericles* (5.1). This evidence

supports the theory that George Wilkins wrote the
original, complete version of *Pericles*. Perhaps
Wilkins helped prepare a surreptitious copy which he
turned over to Henry Gosson, printer of the Quarto
(1609). Gosson is mentioned in the records as having
stood bail for innkeeper George Wilkins in 1611.

448.   Easson, Angus. "Marina's Maidenhead." *Shakespeare
        Quarterly*, 24 (1973): 328-29.

        Boult's remark to Marina, "I must have your
        maidenhead taken off, or the common hangman shall
        execute it" (4.6.127-28), contains a far more sinister
        threat than J.C. Maxwell, editor of the New Cambridge
        Pericles, accounts for in his explanation of Boult's
        play on the word "head" (see item 513). F.D. Hoeniger,
        the Arden editor (see item 528), follows Maxwell.
        Boult's remark is an allusion to Tacitus' account of
        the death of Sejanus' children, particularly the girl,
        who was raped by the executioner before being hanged,
        there being no precedent in Roman law for executing
        virgins. Shakespeare acted in Jonson's *Sejanus*, which
        contains the episode. Boult's comment is not
        word-play; it is a real threat to Marina from the
        sordid world in which she finds herself.

449.   Pease, Ralph William, III. "The Genesis and Authorship
        of *Pericles*." Ph.D. dissertation, Texas A&M
        University, 1972. *Dissertation Abstracts
        International*, 33 (1973): 4358A.

        Shakespeare alone wrote *Pericles*. He wrote acts 1-2
        early in his career and completed acts 3-5 between 1605
        and 1608. The dissertation includes chapters on the
        history of the play, sources, Quarto corruptions,
        authorship, diction, style, and theme.

450.   Wood, James O. "Shakespeare and the Belching Whale."
        English Language Notes, 11 (1973): 40-44.

        Because the metaphor in *Pericles* of the whale that
        swallows and belches (2.1.29-48) belongs to patterns of
        words and images commonly found in Shakespeare's plays,
        the scene incorporating the metaphor is more likely
        Shakespeare's than Day's, as F.D. Hoeniger has argued
        (see item 425, 528). *Pericles* may also be among
        Shakespeare's earliest plays; if so, the whale metaphor

in *Pericles* may underlie the image in other Shakespeare plays.

451.   Wood, James O. "Shakespeare's Hand in *Pericles*."
       Notes and Queries, n.s. 21 (1974): 132-33.

       Editors are wrong to think that 1.1.30-33 in the
       Quarto is incorrect.

452.   Eccles, Mark. "George Wilkins." *Notes and Queries*,
       n.s. 22 (1975): 250-52.

       Roger Prior has established conclusively that the
       innkeeper George Wilkins of St. Sepulchre's Parish who
       testified with Shakespeare in the Belott-Mountjoy suit
       of 1612 was the minor dramatist and author of *The
       Painfull Adventures* (see item 447). Further evidence
       from the Middlesex Sessions shows that George Wilkins
       knew many actors and Henry Gosson, the man who printed
       Pericles. But Prior's portrait of Wilkins as a
       melancholic and violent man is overdrawn and without
       support.

453.   Parks, Stephen. "Shakespeare and His Editors,
       1594-1790: The Catalogue of an Exhibition in the
       Beinecke Library, March-May 1975," *Yale University
       Library Gazette*, 50 (1975): 98-111.

       In the spring of 1975 the Beinecke Library exhibited
       the Daniel-Huth-Cochran copy of Q1 (1609) from the
       Elizabethan Club collection, one of nine known copies,
       in their display of quartos. The three emendations to
       the Quarto are probably those of Scipio Squyer, who
       signed the title page.

454.   Prior, Roger. "Replies," *Notes and Queries*, n.s. 22
       (1975): 561-62.

       The note thanks Mark Eccles (see item 452) for
       corrections to his 1972 article, "The Life of George
       Wilkins" (see item 447), but disagrees that Wilkins was
       often proved innocent of charges brought against him.
       The verdict cannot always be determined. Charges
       without a verdict may be evidence of guilt, but not of
       conclusive guilt.

455. Wood, James O. "The Shakespearean Language of
     Pericles." *English Language Notes*, 13 (1975):
     98-103.

     The word "ayre" in the Shakespearean portion of
     Pericles (3.1.63) is correct, and a passage from the
     so-called non-Shakespearean part (1.4.11-20) is good
     enough for early Shakespeare.

456. Hawkes, Nigel. "Word Detective Proves the Bard Wasn't
     Bacon." *Observer* (London), 14 March 1976, p. 4.

     The new stylometric technique of literary detection
     devised by Andrew Q. Morton (item 466) makes it
     possible to distinguish between authorial styles.
     Morton's system uses a computer to examine the
     frequency of simple word pairs (and the, as if, of
     course, etc.) and to distinguish individual patterns of
     use. A text is typed into the computer, which then
     compiles an alphabetical list of all words, complete
     with preceding and succeeding words. Examination of
     Pericles shows the authorial style consistent
     throughout the play.

457. Hoeniger, F. David. "*Pericles*: Gower's Dramaturgy
     Fitfully Improved by Shakespeare." *Research
     Opportunities in Renaissance Drama*, 19 (1976): 1-2.

     David Bevington reports on a paper that Hoeniger gave
     at the 1975 MLA Seminar, "Critical and Aesthetic
     Problems of Collaboration," which questions whether
     Pericles is either a collaboration or the product of
     reporters. Perhaps the stylistic and dramatic
     differences between acts 1-2 and acts 3-5 are
     intentional. Gower dominates the play in a voice that
     fits his moralizing narrative; only in acts 3-5 does
     Shakespeare allow his own style to emerge. The play is
     "an experimental jeu d'esprit" (p. 2) which acts better
     than it reads. Perhaps the Quarto is "good" instead of
     "bad." See item 472.

458. Hoge, James O., Jr. "Tennyson on Shakespeare: His Talk
     about the Plays." *Texas Studies in Literature and
     Language*, 18 (1976): 147-70.

     The essay reprints Hallam Tennyson's typescript notes
     of his father's remarks on several of Shakespeare's
     plays, including *Pericles*. Tennyson thought that most

of the play, with the exception of Shakespeare's act 5
characterization of Marina, was not Shakespeare's work.
Tennyson agreed that F.G. Fleay's three-act version
retrieves Shakespeare's part but added Shakespearean
passages that Fleay overlooked. See items 392, 393.

459. Marder, Louis. "Stylometric Analysis of the *Pericles*
      Problem." *Shakespeare Newsletter*, 26 (1976): 46.

      A comparison of commonly used word pairs (such as
      "and all," "to be," and "very much") by A.Q. Morton in
      an authenticated Shakespeare text and *Pericles* show
      that only Shakespeare wrote *Pericles*. See items 465,
      466.

460. Prior, Roger. "George Wilkins and the Young Heir."
      Shakespeare Survey, 29 (1976): 33-39.

      In a 1972 article Prior argued from evidence in the
      Greater London Record Office that the innkeeper George
      Wilkins who lived in Cow Cross between 1610 and 1618
      was the minor dramatist and author of *The Painfull
      Adventures* (see item 447). He had also said it likely
      that the writer-innkeeper was the George Wilkins who
      gave evidence with Shakespeare in the Belott-Mountjoy
      suit (1612). This essay presents new evidence to
      confirm the latter hypothesis. In 1614 George Wilkins,
      undoubtedly the innkeeper, gave a signed deposition in
      a Chancery suit. Wilkins' two signatures on the
      deposition match the signature contained in the records
      of the Belott-Mountjoy suit. The essay also includes
      Wilkins' testimony in the 1614 suit involving a ruined
      young heir and his despoiler. A similar situation
      occurs in Wilkins' play, *The Miseries of Inforst
      Marriage* (1607), in which the protagonist, a young heir
      named William Scarborrow, is ruined by low company and
      riotous tavern life. Even though the play predates the
      suit, tavernkeeper Wilkins must have known other
      profligate young heirs.

461. Schrickx, Willem. "*Pericles* in a Book-List of 1619
      from the English Jesuit Mission and Some of the
      Play's Special Problems." *Shakespeare Survey*, 29
      (1976): 21-32.

      George Wilkins wrote acts 1-2 of *Pericles*. At the
      Ghent Rijksarchief, in a 1619 catalogue of books
      belonging to the English Jesuit mission at St. Omer,

the hundredth listing is a quarto of *Pericles*,
presumably a copy of one of the two 1609 quartos or the
1611 quarto. The other listings are works of devotion
and religious polemics; *Pericles* is the only purely
literary work listed. The play may have been included
because it contains religious sentiments likely to
promote Catholic instruction at the seminary. Wilkins
was attracted to the Antiochus theme. Certain speeches
in act 1 and in Wilkins' *Miseries of Inforst Marriage*
are autobiographical; and, too, the story of the
struggle between the tyrant Antiochus and Judas
Maccabeus was in vogue at the time among Catholic and
Protestant apologists alike. Whether acts 1-2
represent a collaborated effort or indicate the
existence of an *Ur-Pericles*, Wilkins is the likeliest
authorial candidate. Perhaps Wilkins was a Catholic
recusant with close ties through marriage to important
Catholics on the continent.

462. Boni, John. "Gower's 'Custom' in *Pericles*:
      Shakespeare's Hand?" *American Notes and Queries*, 16
      (1977): 35-36.

      When Gower uses the noun "custom" to describe the sin
of Antiochus and his daughter, he speaks proverbially,
using "custom" to mean "inurement": "But custom what
they did begin / Was with long use accounted no
sin. . ." (1ch.29-30). Shakespeare probably wrote
these lines; after all, he had used "custom" in its
proverbial sense in *Hamlet*.

463. Michael, Nancy C. "The Relationship Between the 1609
      Quarto of *Pericles* and Wilkins' *Painfull Aduentures*."
      Tulane Studies in English, 22 (1977): 51-68.

      Because the Quarto and Wilkins' *Painfull Aduentures*
are independent reports of the same play, Wilkins'
novel offers a sound means of emending the Quarto.
Wilkins took his novel from Laurence Twine's *Patterne
of Painefull Adventures* and the stage play represented
in the Quarto, not an *Ur-Pericles* later revised by
Shakespeare, as Craig (see items 407, 427) and Muir
(see items 348, 353, 360, 383, 426) separately contend.
The borrowings from Twine, most of which occur in the
chapters corresponding to acts 3-5 in the Quarto,
indicate Wilkins' inability to recall the complex
sequence of events he had seen on stage, not
carelessness, as Edwards argues (see item 413). In the

chapters corresponding to acts 1-2, where the plot is
linear, Wilkins remembered the play easily enough,
using Twine only for embellishment; but in the chapters
covering acts 3-5, which contain the overlapping plots
of Pericles, Thaisa, and Marina, Wilkins was forced to
turn to Twine for direction. While Edwards is correct
to say that emendations of the Quarto based on the work
of a dishonest hack would convey only subjective
opinion, Wilkins' imperfect but guilelessly composed
"History of the Play of Pericles" can be used more
definitively.

464. Wood, James O. "Shakespeare, *Pericles*, and the Genevan
      Bible." *Pacific Coast Philology*, 12 (1977): 82-89.

      The essay reviews the case for Shakespeare's
      authorship of *Pericles* and argues that the scene of
      Pericles' return to Tyre in the Quarto (1.2) is
      correct. The *OED* and the sixth book of Jeremiah (1560
      Geneva) help make sense of Helicanus' speech on
      flatterers. Echoes of the Geneva Bible occur elsewhere
      in *Pericles* and other of Shakespeare's plays. Editors
      should recognize and respect the integrity of the
      Quarto by considering the accruing evidence that
      Pericles is entirely Shakespeare's play.

465. Michaelson, Sidney, Andrew Q. Morton, and Neil
      Hamilton-Smith. *To Couple Is the Custom: A General
      Stylometric Theory of Writers in English*. Edinburgh:
      Edinburgh [University] Department of Computer
      Science, 1978.

      The pamphlet contains an explanation of stylometrics
      and several statistical tables for literary works,
      including *Pericles* (pp. 62-65), similar to those found
      in Morton's lengthier *Literary Detection* (see item
      466). A frequency analysis of commonly used words
      shows that *Pericles* is the work of one author, probably
      Shakespeare.

466. Morton, Andrew Q. "*Pericles*." *Literary Detection: How
      to Prove Authorship and Fraud in Literature and
      Documents*. London: Bowker; New York: Scribner's,
      1978, pp. 184-88.

      A comparison of the frequency and position of often
      used words (e.g., a, and, in, that, the) and word pairs

(e.g., all + any) in acts 1-2 and acts 3-5 of *Pericles* shows no evidence of a mixed authorship.

467. Musgrove, S. "The First Quarto of *Pericles* Reconsidered." *Shakespeare Quarterly*, 29 (1978): 389-406.

In 1952 Philip Edwards argued that the copy for the Quarto was the work of reporters, one for acts 1-2 and another for acts 3-5 (see item 413). F.D. Hoeniger (see item 528) and J.C. Maxwell (see item 513) upheld Edwards' theory. This essay argues that the text to sig. E3r (3.2) is taken from foul papers and that the rest of the text is reported. The spellings "Thaliart" and "Tharsis" in chorus 2 are unique in the play. Because these spellings occur in Gower's *Confessio Amantis*, it may be that a careless compositor was following foul papers. Chorus 1, which contains no evidence of memorial reconstruction, may also derive from a draft. The corrupt scenes involving Thaliard are reported. An examination of sheet B shows that it was printed last. Evidence from the running titles indicates that there was a break in printing. The work of setting the copy for the Quarto was divided between two shops, compositors y and z finishing sheets F-I as planned; meanwhile, compositor x could not finish sheet A until copy for the Thaliard scenes was secured. The sheets may be reassigned as follows: compositor x set sheets A and C-E; compositors y and z set sheets B and F-I. The essay moves next to the eleven different spellings of "Helicanus." In the Shakespearean section, from chorus 3 to the end, four-syllable forms are used exclusively. In acts 1-2 spellings with one, two, and three syllables appear, except for the spelling "Hellicanus" in two stage directions. (These may be printer's corrections.) The spelling differences are authorial. Act 2, scene 4, contains two parts. The second part, the encounter between Helicanus and the lords, is authorial; this would make the first part, 16 lines of dialogue between Helicanus and Escanes, reported matter inserted to fill a gap in the copy. Moving some of the lords' speeches makes sense of another gap in the Quarto (1.2.35). The fullness of the stage directions and the cleanness of the text in the Simonides scenes (2.2-3,5) indicate that they may have been written by someone other than the author of most of acts 1-2; a reporter may also have been involved. The scenes, which seem jumbled,

may have been presented on stage in a different order.
Thus, much of acts 1-2 derive from foul papers. As for
acts 3-5, Edwards is correct: the text from E3r to the
end is reported, and the copy-text must have been
written in prose. The essay reconstructs the encounter
in the brothel between Marina and Lysimachus. The
ambiguous character of Lysimachus may be the result of
textual corruption. Marina's strong speeches to Boult
on the loathsomeness of his profession (4.6.184-96) may
actually belong to Lysimachus. For aesthetic reasons,
the authenticity of lines 19-42, the only passage in
which Lysimachus "talks dirty" (p. 403), may also be
corrupt. Chorus 3 and the first ten lines of 3.1 were
printed from foul papers; the report of acts 3-5 begins
with 1. 11. Wilkins' novel, *The Painfull Aduentures*,
shows that its author knew acts 1-2 of *Pericles* well
but knew the second half of the play from 3.4 only
imperfectly. If Wilkins had a hand in acts 1-2, then
his close knowledge of the play would be explained.
The article ends with seven generalizations based on
the evidence: (1) there was an *Ur-Pericles*, perhaps
written in part by Wilkins; (2) Shakespeare touched up
parts of the working draft for acts 1-2; (3)
Shakespeare wrote acts 3-5; (4) a promptbook was made;
(5) the Quarto was printed surreptitiously, the
printers obtaining a rough draft of act 1 through
3.2.1-10; (6) gaps in the draft were filled with
reported matter, including 3.2-5; (7) the printing,
which was divided between two houses, was the careless
work of at least three compositors.

468.   Evans, Gareth Lloyd. "Kenneth Muir in Conversation
       with Gareth Lloyd Evans." *Shakespeare Quarterly*, 30
       (1979): 7-14.

       Muir has not changed his mind much concerning
Pericles since *Last Periods of Shakespeare, Racine and
Ibsen* (see item 63). He still does not entirely agree
with Philip Edwards that Shakespeare wrote all of
Pericles (see item 413). Perhaps *Pericles* as it was
originally written was one of Shakespeare's earliest
plays, the differences between acts 1-2 and acts 3-5 in
the Quarto representing two different stages of
writing. The considerable textual problems make a
final conclusion impossible.

469. Metz, G. Harold. "A Stylometric Comparison of Shakespeare's *Titus Andronicus, Pericles* and *Julius Caesar.*" *Shakespeare Newsletter*, 29 (1979): 42.

 Results of a stylometric test run at Edinburgh University by A.Q. Morton, S. Michaelson, and N. Hamilton-Smith comparing *Pericles, Titus Andronicus,* and *Julius Caesar* show that Shakespeare wrote all these plays. See items 465, 466.

470. Michael, Nancy C. "The Usefulness of Narrative Sources and the Gower Choruses in Determining a Divided Authorship for *Pericles.*" *Upstart Crow*, 2 (1979): 34-50.

 Stylistic evidence from the major sources, Gower's *Confessio Amantis* and Twine's *Patterne of Painefull Adventures,* and the Gower choruses support textual evidence of a divided authorship. Even though Gower is the play's main source, the use of Twine in acts 3-5 for heightened suspense and increased dramatic tension suggests a dramatist for acts 3-5 distinct from the author of acts 1-2. The differences between the two facile choruses in acts 1-2 and the six more sophisticated choruses in acts 3-5 also indicate a divided authorship: an unknown dramatist, or dramatists, for acts 1-2 and Shakespeare for acts 3-5.

471. Wood, James O. "The Case of Shakespeare's *Pericles.*" *San Jose Studies*, 6, no. 2 (1980): 39-58.

 Pericles is entirely Shakespeare's work, the partial revision of an early play. George Wilkins based *The Painfull Aduentures* on *Pericles,* some of which he remembered seeing, and on Twine's *Patterne of Painefull Adventures,* but he did not write any of *Pericles.* Neither is there an *Ur-Pericles* (see 360). Because the scene of Lysimachus' conversion (4.6) contains language consonant with the unrevised first half of *Pericles,* it is erroneous to piece out the so-called imperfections of the scene with lines borrowed from Wilkins, as recent stage productions have done. F.D. Hoeniger has argued that John Day may have written parts of *Pericles* (see items 425, 528), but Day may have been influenced by *Pericles* instead. The printing errors in the Quarto are not oral errors made by reporters (see item 413). They are transcription errors that witness the printers' failure to read Shakespeare's handwriting in

a crowded revision; in other words, *Pericles* was
printed from "foul papers" (see items 407, 427).
Critics mistake Pericles' Biblical archetype. He is
not Jonah (see item 358) but Lot, who was punished for
pitching his tent on ground polluted by sexual sin.
Criticism that concentrates on Shakespeare's
characteristic wording and spelling may in time confirm
that *Pericles* is indeed a partial revision by
Shakespeare of his own early play.

472.   Hoeniger, F. David. "Gower and Shakespeare."
       Shakespeare Quarterly, 33 (1982): 461-79.

       Textual and stylistic arguments that find *Pericles*
       crudely botched and piecemeal fail to take into account
       the popularity of the play in the seventeenth century
       and its success on twentieth-century stages. The
       signal differences between acts 1-2 and 3-5 are more
       the work of two stylists--Gower and Shakespeare--than
       the result of two or more authors, reporters, or
       compositors. *Pericles* is a "theatrical experiment" (p.
       476), an interplay between storyteller Gower and
       dramatist Shakespeare that plays better than it reads.
       All four romances show Shakespeare's turn from tragedy
       to a new dramaturgy reflecting the narrative, naive,
       and often crude natures of these plays. In the first
       of the romances, *Pericles*, Shakespeare concentrated not
       only on Gower's story but on his medieval manner as
       storyteller as well. Shakespeare's self-consciously
       contrived Gower choruses and episodic plot in acts 1-2
       deliberately (and sometimes playfully) reflect ancient
       Gower's loose plotting and labored rhymes, not
       Shakespeare's spirited pace. The shift from Gower's
       style at act 3 to that of Gower and Shakespeare
       interspersed (less noticeable on the stage than in the
       study) occurs only after the audience has accustomed
       itself to Gower's episodic structure and old-fashioned
       prosody. Seemingly Gower's play, but played before a
       knowing audience, *Pericles* is unique in Shakespeare's
       canon. Heminge and Condell, in fact, left *Pericles* out
       of the First Folio because they feared that future
       readers would misunderstand the technique and intention
       behind the original staged *Pericles*.

473.   Smith, M.W.A. "The Authorship of *Pericles*: An Initial
       Investigation." *The Bard* (London), 3, no. 4 (1982):
       143-76.

Smith says that his stylometric tests of *Pericles* run by computer analysis and based on Hoeniger's Arden edition (see item 528), suggest that Shakespeare only lightly revised acts 1 and 2 but wrote acts 3-5.

474. M[arder], L[ouis]. "Scholars Dispute Pericles Data." *Shakespeare Newsletter*, 33 (Winter 1983): 37-38.

Marder reports on the conflicting results of stylometric analyses conducted by A. Q. Morton and Thomas Merriam, who conclude *Pericles* the work of a single author (see items 465, 466), and M.W.A. Smith, whose tests indicate that acts 1-2 and acts 3-5 are the work of different authors (see items 473, 475).

475. Smith, M.W.A. "The Authorship of *Pericles*: Collocations Investigated Again." *The Bard* (London), 4, no. 1 (1983): 15-21.

Smith provides further statistical evidence that acts 1-2 and acts 3-5 are the work of different authors. See item 473.

476. Smith, M.W.A. "An Initial Investigation of the Authorship of *Pericles*: Statistics Support Scholars: Shakespeare Did Not Write Acts 1 & 2." *Shakespeare Newsletter*, 33 (fall 1983): 32.

In *Literary Detection* (1978), A.Q. Morton presented evidence from 28 word-frequency tests of *Pericles* and concluded that the play is the work of a single author (see item 466). However, stylometric investigations conducted by Smith, and published in 1982, indicate that acts 1-2 and acts 3-5 were written by different authors (see items 473, 475). Because of the corrupt state of the Quarto, Smith ran numerous word tests, considerably more than Morton, including comparisons of word groups in various combinations of the five acts and comparisons of *Pericles* with plays written about the same time, to reach his conclusion.

477. Smith, M.W.A. "Recent Experience and New Developments of Methods for the Determination of Authorship." *Association for Literary and Linguistic Computing*, 11 (1983): 73-82.

Smith includes a review of his computer analysis of sentences in *Pericles* suggesting that acts 1-2 and 3-5

are by different authors (pp. 76-77). The essay
investigates the usefulness of stylometrics in
determining authorship. Smith finds such evidence at
best supportive rather than conclusive. See items 473,
475, 476.

478. Thomas, Sidney. "The Problem of *Pericles*." *Shakespeare
     Quarterly*, 34 (1983): 448-50.

     Thomas thinks Hoeniger's 1982 argument, "Gower and
     Shakespeare" (see item 472), that the peculiarities of
     acts 1-2 are not textual corruptions but Shakespeare's
     stylistics in imitation of medieval Gower is
     wrong-headed bardolatry. Hoeniger surmises that
     Heminge and Condell omitted *Pericles* from the First
     Folio because they sensed that future readers would
     misunderstand Shakespeare's technique and intention;
     such an assumption, Thomas points out, is sheer
     guesswork. Hoeniger's assertion that no other corrupt
     Jacobean text was reprinted as frequently as *Pericles*
     (five times in 26 years) is incorrect: Heywood's *If You
     Know Me*, for instance, was reprinted seven times after
     the 1605 first edition. Hoeniger's critical analysis
     of the play is wrong as well; Thomas argues it
     implausible that Shakespeare would write in a
     deliberately archaic and unsophisticated style for half
     the play before switching abruptly in act 3 to a
     livelier, more accommodating style.

479. Marder, Louis. "Stylometry: The Controversy
     Continues." *Shakespeare Newsletter*, 34 (1984): 28.

     Marder accepts M.W.A. Smith's stylometric evidence
     concerning authorship of *Pericles* (see items 473, 475)
     over that of A.Q. Morton (item 466) and Thomas Merriam
     (item 480). He also reports on the unresolved problems
     debated at the 21-24 August conference on stylometry
     held at Edinburgh University.

480. Merriam, Tom. "Morton vs Smith: An Objective
     Analysis." *Shakespeare Newsletter*, 34 (1984): 5.

     M.W.A. Smith (item 473) has increased the word-habits
     list devised by A.Q. Morton in *Literary Detection* (item
     466). Morton rightly rejects these new lists, untested
     as they are as random variables. Smith's *Pericles*
     tests are irrefutable within the circle of Smith's own
     data. A Shakespeare control is needed. Morton, who

compared *Pericles* with *Titus Andronicus* and *Julius
Caesar* in *Literary Detection*, concluded that *Pericles*
is likely the work of a single author.

481. Morton, Andrew Q. "Stylometry vs Stylometry."
     Shakespeare Newsletter, 34 (1984): 5.

     Hardly anything about authorship can be proved from
     stylometric tests of *Pericles* alone.

482. Smith, M.W.A. "Critical Reflections on the
     Determination of Authorship by Statistics. Part 1:
     Shakespeare, Bacon and Marlowe." *Shakespeare
     Newsletter*, 34 (1984): 4-5.

     Chapter 15 of A.Q. Morton's *Literary Detection* (item
     466) investigates *Pericles*. Morton concludes that one
     author wrote the play. His statistical evidence,
     however, is "unconvincing."

483. Smith, M.W.A. "Critical Reflections on the
     Determination of Authorship by Statistics. Part 2:
     Morton, Merriam and *Pericles*." *Shakespeare
     Newsletter*, 34 (1984): 28, 33.

     The statistical evidence that one dramatist wrote
     Pericles contained in chapter 15 of A.Q. Morton's
     Literary Detection (item 466) and Thomas Merriam's
     "What Shakespeare Wrote in Henry 8" (*The Bard*, 2
     [1979]: 81-98), is faulty. Smith reiterates the
     conclusion of his 1982 essay, "The Authorship of
     Pericles: An Initial Investigation" (item 473), that
     someone, probably Shakespeare, revised acts 1-2 and
     wrote acts 3-5.

484. Metz, G. Harold. "Disputed Shakespearean Texts and
     Stylometric Analysis." *Text: Transactions of the
     Society for Textual Scholarship*, vol. 2. Edited by
     D.C. Greetham and W. Speed Hill. New York: AMS,
     1985, pp. 149-71.

     Stylometry, computer-assisted tests of authenticity
     of authorship, focuses on frequently-used words that
     display individual habits rather than exceptional words
     and phrases. In tests of *Pericles*, stylometrists
     tested 23 habits in acts 1-2 and 3-5 that proved
     consistent enough to suggest that *Pericles* is the work
     of a single author (see items 465, 466). Tests on 17

habits in *Titus Andronicus* indicate that it too is the
work of one dramatist. Comparison between *Pericles* and
Titus shows that the same author wrote both plays.
When stylometrists compared *Julius Caesar* (c. 1599),
written midway between *Titus* (c. 1590) and *Pericles* (c.
1608), to the two plays, the results showed that
Shakespeare wrote all three plays.

See also items 1-11, 14, 17-18, 21, 24-25, 27-28, 30-31,
34-35, 40, 43, 46, 49, 59, 63, 67, 72, 74, 76, 79, 87, 89-90,
98, 115-18, 123, 125, 127, 135, 144, 146, 151, 158, 166, 170,
191, 197, 206, 221, 232, 273, 278, 284, 286, 312, 321, 329,
335, 340, 343, 348, 353-55, 360, 363-64, 366, 374, 383,
388-89, 487-91, 493-96, 498-500, 502-04, 507-09, 512-14,
518-20, 527-28, 533-34, 538, 542, 551, 554, 559-61, 564-67,
570, 576, 686, 701, 703, 710, 736, 756, 789, 794-95, 804,
806-07, 812.

V. BIBLIOGRAPHIES AND CONCORDANCES

485. Smith, Gordon Ross. *A Classified Shakespeare
     Bibliography, 1936-1958*. University Park:
     Pennsylvania State University Press, 1963.

     The *Pericles* section (pp. 761-62) of this subject
     bibliography lists one textual study, two modern
     editions, three articles on textual emendations,
     twenty-two source and analogue studies, one note on
     language, six literary commentaries, and one
     miscellaneous item.

486. Spevak, Marvin. *A Complete and Systematic Concordance
     to the Works of Shakespeare*. 9 vols. Hildesheim:
     Georg Olms, 1968-80.

     This computer-generated concordance and the single-
     volume *Harvard Concordance to Shakespeare* (see item
     492) are based on the texts in *The Riverside
     Shakespeare* (see item 560). The *Pericles* concordance
     (vol. 3, pp. 1398-1427) is prefaced with tables listing
     speech, line, and word totals and followed by a
     concordance to characters preceded by statistics on
     speeches, lines, and words (pp. 1428-83). Volumes 4-6
     hold the collected concordance of Shakespeare's works.
     Volume 7 lists stage directions in Q1-Q4 of *Pericles*
     (pp. 307-11), characters' names that prefix speeches in
     Q1-Q4 (pp. 666-70), and speech prefixes in Q1 (pp.
     773-74).

487. Velz, John W. "The Last Plays." *Shakespeare and the
     Classical Tradition: A Critical Guide to Commentary,*

1660-1960. Minneapolis: University of Minnesota
Press, 1968, pp. 336-54.

The chapter includes some twenty-six studies on or
including *Pericles* among 137 listings for the last
plays.

488.   Howard-Hill, Trevor H. *Shakespearian Bibliography and
       Textual Criticism: A Bibliography*. Index to British
       Literary Bibliography, vol. 2. Oxford: Clarendon,
       1971, pp. 137-38.

       One facsimile edition along with eight notes and
       articles on textual matters are listed in the *Pericles*
       section.

489.   [Howard-Hill, Trevor H., comp.] *Pericles: A
       Concordance to the Text of the First Quarto of 1609*.
       Oxford Shakespeare Concordances. Oxford: Clarendon,
       1972.

       This concordance is based on W.W. Greg's facsimile
       edition of the Malone copy of the Quarto in the
       Bodleian Library (see item 502). A table of act,
       scene, and line numbers coordinates Quarto signatures
       with Edwards' putative compositors x, y, and z (see
       item 413) and with act, scene, and line numbers in
       Greg's facsimile. Corrections for 32 misprints in the
       facsimile are listed.

490.   Berman, Ronald. *"Pericles." A Reader's Guide to
       Shakespeare's Plays: A Discursive Bibliography*. Rev.
       ed. Glenview, Ill.: Scott, Foresman, 1973, pp.
       164-67.

       The *Pericles* section lists titles concerned with the
       text, sources, criticism, and staging. A bibliographic
       essay on the criticism says that *Pericles*
       interpretations generally tend either to be harsh or to
       praise, often with exaggeration, the mythopoeic
       qualities of the play.

491.   Edwards, Philip. "The Late Comedies." *Shakespeare:
       Select Bibliographical Guides*. Edited by Stanley
       Wells. London: Oxford University Press, 1973, pp.
       113-33.

This chapter has sections on the "Texts," "The
Romances as a Group," and "Additional Studies of
Individual Plays." A bibliography ends the chapter.
The summary of *Pericles* studies notes that textual and
authorial questions should precede critical evaluations
and interpretations. Titles essential to the study of
textual and authorial problems and a few recommended
critical studies are named.

492. Spevak, Marvin. *The Harvard Concordance to
      Shakespeare*. Cambridge: Harvard University Press,
      Belknap Press, 1974.

      This is a slightly abbreviated, one-volume edition of
      the data in vols. 4-6 of Spevack's *Shakespeare
      Concordance* (see item 486). The text is also that of
      The Riverside Shakespeare. See item 560.

493. McManaway, James G. and Jeanne Addison Roberts, comps.
      *"Pericles." A Selective Bibliography of Shakespeare:
      Editions, Textual Studies, Commentary*. Washington,
      D.C.: Folger Library, 1975, pp. 145-46.

      The list of essential works published since 1930
      includes for *Pericles* one facsimile edition, four
      textual commentaries, seventeen literary commentaries,
      and cross-references to entries on the canon, the
      comedies, and the romances.

494. Bevington, David, comp. *Shakespeare*. Goldentree
      Bibliographies in Language and Literature. Arlington
      Heights, Ill.: AHM, 1978.

      This selective bibliography, covering Shakespeare
      studies from 1930 to February, 1977, includes in the
      Pericles section 26 items and 47 crosslistings.

495. Kay, Carol McGinnis and Henry E. Jacobs, comps.
      "Selected Bibliography on the Romances."
      Shakespeare's Romances Reconsidered. Lincoln:
      University of Nebraska Press, 1978, pp. 181-215.

      The bibliography lists general works that include
      sections on Shakespeare's romances, studies of romance
      and Shakespeare's romances, and works on each of the
      four romances. The *Pericles* section (pp. 192-95)
      contains 82 items.

496. Jacobs, Henry E., comp. *Cymbeline*. The Garland
      Shakespeare Bibliographies, no. 3. New York:
      Garland, 1982.

      Jacobs includes 133 references and cross references
      to *Pericles* in his Index (pp. 574-75).

See also items 22, 69-70, 72, 96, 103, 119, 123-24, 127, 129,
136-37, 140, 145-47, 151, 154, 157-58, 160, 165, 167, 170,
175, 186, 189, 197-98, 201, 205, 207, 211, 215-16, 226,
231-32, 234-35, 254, 264, 271, 292-93, 300, 320, 328, 330-34,
366, 370, 390, 394, 415, 443-47, 449, 509, 520, 538, 564,
570, 680, 731, 804, 810.

VI. EDITIONS

497. Clark, William George and William Aldis Wright, eds.
    The Works of William Shakespeare. The Globe Edition.
    Cambridge: Macmillan, 1864. (not seen)

498. Round, P.Z., intro. *Pericles: By William Shakspere and
    Others. The First Quarto, 1609, A Facsimile from the
    British Museum Copy, c.12.h.5. By Charles Praetorius
    with Introduction by P.Z. Round*. Shakspere-Quarto
    Facsimiles 21. London: C. Praetorius, 1886.

    The introduction examines the publishing history and
    popularity of *Pericles* in the seventeenth century,
    traces the literary origins of the Apollonius story,
    and discusses Gower's *Confessio Amantis* as the sole
    source of the play. Perhaps Shakespeare began a play
    about Marina, which later became acts 3-5 of *Pericles*;
    Wilkins wrote a new beginning, which became acts 1-2;
    and Rowley wrote act 4, scenes 2, 4, and 5. Wilkins,
    possibly with Rowley's help, wrote the choruses. This
    work has perished. *Pericles* is a hasty report of
    Shakespeare, Wilkins, and Rowley's original.

499. Round, P.Z., intro. *Pericles: by William Shakspere and
    Others. The Second Quarto, 1609, A Facsimile from
    the British Museum Copy . . . By Charles Praetorius,
    introduced by P.Z. Round*. Shakspere-Quarto
    Facsimiles 22. London: C. Praetorius, 1886.

    Pericles consists of an unfinished play by
    Shakespeare (most of acts 3-5) to which George Wilkins
    added acts 1-2 and the Gower choruses and William
    Rowley the brothel scenes (4.2, 5-6).

500. Lee, Sidney, ed. *Shakespeares Pericles: Being a*
      Reproduction in Facsimile of the First Edition 1609
      from the Copy in the Malone Collection in the
      Bodleian Library with Introduction and Bibliography
      by Sidney Lee. Oxford: Clarendon, 1905.

      The introduction examines the history of the
      Apollonius story, the literary inferiority of the text
      (Shakespeare wrote most of act 3 and some of act 4),
      the reception of the play in the seventeenth and
      eighteenth centuries, the publishing and textual
      history, and the ownership and disposition of 74 copies
      of the six quarto editions. The facsimile is a
      collotype reproduction on heavy cream paper with act,
      scene, and line numbers from the 1891 Globe edition.

501. Farjeon, Herbert, ed. *The Comedies, Histories and*
      Tragedies of William Shakespeare. Vol. 28. New
      York: Limited Editions Club, 1940.

      The text derives from a collation of the Quarto with
      the second, third, and fourth quartos. Six wood
      engravings by Stanislas Ostojo-Chrostowski illustrate
      scenes from the play. An appended section of
      commentary reproduces remarks on *Pericles* by William
      Allan Neilson in the Cambridge Shakespeare (see item
      504), Sir Paul Harvey in *The Oxford Companion to*
      English Literature (see item 795), and Georg Brandes'
      1898 essay on *Pericles* in the 1935 edition of
      Shakespeare: A Critical Study (see item 3).

502. Greg, W.W., ed. *Pericles 1609.* Shakespeare Quartos
      no. 5. 1940. Reprint. Oxford: Clarendon, 1963.

      This edition is a facsimile of Q1 taken from the
      Malone copy in the Bodleian Library, Oxford, with act,
      scene, and line numbers added from the 1891 Globe
      edition. The introduction labels the Quarto "bad,"
      names extant copies, and justifies having reproduced
      the Malone copy in spite of its extensive alterations
      in pencil and ink. Because some of the changes are
      hard to detect in reproduction, a list of readings
      obscured in the facsimile is included.

503. *The Complete Works of William Shakespeare, with the*
      Temple Notes, Containing All of the Plays and Poems
      of William Shakespeare, the History of His Life, His

*Will, an Introduction to Each Play, and an Index to
Characters.* Cleveland: World, 1942.

The *Pericles* introduction discusses authorship and
attributes the play to Shakespeare only in part.
Notes, from the 1935 Temple edition, are at the end of
the volume.

504. Neilson, William Allan and Charles Jarvis Hill, eds.
      The Complete Plays and Poems of William Shakespeare.
      New Cambridge Edition. Boston: Houghton Mifflin,
      1942.

      Texts for the plays, based on *The Complete Works of
      William Shakespeare* (1906), are heavily revised. The
      editors open the *Pericles* introduction with a textual
      history. The play is the result of a collaboration
      between an unknown author (acts 1-2) and Shakespeare
      (acts 3-5); all the choruses are not Shakespeare's.
      George Wilkins based his novel, *The Painfull Aduentures*
      (1608), on a manuscript version of *Pericles* and Twine's
      Patterne of Painefull Adventures. "The theme of
      separation and union" (p. 426) links Pericles to *The
      Comedy of Errors, Twelfth Night, Cymbeline, The
      Winter's Tale,* and *The Tempest. Pericles* and the other
      late plays are graver than the early comedies. At the
      end of the late plays, entire families share a joy
      beyond mere happiness, and even the young enter a
      future that is a fulfillment, not a promise.

505. *The Comedies and Tragedies of Shakespeare.* Vol. 2.
      New York: Random House, 1944.

      William Chappell provided the notes, glossary, and
      illustrations. No reference is made to the text in
      this collection.

506. János, Arany, trans. *The Collected Plays of
      Shakespeare.* Vol. 4. Kisfaludy Society. Budapest:
      n.p., 1948. (not seen)

507. Alexander, Peter, ed. *The Complete Works.* Tudor
      Edition. 1951. Reprint. London: Collins, 1966.

      A general introduction precedes the plays. There are
      no individual introductions. Discussions may be found
      in *Alexander's Introductions to Shakespeare* (see item
      76).

508. Craig, Hardin, ed. *The Complete Works of Shakespeare*.
      Chicago: Scott, Foresman, 1951.

      The texts for this collection are based on the Globe
      edition (see item 497). The final group of
      plays--*Pericles, Cymbeline, The Winter's Tale, The
      Tempest*, and *Henry 8*--are prefaced by an essay, "The
      Period of the Romances, 1609-1616," which terms the
      first three plays tragicomedies rather than romances.
      Perhaps the popularity of *Pericles* encouraged
      Shakespeare, Beaumont, and Fletcher to write other
      tragicomedies. Sections on the textual history of
      Pericles, the dates of earliest performance
      (1606-1607), the two main sources, Twine and Gower, and
      the authorship question open the introduction to the
      play. Wilkins based his novel, *The Painfull Aduentures*
      (1608), on a lost play, the same play Shakespeare
      revised as *Pericles*. Wilkins used notes taken at a
      performance of the older play in writing his novel.
      The main differences between the *Ur-Pericles*, as seen
      in Wilkins, and *Pericles* occur in the brothel scenes in
      act 4. In the lost play, Marina converts Lysimachus.
      In *Pericles*, even though traces of the conversion
      remain, Lysimachus claims that he did not come to the
      brothel with a corrupt mind. Shakespeare did not begin
      his important revisions until act 4. *Pericles* is a
      good version of Shakespeare's careful and successful
      revision of the *Ur-Pericles*, even though the large
      amount of verse printed as prose has made others think
      the Quarto "bad." The Quarto was in fact printed from
      a manuscript whose revisions are largely in
      Shakespeare's own hand (see items 407, 427). The play
      has had no recent stage history.

509. Harrison, G.B., ed. *Shakespeare: The Complete Works*.
      New York: Harcourt, Brace, 1952.

      The introduction to *Pericles* contains a summary of
      the textual and authorship problems, a discussion of
      the sources, including the plot of Gower's *Confessio
      Amantis*, and an examination of the relationship between
      Wilkins' *Painfull Aduentures* and the play. If *Pericles*
      belongs to Shakespeare, it is his first play of two
      generations. Perhaps he wrote the four romances partly
      to continue the stage success of a boy actor who played
      Marina, Imogen, Perdita, and Miranda. The texts in
      this collection are based on the 1864 Globe edition

(see item 497). A bibliography is included at the end
of the volume.

510. *Shakespeare: The Complete Dramatic and Poetic Works.*
Philadelphia: Winston, [1952]. (not seen)

511. Bodenstedt, Friedrich, trans. *Sämtliche Werke.* Vol.
4. Heidelberg: Schneider, [1953?]. (not seen)

512. Sisson, Charles Jasper, ed. *The Complete Works.*
[1954.] Reprint. London: Odhams, [1970].

The *Pericles* text, which is based on the Quarto, is
prefaced by a list of doubtful and disputed readings
(pp. 1206-07).

513. Maxwell, J.C., ed. *Pericles, Prince of Tyre.* New
Cambridge Shakespeare. 2nd ed. rev. Cambridge: At
the University Press, 1956.

This edition contains an introduction by Maxwell, a
stage history by C.B. Young (see item 661), the text,
an essay by Maxwell on the copy for the Quarto, textual
notes, and a glossary. Whoever plotted *Pericles*, using
Gower more than Twine, followed his sources with an
intricacy wholly uncharacteristic of Shakespeare.
George Wilkins probably had nothing to do with the
play; he seems to have based his novel, *The Painfull
Aduentures of Pericles* (1608), on the play after
Shakespeare had revised it. There is no external
evidence for an *Ur-Pericles*, and the internal evidence
is weak. Even without an *Ur-Pericles* a
pre-Shakespearean version is probable. Shakespeare
took up the play (c. 1604), left acts 1-2 virtually
untouched, and rewrote acts 3-5. Philip Edwards'
arguments that the differences between the halves of
the play are the result of separate reporters, not
separate authors, is unconvincing (see item 413). The
verse in the two sections is too different to be the
result of reporting, and, too, Wilkins' novel and the
Quarto often resemble one another closely. If
Shakespeare had written all of *Pericles*, surely Heminge
and Condell would have included it in the Folio. The
author of the play that Shakespeare revised remains
unknown. *Pericles* contains many of the themes,
partially developed, found in Shakespeare's other late
romances. The play has the same symbolic quality as
Cymbeline, The Winter's Tale, and *The Tempest.*

Allegorical Pericles, presenter Gower, the fairy-tale
motifs, and the straightforward, low comedy of the
brothel scenes are the hallmarks of Shakespeare's
simple but frequently moving play. An essay following
the text, "The Copy for *Pericles, Prince of Tyre*,
1609," argues that the Quarto is "bad" and reported.
However, the differences between acts 1-2 and acts 3-5
are not reportorial; they are literary. There is also
evidence of stop-press correction and two printing
houses. Because the text is based perforce on the
Quarto, which is a "bad" text, conservative editorial
principles were combined with emendations designed for
general readers.

514. Nunes, Carlos Alberto, trans. *Obras completas de
      Shakespeare*. Vol. 12. San Paulo: Melhoramentos,
      1956.

      A preface to the *Pericles* translation includes
      discussion of the publishing history, the sources, and
      Marina.

515. Schücking, L.L., ed. *Shakespeares Werke: Englisch und
      und Deutsch*. Tempel-Klassiker. Vol. 6. 1956.
      Reprint. Berlin: Tempel, 1961.

      The English text of *Pericles* in the Temple edition
      (1935) and the German text, translated by H.
      Steinitzer, appear on opposite pages. There is no
      introduction.

516. Munro, John, ed. *The London Shakespeare: A New
      Annotated and Critical Edition of the Complete Works
      in Six Volumes*. Vol. 2. New York: Simon and
      Schuster, 1957.

      The *Pericles* introduction concerns critical estimates
      of the play written in the eighteenth, nineteenth, and
      early twentieth centuries. The text, emended from the
      Quarto, follows with notes at the foot of each page.

517. Simić, Zivojin and Sima Pandurović, trans. *Celokupna
      dela* [Complete Works]. Vol. 1. Cetinje: Narodna
      knjiga, 1957. (Serbian—not seen)

518. Harrison, G.B. ed. *The Play of Pericles, Prince of
      Tyre*. Penguin Shakespeare. Harmondsworth: Penguin,
      1958.

The introduction identifies *Pericles*, a play below
Shakespeare's standard, as a work of mixed authorship.
A brief history of the play with a summary of the
Apollonius story in Gower's *Confessio Amantis*, the
chief source for *Pericles*, follows. Wilkins' 1608
novel, *The Painfull Aduentures*, is based on *Pericles*,
which must also have been written in 1608. *Pericles* is
a "bad" quarto, perhaps a piracy or the result of copy
that was hard to read. The editor has prepared a
conservative edition based on the Quarto. Notes and a
glossary follow the text.

519. Hauser, Georg, ed. *Perikles*. Translated by Theodor
      von Zeynek. Klassiker der Bühne, 134-35. Salzburg:
      Stifterbibliothek, 1958.

The afterward (pp. 125-31), discusses *Pericles* as a
paradoxical play combining pantomime and mystery with
realism. With his acute business sense and poetic
genius, Shakespeare put *Pericles* together from
another's or others' story fragments of riddle-solving
and incest, of flight, shipwreck, and comic fishermen,
of a good king (Simonides), of a weak king and a wicked
stepmother (Cleon and Dionyza), of the trials and
triumph of a guiltless man.

520. Fluchere, Henri, ed. *Oeuvres complètes*. Translated by
      Francois-Victor Hugo. Vol. 2. Paris: Gallimard,
      1959.

This volume contains an introduction to each play and
a general bibliography. The introduction discusses
dating (c. 1607-1609) and sources, summarizes the
textual debate and the plot of the play, and concludes
that in *Pericles* life and love triumph in an atmosphere
of miracle and wonder. With its emphasis on love,
Pericles is the opposite of *Antony and Cleopatra*, a
play in which death triumphs.

521. Balser, Karl, Reinhard Buchwald, and Karl Franz
      Reinking, eds. *William Shakespeare*. Translated by
      August Wilhelm Schlegel and Ludwig Tieck. Vol. 1.
      Wiesbaden: Vollmer, 1960. (not seen)

522. Lodovico, Cesare Vico, trans. *Pericle, principe di
      Tiro*. Piccola Biblioteca Scientifico-letteraria 91.
      Turin: Giulio Einaudi, 1960.

There is no introduction.

523. Messiaen, Pierre, trans. *"Périclès, prince de Tyr."*
     Les Tragédies. Vol. 1. Bruges: Desclee de Brouwer,
     [1960]. (not seen)

     Essays and notes are by José Axelrad.

524. Smirnov, A. and A. Anikst, eds. *Polnoe sobranie
     sochinenii* [Complete Collected Works]. Vol. 7.
     Translated by T. Gneditch. Moscow: Iskusstvo, 1960.
     (not seen)

     The editors include an essay on *Pericles* (pp.
     809–16).

525. *Il Teatro di William Shakespeare.* Turin: Giulio
     Einaudi, 1960. (not seen)

526. Kostetzky, Eaghor G., ed. *Makbeta. Korolj. Henri IV.
     Perekl. Theodosy Osmatschka.* Munich: Wydmija "na
     hori," 1961. (Ukranian—not seen)

527. Deninger, Wolfgang, ed. *Shakespeares Werke:
     Vollständige, Ausgabe.* Translated by [Friedrich]
     Bodenstedt et al. Vol. 11. Bongs goldene Klassiker
     Bibliothek. Munich: Bong, [1962?].

     The essay on *Pericles* examines the authorship
     question, comments on the sources for the play and the
     name Pericles, and summarizes the plot. The play is
     almost never staged in Germany.

528. Hoeniger, F.D., ed. *Pericles.* Arden Shakespeare.
     1963. Reprint. London: Methuen; Cambridge: Harvard
     University Press, 1969.

     The introduction includes sections on sources, text,
     authorship, date, stage history, and literary
     interpretation. The section on sources provides a
     history of the Apollonius story from its origins in
     Greek narrative to the major sources for *Pericles*,
     Gower's *Confessio Amantis* and Twine's *Patterne of
     Painefull Adventures*; a discussion of the minor
     sources, such as 2 Maccabees 9 and Sidney's *Arcadia*;
     several analogues; and prototypes of the Gower chorus
     in *Henry 5*, Barnes's *Divil's Charter* (1607), and Day,
     Rowley, and Wilkins' *Travailes of the Three English*

Brothers (1607). The 1609 Quarto, the only substantive
text of *Pericles*, was not set from Shakespeare's foul
papers (see items 407, 427); it is a pirated version.
Two shops, William White's and another, printed the
Quarto, with at least three compositors sharing the
work. Philip Edwards' 1952 bibliographical argument is
correct: the Quarto is the result of corrupt, reported
copy (see item 413). But two reporters, one for acts
1-2 and another for acts 3-5, cannot account for the
differences in the two sections of the play. The
differences are authorial. Wilkins' *Painfull
Aduentures* is not a source for *Pericles*; moreover,
Wilkins based his novel on *Pericles* as we know it in
the Quarto, not on an *Ur-Pericles* (see items 407, 427;
348, 353, 360, 383, 426). The *Painfull Aduentures* is a
hybrid combining Wilkins' memory of *Pericles* as it
appeared on the stage with long sections copied from
Laurence Twine's *Patterne of Painefull Adventures*.
Because Wilkins' "History" of *Pericles* is highly
inaccurate, one should be extremely cautious in
assuming that scenes reported in Wilkins may be more
accurate than those in the Quarto. Even though
external evidence of a mixed authorship is lacking,
stylistic evidence strongly suggests that Shakespeare
wrote only acts 3-5 of *Pericles*. Perhaps he also wrote
some of the later choruses. Arguments that either
Rowley or Heywood wrote acts 1-2 are altogether
unconvincing. The case for Wilkins is stronger, but
Wilkins can hardly have written *Pericles* if he needed
to copy a third of Twine's narrative into his novel.
Textual parallels and similarities in speech patterns
and wording indicate that John Day, not Wilkins, may
have written some of acts 1-2 (see item 425). Evidence
for Day's authorship appears in Appendix B. Written
and staged between 1606 and 1608, *Pericles* probably
followed *Macbeth* and *Antony and Cleopatra* and preceded
Cymbeline and *The Winter's Tale*. The stage history
treats the early popularity of the play and covers
productions from the seventeenth century to 1960.
Pericles and Shakespeare's other romances are plays
with plots about parents and children, actions
involving many years, and atmospheres that suggest
man's helplessness in the face of superior powers. The
first of the romances, *Pericles* was an experiment in
turning narrative into drama. The play follows its
sources unusually closely for Shakespeare and holds its
audience not by suspense but by its chorus, an
evocation of the medieval poet John Gower, author of

the play's chief source, *The Confessio Amantis*. In
Pericles there are few dramatic scenes; the play
emphasizes spectacle and music. Pericles rather than
the plot unifies the play. His "romantic biography"
involves "love, loss, and restoration" (p. lxxix).
Providence more than human actions influences the life
of this good man who suffers his troubles passively.
Marina renews her father. The theme of patience, so
important in *Pericles*, is emphasized in none of the
sources for the play. Shakespeare saw the profundity
in Apollonius' tragicomic story of human suffering
which Gower, Twine, and others had missed. The choric
presenter, the loosely related episodes, the emphasis
on spectacle, the tragicomic structure, the presence of
supernatural deities, and the didactic purpose of the
play show the influence of vernacular saints' plays.
The dramatic form as well as the story and chorus are
medieval. *Pericles* is a secular miracle play. The
heavily emended text, which is based on the Quarto,
follows the introduction. Textual commentary appears
below the text. Four appendices close the edition.
Appendix A contains chapters 11-14 of Twine's *Patterne
of Painefull Adventures*, corresponding to act 4, scenes
1, 3, and 6. Appendix B sets forth Hoeniger's case for
John Day as an author of *Pericles*. Appendix C
reconstructs 1.2.1-52. Appendix D contains
reconstructed verse from five passages of prose and
poor verse.

529.   Saudek, Erik Adolf, trans. *A Midsummer Night's Dream.
       Romeo and Juliet. Hamlet. Othello. Pericles*.
       Deslov: Pokorny, 1963. (Czech--not seen)

530.   Hugo, Francois-Victor, trans. *Théâtre complet*. Vol.
       3. Paris: Garnier, 1964.

       Jean B. Fort provides a general introduction to
       Pericles and textual notes to accompany Hugo's prose
       translation.

531.   János, Arany et al., trans. *Összes művei*. Vol. 2.
       Budapest: Europa Konyvkiadó, 1964. (not seen)

532.   Kim, Jae-Nam, trans. *Sinyok Syeiksup'io chonjip* [The
       Complete Works of Shakespeare]. Vol. 3. 1964.
       Reprint. Korea, 1971.

       The *Pericles* text has no introduction.

533. Leyris, Pierre and Henri Evans, eds. *Oeuvres complètes
      de Shakespeare*. Vol. 11. Paris: Le club francais du
      livre, 1964.

      This bilingual edition of Shakespeare uses the New
      Cambridge text. Philip Edwards wrote an introduction
      in French to *Pericles*, and R.G. Cox provided remarks in
      French on the text, dating and authorship, sources,
      criticism, and staging to 1921. The *Pericles* text, in
      English and and French on facing pages, and two pages
      of notes, in French, follow Cox's paragraphs. Notes
      and a glossary, reprinted from the 1956 New Cambridge
      Pericles (see item 513), appear at the end of the
      volume. Edwards says that the intractable *Pericles*
      text may hide a work entirely by Shakespeare or by him
      only in part. In working with *Pericles* one must not be
      too ingenious in dealing with the edifice behind the
      ruin. *Pericles* is neither sentimental nor realistic.
      Its mixture of times and places, such as the inclusion
      of medieval knights and the cult of Diana, releases
      history from filtering reality. Pericles himself is
      presented only in general terms; the rest of the cast
      are barely characterized. The grotesque and shocking
      brothel scenes are too true for the improbabilities of
      Pericles. The play does not depend on cause and effect
      relationships, even if Pericles seems to bring about
      some of his own suffering. The tempests and
      resurrections in the play are paradigms of human
      experience, not allegory. *Pericles* has meanings
      different from those of Shakespeare's more rigorous
      plays; the same meanings have less importance in
      Pericles. One's attitude toward Marina is the
      touchstone for response to this play in which emotions,
      not actions, are important. The reunion between
      Pericles and Marina brings unexpected happiness and
      reunites father with daughter. As in *Cymbeline*, *The
      Winter's Tale*, and *The Tempest*, the life of the older
      generation in *Pericles* is reaffirmed and restored by
      the new generation.

534. *Pericles 1609*. London: University Microfilms, 1964.

      This microfilm-Xerox copy was taken from the copy of
      the Quarto in the Folger Shakespeare Library,
      Washington, D.C.

535. Sladek, J.V. et al., trans. *Historical Plays II--
      Poems*. Prague: SMKLU, 1964. (not seen)

536. Maxwell, J.C., ed. *Pericles, Prince of Tyre*.
     Cambridge Pocket Shakespeare. Cambridge: At the
     University Press, 1965.

     This edition reprints the 1956 New Cambridge text and
     glossary without the introduction or notes. See item
     513.

537. Praz, Mario, ed. *Tutte le Opere*. 4th ed. Florence:
     Sansoni, 1965.

     Pericles is translated into prose. There is no
     introduction; notes appear at the end of the volume.

538. Schanzer, Ernest, ed. *Pericles, Prince of Tyre*.
     Signet Classic Shakespeare. New York: New American
     Library, 1965.

     This edition includes a prefactory essay on
     Shakespeare by the series editor, Sylvan Barnet, an
     introduction to *Pericles*, the text, and a textual note.
     Comments on the sources for the play, Gower's *Confessio
     Amantis* and Twine's *Patterne of Painefull Adventures*;
     passages from Gower and Twine; and sections from
     discussions of *Pericles* by G. Wilson Knight (see item
     14), Kenneth Muir (see item 426), and M. St. Clare
     Byrne (see item 664) follow. Selective bibliographies
     for Shakespeare and *Pericles* close the edition.
     Because acts 3-5 are superior to acts 1-2, *Pericles* is
     not a collaborated play; instead, Shakespeare must have
     revised someone else's play, beginning with the sea
     storm which opens act 3, and rewritten lines in acts
     1-2. The fact that the only substantive version of
     Pericles is corrupt is complicated by the publication
     of *The Painfull Adventures of Pericles Prince of Tyre*
     (1608), which its author, George Wilkins, offered as an
     accurate history of the play. *The Painfull Adventures*
     is indeed based on the play in performance, but Wilkins
     also copied into it large, unacknowledged portions from
     Twine. Wilkins' novel, which contains clues as to what
     the stage version of *Pericles* was like, can be used to
     correct the Quarto. The Gower choruses that
     Shakespeare wrote begin with act 3; these choruses
     imitate the archaisms of the earlier choruses, but the
     poetry has more vigor and polish. With its Levantine
     names and setting, shipwrecks, adventures, lost and
     found parents and children, and chaste maidens,
     Pericles typifies its origin in Greek romance. It is

also similar in structure to medieval morality plays.
Pericles, like *The Winter's Tale*, the play it most
resembles, focuses doubly on Pericles, the father, and
on Marina, the daughter. Pericles is not an exemplum
of patience, as critics often claim, and J.M.S.
Tomkins' suggestion that Pericles is named after the
Athenian statesman (see item 351) is also incorrect.
Shakespeare's Pericles resembles Pyrocles, the virtuous
prince in Sidney's *Arcadia*, a prose romance similar to
Pericles in several of its incidents. Like Pyrocles,
Pericles is "the pattern of all princely excellences"
(pp. xxxv-vi). Marina is the virtuous princess whose
endurance surpasses even that of her father. Divine
providence is not at work in *Pericles*. Fortune, not
Diana, presides. Pericles credits heaven with the
accidents, good and bad, that befall him, but Gower
always points to fortune. Like the other late
romances, *Pericles* involves a heightened sense of
wonder and a predominant use of fairy-tale mood and
motifs not found in the earlier comedies. Fourteen-
year-old Marina resembles the youthful heroines,
Perdita, aged fifteen, and Miranda, aged sixteen, not
Portia, Rosalind, or Helena. The emphasis in *Pericles*,
more than in Shakespeare's other comedies before or
after, is on the relationship between father and
daughter. *Pericles* and the later comedies emphasize
the reunions of separated families. A publishing
history opens the textual note. The Quarto is between
"good" and "bad"; it is faithful to the original yet
full of errors mainly compositorial, not reportorial.
The text is an emended version of the Quarto with
departures listed at the end of the textual note.
Commentary appears below the text. The note on the
sources explains that Sidney's *Arcadia* was the chief
literary influence on the play. Of the two main
sources, Gower's *Confessio Amantis* and Twine's *Patterne
of Painefull Adventures*, Gower dominates. Yet
Shakespeare seems to have been more interested in
following Twine's motivating idea behind the Apollonius
story, the pattern of adverse fortune, than Gower's
moral contrast between the horrors of unlawful love and
the happiness of honorable love.

539. *Viljams Sekspirs kapoti raksti*. Vol. 5. Riga:
     Latvijas Valsts Izdevnieciba, 1965. (not seen)

540. Lodovici, Cesare Vico, trans. *Teatro*. Vol. 5. Turin:
     Giulio Einaudi, 1966. (not seen)

541. Nakano, Yoshio et al., trans. *Sekai Koten Bungaku
      Zenshu*. Vol. 6. Tokyo: Chikumashobo, 1966. (not
      seen)

      Kazuso Ogoshi translated *Pericles*.

542. Sisson, Charles Jasper, ed. *Pericles Prince of Tyre*.
      Laurel Shakespeare. New York: Dell, 1966.

      The Laurel *Pericles* contains Sisson's text and a
      glossary by Laurence Blonquist. Francis Fergusson, the
      general editor, prefaces the text with an introduction,
      an essay by R.W.B. Lewis, "Pagan and Christian Elements
      in *Pericles*," and a textual note by Sisson. A general
      essay by Fergusson, "Shakespeare and His Theatre,"
      follows the text. Fergusson mentions the main sources
      and reviews the plot in his introduction. Anticipating
      Lewis' essay, he explains the episodic plot as a
      departure for Shakespeare into religious allegory. In
      the "Note on the Text," Sisson says that the Quarto is
      an abridgment set with considerable carelessness from
      "foul papers." He concludes with a list of textual
      emendations. His text is based on the Quarto.
      Assuming that Shakespeare revised somebody else's work
      in acts 1-2, Lewis argues in his essay on the religious
      symbolism of *Pericles* that Shakespeare let much of the
      original acts 1-2 stand because they treat subjects
      that absorbed him: the relationship between fathers and
      daughters, chastity and lust, birth and death, and the
      link between acts of physical creation and poetic
      creation. Like the other late plays, *Pericles* records
      Shakespeare's "basically revised judgment on human
      experience generally" (p. 20) and new moral outlook.
      Shakespeare conveys his altered point of view through
      symbolism. Thus, even though the locale of the play is
      pagan, the bearings are Christian. Diana, who presides
      over most of the action, represents the kind of
      chastity, namely Marina's, that begets lasting
      community; Neptune, who presides over the language,
      rules the very waters of life. The Christianity
      Shakespeare expresses in *Pericles* is more humanistic
      than modern Christianity, which bears the melancholy
      effects of Paul's and Augustine's emphases on original
      sin and the power of evil. The play, and especially
      the recognition scene at Mytilene in act 5, celebrates
      man more than human nature; it celebrates his
      possession of God inside himself.

543. Fukuhara, Rintaro and Yoshio Nakano, eds. *Shakespeare Zenshu*. Vol. 3. Tokyo: Chikumashobo, 1967. (not seen)

    Kazuso Ogoshi translated *Pericles*.

544. Lambin, Georges, trans. *Périclès, prince de tyr*. Collection Shakespeare. Paris: Les Belles Lettres, 1967. (not seen)

545. Ogoshi, Inzo, trans. *Pericles*. World Classics. Tokyo: Chikuma Shobo, 1967. (Japanese—not seen)

546. Ogoshi, Kazuso, trans. *Shakespeare Zenshu 3: Kigeki III* [The Complete Works of Shakespeare 3: Comedies III]. Tokyo: Chikumashobo, 1967. (not seen)

547. Shih-ch'iu, trans. *Sha-shih-pi-ya ch'üan chi*. Vol. 37. [n.p.:] Far East, [1967]. (Chinese—not seen)

548. Harrison, G.B., ed. *Pericles*. New York: Shakespeare Recording Society, [1968].

    This text was prepared to accompany the recording. See item 684.

549. Rotas, Vassilis, trans. *Pericles*. Athens: Icaros, 1968. (not seen)

550. Harbage, Alfred, gen. ed. *William Shakespeare: The Complete Works*. Baltimore: Penguin, 1969.

    James G. McManaway edited *Pericles*. See item 565.

551. Kittredge, George Lyman and Irving Ribner, eds. *Pericles, Prince of Tyre*. New Kittredge Shakespeares. Waltham, Mass.: Ginn, 1969.

    The introduction by Ribner reviews the history of *Pericles*, problems of text and source, and romance structure. The text, largely Kittredge's from his 1936 edition, *The Complete Works*, follows, with commentary by Kittredge and Ribner below the text.

552. Marín, Luis Astrana, trans. *Vida del Rey Enrique V. Pericles*. Madrid: Espasa-Calpe, 1969. (not seen)

553. Fried, Erich, trans. *Erich Fried/Shakespeare-Übersetzungen: Antonius und Kleopatra; Perikles, Fürst von Tyrus*. Vol. 3. Berlin: Klaus Wagenbach, 1970.

Pericles appears without an introduction.

554. Ribner, Irving, and George Lyman Kittredge, eds. *The Complete Works of Shakespeare*. Waltham, Mass.: Xerox, 1971.

Introductions by Ribner replace those Kittredge wrote for the 1939 edition. Even though Shakespeare wrote little, if any, of acts 1-2, he wrote most, if not all, of acts 3-5. Because the Quarto is "bad," the text is heavily emended. Most of the readings follow Kittredge. *Pericles* belongs to the tradition of medieval miracle plays, dramatized saints' lives that used presenters such as Gower to hold together episodic plots and to moralize. Beginning with *Pericles* and continuing in the succeeding romances, Shakespeare added to the ancient formula for fairy-tale romance a parallel plot involving parents and children.

555. Barnet, Sylvan, gen. ed. *The Complete Signet Classic Shakespeare*. New York: Harcourt, Brace, Jovanovich, 1972.

Ernest Schanzer edited *Pericles*. See item 538.

556. Courteaux, Willy, trans. *Verzameld Werk, IV: Comedies II*. Antwerp: De Nederlandsche Boekhandel, 1972. (not seen)

557. János, Arany, trans. *Összes drámai*. Vol. 1. Budapest: Magyar Helikon, 1972. (not seen)

558. Pasco, Richard, intro. *Pericles Prince of Tyre*. London: Folio Society, 1972.

Richard Pasco, who played Pericles in Douglas Seale's 1954 Birmingham production, introduces the play from an actor's point of view. Seale staged a fairy-tale *Pericles* with the Prince as a medieval Ulysses and a father akin to Lear. Included are portions of a review by a Birmingham theatre critic, a letter written by a member of the audience, and notes from Pasco's working copy of the play. The text is that of the New Temple

edition, edited by M.R. Ridley (1935). This edition
also includes eight colored drawings by Richard Moore
of Paul Shelving's costume designs for Seale's
production and a glossary by Jean Rook. See item 600.

559. Craig, Hardin and David Bevington, eds. *The Complete
Works of Shakespeare*. Rev. ed. Glenview, Ill.:
Scott, Foresman, 1973.

Following Craig's practice in the 1951 edition of
grouping the plays by genre within a chronological
period and preceding each group with an introduction
(see item 508), Bevington prefaces the four romances
with an essay, "The Period of Romances." The
introduction to *Pericles* opens with a summary of the
authorship and textual problems. *Pericles* seems a
revival of the stage romances popular in the 1580s, a
revival that set the Jacobean vogue for tragicomedies.
The Gower choruses divide the play into seven episodes
over which Gower presides as a reassuring figure of
providence who promises punishment for the wicked and
reward for the good. The characters are all one-
dimensional. If Pericles, the chivalrous knight of
romance, has a defect, it is the despair from which
Marina rouses him. She is typical of the heroines of
Shakespeare's late romances and folk heroines
generally. Her name suggests loss and recovery; like
Perdita in *Cymbeline*, Marina is a gift from the
hazardous and potent sea. She can convert the sinful
and cure the sick. In her curative powers she is like
Cerimon in *Pericles* and Paulina in *The Winter's Tale*.
Marina is that part of providence which rewards
patience with eventual good. The text, Craig's
revision of the 1864 Globe text (see item 497),
includes changes by Bevington. The notes remain
Craig's for the most part. General remarks by Craig on
the canon, dates, early texts, sources, and stage
history appear in three appendices. Appendix 1
includes an account of the publishing history of
Pericles. Appendix 2 includes discussion of the
sources for *Pericles* and its relationship to George
Wilkins' *Painfull Aduentures*.

560. Evans, G. Blakemore et al., eds. *The Riverside
Shakespeare*. Boston: Houghton Mifflin, 1974.

In the introduction to *Pericles*, Hallett Smith
considers dating problems, possible reasons for the

exclusion of *Pericles* from the First Folio, the
qualitative differences between acts 1-2 and 3-5, and
authorship problems. He also discusses three sources
for the play--Gower's *Confessio Amantis*, Twine's
Patterne of Painefull Adventures, and Sidney's
Arcadia--before turning to interpretation. *Pericles*
has an uneven style: some passages are sophisticated
and elegiac; others are sententious and naive. The
characters are uncomplicated. *Pericles* is a
characteristic romance; as such it is not realistic.
Modern critics emphasize the symbolic quality of the
play and are mainly interested in it as the first of
Shakespeare's romances, yet *Pericles* was popular in the
seventeenth century and has had a twentieth-century
revival. The *Pericles* text is based on the Quarto.
Act and scene divisions are taken from the 1864 Globe
edition (see item 497).

561. Smith, Hallett, intro. *"Pericles Prince of Tyre."* The
      Riverside Shakespeare. Edited by G. Blakemore Evans
      et al. Boston: Houghton Mifflin, 1974, pp.
      1483-1516.

      See item 560.

562. Hodek, Bretislav, trans. *Perikles*. Prague: DILIA,
      [1975?]. (not seen)

      This is a mimeographed actors' edition.

563. Lesberg, Sandy, ed. *The Works of William Shakespeare*.
      Vol. 9. Peebles Classic Library. New York: Peebles,
      1975. (not seen)

564. Edwards, Philip, ed. *Pericles Prince of Tyre*. New
      Penguin Shakespeare. Harmondsworth: Penguin, 1976.

      The introduction explains that the popularity of
Pericles led to the publication of George Wilkins'
novel, *The Painfull Adventures* (1608) and the pirated
Quarto (1609), the only substantive text of the play.
Mere glimpses can be seen in them of the *Pericles*
staged by Shakespeare's company. *Pericles* is a
deliberately artless play based on the story of
Apollonius in Gower's *Confessio Amantis* and another
version in Laurence Twine's *Patterne of Painefull
Adventures*. The Gower choruses, although poorly
recorded in the Quarto, skillfully combine narrative

with pantomime and stage action. The effect is
consciously medieval and nostalgic. The physical
locations of scenes, the formal groupings, ceremonious
action, and music create a sense of actuality rather
than illusion. Even though *Pericles* is a moral tale,
there is little connection between what Pericles does
and what happens to him; the Renaissance fondness for
romance admitted and enjoyed improbabilities and
absurdities. Accordingly, the action in *Pericles*
covers a lifetime, and each scene, removed from the
world of cause and effect, has importance in and of
itself. The sea connects the scattered events in
Pericles' lifetime. Continuity in *Pericles* depends on
relationships, particularly that of father and
daughter. Like Pericles, Marina undergoes ordeals, and
like a fairy-tale princess, in triumphing she has the
power to renew life in others. The focus of Marina's
trials is the brothel scenes, which interject realism
into romance. Such a mixture of genres suggests to the
audience that ideality can live amid and survive the
world of experience. *Pericles* is a vision of marriage,
the sexual union of husband and wife that produces the
stronger and more spiritual affections between parent
and child. For all the many references to the gods in
Pericles, there is no pattern of providence. Instead,
the mysterious restorative powers of Marina and Cerimon
seem divinely inspired. Did Shakespeare write
Pericles? In its attention to the sea and the
relationship between fathers and daughters, *Pericles*
closely resembles *The Winter's Tale* and *The Tempest*.
The only external evidence of authorship is the
titlepage attribution to Shakespeare in the Quarto.
Surely it cannot be argued that *Pericles* as it appeared
on the stage was wholly by Shakespeare, even though the
play seems conceived by one mind, namely Shakespeare's.
Perhaps, then, *Pericles* is a collaborated play.
Shakespeare may have written the first scene in acts
1-2 and most of acts 3-5; his collaborator may have
written most of acts 1-2, the scene between Cleon and
Dionyza (4.3), and the last three choruses in
decasyllables. The identity of the collaborator cannot
be determined. In fact, the problems of *Pericles* admit
no solution. The introduction is followed by a
selection of titles for further reading, the text, and
notes on the text. The edition concludes with "An
Account of the Text." This essay repeats with further
examples the argument that the Quarto text is reported
(see item 413). Although the text for this edition is

conservative, it incorporates many emendations and
alterations from previous editors.

565. McManaway, James G., ed. *Pericles Prince of Tyre*.
      Pelican Shakespeare 38. Rev. ed. 1977. Reprint.
      New York: Penguin, 1979.

      The introduction compares Lear and Pericles,
      characters Shakespeare created about the same time,
      gives a short history of the Apollonius story, mentions
      the continuing popularity of the romance genre during
      the Renaissance, and explains the chief characteristics
      of the genre. An account of the textual and authorial
      problems of *Pericles* follows, along with discussion of
      the relationship between the play and George Wilkins'
      novel, *The Painfull Aduentures of Pericles Prince of
      Tyre* (1608). The introduction also includes remarks on
      dating, court performances, and the popularity of the
      play during the seventeenth century. *Pericles* is
      experimental in content and form. Shakespeare
      concentrated on the relationship between a father and
      daughter, using the Gower choruses to give definition
      and distance to their adventures. Even though *Pericles*
      is a moving play in performance, it has seldom been
      played in the twentieth century. The recognition
      scenes in *Cymbeline*, *The Winter's Tale*, and *The Tempest*
      lack the emotional intensity of Pericles and Marina's
      reunion (5.1). The play is less effective in the study
      than on stage, however, probably because of the
      archaisms of Gower, the colloquial speeches of the
      fishermen and the brothel keepers, and the frequently
      garbled text. Like *Love's Labor's Lost*, *Pericles* is a
      mannered play. The Pelican text is closely based on
      the Quarto. An appendix includes paragraphs on the
      corrupt Quarto and a list of emendations.

566. Wright, Louis B. and Virginia A. LaMar, eds. *Pericles
      Prince of Tyre*. Folger Library General Reader's
      Shakespeare. New York: Simon and Schuster, Pocket
      Books, 1977.

      The *Pericles* section in the general introduction is
      titled "A Greek Romance for Shakespeare's Stage."
      Pericles dates from 1608-1609, a time when plays based
      on Greek romances were beginning to be popular. Most
      critics think Shakespeare wrote only acts 3-5, possibly
      revising someone else's play. Perhaps Heminge and
      Condell left *Pericles* out of the First Folio because of

Editings*Editions* 193

the corrupt text. The play is based on the Apollonius
legend found in Gower and Twine, chief sources for the
play. Pericles is probably an adaptation of the name
Pyrocles in Sidney's *Arcadia*. Like the *Arcadia*, George
Wilkins' novel, *The Painfull Aduentures* (1608),
parallels the play. *Pericles* was successful in its day
because its audience was accustomed to romances.
Shakespeare used the Gower choruses to help explain the
play. *Pericles* never regained its popularity after the
seventeenth century, although George Lillo wrote a
popular revision in 1738. Modern productions
infrequently stage the original version. The text,
which is based on the Quarto, is printed on right-hand
pages with notes and Folger illustrations on the left.

567. Rowse, A.L., ed. *The Annotated Shakespeare*. Vol. 3.
London: Orbis; New York: Clarkson N. Potter, 1978.

The *Pericles* introduction recalls that the Apollonius
story was near to hand in 1607, for in that year
Twine's *Patterne of Painefull Adventures* appeared in a
new edition. That same year Shakespeare's youngest
brother, Edmund, an actor also, was buried in St.
Saviour's, Southwark, near the monument to John Gower.
Pericles, like other of Shakespeare's plays, contains a
reference to monumental sculpture, "yet thou dost look/
Like Patience gazing on king's graves. . ."
(5.1.138-39); and the Gower choruses, Shakespeare's new
idea, form an "archaic framework" (p. 671) for
Pericles' far-flung adventures. The prevalence of sea
references in the play reflects the absorption of
Jacobean London with New World trading ventures. When
George Wilkins published his novel, *The Painfull
Aduentures of Pericles Prince of Tyre* (1608), he had
more than a pecuniary interest in Shakespeare's play;
Wilkins and Shakespeare had mutual friends, the
Monjoies, who later took lodgings in Wilkins' Turnmill
Street tavern, a meeting place for theatre people.
Pericles was popular for its spectacle and bawdy.
Studies of "the *Pericles* problem" involving the Quarto
and its publishing history can be dismissed. The text
is poor because the 1608 plague, which closed the
theatres for eighteen months and disrupted theatre
life, sent Shakespeare home to renew his family life.
When he returned to London, he became absorbed in
writing plays for Blackfriars, his company's indoor
theatre. Texts, taken from the 1900 Globe edition, are
illustrated with woodcuts, engravings, and photographs.

568. Simić, Zivojin and Sima Pandurović, trans. *Celokupna dela 4* [Collected Works]. Beograd: Bigz, Narodna knjiga, Nolit, Rad, 1978. (Serbian--not seen)

Borivoje Nedić introduces *Pericles.*

569. Odashima, Yushi, trans. *Shakespeare Kenshu.* Vol. 6. Tokyo: Hakusuisha, 1979. (not seen)

570. Bevington, David, ed. *The Complete Works of Shakespeare.* 3rd ed. rev. Glenview, Ill.: Scott, Foresman, 1980.

This edition groups the plays as comedies, histories, tragedies, and romances. Hardin Craig's essays have been omitted. The *Pericles* introduction remains that of the second edition (see item 559) except for a paragraph on one-dimensional characterization and paired opposites rewritten to emphasize the incest motif and Shakespeare's continuing dramatic interest in the relationship between fathers and daughters. Thelma N. Greenfield served as the *Pericles* advisor. Short bibliographies for the romances and *Pericles* are included at the end of the volume. The *Pericles* text is an emended version of the Quarto.

571. Giuliani, Alfredo, trans. *Pericle, Principe di Tiro.* Genoa: Ed. del Teatro di Genova, 1982. (Italian--not seen)

The edition includes an introduction, "Pericle: Teatro come felicità," by Franco Marenco. William Gaskill directed a production of *Pericles,* in Giuliana's translation, by Teatro di Genova in April, 1982, with Paulo Graziosi as Pericles and Elisabetta Pozzi as Marina. See item 637.

572. Komrij, Gerrit, trans. *Pericles.* Amsterdam: International Theatre Bookshop, 1982. (Dutch--not seen)

573. Berwińska, Krystyna, trans. *Perykles.* Warsaw: Pánstowowy Institute Wydawniczy, 1983. (not seen)

574. Słomcyzńki, Maciej, trans. *Perykles, władca Tyru.* Afterword by Juliusz Kydrýnki. Krákow: Wydawnictwo Literackie, 1983. (not seen)

575. Kot, Josef, trans. *Perikles*. Bratislava: Tatran, 1984. (Slovakian--not seen)

Alois Bejblík wrote the afterward, critical commentary, and notes for this translation.

576. Wilders, John, et al. *Pericles*. The BBC Television Shakespeare. London: BBC, 1984.

The edition opens with a Preface (pp. 7-8) and Introduction (pp. 9-16) by John Wilders, an essay on the production by Henry Fenwick (pp. 17-27), a cast and crew list (pp. 28-29), and an essay on the text by David Snodin (pp. 30-31). The Preface is a brief history of the play: its text, dating, sources, and productions. In his Introduction, Wilders identifies the text of *Pericles*, the 1609 Quarto, as poorly printed and the work of two, unequally talented authors. The play is a collaboration between a third-rate writer, who wrote acts 1-2, and Shakespeare, who wrote acts 3-5. Perhaps Shakespeare finished the play begun by someone else, or perhaps the two dramatists collaborated. In either case, the play is unified, in large part because of the presence throughout the play of ancient Gower as Chorus. Through Gower, Shakespeare offers his audience, not a realistic story like *Julius Caesar*, but an episodic myth or folktale. Simple and passive Pericles is a good man beset by misfortune. The audience perceives the power of Marina through her effect on others. She is Shakespeare's most saintly character. The fishermen and brothel inmates are the realistic characters of *Pericles*. Pericles, Marina, and Gower as Chorus link the self-contained episodes that make up the play. *Pericles* is an experimental play resembling the religious narratives depicted in church murals and stained-glass windows dating from the middle ages. *Pericles* was popular in Shakespeare's day because it concerns familial ties, the power of the elements, and supernatural wonders. Perhaps the response to *Pericles* is religious. In his essay, "The Production," Henry Fenwick says that most of the actors for the BBC production came to *Pericles* knowing little about it, yet they soon found that the power of the play lies in its eventful story. Director David Jones used different sets and costumes for each of the several countries in *Pericles*. Not water but sand dunes suggested the sea. Jones deleted only a little from the text (including lines from Gower's choruses).

Instead, he added two pages of Lysimachus' conversion
in the brothel from Wilkins' *Painfull Aduentures* (item
353) and had the riddles in Twine's *Patterne of
Painefull Adventures* (item 366) set to music and sung
by Marina to Pericles in the recognition scene.
Because it is a narrative drama, *Pericles* played well
on a small screen. On television the narrative moved
from one detailed setting to the next without
confusion. In the textual essay, David Snodin says
that the BBC text is that of Peter Alexander for the
1951 *Complete Works* (item 507). Additions and
substitutions from Wilkins and Twine are indicated in
the margins. Lines in the margin indicate cuts. Scene
numbers and descriptions are based on the camera
script. Stage directions appear when they differ
greatly from those in Alexander's text.

577. Nolte, G. "William Shakespeare, Pericles, Fürst von
     Tyrus: Deutsche Prosübersetzung mit Anmerkungen und
     Szenenkommentar" [William Shakespeare, Pericles,
     Prince of Tyre: A German Prose Translation with
     Annotations and a Commentary on the Scenes]. Ph.D.
     dissertation, Universität Marburg, 1982.
     Dissertation Abstracts International, 46 (1985):
     10/184C.

     This *Pericles* translation is based on the 1969
     Complete Pelican Shakespeare, edited by Alfred Harbage
     (item 550). The translation is in prose, and the
     annotations attempt a literal rendering of *Pericles*.

See also items 353, 390, 394, 399, 401, 405, 407-09, 413,
415-18, 421, 426-27, 438, 445-56, 453, 467, 471-72, 478,
485-86, 488-89, 491-96, 701.

VII. STAGE HISTORY AND RECORDED PERFORMANCES

PRODUCTIONS

578. January or February 1661. The Cockpit, London. The Duke's Company. Directed by William Davenant. Pericles = Thomas Betterton.

579. 1661. Salisbury Court Theatre, Whitefriars, London. The Duke's Company.

580. June 1661. Lincoln's Inn Fields, London. The Duke's Company.

581. August 1738. Theatre Royal, Covent Garden, London. *Marina*. Adapted by George Lillo. Pericles = Stephens. Thaisa = Mrs. Marshall. Marina = Mrs. Vincent.

582. 14 October 1854. Sadler's Wells, London. Directed by Samuel Phelps. Pericles = Samuel Phelps. Thaisa = Miss Cooper. Marina = Miss Heraud.

583. October 1882. Munich. Directed by Ernst Possart. Music by Karl von Perfall.

584. April 1900. Memorial Theatre, Stratford-upon-Avon. Adapted by John Coleman. Directed by Frank Benson. Pericles = John Coleman. Thaisa = Lily Brayton. Marina = Lilian Braithwaite. Cleon = Oscar Asche.

585. 1904. Munich.

586. 22-23 April 1920. Northampton, Massachusetts. Smith
      College Theatre Workshop. Adapted and directed by
      Samuel Atkins Eliot, Jr.

587. May 1921. The Old Vic, London. Directed by Robert
      Atkins. Pericles = Rupert Harvey. Marina = Mary
      Sumner. Gower = Robert Atkins.

588. 1924. Nationaltheater, Mannheim.

589. 1924. Stadttheater, Kiel.

590. 14 March 1926. New Scala, London. Fellowship of
      Players. Directed by Terence O'Brien. Pericles =
      Philip Desborough. Marina = Nancy Harker.

591. 1929. Maddermarket Theatre, Norwich. Norwich Players.
      Directed by Nugent Monck.

592. February 1933. Festival Theatre, Cambridge. Directed
      by Noel Iliff. Pericles = Godfrey Renton. Marina =
      Vivienne Bennett. Helicanus, Cerimon = Noel Iliff.

593. 29 June – 4 July 1936. Pasadena Playhouse, Pasadena,
      California. Directed by Gilmor Brown.

594. June 1939. Open Air Theatre, Regent's Park, London.
      Directed by Robert Atkins. Pericles = Robert
      Eddison. Thaisa = Sylvia Coleridge. Marina =
      Margaret Vines.

595. August and September 1947. Stratford-upon-Avon. Royal
      Shakespeare Company. Directed by Nugent Monck.
      Pericles = Paul Scofield. Marina = Daphne Slater.

596. 2 July 1950. Rudolf Steiner Hall, London. Under
      Thirty Group. Directed by John Harrison. Pericles =
      Paul Scofield. Marina = Daphne Slater. Bawd =
      Beatrix Lehmann.

597. 11 March 1952. Globe Theatre, London. Royal Academy
      of Dramatic Art. Directed by Robert Atkins.

598. 1954. Antioch, Ohio. Directed by Arthur Lithgow.

599. June and July 1954. Birmingham Repertory Theatre,
      Birmingham. Directed by Barry Jackson. Pericles =

Richard Pasco. Marina = Doreen Aris. Gower = Bernard Hepton.

600. 1955. Birmingham Repertory Theatre, Birmingham. Directed by Douglas Seale.

601. 1957. Ambigu, Paris. Adapted by Léon Ruth. Directed by René Dupuy.

602. 1957. Ashland, Oregon. Ashland Shakespeare Festival.

603. 1958. Royal Court, London. Royal Shakespeare Company. Directed by Tony Richardson.

604. 1958. Stratford-upon-Avon. Royal Shakespeare Company. Directed by Tony Richardson. Pericles = Richard Johnson. Marina = Geraldine McEwan. Gower = Edric Connor. Bawd = Angela Baddeley. Boult = Patrick Wymark.

605. April 1960. Barnard College, New York.

606. May 1960. Gniezno, Poland.

607. July 1963. Festival Hall, Hollywood. Hollywood Shakespeare Festival. Directed by David Bond.

608. 1967. Ashland, Oregon. Oregon Shakespeare Festival. Directed by Nagle Jackson. Pericles = Tom Donaldson. Marina = Jo Ann Bayless. Gower = Philip Davison. Antiochus = Glen Mazen.

609. 1969. Stratford-upon-Avon. Royal Shakespeare Company. Directed by Terry Hands. Pericles = Ian Richardson. Thaisa, Marina = Susan Fleetwood. Gower = Emrys James. Dionyza, Bawd = Brenda Bruce.

610. July-August 1973. Boulder, Colorado. Colorado Shakespeare Festival. Directed by James Sandoe. Pericles = William McLaughlin. Marina = Anne L. Sandoe.

611. 1973. Edinburgh. Edinburgh Arts Festival. Prospect Theatre Company. Directed by Toby Robertson and Eleonor Fagan. Pericles = Derek Jacobi. Marina = Marilyn Taylerson.

612. 1973. The Roundhouse, London. Prospect Theatre
      Company. Directed by Toby Robertson.

613. 1973. Stratford, Ontario. Directed by Jean Gascon.
      Pericles = Nicholas Pennell. Marina = Pamela Brook.
      Gower = Edward Atienza.

614. 1974. Comédie Française, Paris. Directed by Terry
      Hands.

615. 1974. Delacorte Theatre, Central Park, New York.
      Directed by Edward Berkeley. Gower = Bernard Hughes.

616. December 1975. Berkeley, California. Berkeley
      Shakespeare Festival. Directed by J.D. Trow.
      Pericles = Randall Duk Kim. Thaisa = Charlotte
      Moore. Marina = Marybeth Hurt.

617. January 1977. Kecskemet, Hungary. Directed by Jozsef
      Ruszt.

618. 1978. Berlin. Théâtre National Populaire, Lyon.
      Directed by Roger Planchon.

619. 1978. Théâtre des Amandiers, Nanterre. Théâtre
      National Populaire, Lyon. Directed by Roger
      Planchon.

620. March 1978. Nationaltheater, Weimar, East Germany.
      Directed by Heinz-Uwe Haus. Translation by Johann
      Joachim Eschenburg. Pericles = Manfred Heine.
      Thaisa, Marina = Silvia Kuziemski.

621. 1978. Deutsches Nationaltheater, Rudolstadt, East
      Germany. Directed by Heinz-Uwe Haus. Pericles =
      Manfred Heine. Thaisa, Marina = Silvia Kuziemski.

622. 1978. Tokyo.

623. 4 April 1979. The Other Place, Stratford-upon-Avon.
      Royal Shakespeare Company. Directed by Ron Daniels.
      Pericles = Peter McEnery. Marina, Antiochus'
      daughter = Julie Peasgood. Gower = Griffith Jones.

624. 1979. Central Park, Louisville, Kentucky. Directed by
      Gary McKim. Pericles = Michael Horenkamp. Marina =
      Debra Hale.

625. 1979. The Warehouse, London. Royal Shakespeare
      Company. Directed by Ron Daniels.

626. August 1979. John Hinkel Park Amphitheatre, Berkeley,
      California. Berkeley Shakespeare Festival. Directed
      by Julian López-Morillas. Pericles = Kevin Gardiner.
      Thaïsa = Beth Sweeney. Marina, Lychorida = Tracy
      Donahue. Gower = Barry Kraft.

627. 1979. Tokyo.

628. October 1979. Tuscaloosa, Alabama. University of
      Alabama Players.

629. 15 May 1980. The Warehouse, London. Royal Shakespeare
      Company. Directed by Ron Daniels. Pericles = Peter
      McEnery. Marina = Julie Peasgood. Gower = Griffith
      Jones.

630. 13 June 1980. Herod Atticus Theatre, Athens.
      Translated by Alexis Rosolimos. Directed by Alexis
      Solomos.

631. 9 July - 23 August 1980. Royall Tyler Theatre,
      Champlain, Vermont. Champlain Shakespeare Festival.
      Directed by Edward J. Feidner. Pericles = Paul
      D'Amato. Thaïsa = Stacey Gladstone. Marina =
      Jennifer O'Rourke.

632. 9 August - 6 September 1980. Theatre 62, Adelaide.
      State Theatre Company. Directed by Nick Enright,
      Nigel Levings, and Richard Roberts. Pericles = Wayne
      Jarratt. Marina, Lychorida = Vanessa Dowling.
      Thaïsa, Dawd = Susan Lyons. Dionyza, Diana = B.J.
      Cole.

633. 5 December 1980 - 7 May 1981. The Theatre in the
      Bowery, New York City. Jean Cocteau Repertory
      Company. Directed by Toby Robertson. Pericles =
      Elton Cormier. Marina = Deborah Houston. Gower =
      Craig Smith.

634. March 1981. Deutsches Schauspielhaus, Hamburg.
      Translated by Erich Fried. Directed by Augusto
      Fernandes. Pericles = Matthias Fuchs. Thaïsa,
      Marina = Elisabeth Seiler. Gower, Cerimon = Karl
      Heinz Stroux. Antiochus, Simonides, Lysimachus =
      Peter Gavajda.

635. 1981. Stuttgart.

636. 1982. Giulesti Theatre, Bucharest.

637. 1982. Teatro di Genova, Genoa. Translated by Alfredo
      Giuliani. Directed by William Gaskill. Pericles =
      Paolo Graziosi. Thaisa = Enrica Origo. Marina =
      Elisabetta Pozzi.

638. July 1982. Todd Union Theatre, Rochester, New York.
      University of Rochester Summer Theatre.

639. 2 December 1982. Théâtre du Ranelagh, Paris. La
      Compagnie Eden Théâtre. Translated by Marika
      Princay. Directed by Jean-Michel Noiret.

640. April 1983. American Place Theatre, New York. The
      American Acting Company of New York. Directed by
      Toby Robertson. Music by Carl Davis and Jim
      Cummings. Pericles = Tom Hewitt. Thaisa, Marina =
      Ronna Kress. Gower = J. Andrew McGrath.

641. 1983. Paramount Arts Centre, Aurora, Illinois. The
      Acting Company of New York. Directed by Toby
      Robertson. Pericles = Tom Hewitt. Thaisa, Marina =
      Ronna Kress. Gower = J. Andrew McGrath.

642. October 1983. Boston. Boston Shakespeare Company.
      Directed by Peter Sellars. Pericles = Ben Halley,
      Jr. Thaisa, Diana = Sandra Shipley. Marina =
      Jeannie Affelder. Gower = Brother Blue.

643. 31 October - 26 November 1983. Theatre Royal,
      Stratford East, England. Directed by David Ultz.
      Pericles = Gerard Murphy. Antiochus' daughter,
      Thaisa, Marina = Felicity Dean. Dionyza, Diana =
      Darlene Johnson. Antiochus, Cleon, Lysimachus =
      Brian Protheroe. Gower = Martin Duncan.

644. 1983 (Great Britain); June 1984 (USA). BBC Television/
      Time-Life Series. Directed by David Jones.
      Pericles = Mike Gwilym. Thaisa = Juliet Stevenson.
      Marina = Amanda Redman. Gower = Edward Petherbridge.

645. February 1984 - January 1985. On tour in England.
      Cheek by Jowl Theatre Company. Directed by Declan
      Donnellan. Pericles = Andrew Collins. Antiochus'

daughter, Marina = Amanda Harris. Cleon, Cerimon,
Boult = Duncan Bell.

646. March 1984. Andrej Bagar Theatre, Nitra, Yugoslavia.
      Directed by Josef Bednárik. Slovak trans. by Josef
      Kot. Adapted by J. Bednárik and Darina Karova.
      Pericles = Peter Staník. Thaisa = Eva Pavlíková.
      Marina = Eva Matejková.

647. August 1984. Parade Theatre, Kensington, New South
      Wales; Playhouse Theatre, Canberra, Australian
      Capital Territory. National Institute of Dramatic
      Art. Directed by Nick Enright. *Sea Changes*: a
      double bill, consisting of short versions of *Pericles*
      and *The Comedy of Errors*. Pericles = Steve Shaw.
      Thaisa = Antoinelle Blaxland. Marina = Fiona
      Stewart. Gower = Jenny Vuletic.

648. 11 February – 8 June 1985. Denver, Colorado. The
      Denver Center Theatre Company. Directed by Laird
      Williamson. Pericles = Byron Jennings. Thaisa =
      Carol Halstead. Marina = Robynn Rodriguez.

REVIEWS AND STAGE HISTORY

649. Meissner, Alfred. "Shakespeare's 'Perikles, Fürst von
      Tyrus' auf der Münchener Bühne." *Shakespeare
      Jahrbuch*, 18 (1883): 209–14.

      Director Ernst Possart introduced fairy-tale *Pericles*
      to the German stage on 20 October 1882 in Munich. Karl
      von Perfall provided the music (item 803). Possart
      replaced the scene in Antiochus' court with a narrative
      version told to Helicanus by Pericles. Likewise, the
      brothel scenes in act 4 were removed. Instead,
      Lysimachus rescued Marina from a slave-market and
      placed her in honorable surroundings. The production
      was lavishly staged with a sea of painted cloth,
      electric lights and machines, and well-orchestrated
      sound effects. After four performances, King Ludwig
      asked for a private staging.

650. Phelps, William May and John Forbes-Robertson. *The
      Life and Life-Work of Samuel Phelps*. London: Sampson
      Low, Marston, Searle, and Rivington, 1886.
      Photocopy, Ann Arbor: University Microfilms, 1969,
      pp. 139–47.

This account of Samuel Phelps's 1854-1855 season at
Sadler's Wells includes reviews of *Pericles* by Henry
Morley in the *Examinder*, Douglas Jerrold in *Lloyd's
Weekly London News*, and John Oxenford in *The Times*.

651. Morley, Henry. *The Journal of a London Playgoer*.
      Victorian Library Edition. 1891. Reprint.
      Leicester: Leicester University Press, 1974, pp.
      78-84.

      On 14 October 1854 Morley saw Samuel Phelps's
      production of *Pericles* at Sadler's Wells and wrote an
      account in his journal. Phelps's Eastern spectacle
      draped with exotic trappings an inferior play
      containing some fine poetic passages. In place of
      Gower, Phelps added explanatory passages of his own to
      several scenes; he also combined the two brothel
      scenes. Taking the lead himself, Phelps played the
      Prince as a melancholy man "pursued by evil fate" (p.
      82). The most outstanding feature of the production
      was the elaborate Sadler's Wells scenery and machinery.
      Phelps staged *Pericles* as a sea story complete with
      rolling billows, whistling winds, and a tossing ship.
      Banks of rowers pulled Pericles to Ephesus for the
      final scene while behind them a panorama gave the
      audience the sensation of moving on water. Costumes
      and scenes were Roman, Greek, and Assyrian. Without
      the dazzle of spectacle the play would not have
      succeeded "as a mere acted play" (p. 84).

652. Odell, George C.D. *Shakespeare--from Betterton to
      Irving*. 2 vols. 1920. Reprint. New York: Benjamin
      Blom, 1963.

      Pericles was performed three times on the English
      stage between the Restoration and the end of the
      nineteenth century. Volume 1 records two productions:
      early in the 1660s Sir William Davenant's company, the
      Duke's, performed the play at the Cockpit, and in 1738
      Marina, George Lillo's adaptation, was performed at
      Covent Garden. A description of Samuel Phelps's 1854
      Sadler's Wells production appears in volume 2.

653. Haddon, Archibald. *Green Room Gossip*. London: Stanley
      Paul, 1922, pp. 60-61.

Robert Atkins' 1921 production of *Pericles* at the Old
Vic was the first London production since Samuel
Phelps's 1854 production at Sadler's Well.

654. Asche, Oscar. *Oscar Asche: His Life, by Himself.*
      London: Hurst and Blackett [1929], pp. 88-89.

      This autobiography includes an unflattering account
      of Frank R. Benson's 1900 Stratford-upon-Avon
      production of *Pericles*, rewritten by John Coleman, in
      which Asche played Cleon to Coleman's Pericles.

655. Day, Muriel C. and J.C. Trewin. *The Shakespeare
      Memorial Theatre.* London: Dent, 1932, pp. 85-88.

      The book includes a description of Frank R. Benson's
      1900 *Pericles* production, the first at Stratford-upon-
      Avon. Benson staged John Coleman's adaptation, written
      15 years earlier, with Coleman as the Prince, during a
      week-long festival that included four other Shakespeare
      plays. Coleman removed act 1 and Gower and revised
      acts 2 and 4 considerably. Opinion was divided over
      the result.

656. Crosse, Gordon. *Fifty Years of Shakespearean
      Playgoing.* London: Mowbray, 1941, pp. 68-69, 77,
      142-43.

      The book contains two references to *Pericles*
      productions. Actresses in *Pericles* are mentioned in a
      discussion of Robert Atkins' direction of the Old Vic,
      1920-1925. The description of the Shakespeare
      productions at the Open Air Theatre in Regent's Park
      includes Atkins' 1939 revival of *Pericles*, which
      included five ballets: one of Diana worship at the
      beginning of the play, a ballet at Tyre to cheer
      Pericles after his return from Antioch, another of
      starving people at Tharsus, a knights' ballet at
      Simonides' court, and a ballet representing a sea
      storm. The scene with Simonides, Pericles, and Thaisa
      (2.4) was an amusing parody of the relations between
      Prospero, Ferdinand, and Miranda.

657. Ellis, Ruth. *The Shakespeare Memorial Theatre.*
      London: Winchester, [1948], pp. 136-37.

Appendix A contains the cast list for Frank R.
Benson's 1900 Stratford-upon-Avon production of
Pericles.

658. Hogan, Charles Beecher. *Shakespeare in the Theatre,*
     1701-1800: A Record of Performances in London,
     1701-1750. Oxford: Clarendon, 1952, pp. 374-75.

     A section on *Pericles* summarizes the differences
     between George Lillo's *Marina* (1738) and the last two
     acts of *Pericles* and names the cast in Lillo's Covent
     Garden production.

659. Nagler, A.M. "Phelps' *Pericles.*" *A Source Book in*
     Theatrical History (Sources of Theatrical History).
     1952. Reprint. New York: Dover, 1959, pp. 479-80.

     This section quotes Henry Morley's description of
     Samuel Phelps's 1854 production of *Pericles* at Sadler's
     Wells in *The Journal of a London Playgoer* (see item
     651).

660. García Lora, José. "Pericles y Apolonio (Con Motivo de
     una Representacion.)" *Suplemento de Insula* (Madrid),
     no. 111 (15 March 1955): 1-2.

     This review gives a history of the Apollonius legend,
     a description of the 1954 Birmingham production of
     Pericles, and a comparison of Shakespeare's play with
     the Spanish version of the story, *Libro de Apolonio.*
     Samuel Singer was the first to find the name *Perillie*,
     meaning "shipwrecked" in Spanish, given the hero in a
     French version of the story. See item 337.

661. Young, C.B. "The Stage-History of *Pericles.*"
     Pericles, Prince of Tyre. Edited by J.C. Maxwell.
     New Cambridge Shakespeare. 2nd ed. rev. Cambridge:
     At the University Press, 1956, pp. xxx-xl. See item
     513.

     This 1954 essay treats *Pericles* productions in
     England from the early 1600s to 1954 and mentions
     American productions at Smith College in 1920 (see item
     794) and the Pasadena Playhouse in 1936.

662. Griffin, Alice. "Theatre, U.S.A." *Theatre Arts*, July
     1957, pp. 70-72, 94.

This review mentions the Oregon 1957 Shakespeare
Festival production of *Pericles*.

663. Brien, Alan. "Theatre: Space Opera." *Spectator*, 18
July 1958, pp. 85-86.

Flash Gordon comics may have influenced the sets for
Tony Richardson's 1958 *Pericles* production at
Stratford-upon-Avon. The reunion at Mytilene was
tedious; the play itself is forgettable.

664. Byrne, M. St. Clare. "The Shakespeare Season at the
Old Vic, 1957-58 and Stratford-upon-Avon, 1958."
Shakespeare Quarterly, 9 (1958): 520-23.

This review of Tony Richardson's 1958 Stratford-upon-
Avon production of *Pericles* includes descriptions of
Loudon Sainthill's shipboard setting and Graeco-
Byzantine costumes. Edric Connor portrayed a West
Indian Gower. Angela Baddeley and Patrick Wymark
played the Bawd and Boult with straightforward
simplicity. The cast, including Richard Johnson as
Pericles, did not always deliver their lines forcefully
enough.

665. Hewes, Henry. "Broadway Postscript: Directors at
Work." *Saturday Review*, 41 (20 Sept. 1958): 31.

Tony Richardson's 1958 Stratford-upon-Avon production
was a light opera version with a Carribean Gower who
chanted his lines and Calipso-singing galley slaves who
rowed.

666. Matthews, Harold. "The Gauds of *Pericles*." *Plays and
Players*, August 1958, p. 26.

Director Tony Richardson swapped Gower, the medieval
bore, for a Negro singer, Edric Connor, in his 1958
Stratford-upon-Avon production of *Pericles*. The
gaudily staged brothel scenes kept the audience from
settling down for the quieter recognition scenes.
Photographs of the production by Angus McBean precede
the review (pp. 24-25).

667. "Pericles at Stratford: Music Removes Absurdities."
London Times, 9 July 1958, p. 6.

Tony Richardson, director of the 1958 Stratford-upon-
Avon production of *Pericles*, used plenty of music
played on ancient and exotic instruments and a chanting
Gower to enliven the first two acts until the lyrical
language that opens act 3 proclaimed itself.
Richardson set *Pericles* inside a rowing galley,
performing it as a fantasy that unfolds before the eyes
of simple sailors accustomed to romantic sea tales of
loss and recovery. At act 3, after the musical acts
were past, the actors, led by Richard Johnson, a
resounding and heroic Pericles, took over. Geraldine
McEwan was perhaps too sophisticated a Marina in the
brothel scenes, dominated by Angela Baddeley. But in
the recognition scene, McEwan rang true in the keenness
of her joy.

668. Veelo, G. Van. "Pericles in Stratford. Het
     Shakespeare Festival te Stratford on Avon 1958."
     Levende Talen, 198 (1958): 506-12. (Dutch--not seen)

669. Worsley, T.C. *"Pericles."* *New Statesman*, 56 (19 July
     1958): 80, 82.

     Tony Richardson's outstanding 1958 production of
     Pericles at the Royal Court featured an African Gower,
     who told his story to a spellbound ship's crew.
     Actions on stage were the sailors' imaginings. Loudon
     Sainthill designed his gandy sets to match the violence
     and crudities in Richardson's conception of the play.

670. Brahms, Caryl. "Not in the Folio." *Plays and Players*,
     August 1959, p. 12. (not seen)

     This is a review of Tony Richardson's 1958 *Pericles*
     production at Stratford-upon-Avon.

671. McBean, Angus. *Shakespeare Memorial Theatre 1957-1959:
     A Photographic Record with an Introduction by Ivor
     Brown and Photographs by Angus McBean*. New York:
     Theatre Arts, 1959.

     This collection contains eleven photographs from Tony
     Richardson's 1958 Stratford-upon-Avon production, with
     Richard Johnson as Pericles, Edric Connor as Gower, and
     Geraldine McEwan as Marina, and describes Richardson's
     production along with Loudon Sainthill's set.

672. Phillabaum, Corliss E. "Panoramic Scenery at Sadler's Wells." *Ohio State University Theatre Collection Bulletin*, 6 (1959): 20-25.

This essay discusses panoramas in Samuel Phelps's productions of *Pericles* (1854), *Timon of Athens* (1851 or 1856), and *The Tempest* (1849) at Sadler's Wells. Phelps used two types of panoramas in act 5 of *Pericles*: a sea and landscape which moved during Pericles' voyage to Ephesus by means of a painted strip of material attached to large cylinders and wound from one side of the stage to the other and painted flats which moved along grooves to mask Diana's approach in the recognition scene (5.1).

673. Jackson, Peter. "Obscurity to Limelight." *Plays and Players*, August 1960, pp. 8-9. (not seen)

This is a review of Loudon Sainthill's settings for Tony Richardson's 1958 productions of *The Tempest* and *Pericles* at Stratford-upon-Avon.

674. "American Shakespeare Festival Programs--1963." *Shakespeare Newsletter*, 13 (1963): 23.

Included in this listing is the Hollywood Shakespeare Festival production of *Pericles*, directed by David Bond, which opened 13 July 1963 in Festival Hall.

675. Trewin, John C. *The Birmingham Repertory Theatre 1913-1963*. London: Barrie and Rockliff, 1963.

The book includes a brief account of Barry Jackson's 1954, uncut version of *Pericles* with Richard Pasco as the Prince and Bernard Hepton as Gower.

676. Knight, G. Wilson. *Shakespearian Production: With Especial Reference to the Tragedies*. Evanston: Northwestern University Press, 1964, pp. 155, 259.

Sensitive and careful planning must precede the staging of the scenes of death and rebirth in *Pericles*. Tony Richardson's set for the 1958 production at Stratford-upon-Avon used dissolving techniques to suit the dream-like sequence of events. Lighting and costuming gave Marina a mystic gleam for her reunion with Pericles.

677. *Pericles, Prince of Tyre.* Directed by George Rylands.
      With Frank Duncan, William Squire, and Tony Church.
      The Marlowe Dramatic Society and Professional
      Players. London: Decca Records, Argo Division, 1964.

      This recording features Frank Duncan as Antiochus,
      William Squire as Pericles, Tony Church as Gower,
      Janette Richer as Thaisa, and Prunella Scales as
      Marina.

678. Trewin, John C. *Shakespeare on the English Stage
      1900-1964: A Survey of Productions Illustrated from
      the Raymond Mander and Joe Mitchenson Theatre
      Collection.* London: Barrie and Rockliff, 1964.

      Several productions of *Pericles* are mentioned: the
      1900 Stratford-upon-Avon production, adapted by John
      Coleman; Robert Atkins' 1921 Old Vic production;
      Atkins' 1939 Open Air Theatre production in Regent's
      Park; the 1947 Stratford-upon-Avon production, directed
      by Nugent Monck; a 1950 production in the Rudolf
      Steiner Hall, Baker Street, directed by John Harrison;
      Douglas Seale's 1955 Birmingham production; and the
      1958 Stratford-upon-Avon production, directed by Tony
      Richardson.

679. Willy, Margaret. "Shakespeare on Record." *English*, 15
      (1964): 57-60.

      This review for a general audience approves of the
      nine recordings of Shakespeare plays which completed
      the Argo Shakespeare series: *Titus Andronicus, Pericles*
      (see item 677), the Henry 6 plays, *Richard 3, The
      Comedy of Errors, The Merry Wives of Windsor,* and *All's
      Well That Ends Well.*

680. Shattuck, Charles H. *The Shakespeare Promptbooks: A
      Descriptive Catalogue.* Urbana: University of
      Illinois Press, 1965.

      This volume contains descriptions of the promptbook
      for Samuel Phelps's 1854 production of *Pericles* at
      Sadler's Wells, now in the Folger Shakespeare Library,
      Washington, D.C., two transcriptions of the promptbook,
      one in the Folger, the other in the Shakespeare Centre
      Library, Stratford-upon-Avon, and the promptbooks from
      Nugent Monck's 1947 and Tony Richardson's 1958

productions at Stratford-upon-Avon. The latter two
promptbooks are in the Shakespeare Centre Library.

681. Glackin, William C. "Rarely Staged 'Pericles' Shines."
      Sacramento Bee, 24 August 1967, p. C5.

      Under Nagle Jackson's direction, seldom-seen *Pericles*
      received a stylish and witty staging at the Oregon
      Shakespeare Festival in Ashland. *Pericles* is a fairy
      tale only partly written by Shakespeare. Probably
      little of acts 1-2 are by Shakespeare, but acts 3-5 are
      his entirely. Jackson moved the prosaic first two acts
      quickly from Antioch, with gates adorned by a string of
      heads, to a starving Tharsus full of citizens draped in
      black. Helping the action along was Philip Davison's
      believable and personable Gower. Jackson's outstanding
      scenes took place in a brothel curtained with beads
      where the disreputable and comic crew both threatened
      and amused the audience with their antics. For all the
      foolishness of the brothel scenes, Joanne Bayless moved
      the audience with her Marina's simple and beautiful
      spirit. Tom Donaldson as Pericles brought a personal
      force to his slow and sceptical resurrection in the
      recognition scene between father and daughter.

682. Hewes, Henry. "The Shakespeare Trail." *Saturday
      Review*, 50 (2 September 1967): 38.

      This 1967 production, directed by Nagle Jackson, was
      the second *Pericles* staged by the Oregon Shakespeare
      Festival. The play began with Elizabethan folk dances
      and ballads performed near the entrance to the open-air
      theatre, a reconstruction of Shakespeare's Fortune.
      Jackson's production was full of humor and "fairy-tale
      atmosphere." Glen Mazen played a Fu Manchu Antiochus
      with a Max Sennet pack to chase the virtuous and
      discerning Pericles, played by Tom Donaldson, from
      Antioch. The brothel scenes too were played with humor
      when Joanne Bayless' graceful Marina lectured her
      would-be seducers on chastity. The recognition scene,
      for all its implausibility, was moving.

683. Nichols, Dorothy E. "The Oregon Shakespeare Festival,
      1967." *Shakespeare Quarterly*, 18 (1967): 421-23.

      The outstanding acting and spectacle in Nagle
      Jackson's 1967 production of *Pericles* at Ashland caused

Nichols to question her belief that Shakespeare wrote
none of the play.

684. *Pericles*. Directed by Howard Sackler. With Paul
      Scofield, Felix Aylmer, Judi Dench, John Laurie,
      Miriam Karlin. . . . The Shakespeare Recording
      Society. New York: Caedmon, [1968]. (not seen)

685. Esslin, Martin. "Was kommt nach Peter Brook?
      Shakespeare in England: *Hamlet* im Centre 42, *Pericles*
      in Stratford and *Vorlorene Liebesmüh* im Londoner
      National Theater." *Theater Heute*, June 1969, pp.
      32-35.

      This review concerns the new generation of
      Shakespeare actors, directors, and spectators. Terry
      Hands's 1969 Stratford-upon-Avon production of *Pericles*
      was an unashamed parable of man's dual nature.
      Departing from the Brechtian and Absurdist productions
      of older Stratford directors Peter Hall and Peter
      Brook, Hands transformed fairy-tale *Pericles* into a
      neo-Platonic allegory of the soul's journey from sin to
      redemption. Ian Richardson graced the production with
      his simple rather than commanding Pericles.

686. Roberts, Peter. "First of a Cycle?" *Plays and
      Players*, May 1969, pp. 18-23.

      Terry Hands used the Quarto with emendations and
      additions from George Wilkins' *Painfull Aduentures* for
      his *Pericles* production at Stratford-upon-Avon. The
      doubled parts of Thaisa and Marina in *Pericles* and
      Hermione and Perdita in Trevor Nunn's production of
      The Winter's Tale, which also opened in Stratford
      during the summer of 1969, emphasized the similarities
      between the two romances. Hands presented the themes
      of time and love by contrasting Gower's medieval garb
      with the state of undress, resembling Renaissance
      painting, worn by the other characters and by showing
      the many attractions, false and true, called love.
      Especially noteworthy were Ian Richardson's restrained
      and commanding Pericles and Brenda Bruce's vivid
      Dionyza and Mytilene Bawd. Less effective was Emrys
      James, who used a Welsh accent rather than voice
      quality to underscore Gower's antiquity.

687. Speaight, Robert W. "Shakespeare in Britain."
      Shakespeare Quarterly, 20 (1969): 435-41.

Emrys James played a Welsh Gower and doubled as
Helicanus in Terry Hands's admirable 1969 production of
Pericles at Stratford-upon-Avon; Susan Fleetwood
doubled Thaisa-Marina less convincingly. Ian
Richardson was a graceful and moving Pericles.

688. "Stratford-upon-Avon Season Features Comedy and
Romance." *Shakespeare Newsletter*, 19 (1969): 21.

Included is a review of Terry Hands's 1969 production
of *Pericles* with phrases quoted from favorable
newspaper reviews.

689. Krag, Helena. "Moderne Shakespeare-tolkning i
Stratford" [Modern Shakespeare Interpretation at
Stratford]. *Samtiden* (Oslo), 79 (1970): 227-31.
(not seen)

The review includes notes on Terry Hands's 1969
Pericles production at Stratford-upon-Avon.

690. Sprague, Arthur Colby and J.C. Trewin. *Shakespeare's
Plays Today: Some Customs and Conventions of the
Stage*. Columbia: University of South Carolina Press,
1971, pp. 44-45.

Nugent Monck cut act 1 from the 1947 production of
Pericles at Stratford-upon-Avon because he thought the
act irrelevant and not Shakespeare's work.

691. Crouch, J.H. "The Colorado Shakespeare Festival—
1973." *Shakespeare Quarterly*, 24 (1973): 416-18.

James Sandoe's production of *Pericles* was excellent,
but the play is careless.

692. Elsom, John. "Theatre: Edinburgh Camp." *Listener*, 90
(1973): 294.

Toby Robertson and Eleanor Fagan's 1973 production of
Pericles set in a homosexual brothel was a travesty.

693. Hughes, Catharine. "New York." *Plays and Players*, 21,
no. 2 (1973): 45.

The play is tiresome and so was Edward Berkeley's New
York Shakespeare Festival production.

694. Jackson, Berners W. "Shakespeare at Stratford, Ontario, 1973." *Shakespeare Quarterly*, 24 (1973): 405-10.

Even though *Pericles* pleased large audiences from its 1973 mid-summer opening, it was treated grudgingly by critics. Nevertheless, Jean Gascon's straightforward production compared favorably with Toby Robertson's Edinburgh production, set entirely in a brothel. Jeremy Gibson edited the play for Gascon (see item 701), and Nicholas Pennell played a simple Pericles, a man more remarkable for what happens to him than for himself.

695. Lambert, J.M. "Plays in Performance." *Drama*, 111 (1973): 14-37.

The essay reviews 37 plays from the 1973 London theatre season, including the season's "oddity" (p. 32), Toby Robertson's production of *Pericles* at the Roundhouse, set entirely in an all-male brothel. The production, mainly enjoyable, jarred in certain scenes, such as the final one. The production was filled with music and gymnastics. Derek Jacobi made Pericles' story and poetry haunting.

696. Nightingale, Benedict. "Vice Squad." *New Statesman*, 31 August 1973, p. 294.

The Prospect Theatre Company's ironic *Pericles* at the 1973 Edinburgh Festival with its homosexual brothel and inmates borrowed from Lawrence Durrell's Alexandria was deplorable. The power of the recognition scene played by Derek Jacobi as Pericles and Marilyn Taylerson as Marina revealed the simple and moving story beneath the cynical veneer applied by director Toby Robertson.

697. Oliver, Cordelia. "Edinburgh 1." *Plays and Players*, 21, no. 1 (1973): 64-65.

Toby Robertson staged a likable "forbidden picturebook" production of *Pericles* for the 1973 Edinburgh Arts Festival, with Derek Jacobi and Marilyn Taylerson as a moving and simple Pericles and Marina.

698. Rubin, Don. "'Buy Canadian' or 'By Canadian': Stratford Festival." *Performing Arts in Canada*, 10, no. 3 (1973): 24-25.

Pericles was Jean Gascon's only successful production during the 1973 summer season at Stratford, Ontario.

699. Speaight, Robert. *Shakespeare on the Stage: An Illustrated History of Shakespearian Performance.* London: Collins, 1973, pp. 253-54.

Director Tony Richardson's 1958 Stratford production turned improbable *Pericles* into a sailor's yarn sung by West Indian Edric Connor as Gower. Richardson treated the play as an opera libretto backed by colorful settings, abundant music, and solid performances.

700. Trewin, John C. "Theatre: Profit and Loss." *Illustrated London News,* no. 6904 (1973): 100.

This is a review of several London productions. Toby Robertson's 1973 Prospect Theatre Company production of *Pericles* at the Roundhouse was cluttered, by Derek Jacobi as Pericles and Marilyn Taylerson as Thaisa-Marina maintained a simple grace.

701. Wylie, Betty Jane. "Play-Doctoring the Text of *Pericles.*" *Shakespeare Newsletter,* 23 (1973): 56.

This essay concerns the textual changes in Jean Gascon's 1973 production of *Pericles* at Stratford, Ontario. Jeremy Gibson, Gascon's textual editor, added original and rewritten lines, made cuts in acts 1-2, and included passages from Wilkins' *Painfull Aduentures* to the brothel scenes. Gibson used the Arden *Pericles* (see item 528), Bullough's *Narrative and Dramatic Sources of Shakespeare* (see item 366), and Wilkins' novel (see item 353) to prepare the play script.

702. Barnes, Clive. "Stratford Shakespeare a Simple Romance." *New York Times.* 6 June 1974, p. 49, col. 4.

Although the story was crisply and entertainly told, Jean Gascon's 1973 Stratford, Ontario, production of *Pericles* lacked depth. More emphasis should have been placed on the sexual issues of the play. Nicholas Pennell's Pericles was lightweight; Edward Atienza affected tiresomeness as Gower; and Leslie Hurry's settings were uninteresting.

703.   Galey, Matthieu. "Shakespeare, les yeux fermés.
       Périclès de Shakespeare à la Comédie-Française." *Les
       Nouvelles littéraire*, no. 2419 (1974): 19.

       This is a review of Terry Hands's production of
       Pericles by the Comédie-Francaise. Because of its
       authorship problems, the play is the province of
       theatre directors. Modern audiences are not the
       innocent spectators of the seventeenth and eighteenth
       centuries who saw *Pericles* more often than they saw
       Hamlet. Now *Pericles* must be produced either as a
       parody or as an esoteric play. Hands chose to produce
       the latter and succeeded, except for the scenery.

704.   Jackson, Berners W. "Shakespeare at Stratford,
       Ontario, 1974." *Shakespeare Quarterly*, 25 (1974):
       395-400.

       For its 1974 season the Shakespeare Festival staged
       three seldom-performed plays: *Love's Labor's Lost*, *King
       Lear*, and *Pericles*. Jean Gascon's production of
       Pericles with Nicholas Pennell as Pericles, Martha
       Henry as Thaisa, and Pamela Brook as Marina, was
       carried over from the past summer. The resulting cast
       changes in minor parts altered a few episodes only
       slightly. The performances of the three principals
       were firm and sure; the production was well integrated
       and successful.

705.   Jorgens, Jack J. "New York Shakespeare Festival,
       Summer 1974." *Shakespeare Quarterly*, 25 (1974):
       410-14.

       Edward Berkeley's 1974 production of *Pericles* at the
       Delacorte Theatre in Central Park was unsuccessful as
       pure entertainment. Performed by a troupe of traveling
       actors who entered and left on covered wagons, the play
       was preceded with tumbling, juggling, and clowning.
       Costumes and scenes were colorful and lavish: black
       jewels and gowns in Antioch, green-masked zombies in
       Tharsus, Pentapolis in green and gold, and the brothel
       scenes in red and white. Bernard Hughes's wry and
       skeptical Gower was excellent, but Berkeley's
       playfulness robbed *Pericles* of its symbolic power.

706.   Maddocks, Melvin. "Stratford Solution." *Time*, 103 (17
       June 1974): 72, 74.

In a review of the 1974 summer festival at Stratford, Ontario, Maddocks says that Jean Gascon's worthy treatment of the flawed *Pericles* avoided embarrassment without achieving a triumph.

707. Michener, Charles. *"Pericles* Regained." *Newsweek,* 15 July 1974, p. 91.

The first lines of poetry at the beginning of act 3 turn *Pericles* into a worthy successor to *King Lear* and a precursor to *The Tempest.* The review approves the set, costumes, direction, music, and acting in Edward Berkeley's 1974 Central Park production.

708. Miklaszewski, Krzysztof. "Edynburg jaki jest." *Teatr* (Warsaw), 29, no. 1 (1974): 20-22. (not seen)

This essay reviews Toby Robertson's 1973 Edinburgh Arts Festival production of *Pericles.*

709. Obraztsova, A. "'Prospect' at Home and Visiting." *Teatralnayazhyzn,* no. 17 (1974): 27-29. (Russian-- not seen)

The essay reviews Toby Robertson's Prospect Theatre Company productions of *Pericles* and *Twelfth Night.*

710. Pettigrew, John. "Stratford's Festival Theatre, 1973." *Journal of Canadian Studies,* 9 (1974): 3-9.

Despite the crudities and corruptions of *Pericles,* Jean Gascon's straight-forward production succeeded as underplayed spectacle. To prepare a smooth, playable text, Jeremy Gibson, Gascon's textual adviser, cut Escanes' part, omitted Lysimachus' speech giving his reasons for coming to the brothel, added lines for Lysimachus and the other brothel visitors, and cut considerably the final scene. Ensemble acting, which Gascon used, is necessary for a successful production of *Pericles.* Particularly effective was Edward Atienza's confident and engaging Gower, who strolled about the stage as "the writer, director, lighter, and chief star of the play. . ." (p. 7).

711. Senart, Philippe. "La Revue Théatrale." *La Nouvelle revue des deux mondes,* 4 (1974): 184-86.

This is a review of Terry Hands's 1974 production of
Pericles for the Comédie-Française. *Pericles* is a
pilgrimage to the source of happiness, a quest for the
grail; it is also a melodramatic novel. Instead of
staging the play in a fitting popular style, Hands gave
Pericles the reverent handling that should be reserved
for masterpieces. Some of his absurd ideas included
making the fishermen in act 2 talk like the country
people of Normandy and having the actors of the
Comédie-Francaise appear all but undressed. The
production was a spectacle in the worst taste.

712. Stedman, Jane W. "Pericles, Prince of Tyre."
      Educational Theatre Journal, 26 (1974): 532–34.

      Set in a transvestite brothel, Toby Robertson's
      Prospect Theatre production of *Pericles* at Her
      Majesty's Theatre in London is sometimes innovative but
      more often confounding. Yet Derek Jacobi as Pericles
      offers genuine emotion rather than shock. His
      Pericles, every inch a Renaissance king, is a husband
      and father in grief and joy alike.

713. Bartoshevich, A.V. "Perikles Trafal'garskoj ploscadi."
      Teatr (Moscow), 6 (1975): 126–27. (not seen)

      The essay presents an interpretation of *Pericles* and
      reviews Toby Robertson and Eleanor Fagan's production
      at the 1973 Edinburgh Festival.

714. Montagna, Barbara Jean. "1973–74 Stage Interpretations
      of *Pericles*." Ph.D. dissertation, University of
      Michigan, 1974. *Dissertation Abstracts
      International*, 36 (1975): 601A.

      This dissertation is a record of *Pericles* productions
      at the Shakespeare Festival, Stratford, Ontario, the
      Edinburgh Arts Festival, and the New York Shakespeare
      Festival. The account includes a stage history,
      staging descriptions, interviews with producers,
      reviews, and photographs.

715. Salgado, Gāmini. *Eyewitnesses of Shakespeare: First
      Hand Accounts of Performances 1590–1890*. London: Cox
      and Wyman; New York: Barnes and Noble, 1975.

      "Part I: 1590–1700" contains quotes from the
      anonymous pamphlet *Pimlico or Run Red-Cap* (1609) on the

popularity of *Pericles*, Gerrand Herbert's account of
the 1619 court performance, and John Downes' remarks in
Roscius Anglicanus (1708) on Betterton's *Pericles*.
"Part Two--to 1890" includes Henry Morley's diary
account, from *The Journal of a London Playgoer* (see
item 651), of Samuel Phelps's 1854 production at
Sadler's Wells.

716. Booth, Stephen. "Shakespeare in California and Utah."
      Shakespeare Quarterly, 28 (1977): 229-44.

      J.D. Trow's successful Berkeley Shakespeare Festival
      production of *Pericles*, which opened in December, 1975,
      matched a straightforward, perceptive Pericles with a
      versatile and officious Gower.

717. Foulkes, Richard. "Samuel Phelps's *Pericles* and
      Layard's Discoveries at Nineveh." *Nineteenth-Century
      Theatre Research*, 5, no. 2 (1977): 85-92.

      Inspired by Austen Henry Layard's Nineveh discoveries
      assembled for the Great Exhibition of 1851, Charles
      Kean produced Byron's *Sardanapalus* in 1853 and Samuel
      Phelps produced *Pericles* in 1854. Unlike Kean's
      pedantically researched and staged *Sardanapalus*, Phelps
      used Assyrian stage designs only at theatrical
      highpoints in *Pericles* and never with historical
      accuracy. The principal motif was the sea, not
      land-locked Nineveh. Phelps used the discoveries
      particularly in constructing an elaborate Assyrian
      court for Simonides in act 2. He also used the
      discoveries in act 1 for the Tharsus scenes, which he
      rearranged into harbor scenes, and in designing
      Pericles' ship for act 5. Phelps's production, without
      Gower and with a poorhouse instead of a brothel, ran
      for 54 performances.

718. Styan, J.L. *The Shakespeare Revolution: Criticism and
      Performance in the Twentieth Century*. Cambridge: At
      the University Press, 1977, p. 223.

      Christopher Morley designed a white, three-sided box
      lit from above with harsh light as the set for Terry
      Hands's 1969 *Pericles* production at Stratford-upon-
      Avon.

719. Evans, Gareth Lloyd and Barbara Lloyd Evans.
      Everyman's Companion to Shakespeare. London: Dent,
      1978.

      Pericles is mentioned in discussions of Samuel Phelps
      (pp. 125, 201), Nugent Monck (p. 165), and Paul
      Scofield (p. 202). The book also includes remarks on
      the text and sources and a plot summary (pp. 243–44).

720. Goldberg, Henryh and Rainer Kerndl. "Shakespeare
      phantasievoll inszeniert. Hohe Darstellungskultur
      des TNP aus Frankreich." *Neues Deutschland*, 14–15
      October 1978, p. 11.

      Roger Planchon, director of the Théâtre National
      Populaire of Lyon, on tour in East Germany at the 22nd
      Berlin Festival elevated *Pericles* from a fantastic
      fairy tale to a lavish allegory of human greatness and
      capability. The production drew on classical stage
      interpretations and on clichés, ironically played, from
      film and television.

721. Pálffy, Istvan. "Shakespeare in Hungary." *Shakespeare
      Quarterly*, 29 (1978): 292–94.

      During the 1976–77 theatre season, devoted
      Shakespeare plays rarely seen in Hungary, Jozsef Ruszt
      directed a production of *Pericles*, which opened in
      Kecskemet on 21 January 1977.

722. Pietzsch. Ingeborg. "Gäste aus Frankreich. T[héâtre]
      N[ational] P[opulaire Lyon] mit Molière and
      Shakespeare" [*Pericles* and *Antony and Cleopatra*].
      Theater der Zeit, 32, no. 12 (1978): 48–50.

      Director Roger Planchon and the TNP on tour presented
      Pericles to Berliners as an ironic fairy tale for
      moderns in which Prince Pericles performed his
      incredible hero's tasks in a dream landscape strewn
      with relics of modernity and antiquity. Under silver
      light the characters moved amid pink plastic wrap,
      outré shapes, urban litter, and the broken heads of old
      gods. Pericles and Marina represented pure love
      pursued in a world of refined incest. Planchon's
      modern folkdrama, which showed the influence of Brecht,
      Freud, film, and modern literature, brought its
      audience the excitement of novelty, questions, and
      doubts.

723. Sandier, Gilles. "Planchon et Shakespeare." *La Quinzaine Littéraire*, 292 (1978): 20.

    This is a review of Roger Planchon's productions of *Pericles* and *Antony and Cleopatra* at the Théâtre des Amandiers, Nanterre. Because Planchon is more gifted in historical analysis than in rendering fairy tales, *Antony and Cleopatra* is a more successful production than *Pericles*. The Prince's journey, like those of Ulysses and Arthur's knights, leads to the mysterious sources of human destiny. The play is a poet's dream that must be staged with delicacy. Instead, Planchon's modern contraptions and gadgets contravened imagination and dream. This heavy and ugly production had no magic and no music. Better to have seen *Antony and Cleopatra* twice than *Pericles* at all.

724. Scheller, Bernhard. "Der Verwickelte Pericles. 'Perikles Fürst von Tyrus' von Shakespeare am Deutschen Nationaltheater Weimar." *Theater der Zeit*, 33, No. 7 (1978): 41–42.

    Instead of treating *Pericles* as a fairy tale, a musical, or a parody, Heinz-Uwe Haus directed a stark production at the Deutsches Nationaltheater, Weimar, in a prose translation by Johann Joachim Eschenburg. Haus said that Shakespeare in his plays made concrete the discomfort of his contemporaries in order to point out the inner tensions of that society. The result on stage, however, is an overly aesthetic production of *Pericles* consisting of undifferentiated costuming from various times and places, markedly artificial dumb shows, speeches in monotone, and unsynchronized spoken choruses. Consequently, Manfred Heine's Pericles was inexact and unfocused. Sylvia Kuziemski, doubling the roles of Thaisa and Marina, could not convey more than the girlish allure of womanhood.

725. Stephan, Erika. "Shakespeare-Tage 1978: *Pericles* und *Sommernachtstraum*." *Sonntag 32*, 20 (14 May 1978): 4. (not seen)

    This is a review of productions of *Pericles* and *A Midsummer Night's Dream* at the Nationaltheater of Weimar and Rudolstadt.

726. Trewin, J.C. "*Pericles, Prince of Tyre* (1607-8)."
      Going to Shakespeare. London: Allen and Unwin, 1978,
      pp. 244-50.

      The chapter discusses *Pericles* briefly as an actor's
      play and mentions English productions in 1854, 1900,
      1921, 1939, 1947, 1955, 1958, 1969, and 1974.

727. Aire, Sally. "*Pericles*." *Plays and Players*, 26, no. 8
      (1979): 21, 23.

      Ron Daniels achieved a simple and moving production
      of *Pericles* at the Other Place, Stratford-upon-Avon, by
      staging the play inside the stark confines of a "cosmic
      circle" and dressing his characters in black, white, or
      grey, according to their morals. Peter McEnery's
      honest and passionate Pericles moved in his stage
      journey from the black incest of Antioch to Diana's
      white shrine at Ephesus. Defects in this otherwise
      outstanding production included Julie Peasgood's
      somewhat wooden Marina, Griffith Jones's sometimes
      inaudible Gower, and inferior music and dances.

728. Billington, Michael. "The Other Place: *Pericles*."
      Observer, 1979.

      Under Ron Daniels' direction, *Pericles* became a
      simple fairy tale of good and bad robed explicitly in
      black and white. The set was a wooden circle to which
      stage props were brought (skulls on poles in Antioch, a
      slanting rope for a lifeline in Pericles' storms at
      sea). Percussion sustained the blank verse in acts
      1-2. Peter McEnery played the handsome hero of faery,
      and Julie Peasgood's Marina was pure, not coy, in her
      virginity.

729. Cushman, Robert. "Merry Stratford." *Observer*, 8 April
      1979.

      Pericles stayed plain and dull, especially acts 1-2,
      despite the clever staging and largely competent acting
      directed by Ron Daniels.

730. Drury, Alan. "Farcical Demands." *Listener*, 101 (12
      April 1979): 523-24.

      This essay reviews the 1979 *Merry Wives of Windsor*
      and *Pericles* productions at Stratford-upon-Avon. Ron

Daniels wisely cut sections from *Pericles*, performed at
the Other Place with simple staging and acting.

731. Halstead, William P. *Shakespeare as Spoken: A
     Collection of 5000 Acting Editions and Promptbooks of
     Shakespeare.* Vol. 12. Ann Arbor: University
     Microfilms, 1979.

     The *Pericles* section opens with a bibliography of
     works used totally or partially as playing scripts,
     beginning with Wilkins' *Painfull Adventures* (1608) and
     ending with the promptbooks for Edward Berkeley's 1974
     New York Shakespeare Festival production and an
     undated, uncollated script in German. *Pericles* is
     collated with the twelve promptbooks for productions by
     Samuel Phelps (1854 and 1954), Henry Irving and Frank
     A. Marshall (1888), the Memorial Theatre (1890), Nugent
     Monck (1929 and 1951), Douglas Seale (1954), Toby
     Robertson (1958 and 1973), Terry Hands (1969), Jean
     Gascon (1973), and Edward Berkeley (1974). Appendix C,
     a list of Shakespeare plays produced by Shakespeare
     theatres from 1955 to 1974, includes nineteen
     productions of *Pericles*.

732. Hartwig, Joan. "Shakespeare in Central Park,
     Louisville." *Shakespeare Quarterly*, 30 (1979):
     208-10.

     Poor direction and acting marred the 1979 summer
     production of *Pericles* presented by the Committee for
     Shakespeare in Central Park.

733. Haus, Heinz-Uwe. "Aus der Konzeption der Weimarer
     Pericles-Inszenierung." *Shakespeare Jahrbuch*
     (Weimar), 115 (1979): 77-82.

     This essay is the director's account of the Brechtian
     treatment he gave his 1978 Marxist production of
     Pericles to show the adversities in man's life.

734. Maguin, Jean-Marie. "*Pericles*." *Cahiers
     Elisabéthains*, 16 (1979): 99-101.

     Because it is seldom staged, *Pericles* suffers from
     preconceived ideas more than other Shakespeare plays.
     Using a circular playing area, director Ron Daniels
     kept his 1979 production at the Other Place, Stratford-
     upon-Avon, starkly simple. Music pervaded the

production: Gregorian harmony sounded for Pericles'
music of the spheres; other music was modern.
Revelations took place in the spot-lit center of the
playing circle. Peter McEnery as Pericles and Julie
Peasgood as Marina were excellent. With a cast of
fourteen there was much doubling of parts, some actors
taking as many as six roles.

735. Metscher, Thomas. "Shakespeares Spätstücke, als
      episches Theater betrachtet." *Shakespeare Jahrbuch*
      (Weimar), 115 (1979): 35-50.

      Although the essay concentrates mainly on *The Tempest*
      in its argument that Shakespeare's romances are
      especially prototypical of Brecht's epic theatre,
      Pericles, *Cymbeline*, and *The Winter's Tale* are
      mentioned. Shakespeare's unconfined treatment of time
      and distance in *Pericles* is characteristic of Brechtian
      theatre, as are the non-verbal dumb shows, ballets and
      music, the detached Gower choruses, and the dialectic
      of the fishermen scene (2.1).

736. Mulryne, J.R. "'To Glad Your Ear and Please Your
      Eyes': *Pericles* at the Other Place." *Critical
      Quarterly*, 21, no. 4 (1979): 31-40.

      Previous productions of *Pericles* often used spectacle
      and the proscenium arch to maintain distance between
      play and audience. Ron Daniels' successful 1979
      production was performed on a small stage open on three
      sides to the audience. Daniels used Philip Edwards'
      Penguin edition (see item 564) as the basis for the
      script, incorporating into his stage version many of
      the changes that Terry Hands made for the 1969 Royal
      Shakespeare production. Although Daniels made fewer
      changes than Hands, he found some alteration necessary,
      including the addition of lines from Twine's novel to
      several scenes. He doubled many parts, most
      importantly those of Antiochus' daughter and Marina,
      instead of Thaisa and Marina as Hands had done.
      Daniels proved more inventive in the first half of the
      play when Pericles faces uncertainty than in the second
      half with its movement toward reconciliation.

737. Planchon, Roger. "Trembler devant Shakespeare."
      Cahiers Elisabéthains, 16 (1979): 59-68.

The director discusses *Antony and Cleopatra* and *Pericles*, which he produced for the Théâtre National Populaire. Shakespeare patched up an ancient play to create *Pericles*. Perhaps what has happened in Hollywood to the works of Fitzgerald and Faulkner may help us understand that Shakespeare's *Pericles* in its turn was also patched up. Shakespeare's late plays, like the scissors-art of Matisse in his late years, inspire new artists more than the earlier works. Despite its mutilated text, *Pericles* possesses an organic life enriched by the poignant theme of incest, one of the first fables of man. Antiquated things, such as *Pericles*, are particularly suited for adaptation in such a cynical and cruel age as our own. The theatre should not turn away from the marvelous, psychology, and moral debate. Modern poetry and painting have not done so. Surely fairy tales are dreams whose phantom personages search for a magic dawn in which to lose themselves. Such is the dream of youth.

738. Yamamoto, Hiroshi. "Adaptation of Shakespeare in Japan." *Renaissance Bulletin*, 6 (1979): 4-8.

Tokyo audiences saw *Pericles* performed in 1978 and 1979.

739. Clarus, Babis. *Vradini*, 16 June 1980, n.p. (Greek-- not seen)

Clarus reviews director Alexis Solomos' *Pericles*, translated by Alexis Rosolimos, performed 13 June 1980 at the Herod Atticus Theatre in Athens.

740. Dromazos, S.I. *Kathemerini*, 19 June 1980, n.p. (Greek--not seen)

Dromazos reviews director Alexis Solomos' *Pericles*, translated by Alexis Rosolimos, performed 13 June 1980 at the Herod Atticus Theatre in Athens.

741. Georgosopoulos, K. *Vima*, 18 June 1980, n.p. (Greek-- not seen)

Georgosopoulos reviews director Alexis Solomos' *Pericles*, translated by Alexis Rosolimos, performed 13 June 1980 at the Herod Atticus Theatre in Athens.

742. Jacobs, Laurence H. "Shakespeare in the San Francisco
      Bay Area." *Shakespeare Quarterly*, 31 (1980): 274-78.

      Julian López-Morillas' production of *Pericles* was the
      highlight of the 1979 Berkeley Shakespeare Festival
      summer season. With a cast of nine actors, there was
      much doubling, tripling, and swaping of roles.
      Pericles was played by three actors; Gower served as
      stage manager in the Noh-style production. The company
      gave a repeat performance at the MLA convention in
      December.

743. Margaritas, A. *Ta Nea*, 21 June 1980, n.p. (Greek--not
      seen)

      Margaritas reviews director Alexis Solomos' *Pericles*,
      translated by Alexis Rosolimos, performed 13 June 1980
      at the Herod Atticus Theatre in Athens.

744. Morley, Sheridan. "Tyre Marks." *Punch*, 11 June 1980,
      p. 932.

      Ron Daniels' Royal Shakespeare Company production of
      Pericles, played in London at the Warehouse, was a
      skillful staging of a silly play. Griffith Jones
      portrayed a theatrical and spellbinding Gower.

745. Nightingale, Benedict. "Sexual Pain." *New Statesman*,
      23 May 1980, p. 791.

      This review mentions disparagingly Ron Daniels'
      production of *Pericles*, played in London at the
      Warehouse.

746. Pearce, G.M. *"Pericles."* *Cahiers Elisabéthains*, 18
      (1980): 93-94.

      Director Ron Daniels successfully moved his *Pericles*
      production from Stratford to the Warehouse in London.
      Music was vital to both productions. With the
      musicians playing in the gallery because of the smaller
      quarters at the Warehouse, the players acted within the
      formal confines of a "magic circle." Ritualistic
      presentation made the fantasies of *Pericles* more
      acceptable.

747. Roberts, Alan. *The Advertiser* (Adelaide, Australia),
      15 August 1980, p. 17. (not seen)

Roberts reviews directors Nick Enright, Nigel Levings, and Richard Roberts' production of *Pericles* at Theatre 62, Adelaide, from 9 August through 6 September 1980.

748. Sotiriadis, H. *Exormisi*, 29 June 1980, n.p. (Greek--not seen)

Sotiriadis reviews director Alexis Solomos' *Pericles*, translated by Alexis Roslimos, performed 13 June 1980 at the Herod Atticus Theatre in Athens.

749. Themelis. *Rizospastis*, 21 June 1980, n.p. (Greek--not seen)

Themelis reviews director Alexis Solomos' *Pericles*, translated by Alexis Rosolimos, performed 13 June 1980 at the Herod Atticus Theatre in Athens.

750. Trewin, J.C. "Revealing a Character." *Illustrated London News*, July 1980, p. 80.

Ron Daniels' Stratford production of *Pericles* moved successfully to smaller quarters at London's Warehouse Theatre. This production and its cast showed concern for language. It is therefore unfortunate that Daniels' sea storm was louder than Pericles' speech, "Thou god of this great vast."

751. Wallach, Susan Levi. "Berkeley Shakespeare Festival." *Theatre Crafts*, 14, no. 4 (Sept. 1980): 26, 122.

The 1979 Berkeley Shakespeare Festival production of *Pericles* won the Bay Area Critics Circle awards for best production, direction, and costume design.

752. Ward, Peter. "A *Pericles* sans Luxury." *The Australian* [Adelaide], 18 August 1980, p. 10.

Pericles demands a more formal style than the bedtime story for adults offered Adelaide at Theatre 62 by the South Australian State Theatre Company, directed by Nick Enright. Wayne Jarratt gave a satisfactory performance as Pericles, and the recognition scene was moving.

753. Warren, Roger. "Shakespeare at Stratford and the
      National Theatre, 1979." *Shakespeare Survey*, 33
      (1980): 169-80.

      Pericles at Stratford-upon-Avon and *As You Like It* at
      the National Theatre, London, were the outstanding
      productions of 1979. Ron Daniels' production of
      Pericles at the Other Place used no set and simple
      costumes. The scene at Pentapolis was too elaborate,
      but the brothel and reunion scenes were effective.
      Daniels made cuts involving Helicanus and added
      portions from Wilkins' *Painfull Aduentures* to the
      brothel scenes and the reunion of Pericles and Marina.

754. Babula, William. *Shakespeare in Production, 1935-1978*.
      New York: Garland, 1981, pp. 251-54.

      The *Pericles* section lists six major productions:
      those of Tony Richardson at Stratford-upon-Avon in
      1958, Nagle Jackson at Ashland, Oregon, in 1967, Terry
      Hands at Stratford-upon-Avon in 1969, Toby Robertson in
      1973 at the Roundhouse, London, Jean Gascon in 1973 at
      Stratford, Ontario, and Edward Berkeley in 1974 at the
      Delacorte Theatre, New York. Babula follows each
      listing with a summary of one, two, or three reviews.

755. Brissenden, Alan. "Shakespeare in Adelaide,"
      Shakespeare Quarterly, 32 (1981): 363-64.

      When directors Nick Enright, Nigel Levings, and
      Richard Roberts cut the first three scenes from the
      State Theatre Company production of *Pericles*, staged
      from 9 August through 6 September 1980 at Theatre 62 in
      Adelaide, they did no structural harm, but the sinister
      theme of incest between father and daughter was lost.
      The smallness of the double-sided stage insured
      audience awareness of the doubling of parts: Thaisa and
      the Bawd, Boult and Cerimon, Lichorida and Marina,
      Dionyza and Diana. Wayne Jarratt lifted the production
      beyond itself with his grasp of poetic delivery and his
      sensitive portrayal of a prince of romance.

756. Ehrich, Brigitte. "Dichter im Computer-Test."
      Hamburger Abendblatt, 24 March 1981, p. 9.

      Those who saw *Pericles* staged by director Augusto
      Fernandes at the Hamburg Schauspielhaus in the modern
      translation by Erich Fried knew *Pericles* to be

authentic. Translator Fried thinks that *Pericles* was published from an unrevised text. Computer tests which analyze common word-pairs confirm the play as Shakespeare's. Director Fernandes staged *Pericles* as an oriental fairy tale lightly sketched so that the audience might travel in its imagination with Pericles.

757. Fox, Terry Curtis. "The Right Rite." *Village Voice,* 31 Dec. 1980 - 6 Jan. 1981, p. 67.

In its American debut by the Jean Cocteau Repertory of New York, Toby Robertson's production of *Pericles* managed to find the heart of the play. Always extremes were accentuated: the play was set in a brothel; Gower appeared as a *"Cabaret*-MC"; false lovers were played by men dressed as women and women dressed as men. Robertson's *Pericles* was "a rite of purification" for which characters walked in and out of different sexual roles. At the end of the play, the brothel inmates on the left of the stage joined in a joyous song with the characters standing in white on the righteous side.

758. Karasek, Hellmuth. "Märchen-Wahrheit." *Theater Heute,* 22, no. 5 (1981): 23-25.

Augusto Fernandes' 1981 Hamburg production of *Pericles* at the Deutsches Schauspielhaus presented a recognition scene between Pericles and Marina that was both a coup de theatre and a lesson in worldly experience and utopian hope. *Pericles,* like Shakespeare's other late romances, concerns the fairy-tale theme of old age. Accordingly, Fernandes' emphasis was on the recognition between Pericles and Marina, the young daughter in the father's arms. Gower merely recounted to the audience the later reunion of Pericles and Thaisa at Ephesus as a dream-vision. Marina in Pericles' arms brought the audience back to the incest between Antiochus and his daughter at the beginning of the play. Fernandes presented the opening scene as an oriental enigma responsible for the errors and wanderings that make up the rest of *Pericles.* Karl-Heinz Stroux as Gower gave an ironic and distanced recounting of the accidents that come to a happy end. Shakespeare's late romances may be more interesting for form than content.

759. Rothwell, Kenneth S. "Champlain [Vermont] Shakespeare Festival." *Shakespeare Quarterly,* 32 (1981): 185-87.

Edward J. Feidner directed a Brechtian epic theater
production of *Pericles* for the 1980 Champlain
Shakespeare Festival, complete with tableaux,
illustrations, and distancing effects. Settings often
suggested the Far East more than the Levant with Paul
D'Amato's Pericles a wandering Marco Polo. Motifs from
street theatre and Chinese theatre (marching, clapping,
waving plumes and streamers, percussive music)
contributed to the theatrical and deliberately naive
stage effects.

760.   Warnecke, Klare. "Der Zadek--Aufguss eines
       Argentiniers." *Die Welt*, 6 April 1981, p. 23.

A director must understand *Pericles* as symbolic of
the mysterious workings of destiny, not as a mere
spectacle and a collection of grotesque scenes. Yet
Argentine director Augusto Fernandes gave Hamburgers a
1981 production of *Pericles* that was all surface
paraphernalia and clamor with no regard for the wonders
and awesome seriousness at work in this play about
patience. Granted that there was much to amuse in
Fernandes' spectacle; nevertheless, this parody of
Shakespeare missed the spiritual power of *Pericles*.
The successful director of the evening was the engaging
Gower played by Karl-Heinz Stroux, whose wit and
comedic talent come from the old school. Stroux
managed as well to strike sparks from Erich Fried's new
translation, which remains inferior to that of Tieck.

761.   Winzer, Klaus-Dieter. "Regie, Reisen und das Resümee:
       Über Inszenierungserfahrungen des Heinz-Uwe Haus."
       Nationalzeitung Berlin (West), 1 August 1981, p. 4.
       (not seen)

762.   Albala, Radu. "Pericle de Shakespeare pe scena
       teatrului Giulesti [Shakespeare's *Pericles* at the
       Giulesti Theatre]." *Theatrul* (Bucharest), 1 (1982):
       32-34. (Romanian--not seen)

763.   Habicht, Werner. "Romance and History on Some West
       German Stages." *Shakespeare Quarterly*, 33 (1982):
       510-13.

Pericles was revived for West German audiences
several times in 1981, most notably by the Deutsches
Schauspielhaus, Hamburg, in Erich Fried's translation.
Pericles, played by Matthias Fuchs, made his way

through a spectacular and stylized fairy-tale world.
Veteran actor Karl-Heinz Stroux, presented an aged
Gower both knowing and naive who charmed his audience
into belief with his tale and his acts (as Cerimon he
restores Thaisa). The considerable doubling of parts
(Antiochus/Simonides/Lysimachus, Dionyza/Lychorida/
Bawd/Neptune, Gower/Cerimon, Helicanus/Cleon, Thaisa/
Marina) often suggested thematic patterns. Diana's
appearance in the recognition scene was omitted, Gower
summarizing her role at the end of the play.

764. Silvestru, Valentin. "Pericle." *Romania Literara*, 3
      (1982): 6. (Romanian--not seen)

      Silvestru reviews a realistic and stylized production
      of *Pericles* at the Giulesti Theatre.

765. Baker, Nick. "Youthful Image." *Times Educational
      Supplement*, 11 November 1983, p. 22.

      Pericles has more substance than David Ultz's 1983
      production at the Theatre Royal, Stratford East.
      Martin Duncan's youthfully-portrayed Gower delivered
      clockwork parodies of Chaucerian rhyme. The music
      likewise was jerky of tempo. Costumes were colored
      according to kingdom. Gerard Murphy's credible
      Pericles remained unaccountably divorced from the
      production.

766. Barthos, Michael W. "Pericles, Prince of Tyre."
      Shakespeare Bulletin (formerly *Bulletin of the New
      York Shakespeare Society*), 1, no. 12 (June 1983):
      5-6.

      Barthos reviews a performance of director Toby
      Robertson's *Pericles* production played in Aurora,
      Illinois, by John Houseman's Acting Company of New York
      on tour. Robertson presented *Pericles* as a psychodrama
      set in "an institution," according to program notes.
      Although the *Cabaret* style and often transvestite
      characters came close to burlesque, the production
      never descended into tastelessness. Robertson's
      Pericles was filled with music, song, and dance. The
      cast included Tom Hewitt as Pericles, J. Andrew McGrath
      as Gower, and Ronna Kress as Thaisa and Marina.

767. Boxill, Roger and Arthur Ganz. "Shakespeare in New
     York City." *Shakespeare Quarterly*, 34 (1983):
     472-76.

     Toby Robertson set his production of *Pericles* in a
     brothel when he staged it for the Jean Cocteau
     Repertory in 1980. Three years later, in April 1983,
     he and the Acting Company of New York presented it in
     an asylum. At the end of Robertson's send-up, the
     actors exchanged their costumes for the pajamas they
     first appeared in, and Gower, a cabaret M.C., sang his
     Epilogue to the same pseudo-Kurt Weill tune the
     audience had heard him sing many times before. Clever
     miming and the representation of the fishermen as a
     circus act of tumbling clowns were reminiscent of the
     ingenious staging techniques of Trevor Nunn's *Nicholas
     Nickleby* and Peter Brook's *Marat/Sade*. But Robertson
     turned romance to camp with the perversions of
     transvestite daughters for Antiochus and Cleon,
     Antiochus as a drag queen, and a sado-masochistic
     Boult. The family scene at the end of the play hinted
     at a repetition of the incest Pericles ran from at the
     first of the play, but it formed no integral part of
     the production.

768. Gordon, Giles. "Ace." *Spectator*, 12 November 1983, p.
     34.

     Even though undercast (Brian Protheroe played all the
     kings, Darlene Johnson played all the queens, and
     Felicity Dean played Thaisa and Marina), David Ultz's
     1983 production of *Pericles* at the Theatre Royal,
     Stratford East, was popular fun because of Ultz's
     designs. Hanging against a black brick stage were
     fruit, foliage, and seagulls. Five packing cases
     opened up to reveal Antioch, Tharsus, Pentapolis,
     Ephesus, and Mytilene.

769. Gussow, Mel. "Stage: Acting Company." *New York Times*,
     24 April 1983, Section 1, p. 53.

     In 1981 Toby Robertson staged a production of
     Pericles for the Jean Cocteau Repertory that was a
     mixture of Genet's *The Balcony* and the musical *Caberet*.
     His 1983 "deconstructionist" production for the Acting
     Company at the American Place Theatre was an
     androgynous and eccentric version of *Pericles* set in a
     madhouse. The proficient and poised acting, however,

outweighed the zany direction; and the singing, begun by J. Andrew McGrath as Gower, warranted a musical *Pericles* someday.

770. Kroll, Jack. "Daring to Be Different." *Newsweek*, 14 November 1983, p. 83.

In his first season as artistic director for the Boston Shakespeare Company, Peter Sellars turned his 1983 low-budgeted promotion of *Pericles* into an energetic and imaginative success. In the erotic and poetic episode in Antioch, a muscular Antiochus introduced his alluring daughter to Prince Pericles, played effectively by Ben Halley, Jr., in the nineteenth-century grand manner. As Gower, Boston street performer Brother Blue used jive cadences to tell the tale. A swinging light in the scene of Marina's sea-birth suggested a dizzying storm at sea. Sellars mixed bawdy vulgarity and chaste romanticism in the brothel scenes. Pericles' loss of Marina threw him into a skid-row withdrawal from life before he woke in the emotional recognition scene.

771. Lieblein, Leanore. "*Périclès, Prince de Tyr.*" *Educational Theatre Journal* (Columbia, Mo.), 35 (May 1983): 262-63.

Lieblein reviews director Jean-Michel Noiret's *Pericles* adaptation by La Compagnie Eden Théâtre at the Théâtre du Ranelagh, Paris, 2 December 1982. Gianni Vianello's staging, a black box filled with ancient ruins and modern junk, set the tone for Noiret's heavily emended, reshuffled, and undercutting version, translated by Marika Princay. In contrast to earlier grotesqueries, the reunion with Thaisa was played seriously, but too late.

772. Lubbock, Tom. "*Pericles*: Stratford East," *Plays and Players*, December 1983, p. 42.

If *Pericles* is a bad play, then better to neglect it than play it for laughs as did director David Ultz. Few serious passages were heard, and those few seemed chosen. As a consequence, the truly comic scenes suffered from the almost constant mockery.

773. Burgess, Tyrrell. "No Skimping." *Times Educational Supplement*, 5 October 1984, p. 26.

Director Declan Donnellan and the seven-person Cheek
by Jowl Theatre Company on tour in England in 1984 and
1985 staged a thoughtful and spirited *Pericles* with few
actors, costumes, or sets. *Pericles* is so seldom
performed that seeing a performance is like seeing a
new Shakespeare play.

774. Burrows, Jill. "Match Play." *Times Educational
     Supplement*, 17 February 1984, p. 25.

Declan Donnellan directed the six-person Cheek by
Jowl Theatre Company in a "placard presentation" of
Pericles that toured England in 1984 and 1985.
Donnellan achieved clarity in *Pericles* at the expense
of depth.

775. "Two Plays Suit NIDA Players, Director Says," *Canberra
     Times*, 14 August 1984, p. 12.

Under the direction of Nick Enright, graduating
students from Australia's National Institute of
Dramatic Arts performed two Shakespeare plays suited to
the vitality and musical aptitudes of the group--*The
Comedy of Errors* and *Pericles*. The two plays,
presented as "Sea Changes," have in common the theme of
a husband and wife reunited after years of separation
and trials. *Pericles* was trimmed, including much of
the opening scenes, to give it a playing time of an
hour and a half. *The Comedy of Errors*, already brief,
was cut slightly to play in an hour and a quarter.
Saturday audiences saw both plays with a dinner
interval between. "Sea Changes" played for two weeks
in Sydney before traveling to Canberra's Playhouse for
a week. From Canberra, the production moved to
Newcastle.

776. F-a. *Hlas l'udu*, 16 March 1984. (not seen)

This is a review of Josef Bednárik's 1984 production
of *Pericles* in Nitra, Yugoslavia, at the Andrej Bagar
Theatre.

777. Hageman, Elizabeth H. "Shakespeare in Massachusetts,
     1983," *Shakespeare Quarterly*, 35 (1984): 224.

Peter Sellars directed the Boston Shakespeare Company
production of *Pericles* (6-30 October 1983) in a
"deconstructive method." A twentieth-century Gower

called Brother Blue narrated while an African Pericles
spoke eloquent rhetoric to nonsense characters in
assorted costumes (fishermen in plaid shirts, Simonides
in evening dress, knights in business suits). The mood
of the scenes that Pericles wandered into were
patternless and his Marina woodenly acted.

778.   Hewitt, Hope. "'Pericles' a Bit of a Marathon,"
       Canberra Times, 17 August 1984, p. 31.

       Uneven and emblematic *Pericles* made a challenge for
       graduating students of the National Institute of
       Dramatic Arts. Director Nick Enright responded by
       cutting the text severely, including many of Gower's
       couplets, suffusing what was left with music, and
       doubling many roles. But too much compression led to
       too many laughs and a pell-mell pace. What poetry
       there is in *Pericles* lacked fire and conviction and
       could barely be heard above the youthful romp.

779.   Kemp, Peter. "Between Crest and Trough." *Times
       Literary Supplement*, 21 December 1984, p. 1476.

       What made fantastic and various *Pericles* succeed for
       the audience of the BBC television series was David
       Jones's lavish and naturalistic production. Each
       setting was given full treatment and contrasted with
       the other. Thus, Antioch was full of sharp grilles,
       weapons, plants, and discordant music, whereas
       Pentapolis was a white and gold court filled with
       harmonies. The link between the disparate places was
       kingship and parenthood. The first half of the play
       followed the trials of the father, the second half
       those of the daughter. Amanda Redman was an innocent
       and courageous Marina; Mike Gwilym's Pericles was
       energetic and yet wary of life's blows. Most
       impressive was Edward Petherbridge's melancholy and
       Celtic-accented Gower. Because the production strove
       for verisimilitude, Marina's age was raised from 14 to
       16 and source material in prose was added to Marina and
       Lysimachus' discussion in the brothel.

780.   Kippax, H.G. *Sydney Morning Herald*, 3 August 1984, p.
       10. (not seen)

       This is a review of "Sea Changes," Nick Enright's
       1984 production in Australia of *The Comedy of Errors*
       and *Pericles*.

781. Mačugová, Gizela. *Ľud*, 19 May 1984. (not seen)

This is a review of Josef Bednárik's 1984 production of *Pericles* in Nitra, Yugoslavia, at the Andrej Bagar Theatre.

782. *National Times* (Sydney), 27 July - 2 August 1984, p. 32. (not seen)

This is a review of "Sea Changes," Nick Enright's 1984 production in Australia of *The Comedy of Errors* and *Pericles*.

783. *National Times* (Sydney), 3-9 August 1984, p. 31. (not seen)

This is a review of "Sea Changes," Nick Enright's 1984 production in Australia of *The Comedy of Errors* and *Pericles*.

784. *National Times* (Sydney), 17-23 August 1984, p. 34. (not seen)

This is a review of "Sea Changes," Nick Enright's 1984 production in Australia of *The Comedy of Errors* and *Pericles*.

785. Štefko, Vladimír. *Nové slovo*, 17 May 1984. (not seen)

This is a review of Josef Bednárik's 1984 production of *Pericles* in Nitra, Yugoslavia, at the Andrej Bagar Theatre.

786. Valo, Peter. *Pravda*, 15 March 1984. (not seen)

This is a review of Josef Bednárik's 1984 production of *Pericles* in Nitra, Yugoslavia, at the Andrej Bagar Theatre.

787. Vrbka, Stanislav. *Film a divadlo*, 3 August 1984. (not seen)

This is a review of Josef Bednárik's 1984 production of *Pericles* in Nitra, Yugoslavia, at the Andrej Bagar Theatre.

788. Vydrová, Monika. *Tvorba* (Prague), 50 (1984). (not seen)

This is a review of Josef Bednárik's 1984 production of *Pericles* in Nitra, Yugoslavia, at the Andrej Bagar Theatre.

789. Warren, Roger. "Shakespeare in England." *Shakespeare Quarterly*, 35 (1984): 337-38.

Director David Jones added sections from Wilkins' *Painfull Aduentures* (item 353) to lengthen his 1983 BBC television production of *Pericles*. Set designer Don Taylor provided naturalistic settings for the various Mediterranean locations as each episode rather tediously unfolded. As usual, acts 1-3 were lively only at Thaisa's marriage to Pericles and Cerimon's revival of Thaisa. Meanwhile, at the Theatre Royal, Stratford East, director David Ultz staged a very different *Pericles*. Gerard Murphy as Pericles kept meeting the same people wherever he went. Brian Protheroe played all the rulers: Antiochus, Cleon, Simonides, and Lysimachus. Felicity Dean played all three daughters. Martin Duncan played a young Gower. The young Pericles in silver armor, Cerimon in a cone of a wizard's hat, and Cleon as buffoon and clown moved about like characters in a children's book in the primitive sets designed by director Ultz. Each country was a different color, and large packing crates served as moveable scenery. The additions to the BBC television production from Wilkins' novel made Jones's brothel scenes more convincing than Ultz's. See item 576. The Stratford East production was livelier than the BBC production, but the comic tone of Ultz's production made it hard for the audience to take seriously the reunion scene between Pericles and Marina.

790. Sacksteder, William. "A *Pericles* in Denver." *Shakespeare Quarterly*, 36 (1985): 472-74.

In the 1985 production by the Denver Center Theatre Company, groups of characters, the entire cast, or individuals spoke Gower's part. Diana's statue spoke the Epilogue. Director Laird Williamson sped and unifed this *Pericles* by emphasizing choric and epic qualities at the expense of text and history. Scenes shifted by means of swiftly opening and closing flats; stage devices (nautical ropes, veils, curtains) were dropped through open ceilings; colored floor coverings indicated courts, brothel, ship, or temple. The

assembled cast wore nondescript coverings until
stepping forth in character costumes for the various
scenes. Byron Jennings as Pericles and Robynn
Rodriguez as Marina played parts ranging from youth to
mature seriousness.

See also items 28, 32, 37, 48, 50-51, 69, 72, 80, 86, 91, 93,
95, 105, 109, 111-12, 115, 118-19, 134, 136, 138, 140-41,
147-48, 153-54, 158-59, 163, 166, 169, 178, 182-83, 189,
198-99, 207, 218, 221, 225, 236, 248, 265-66, 270-71, 273,
292, 302, 316-19, 321, 325, 333, 351, 387, 390, 405-07, 411,
424, 431, 443, 446, 450, 461, 472, 478, 486, 490, 494-96,
509, 513, 527-28, 533, 558-61, 564-67, 571, 576, 793-94, 805,
807, 816.

791. Lillo, George. *Marina: A Play of Three Acts. As It Is Acted at the Theatre Royal in Covent-Garden. Taken from Pericles Prince of Tyre.* 1738. Reprint. London: Cornmarket Press, 1969.

This adaptation is based on acts 4-5. When the play opens the murderer Leonine and Philoten, Queen of Tharsus, are plotting the death of Marina. But pirates rescue her and take her to a brothel in Ephesus. In act 2 Leonine, who has not told Queen Philoten of Marina's escape from death, tries to blackmail her into marrying him. Pericles arrives and is told that his daughter is dead. He leaves Tharsus, having given himself up to blind fortune and vowing not to return to Tyre. Leonine and Philoten murder each other. Back in Ephesus, Lysimachus attempts to seduce Marina, but she converts him to goodness instead. Boult, who has been bribed to goodness with gold, helps Marina escape the brothel. He takes her to the Temple of Diana, presided over by Thaisa, who was washed ashore years earlier and revived by Lysimachus' father. Act 3 opens with Pericles' arrival at the temple. Father, mother, and daughter come face to face and at last recognize one another. The play ends with Pericles and Thaisa reunited and Lysimachus and Marina betrothed.

792. Lamb, Charles and Mary. "*Pericles, Prince of Tyre.*" *Tales from Shakespeare.* 1807. Reprint. New York: Hart, 1976, pp. 302-19.

This prose adaptation for children omits the nature of Antiochus' secret, the brothel episode, and the shove or slap Pericles gives Marina when she addresses

him on board his ship in Mytilene. Except for these
omissions, the adaptation follows the original closely.

793.   Genest, John. *Some Account of the English Stage from
       the Restoration in 1660 to 1830*. Vol. 3. Burt
       Franklin Research and Source Work Series 93. 1832.
       Reprint. New York: Burt Franklin, [n.d.], pp.
       561-67.

       This volume lists the cast for *Marina*, George Lillo's
       1738 adaptation of *Pericles*, and gives plot synopses of
       Pericles and *Marina*.

794.   Eliot, Samuel Atkins, Jr. "*Pericles*." *Little Theatre
       Classics*. Vol. 3. Boston: Little, Brown, 1921, pp.
       115-77.

       This adaptation of *Pericles* was performed 23 April
       1920 by the Smith College Theatre Workshop. The
       introduction discusses the production and its costuming
       in terms of the history of the *Pericles* text, the
       Apollonius story, and the stage adaptations by George
       Lillo (1738) and Samuel Phelps (1854). Separate
       sections contain remarks on staging and
       characterization. Eliot's play in three scenes opens
       with Cleon's exclamations against Dionyza's plan to
       murder Marina. Later, when the murderer Leonine tries
       to cut Marina's throat, she is rescued by Lysimachus,
       the pirate-governor of Mytilene. Scene 2 opens aboard
       a ship in Mytilene, where Lysimachus sends for Marina
       to help cure a sick man. While those on board await
       Marina's arrival, Helicanus tells the man's story in a
       flashback. When Marina arrives, she recognizes and
       restores her father to life. While the recovered
       Pericles sleeps, Diana visits him in a dream and tells
       Thaisa's story in a second flashback. The goddess
       orders him to her temple nearby, where, in scene 3,
       Pericles and Marina rejoin Thaisa.

795.   Harvey, Paul, ed. "*Pericles, Prince of Tyre*." *The
       Oxford Companion to English Literature*. 2nd ed.
       rev. Oxford: Clarendon, 1940, pp. 604-05.

       The entry gives background information and a plot
       summary.

796.   Eliot, T.S. "Marina." *The Complete Poems and Plays*.
       New York: Harcourt, Brace, 1950, pp. 72-73.

One of the four Ariel poems, "Marina" was published
first in September, 1930.

797. Olive, W.J. "Davenport's Debt to Shakespeare in *The
City-Night-Cap*." *Journal of English and Germanic
Philology*, 49 (1950): 333-44.

Robert Davenport imitated a number of Shakespeare's
plays in *The City-Night-Cap* (c. 1624); for instance, he
followed the Marina plot in *Pericles* closely.

798. Germer, Rudolf. "Die Bedeutung Shakespeares für T.S.
Eliot." *Shakespeare Jahrbuch* (Weimar), 95 (1959):
112-32.

"Marina," which was inspired by the recognition scene
in *Pericles* (5.1.81-165), is the one Eliot poem which
expresses pure joy.

799. Halliday, Frank E., comp. *Unfamiliar Shakespeare:
Scenes from the Less-Known Plays, Chosen, with an
Introduction, by F.E. Halliday*. London: Duckworth,
1962.

The compiler says that he has selected a group of
first-rate scenes from the second rank of Shakespeare's
work: the Henry 6 plays, *Titus Andronicus*, *The Comedy
of Errors*, *The Two Gentlemen of Verona*, *Love's Labor's
Lost*, *Venus and Adonis*, *The Rape of Lucrece*, Sonnets
17, 130, and 2, *All's Well That Ends Well*, *Timon of
Athens*, *Pericles*, and *The Two Noble Kinsmen*. Following
general remarks on the background of *Pericles* and a
plot summary, three passages are included: "The Lament
of Pericles for Thaisa" (3.1.1-69), "The Revival of
Thaisa" (3.2.26-116), and "Pericles and Marina"
(5.1.60-198).

800. Harbage, Alfred. *"Pericles." William Shakespeare: A
Reader's Guide*. New York: Farrar, Straus and Giroux,
Noonday Press, 1963, pp. 438-39.

This synopsis calls *Pericles* "peripatetic" (p. 439)
but charming in parts. The play includes most of the
major themes of the later romances.

801. Zukofsky, Celia. *Bottom: On Shakespeare*. Vol. 2.
[Austin:] Ark Press, for the Humanities Research
Center [University of Texas], 1963.

The volume is devoted to a background score of
Pericles for voices, oboe, English horn, clarinet, bass
clarinet, lute, and cello.

802. Boustead, Alan, comp. *Music to Shakespeare: A
      Practical Catalogue of Current Incidental Music, Song
      Settings and Other Related Music*. New York: Oxford
      University Press, 1964, p. 18.

      This book notes the existence of incidental music to
      Pericles by J. Hotchkiss.

803. Dean, Winton, Dorothy Moore, and Phyllis Hartnoll,
      comps. "Catalogue of Musical Works Based on the
      Plays and Poetry of Shakespeare." *Shakespeare in
      Music: Essays by John Stevens (and others) with a
      Catalogue of Musical Works*. Edited by Phyllis
      Hartnoll. 1964. Reprint. London: Macmillan; New
      York: St. Martin's 1967. pp. 243-90.

      The compilers list two pieces based on *Pericles*: an
      unperformed opera, c. 1915, "Pericle re di Tiro,"
      composed for London performance by Guilio Cottrau
      (1831-1916) and untitled incidental music for the
      theatre by Karl von Perfall (1824-1907). See item 649.

804. Nugent, Elizabeth M. *"Pericles." Shakespeare's
      Troilus and Cressida, Titus Andronicus, Timon of
      Athens, Pericles, and Cymbeline*. Monarch Review
      Notes and Study Guides. New York: Monarch, 1965, pp.
      96-122.

      This chapter includes mention of sources, a plot
      synopsis, a scene-by-scene summary, character sketches,
      remarks on critical opinion, two essay questions with
      answers, and a four-item bibliography.

805. Ruth, Léon, adapt. *Périclès, prince de Tyr: tragi-
      comédie en cinq actes et vingt-six tableaux*.
      Microcard edition. Paris: n.p., 1967. *Théâtre:
      Avant-scène*, no. 386-87, pp. 10-37. (not seen)

      This adaptation was performed at the Ambigu, Paris,
      in October 1957.

806. Usherwood, Stephen. *"Pericles." Shakespeare Play by
      Play*. London: Dent, Phoenix House, 1967, pp. 88-89.

The entry includes background information and a plot summary.

807. Frost, David Leonard. "Beaumont and Fletcher: 'Crows and Daws.'" *The School of Shakespeare: The Influence of Shakespeare on English Drama 1600-42.* Cambridge: At the University Press, 1968, pp. 209-45.

It was a mistake ever to assume that Beaumont and Fletcher influenced Shakespeare, for *Pericles* predates any of Beaumont and Fletcher's plays said to have influenced him. When Shakespeare turned to old romance, he made a hit of *Pericles*; Fletcher's *Faithful Shepherdess*, modelled on foreign and newly fashioned pastoral tragicomedy, failed to please. The argument that Shakespeare began to write romances for performance at the newly acquired Blackfriars is wrong also; *Pericles*, clearly a romance, is a Globe play. Shakespeare's return to romance was his own. Perhaps he hoped to rival Sidney and Spenser, the greatest romance writers of his day. Sidney's, Spenser's, and Shakespeare's romances call for protracted and unusual adventures out of which moralizing and allegorical messages may be drawn. By contrast, Beaumont and Fletcher avoid multi-plotted stories, lengthy time spans, spectacle, and underlying meaning. The chapter discusses the influence of *Cymbeline* on *Philaster*, the differences between Fletcher and Shakespeare in *The Two Noble Kinsmen* and *Henry 8*, and Beaumont and Fletcher's debt to Shakespeare.

808. Urwin, George Glencairn, comp. *The Neglected Shakespeare.* London: Blackie, 1969.

The compiler excerpts passages from eighteen of Shakespeare's lesser known plays. A brief introduction prefaces each play. The *Pericles* excerpt is act 3, beginning with the dumb show and chorus.

809. Wilson, Snoo. "Pericles the Mean Knight" [1972]. Unpublished Manuscript. Cline Goodwin Associates, 79 Cromwell Rd., London, S.W. 7. (not seen)

810. Wilson, Gary H. "The Shakespearian Design of T.S. Eliot's Poetry." Ph.D. dissertation, Temple University, 1973. *Dissertation Abstracts International*, 34 (1973): 794A-95A.

"The Love Song of J. Alfred Prufrock" is a modern
Hamlet; The Tempest is the key to "The Wasteland."
With "Marina" (1930), a poem completely dependent on
Pericles, Eliot said goodbye to Shakespearean design
and began his religious period, which culminated in the
Four Quartets.

811. Fühmann, Franz. *Shakespeare-Märchen: Für Kinder
     Erzählt von Franz Fühmann*. Berlin: Kinderbuch, 1976.
     (not seen)

812. Zesmer, David M. "Romances: *Pericles*." *Guide to
     Shakespeare*. New York: Barnes and Noble, 1976, pp.
     407-14.

     The chapters offer a history, plot summary, and
     analysis of *Pericles*. The main theme is man's lack of
     control over his destiny.

813. Drucker, Trudy, ed. "Introduction." *The Plays of
     George Lillo*. Eighteenth-Century Drama, 27. Vol. 1.
     1775. Reprint. New York: Garland, 1979, pp.
     xiii-xv.

     Using only act 4 of *Pericles* in writing *Marina*
     (1738), Lillo added characters, speeches, and a new
     scene to teach his audience moral lessons in taking
     action against despair. Because he believed in the
     power of human will, Lillo eliminated supernatural
     events. Even though the play ends happily, Lillo
     called his play a tragedy. A selected bibliography at
     the end of the essay lists no studies of *Marina*.

814. Hampton, Richard and David Weston, narr.
     Shakespeare--The Wonder of Our Stage. A Program of
     Recordings at the Old Vic. London: Encyclopaedia
     Britannica, 1980. (not heard)

     This recording, available on tape from the National
     Theatre, contains extracts read by Timothy West and
     Judi Dench and songs performed by the Musica Antiqua
     from several plays, including *Pericles*.

815. Heaney, Seamus. "'The Fire i' the Flint': Reflections
     on the Poetry of Gerard Manley Hopkins."
     Preoccupations: Selected Prose 1968-78. New York:
     Farrar, Straus and Giroux; London: Faber and Faber,
     1980, pp. 79-97.

In a lecture from 1974, Heaney speaks briefly of T.S.
Eliot's knowledge of *Pericles* as liberator rather than
limiter of "the scope" of "Marina" (p. 82).

816. Beckerman, Bernard. "Schemes of Show: A Search for
Critical Norms." In *The Stage and the Page: London's
"Whole Show" in the Eighteenth-Century Theatre*.
Edited by George Winchester Stone, Jr. Publications
from the Clark Library Professorship, UCLA 6.
Berkeley: University of California Press, 1981, pp.
209-28.

Considered as a subdivision of theatre, drama is
"*fictional* presentation" (p. 210) combining word and
gesture in acts of wonder and truth. By studying the
words in and left out of a dramatic text or a text
about drama, one can perceive, at least partially, the
dynamics of performance. The unit of performance is
the scene. Analysis of stage performance by scene,
or scheme of activity, is especially needful in
understanding eighteenth-century theatre with its mixed
evenings of various scenes or "turns." In dramatic
presentation the illusion of timelessness is set
against the onrush of action. This can be illustrated
in George Lillo's simply-plotted plays. The two major
motifs in Lillo are the yielding of a moral individual
to commit murder, as in *Fatal Curiosity*, and the
successful resistance of a moral individual to such
pressures, as in *Silvia* and more fully in *The Christian
Hero*, *Elmerick*, and *Marina*. In *George Barnwell* and
Fatal Curiosity, important secondary characters
represent the patient hero. Lillo counterbalances the
thrust of his simple plots with scenes that may seem
mere posturing but are renderings of the passions
calmed. *George Barnwell* contains scenes of hasty
action contrasted with fixed images of guilt and
repentance. In *Marina*, Lillo's adaptation of *Pericles*
(item 791), the heroine preserves her virtue. In
adapting *Pericles*, Lillo dealt only with the Marina
scenes, staying closest to Shakespeare in the two
brothel scenes which form the heart of his adaptation.
Boult's assault on Marina's virtue is counterbalanced
in *Marina* with a call to higher powers by Marina that
makes her an icon of morality. This emblemizing
tendency in *Marina* is fully developed in *The Christian
Hero* and *Elmerick*. The reader can stop the action of a
poem or novel by stopping from time to time as he
reads. In dramatic presentation, it is the actor who

controls the pace of the action. In Lillo, for
example, action slows or stops to depict a moment of
moral perfection. Readings of plays should take scene
units into account. Thus the reader can "see" and
"feel" the dynamics of dramatic performance.

See also items 16, 19, 44, 64, 93, 97, 131, 134, 139, 142,
144, 216, 298, 446, 458, 528, 583, 647, 652, 658.

accident. 272 538
acting. 166 409 558 576
Acting Company of New York. 766-67 769
action. 108 249 333 443 564 816
adultery. 276 313
adventure. 303 807
Aeschylus. 20
aesthetic criticism. 151
aesthetics. 168 457 724
Affelder, Jeannie. 642
Agnes, St. 111
Aire, Sally. 727
Alabama, University of. 628
Albala, Radu. 762
Alexander, Peter. 59 76 507 576
Alexandria. 372 696
allegory. 25 34 40 42 67 111 176 277 513 542 685 720 807
Amans. 329
American Acting Company, New York. 640
Anaya Valdepena, Gabriel. 77
Andretta, Richard A. 231
Andrews, John Frank. 445
Anikst, Alexander. 245 524
Anniah Gowda, H.H. 229
anthropology. 25
Antioch. 372 681
Antioch scenes. 112 201 649
Antiochus. 27 47 58 172 314 363
Antiochus and daughter. 36 137 171 219 238 250 267 276
    280 284 304 321 352 461
Antiochus the Great. 431
Antiochus' daughter. 62 116 122 125 149 179 252 327 462
    758
Antiochus' death. 373
Antiochus' riddle. 355 372
Aoyama, Seiko. 195
Aphrodite. 179
Apollo. 186

Apollonian and Dionysian. 179
Apollonius. 81 140 162 170 193 209 261 329 363
Apollonius legend. 337 339 341 359 370 399 415 424 498 500
    518 528 538 564-67 600 794
Apollonius of Tyre. 337-39 341 344 346 350 355 359 363 368
    381 660
Arakawa, Mitsuo. 164
Araki, Kazuo. 47
Arcadia. 25 337 366 376 528 538 560 566 807
archetypes. 196 200
Aris, Doreen. 599
Aristotle. 442
Armstrong, Edward A. 12
art. 108-09 113 118 128 130 160 167-68 189 196 216 219 287
    292 297 317 321 367 686
Arthos, John. 28
artifice. 127 158 165 189 219
artificiality. 95-96 127
artist. 127 213 271 292 308 319
artistry. 14 22 108 113
artlessness. 27
asceticism. 111 312
Asche, Oscar. 584 654
Ashland (Oregon) Shakespeare Festival. 602 608 662 681-83
    734
assonance. 439
Assyria. 717
Athenaeum. 335
Athens. 630 739-41 743 748-49
Atienza, Edward. 613 702 710
Atkins, Robert. 587 594 597 653 656 678
Auberlen, Richard. 110
Auden, W.H. 78
audience. 25 27 48 56 91 93 114 127 136 158 167 172 178
    191 198-99 205 265-66 270-71 277 292 300 302 308 319
    333 349 472 528 564 566 679 703 756
Augustine, St. 542
Australia. 632 647 747 752 755 775 778 780 782-84
authorial presence. 129
authorship. 146 151 158 170 197 206 312
Autolycus. 142 292
Axelrad, José. 523
Aycock, Wendell M. 303
Aylmer, Felix. 684

Babula, William. 127 196 754
Bacon, Sir Francis. 176 306 482
Bacon, Wallace Alger. 9
Baddeley, Angela. 604 664 667
Baker, Herschel. 142 298
Baker, Nick. 765
Balser, Karl. 521
Barber, C.L. 121
Barber, Vivian Ann Greene. 290
Barker, Gerard D. 363
Barnard College, New York. 605
Barnes, Barnabe. 199 528
Barnes, Clive. 702
Barnet, Sylvan. 538 555
baroque. 196
Barratt, Harold S. 211
Barthos, Michael W. 766
Barton, Anne [Righter]. 65 134
Bartoshevich, A.V. 713
Bassanio. 137
Bates, Paul A. 316
Bawd. 67 370
bawdy. 177 567
Bayless, Jo Ann. 608 681-82
BBC Television. 576 644 779 789
Beaumont and Fletcher. 25 37 66 94 143 169 340 508 807
Becker, Marvin B. 212
Beckerman, Bernard. 816
Bednárik, Josef. 446 646 776 781 785-88
Beethoven. 74
Beinecke Library. 453
Bejblík, Alois. 575
Bell, Duncan. 645
Belott-Mountjoy lawsuit. 343 402 447 452 460 567
Bender, Robert Morton. 69
Beneke, Jürgen. 197
Bennett, Vivienne. 592
Benson, Frank. 584 654-55 657
Bentley, Gerald Eades. 438
Berkeley, Edward. 615 693 705 707 731
Berkeley Shakespeare Festival. 616 626 716 742 751 754
Berlin Festival. 720 722
Berman, Ronald. 490
Berry, Francis. 91
Berwińska, Krystyna. 573

Betterton, Thomas. 578 715
Bevington, David. 255 457 494 559 570
Biggins, D. 423
Billington, Michael. 728
biography. 48 73
Birmingham Repertory Theatre. 599–600 660 675 678
Blackfriars. 112 138 567 807
Bland, D.S. 29
Blaxland, Antionelle. 647
Blondquist, Laurence. 542
Blue, Brother. 642 770 777
Blue, William R. 303
Bluestone, Stephen Edward. 165
Bodenstedt, Friedrich. 511 527
Bodleian Library. 489 500 502
Boethius. 61 99 122 140 171
Bond, David. 607 674
Boni, John. 462
Boose, Lynda E. 304
Booth, Stephen. 716
Boston Shakespeare Company. 642 770 777
Bosworth, Denise Mary. 291
Boult. 98 448
Boustead, Alan. 802
Bowers, J.L. 92
Boxill, Roger. 767
Brahms, Caryl. 670
Braithwaite, Lilian. 584
Brandes, Georg. 3 501
Brayton, Lily. 584
Brecht, Bertolt. 685 722 733 735 759
Brien, Alan. 663
Brissenden, Alan. 755
Bristol University. 139
British Museum. 51 353 498–99
Brockbank, J.P. 135
Broner, E.M. 284
Brook, Pamela. 613 704
Brook, Peter. 685 767
brothel keepers. 565
brothel scenes. 2 3 5 21 26–27 31 34 36 67 74 79 98 111–
    12 118 166 177 244 306 347 362 365 383 386 392 396 407
    412 418 427 467 508 513 533 564 576 649 651 666–67 681–
    82 692 695–96 712 717 757 767 779 789 792 816
Brown, Gilmor. 593

Brown, Ivor. 671
Brown, John Russell. 91 98
Browne, Gordon. 216
Browning, Andrew Holt. 331
Brownlow, Frank W. 232
Bruce, Brenda. 609 686
Brunner, Karl. 43
Bucharest. 636 762 764
Buchwald, Reinhard. 521
Bullough, Geoffrey. 366 430 701
Burbage, Richard. 351
Burgess, Tyrrell. 773
Burrows, Jill. 774
Burton, Robert. 137
Busche, Alexander van den. 347 350 365-66
Byrne, M. St. Clare. 538 664
Byron, Lord. Sardanapalus. 717

Cabas, Victor Nicholas, Jr. 213
Calderón de la Barca. 303 305
Caldwell, Ellen Marie. 292
Calendar of State Papers. 387
Cambridge Festival Theatre. 592
Cardenio. 251
Carpenter, Nan Cooke. 214
Cary, Cecile Williamson. 309
Castiglione. The Courtier. 292
Catholic recusants. 461
ceremony. 89 370
Cerimon. 23 38 54 56 90 168 171 242 268 284 396 559 564
Chambers, E.K. 74 78 396 399
Champlain (Vermont) Shakespeare Festival. 631
Chappell, William. 505
characters. 93 106-08 116 123 133 135 161 180 205 237
    264 278 300 303 315 328 349 409 426 443 503 570 794
chastity. 67 257 296 312 383 443 542 682
Chatterton. 135
Chaucer, Geoffrey. 374
Cheek by Jowl Theatre Company. 645 773-74
Chettle, Henry. 199
children. 73 226 237 239 554 564
Cholmeley's Players. 405
Christian. 14 19 25 36 38 42 52 68 70 89 97 132 179 196
    261 367 372 381 542
Christopher, St. 405

chronology. 389 559
Chujo, Kazuo. 47
Church, Tony. 677
Clarence. 135
Clark, William George. 497
Clarus, Babis. 739
Cleon. 654
Cleon and Dionyza. 7 244
Clyomon and Clamydes. 160
The Cockpit. 578 652
(Jean) Cocteau Repertory Company. 633 757 767 769
Cohen, Walter. 305
Cole, B.J. 632
Coleman, John. 584 654-55 678
Coleridge, Samuel Taylor. 1
Coleridge, Sylvia. 594
collaboration. 3 158 232 343 353 426 433 457 461 467 504
    538 564 576
Collier, John Payne. 335
Collings, R.L.E. 215
Collins, Andrew. 645
Colman, E.A.M. 177
Colman, Elizabeth Lee. 153
Colorado Shakespeare Festival. 610 648 691 790
Comédie Française. 614 703 711
comedies.
    dark. 141
    early. 42 96 104 115 149 157 175 177 504
    festive. 121 194
    final. 70 184
    forgiveness. 94
    late. 25 70 104 112 258 363 491 538
    low. 244 513
    problem. 301
    romantic. 302 331 349
    Shakespeare. 93 96 174 205 208 299 310 494
comedy. 143 158
comic. 57 108
Comito, Terry. 378
compositors. 413 416 445 467 472 489 528 538 756
computers. 456 473 477 479-84 486 492
conclusions. 300
Confessio Amantis. 26 140 170 209 264 329 338-39 348
    351-52 355 360 366 369-70 409 415 426 433 444 470 498
    518 528 538 560 564 566

Connor, Edric. 604 664 666 671 699
Cook, Ann Jennalie. 233
Cooper, Miss. 582
copiousness. 231
Cordelia. 111 121 155 237 261
Coriolanus. 237
Cormier, Elton. 633
Corneille, Pierre. 3
Cornett, Patricia Ann Laping. 198
Cortes, Hernando. 361 426
costume. 316 576 651 664 676 686 724 751 790 794
Cottrau, Guilio. 803
court. 103 159 176
Courteaux, Willy. 556
Covent Garden. 652 658
Cowl, Richard P. 397
Cox, Clyde Perry, Jr. 136
Cox, R.G. 533
Craig, Hardin. 11 363-64 407-09 416 427 463 508 559 570
Cravens, Sydney P. 303
Cressida. 237
Crosse, Gordon. 656
Crouch, J.H. 691
Crow, Charles. 185 193
Csetneki, Gabor. 248
Cummings, Jim. 640
cupidity. 253
Cushman, Robert. 729
Cutts, John P. 116-17 376 424 428
Cymbeline. 133 149 201 313

D'Amato, Paul. 631 759
Danby, John F. 25
dance. 51 62 158 293 309 656 682 735
Daniel, Samuel. 152 380 428
Daniels, Ron. 623 625 629 727-30 734 736 744-46 750 753
daughter. 58 251 280 299
Davenant, William. 652
Davenport, Robert. 797
Davidson, Cathy N. 284
Davies, Sir John. 137
Davis, Carl. 640
Davison, Philip. 608 681
Dawkins, R.M. 345
Day, John. 366 405 425 439 447 450 471 528

Day, Muriel C. 655
Dean, Felicity. 643 768 789
Dean, John. 249 264 382
Dean, Winton. 803
death. 6 7 14 90 135 179 205 254 321 333 676
Deese, Ethel Helen. 234
Delacorte Theatre, New York. 615 705 707 734
Delius, Nicholaus. 391
Dench, Judi. 684 814
Deninger, Wolfgang. 527
Denis, St. 130
denouement. 66
Desborough, Philip. 590
Desdemona. 111 155 261
design. 189 768
devices. 193 317 336 369 380
The Devil's Charter. 199 528
dialogue. 105
Diana. 116 169 185-86 201 252 264 308 321-22 383 410 426
    429 533 538 542 656 727 763 790
    vision of. 49 62 122 288 424 428
Dickey, Stephen John. 328
Dickson, George B. 402
diction. 331 449
Dionyza. 2 36 312
direct address. 271
Dis. 111
disguise. 200 231
distancing. 91-92 319 759
Dobrée, Bonamy. 55
Donahue, Tracy. 626
Donaldson, Tom. 608 681-82
Donnellan, Declan. 645 773-74
doubling. 207 686-87 700 724 734 736 742 755 763 768 778
    789
Dowling, Vanessa. 632
Downes, John. 715
Doyle, Charles Clay. 250
drama.
    medieval. 42 70 127 149 189 196 321 528 554
    modern. 134
    narrative. 576
    Renaissance. 297 311 319
dramatic construction. 109 235 247 816
dramatic performance. 816

dramaturgy. 270
dream. 19 128 168 180 276 333 758
Drew, Elizabeth. 16
Dromazo, S.I. 740
Drucker, Trudy. 813
Drury, Alan. 730
Dryden, John. 390
Duk Moraud. 111
The Duke's Company. 578-80 652
dumb shows. 28 56 62 86 89 91 104 158 160 219 264 297 317
    443 724 735
Dunbar, Mary Judith. 235 317
Duncan, Frank. 677
Duncan, Martin. 643 765 789
Dunn, Catherine M. 122
Dupuy, Rene. 601
Durrell, Lawrence. 696
Durrett, Carlos William. 70
Dutz, Ingold. 216

Easson, Angus. 448
Eastman, Arthur M. 78
Eccles, Mark. 452 454
Eddison, Robert. 594
Edinburgh Arts Festival. 611 692 696-97 713-14
Edinburgh University. 16 44 139 465 469 479
Edwards, Philip. 48 118 221 278 413 416-18 463 467-68 489
    491 513 528 533 564 736
Eggers, Walter Frederick, Jr. 154 199 265
Ehrich, Brigitte. 756
Ellis-Fermor, Una. 20
Eliot, Samuel Atkins, Jr. 586 794
Eliot, T.S. 16 19 44 64 93 131 139 796 798 810 815
    "Marina." 16 796 798 810 815
Elizabeth (daughter, James 1). 176
Elizabethan. 25 51 61 277 320
Ellis, Ruth. 657
Elsom, John. 692
Elton, William. 347 350
emblem. 101 172 193 292 297 300 322 336 369 375 380
Empric, Julienne Helen. 178
Empson, William. 79
Enright, Nick. 632 647 747 752 755 775 778 780 782-84
Ephesus. 190 383
epic poem. 3

epilogue.   36 199 242 268 319 326 374 391 790
epiphany. 169
episodic. 90 105 528 559 576
Erasmus.   292 386
Escanes.   379 710
Eschenburg, Johann Joachim.   620 724
Esslin, Martin.   685
Euripides. 20
Eustace, St. 155
Evans, Barbara Lloyd. 719
Evans, Bertrand. 56 354
Evans, G. Blakemore. 486 492 560-61
Evans, Gareth Lloyd. 166 468 719
Evans, Henri. 533
Everyman. 111
evil.   14 17 20 27 31 90 227 242 312-14 542
Ewbank, Inga-Stina. 278 318
exempla. 374
experience. 300
experiment.   32 34 41 157-58 189 232 265 288 300 341 366
    457 472 528 564 576

Fabiny, Tibor. 322
The Faerie Queene. 18 155 290 311 362 807
Fagan, Eleanor. 611 692 713
fairy tales.   46 73 513 538 558 649 681-82 720 722-23 728
    737 756 758 763
faith. 90 261 363
Falconer, Alexander Frederick. 80
family.   34 197 280 287 294 332 504 538 576
famine. 47 276 307 387
fantasy. 145 161 190 200
Farjeon, Herbert. 501
fate. 63 760 812
father. 151 257 267 280 558
father and daughter.   23 58 129 134 149 162 175 179 194
    244 251 253 256 258 267 276 278 304 435 538 542 564-
    65 570 758 779
feast. 111 291
Feidner, Edward J. 631 759
Feldman, A. Bronson. 35
Fellowship of Players. 590
Felperin, Howard Michael. 100 111 155
Fenwick, Henry. 576
Ferdinand. 656

Fergusson, Francis. 443 542
Fernandes, Augusto. 634 756 758 760
fertility. 30 149 211 283
festival plays. 23 121 194
Fischer, Walther. 36
fishermen. 269 370 565 576 711
fishermen scene. 27 244 429 735
Fleay, Frederick G. 392–93 414 458
Fleetwood, Susan. 609 687
Flenberg, Nona. 306
Fletcher, John. 66 152
Flower, Annette C. 200
Fluchère, Henri. 30 520
Folger Shakespeare Library. 534 566 680
Folio.
   F1 (1623). 59 427 478 560 566 670
   F3 (1664). 421
folk custom. 219 245
folk drama. 96 229 722
folk literature. 316
folk tales. 36 316 576
folklore. 56 73 167 231 238
Forbes-Robertson, John. 650
Ford, Boris. 40
Ford, Jane M. 217
Fort, Jean B. 530
fortune. 13–14 56 63 170 268 538
Fossen, Richard Van. 255
Foulkes, Richard. 717
Fox, Jonathan Roy. 201
Fox, Terry Curtis. 757
Frey, Charles. 236 251
Fried, Erich. 553 634 756 760 763
Frost, David Leonard. 807
Frye, Northrop. 78 93 218
Fuchs, Matthias. 634 763
Fühmann, Franz. 811
Fukuhara, Rintaro. 543
Furnivall, F.J. 393 414
Füssli, J.H. 216

Gajdusek, R.E. 179
Galey, Matthieu. 703
games. 167
Ganz, Arthur. 767

Garber, Marjorie Beth. 128 180 237
García Lora, José. 81 660
Gardiner, Kevin. 626
Garrett, Robert Max. 341
Gascon, Jean. 613 694 698 700 702 704 706 710 731 734
Gaskill, William. 571 637
Gavajda, Peter. 634
Gearin-Tosh, Michael. 373
generations. 73 87 91 218 283 509 533
Genest, John. 793
Genet, Jean. 769
Geneva Bible. 385 464
Geoffrey of Viterbo. Pantheon. 355
Georgosopoulos, K. 741
Germer, Rudolf. 798
Gesner, Carol. 357 370
Gesta Romanorum. 338
Ghent Rijksarchief. 461
Gibson, Jeremy. 694 701 710
Gibson, Richard Joseph. 157
Gilbert, Miriam. 266
Gilroy-Scott, N.W. 374
Gira, Catherine R. 252
Gittings, Robert. 55
Giuliani, Alfredo. 571 637
Giustinian. 387
Glackin, William C. 681
Gladstone, Stacey. 631
Glazier, Plyllis Gorfain. 167 219 238
Globe. 154 207 807
Gneditch, T. 524
Goddard, Harold C. 24
gods. 185 190 196 269 367 528 564
Goepp, Philip H., II. 344 368
Goldberg, Henryh. 720
The Golden Legend. 321
Goneril. 121
good. 30
good and evil. 20 67 316
Goolden, P. 355
Gordon, Giles. 768
Gorfain, Phyllis. 167 219 238
Gosson, Henry. 411 416 426 447 452
Gower.
    African/Carribean. 665 667 669 699

ancient. 114 189 329 374 576 686
antique style. 409
archaic. 565 567
artless. 135
character. 326
Choruses. 27 38 40 50 56 90-91 105 113 155 162 189 191
    196 219 264 286 306 319 329 341 354 370 374 391-92
    396 400 444 446 462 470 472 478 498-99 504 508-09
    513 528 538 559 564-67 576 651 655 724 790
distanced. 287 735 758
emblem. 193
John. 120 341 374 528 567
naive. 272
narrator. 56 111 165 168 232 257 266 302 457 564
presenter. 109 160 199 326 513 528 554 757
rational. 191
resurrected. 321 443
storyteller. 200 316 472
surrogate Shakespeare. 179 271
voice of story. 325
without. 717
Graves, T.S. 387
Gray, J.C. 323 325
Graziosi, Paulo. 571 637
Great Exhibition (1851). 717
Greek plays. 82
Green, Henry. 336 380
green world. 96
Greene, Gayle. 251
Greene, Guy Shepard. 343
Greene, Robert. 95
Greenfield, Thelma N. 102 367 570
Greer, Richard Allen. 156
Greetham, D.C. 484
Greg, W.W. 421 489 502
Griffin, Alice. 662
Grissill. 111 155
Grodal, Torben Kragh. 181
Guicciardini. 199
Guidi, Augusto. 41-42 45 71
Gunpowder Plot 176
Gussow, Mel. 769
Gwilym, Mike. 644 779

Habicht, Werner. 429 763

Hackett, Michael Joseph, III. 293
Haddon, Archibald. 653
Hageman, Elizabeth H. 777
Haight, Elizabeth Hazelton. 346
Hale, Debra. 624
Halio, Jay L. 255 317-18
Hall, John. 396
Hall, Peter. 685
Halley, Ben, Jr. 642 770
Halliday, Frank E. 799
Halstead, Carol. 648
Halstead, William P. 731
Hamburg. 634 756 758 760 763
Hamilton, Guy. 30
Hamilton-Smith, Neil. 465 469
Hamlet. 137
Hampton, Richard. 814
Hands, Terry. 609 614 685-89 703 711 718 731 736 754
Harbage, Alfred. 26 550 577 800
Harder, Harry R. 123
Harding, D.W. 267
Harker, Nancy. 590
harmony. 20 61 73 122 192 309 377
Harris, Amanda. 645
Harris, Bernard. 91 98
Harrison, G.B. 78 509 518 548
Harrison, John. 596 678
Hartnoll, Phyllis. 803
Hartwig, Helen Joan. 119 158 732
Harvey, Sir Paul. 501 795
Harvey, Rupert. 587
Hasegawa, Mitsuaki. 268-69 279
Hastings, William T. 388
Haus, Heinz-Uwe. 316 620 724 733 761
Hauser, Georg. 519
Hawkes, Nigel. 456
Heaney, Seamus. 815
Heckscher, William S. 130
Heims, Neil Stephan. 253
Heine, Manfred. 621 724
Helena. 194 538
Helicanus. 150 176 436 464 467 649
Heminge and Condell. 59 421 472 478 513 566
Henry, Martha. 704
Hepton, Bernard. 599 675

Heraud, Miss. 582
Herbert, Gerrand. 715
Hermia. 237
Hermione. 68 288 332-33
hero. 52 133 249 260-61 287 290 299 303 308 351 370 381
    443 722
Herodotus. 382
heroine. 29 73 157 162 233-34 267 273 308 370 538 559
Herrick, Marvin T. 37
Hewes, Henry. 665 682
Hewitt, Hope. 778
Hewitt, Tom. 640 766
Heywood, Thomas. 353 360 411-12 442 478 528
Hibbard, G.R. 311 322 325
Hikichi, Masatoshi. 202 220
Hill, Charles Jarvis. 504
Hill, W. Speed. 484
Hillman, Richard Wright. 254 329
Hiraiwa, Norio. 101
history. 305 331
history plays. 42 107 320
Hodek, Bretislav. 562
Hoeniger, F. David. 32 221 255 323 366 425 428 448 450
    457 467 471-73 478 528 701
Hogan, Charles Beecher. 658
Hoge, James O., Jr. 658
Hollywood Shakespeare Festival. 607 674
Homan, Sidney R. 168
homosexuality. 121
Honigmann, E.A.J. 431
Hopkins, Gerard Manley. 815
Horenkamp, Michael. 624
Hotchkiss, J. 802
Houseman, John. 766
Houston, Deborah. 633
Howard-Hill, Trevor H. 488-89
Howarth, Herbert. 60
Howarth, R.G. 92
Hoy, Cyrus. 169 256
hubris. 268
Hughes, Bernard. 615 705
Hughes, Catherine. 693
Hugo, Francois-Victor. 520 530
Hulme, Hilda M. 422
humanism. 143 316

humility. 14
humor. 26 244 370 682
Hungary, Kecskemet. 617 721
Hunt, Maurice Arthur. 137
Hunt, Percival. 408
Hunter, G.K. 278
Hunter, Robert Grams. 94
Hurry, Leslie. 702
Hurt, Marybeth. 616
husband and wife. 564 775

Ibsen, Henrik. 20 63 318
Ichikawa, Mariko. 270
icon. 130
iconography. 317 322
identity. 200
Iliff, Noel. 592
Il'in, M.V. 203-04
illusion. 178 183 231 298 333
imagery. 18 32 68 197 317
    alchemy. 321
    appetite. 236
    breath. 12
    childbearing. 121
    darkness and love-making. 12
    death. 12 321 432 434
    destruction. 380
    disease. 74
    drones and kings. 12
    dying knight reborn. 152
    eating. 236 307
    evil. 7
    famine. 307
    fertility. 283
    flower. 283 441
    food. 307
    generational. 283
    gold. 283
    hope. 336
    hunger. 236
    jewels. 6 39 67 125 321 441
    kings. 12 441
    kingship. 7
    medieval. 321
    music. 6 432

Patience. 2
pregnancy. 283
presentational. 317
purgation. 321
resurrection. 125 321 336
riches. 432
running. 441
sea. 121 135 429
sea floors. 39
sexual. 121
ships. 283
shipwrecks. 14 39
sin. 434
sleep. 432
sun-king. 441
tempest. 6 14
treasure. 39
tree. 441
vegetation. 441
verbal. 317
violets and breath. 12
violets and death. 12
voyages. 14
whale. 429
immortality. 135 254
Imogen. 29-30 61 67 211 333 340 509
impresa. 130 380
incest. 35-36 58 112 121 149 167 179 194 217 238 244 251
253 267 276 280 284 304 312-13 321 519 538 570 722 727
737 755 758 792
Ingram, R.W. 102
innocence. 89 233 312
Ino, Mikio. 182
interludes. 102
irreality. 110
irony. 56 141
Irving, Henry. 731
Isabella, 340
Ishikawa, Minoru K. 183
Italy, Genoa. 571 637

Jachimo. 292
Jachmann, Jochen. 120
Jackson, B.W. 82
Jackson, Barry. 599 675

Jackson, Berners W.   694 704
Jackson, MacD. P.   379
Jackson, Nagle.   608 681-83 754
Jackson, Peter.   673
Jacobean.   25 42 48 74 169 378 559 567
Jacobi, Derek.   611 695-97 700 712
Jacobs, Henry E.   256 495-96
Jacobs, Laurence H.   742
Jacquot, Jean.   159
James, David G.   7 8
James, Emrys.   609 686-87
James 1.   176 267 293 387
János, Arany.   506 531 557
Jarrett, Wayne.   632 782 755
jealosy.   73 266
Jennings, Byron.   648 790
Jeremiah.   464
Jerrold, Douglas.   650
jewels.   6 39 67 125 321 441
Job.   200 363
Johnson, Darlene.   643 768
Johnson, Richard.   604 664 667 671
Johnson, Samuel.   390
Jonah.   124 358 429 471
Jones, David.   644 779 789
Jones, Griffith.   623 629 727 744
Jones-Davies, M.T.   297
Jonson, Ben.   78 101 341 448
Jorgens, Jack J.   705
Juliet.   19 237
Jupiter.   169 186
justice.   38 127

Kahn, Coppélia Huber.   280 288 293 443
Kai, Hiromi.   295
Kane, Robert J.   352
Karasek, Hullmuth.   758
Karlin, Miriam.   684
Karova, Darina.   646
Kataoka, Arika.   324
Katherine.   332
Kau, Joseph.   380
Kaul, Mythili.   103 307
Kawachi, Yoshiko.   138
Kawakami, Akiko.   281

Kay, Carol McGinnis. 256 495
Kean, Charles. 717
Kentucky, Louisville. 624 732
Kermode, Frank. 72
Kerndl, Rainer. 720
Keyes, Laura Catherine. 296
Khan, Maqbool H. 257
Kiasashvili, N. 204
Kiefer, Harry Christian. 61
Kiel, Stadttheater. 589
Kim, Jae-Nam. 532
Kim, Randall Duk. 616
King's Men. 147
kings. 7 12 40 107 194 313 363 441
Kippax, H.G. 780
Kirchmannus, Johan. 373
Kirsch, Arthur C. 112
Kirschbaum, Leo. 401
Kittredge, George Lyman. 551 554
Klebs, Elimar. 339 368
Knapp, Peggy Ann. 377
Knight, G. Wilson. 6 8 14 79 97 139 538 676
knights. 193 533
knights' dance. 51 62 376 419 656
knights' devices. 336 380
knights' scene. 297 809
knowing. 137
knowledge. 128 278
Knowles, Richard Paul. 271 308 319
Kohl, Norbert. 104
Komrij, Gerrit. 572
Konishi, Eirin. 131
Kostetzky, Eaghor G. 526
Kot, Josef. 575 646
Kraft, Barry. 626
Krag, Helena. 689
Kress, Ronna. 640 766
Kroll, Jack. 770
Kuhnert, Reinhard. 132
Kuziemski, Silvia. 621 724
Kydrýnki, Juliusz. 574

Lake, D.J. 439-40 442
LaMar, Virginia A. 566
Lamb, Charles and Mary. 792

Lambert, J.M.   695
Lambin, Georges.   433 544
language.   65 113 133 162 243 278 297 300 331 455 471 542
    750
laughter.   98
Laurie, John.   684
Laurence, Harold Whitney.   140
Layard, Henry Austen.   717
Lear, King.   323 558 565
Lee, Sidney.   500
Leech, Clifford.   21 49 66 82 159
Leggatt, Alexander.   184 325
Lehman, Benjamin H.   354
Lehmann, Beatrix.   596
Lenz, Carolyn Ruth Swift.   251
Lenz, J.M.R.   144
Leonard, Nancy Scott.   170
Leonine.   150
Leontes.   73 133 142 149 201 313
Lesberg, Sandy.   563
Levings, Nigel.   632 747 755
Levith, Murray J.   384
Levitsky, Ruth Mickelson.   52
Lewis, R.W.B.   542
Leyris, Pierre,   533
Lieblein, Leanore.   771
Lief, Madelon Jean.   330
lighting.   676
Lillo, George.   813 816
    Marina.   338-39 566 581 652 658 791 793 813 816
Limouze, Henry S.   309
Lincoln's Inn Fields.   580
linguistics.   276
Link, L.T.   239
Lithgow, Arthur.   598
Lloyd, Bertram.   404
Lodovico, Cesare Vico.   522 540
London Library.   51 353 498-99
London Record Office.   447 460
Long, John H.   62 419
López de Gomara, Francisco.   361
López-Morillas, Julian.   626 742
loss.   67 75 111 170
Lot.   471
love.   6 7 34 212 275 303 520 686

chaste. 140
conjugal. 77
constancy. 172
disguised. 179
heterosexual. 280
honorable. 538
passion. 222
Lubbock, Tom. 772
Ludwig 2. 649
Lüthi, Max. 46
Lychorida. 2
Lydgate, John. 199
Lyons, Susan. 632
Lysimachus. 26 252 272 362 364 407 415 424 427 467 471
    508 576 649 710
Lyly, John. 95

Macbeth. 325
Macbeth, Lady. 312
Maccabees 1 and 2. 352 373 528
Maccabeus, Judas. 461
Mackail, J.W. 295
Mačugová, Gizela. 781
Maddermarket Theatre, Norwich. 591
Maddocks, Melvin. 706
madness. 122 278 323
magic. 68
Maguin, Jean-Marie. 297 734
Maitra, Sitangshu. 57
Malone, Edmond. 390 419 500 502
Mander, Raymond. 678
Mann, Thomas. 142 298
mannerism. 169 565
Mannheim, Nationaltheater. 588
Marder, Louis. 459 474 479
Marenco, Franco. 571
Margaret, St. 384
Margaritas, A. 743
Marin, Luis Astrana. 552
Marina. 21 23 27 29-31 34 36 38 56 59 61 67-68 90 92 118
    121 134 155 158 165 168 179 191 200 211 227 232-34 252
    267-69 278 280 286 292 306 312 322 333 340 361 364 367
    392-93 443 448 458 467 498 508-09 514 528 533 538 542
    559 564 576 649 667 797 816
"Marina." 16 796 798 810 815

<u>Marina</u>. 338-39 566 581 652 658 791 793 813 816
Marina and Lysimachus. 176
Marina and Pericles. 244 278 280
Marina's song. 51 62 122 171
Marlowe, Christopher. 482
Marlowe Dramatic Society. 677
marriage. 211 233 304 564
Marsh, Derick R.C. 67 222
Marshall, Frank A. 731
Marshall, Mrs. 581
Martin, Walther. 83
<u>Mary Magdelene</u>. 321
Mashita, Yasutoshi. 84-85
masque. 50-51 89 95 159 218 293 322
Matejková, Eva. 646
Matthews, Harold. 666
Matthews, Honor. 68
maturity. 100 263
Mauch, Russell C., II. 205
Maurer, Oscar. 414
Maxwell, J.C. 448 467 513 536 661
Mazen, Glen. 608 682
McBean, Angus. 666 671
McEnery, Peter. 623 629 727-28 734
McEwan, Geraldine. 604 667 671
McGrath, J. Andrew. 641 766 769
McIntosh, William A. 171
McIver, Bruce. 256
McKim, Gary. 624
McLaughlin, William. 610
McMahan, C.E. 223
McManaway, James G. 389 417 493 550 565
McNeir, Waldo F. 102 326
medicine. 54
medieval. 92
    drama. 290
    literature. 140
    romance. 290
    sermons. 140
    setting. 431
Megaw, Robert N.E. 22
Mehl, Dieter. 86 105
Meissner, Alfred. 649
melancholy. 122 323 369 375 651
Melanchthon, Philipp. 375

Melchiori, Barbara. 58
Melchiori, Giorgio. 52
Merriam, Thomas. 474 478-80 483
Messiaen, Pierre. 523
Meszaros, Patricia K. 309
metamorphosis. 128 180
metaphor. 111 135 180 197 219
  book and child. 226
  constant helmsmen. 173
  death. 135 443
  feminine. 283
  loss and recovery. 170
  man-as-tree. 441
  music. 377
  rebirth. 179 443
  sea. 135
  sea as fortune. 264
  ships. 173
  storms. 377
  tempest. 443
  viol. 327
  whale. 450
metapoetry. 167 219
metatheatre. 219
metrics. 391-92
Metscher, Thomas. 735
Metz, G. Harold. 469 484
Michael, Nancy Carolyn. 446 463 470
Michaelson, Sidney. 465 469
Michener, Charles. 707
Mickov, Georgi. 240
Middlesex Sessions. 452
Miklaszewski, Krzysztof. 708
Millman, Laurence. 206
Milward, Peter. 87
Mincoff, Marco. 224
miracle play. 18 32 109 111 155 212 308 528 554
miracles. 18 27 67 158 232 370 520
Miranda. 29-30 59 211 233 313 340 509 538 656
Mirek, Roman. 106
Mitchenson, Joe. 678
Miyauchi, Bunshichi. 133
Mohan, Laxmikant. 107
Mommsen, Tycho. 335 418
Monck, Nugent. 591 595 678 680 690 719 731

Montagna, Barbara Jean. 714
Montaigne, Michel de. 292
Moore, Charlotte. 616
Moore, Dorothy. 803
Moore, Richard. 558
morality plays. 14 331 538
More, Thomas. 292
Morley, Christopher. 718 744
Morley, Henry. 650-51 659 715
Morton, Andrew Q. 456 459 465-66 469 474 476 479-83
mothers. 267 280
mothers and daughters. 284
motifs.
    death and revival. 152
    dream. 180
    emblematic. 292
    fairy-tale. 513 538
    incest. 570
    journey. 236
    romance. 71
    sea. 717
"mouldiness." 200
Mowat, Barbara A. 225 241
Mucedorus. 112
Muir, Kenneth. 63 185 272 278 317-18 348 353 360-61 383
    410 418 426 429 463 468 538
Mulryne, J.R. 736
Munday, Anthony. 199
Munich. 583 585 649
Munro, John. 406 411 516
Murphy, Gerard. 643 765 789
Musaki, Tsuneo. 310
music. 6 18 51 61-62 73-74 93 102 122 136 139 153 158 162
    166 171 212 214 218 221 264 278 281 287 293 309 322-23
    327 369 375 377 432 528 564 576 649 667 695 699 734-35
    746 769 801-03 814
music of the spheres. 20 28 62 68 122 171 232 257 309 322
    422 734
Musica Antiqua. 814
Musgrove, S. 467
mystery. 519
mystery plays. 89 381
myth. 7 89 97 115 128 180 186 218 377 381 490 576
mythology. 48 79

Nagata, Yoshiko. 242
Nagler, A.M. 659
Nakabayhashi, Kenji. 243 259
Nakamura, Yasuo. 282
Nakano. Yoshio. 541 543
Nakanori, Koshi. 285
names. 346 370 384-85 399 420 426 431 486 527 538 559 566 660
Narasimhaiah, C.D. 75
narrative.
    episodic. 49 66
    exposition. 56
    Greek. 528
    poem. 56
    romantic. 28
    structure. 71 325
Nathan, Norman. 358
National Theatre, London. 753 814
nature. 28 143 196 218 297
Naumann, Walter. 260
Nedic, Borivoje. 568
Neely, Carol Thomas. 251
Neiditz, Minerva Heller. 186
Neilson, William Allan. 501 504
Nelson, Thomas Allen. 108
Neoplatonism. 122 214 685
Neptune. 185 542
Ness, Frederic W. 403
New Scala, London. 590
New York, Rochester. 638
New York Shakespeare Festival. 693 705 714 731
Nicholl, James Robert. 141
Nichols, Dorothy E. 683
Nicoll, Allardyce. 27 50
Nightingale, Benedict. 696 745
Niki, Hisae. 244
Nineveh. 717
Noiret, Jean-Michel. 639 771
Noling, Kim Hunter. 332
Nolte, G. 577
non-naturalistic. 128
North, Sir Thomas. 379
Norwich Players. 591
Nosworthy, J.M. 51
Nowottny, Winifred. 365

Nudd, Rosemary. 333
Nugent, Elizabeth M. 804
Nunes, Carlos Alberto. 514
Nunn, Trevor. 686 767

Obraztsova, A. 709
O'Brién, Terence. 590
Odashima, Yushi. 569
Odell, George C.D. 652
OED. 464
Odysseus. 90 367 558
The Odyssey. 249
Oedipus. 367
Ogoshi, Inzo. 545
Ogoshi, Kazuso. 289 541 543 546
Ohio, Antioch. 598
The Old Vic, London. 587 653 656 678 814
Oliphant, E.H.C. 398
Olive, W.J. 797
Oliver, Cordelia. 697
onomastics. 346 370 384-85 399 420 426 431 527 538 559 566
    660
opera. 93 297 665 699 803
Ophelia. 237
Oppel, Horst. 33
The Orator. 347 350 365-66
order. 30 184 190-91 219 325
Oregon, Ashland. 435 602 608 662 681-83 734
Origo, Enrica. 637
O'Rourke, Jennifer. 631
Orpheus. 377
Ostojo-Chrostowski, Stanislas. 501
Ostrowski, Witold. 371
The Other Place, Stratford-upon-Avon. 623 727-30 734 736
    753
Otsuka, Takanobu. 47
Ovid. 432
Oxenford, John. 650
Oxford, Earl of. 35
Ozu, Jiro. 285

Pafford, J.H.P. 73
paganism. 275 542
The Painfull Aduentures. 63 335 337-39 343 348 351 353 360
    363 366 379 388 395 399-400 406-09 411 413 415 418 424

426-27 430 447 452 460 463 467 470-71 504 508-09 513 518
528 538 559 564-67 576 686 701 731 753 789
Pálffy, Istvan. 721
Palmer. D.J. 25 317-18 363
Panaitescu, V. 187
Pandurovič, Sima. 517 568
pantomime. 86 105 297 519 564
parable. 14 111
Paradin, George. 369 375 436
parents. 73 237 554 564
Paris. 179
Paris, Ambigu. 601 805
Paris, Théâtre du Ranelagh. 639 771
Parker, M.D.H. 38
Parks, Stephen. 453
Parrott, Thomas Marc. 411-12
Pasadena Playhouse. 593 661
Pasco, Richard. 558 599 675
passivity. 14 109 113 174 249 269 528 576
pastoral. 47 69 71 164
patience. 25 52 90 130 162 199 209 242 257 261 272 287 300
351 363 367 443 528 538 559 567 760
The Patterne of Painefull Adventures. 26 170 264 335 338-
39 348 351-53 360 366 369 376 388 400 407 409 411 413
415 418 426-27 463 470-71 504 508 513 528 538 560 564
566-67 576 736
Paul, St. 372 542
Paulina. 559
Pavlíková, Eva. 646
Peacham, George. 341
Pearce, G.M. 746
The Pearl. 321
Pease, Ralph William, III. 449
Peasgood, Julie. 623 629 727-28 734
Pennell, Nicholas. 613 694 702 704
Pentapolis. 111 385 433
Perdita. 29-30 61 68 121 211 233 267 305 340 509 538 559
Perez Gallego, Candido. 188
Perfall, Karl von. 583 649 803
Pericles. 14 34 38 58-59 73 92 113 121 133 137 142 149
151 155 172-74 179 191 200-01 249 257 267-69 278 280
282 284 287 300 304 313 322 333 351 367 372 415 443 513
519 528 533 538 558-59 564-65 576 651 654-56 660 667
Pericles and Marina. 19 538
Pericles of Athens. 335 351 372 538

Perry, Ben Edwin. 368
Peterson, Douglas L. 172–73
Petherbridge, Edward. 644 779
Pettet, E.C. 39 349
Pettigrew, John. 710
Phelps, Samuel. 582 650–53 659 672 680 715 717 719 731
    794
Phelps, William May. 650
Philaster. 340 807
Phillabaum, Corliss E. 672
Pickford, T.E. 381
picture. 91 172 207 297
Pietzsch, Ingeborg. 722
Pinciss, G.M. 311
Piot, Lazarus. 347 350 365–66
pirates. 426 518 528 564
plague. 72 567
Planchon, Roger. 618–19 720 722–23 737
Platonism. 287
Plautus. 356
plays.
    classical Indian. 229
    final. 4 5 14 59 65 72 74 91 158
    last. 6–8 17 22 30–31 40 55 63 67–69 71 75 79 87–88
        97–98 102–03 114–18 123–24 143 145 159 168 185 190 198
        201–03 227–29 245 268 271 274 277 283 285 287 308 310
        313 325 333 360 362 487
    late. 29 34 42 137 148 153 160 193 242–43 259 276 293
        333 504 635
    later. 3 11 89 179 186
    miracle. 18 32 109 111 155 212 308 528 554
    morality. 14 331 538
    mystery. 89 381
    play-within-play. 167 178
plot. 71 73 93 147 167 170 175 206 219 236 278 300 340
    346 435 443 463 472 527–28 542 554 791–95 797 799 804
    806–07 812
Plummer, Denis Lee. 226
Plutarch. 351 367 373 379 384–85
pneumatology. 214
poetry. 2 4 15–16 19 34 44 55 67 76 125 139 144 153 212
    226 259 309 403 430 443 810
Pollard, Alfred W. 394 421
Portia. 538
Possart, Ernst. 583 649

Posthumous. 201
Potts, Abbie Findlay. 362
Pozzi, Elizabetta. 571 637
Praetorius, Charles. 498-99
Praz, Mario. 537
pregnancy. 54 226
presentation. 265
Priapus. 264
Price, Roger Carson. 207
Princay, Marika. 639 771
printing houses. 413 417 467 513 528
Prior, Róger. 447 452 454 460
private theatres. 69 112
Priyadarsika. 229
prologue. 26 28 167
prose. 2 153 792
Proserpine. 111 428
Prospect Theatre Company. 611-12 696 700 709 712
Prospero. 11 59 133 142 149 254 271 292 313 333 656
Protheroe, Brian. 643 768 789
proverbs. 167
providence. 38 56 63 109 125 142 158 170 173 183 185 189
    196 242 261 268 272 280 290 294 300 308 317 329-30 349
    369 528 538 559 564
psychology. 107 263 280 288 294 328 333
psychosomatic. 223
public stage. 69 112
Pukstas, Daniel Joseph. 320
Puritanism. 79
purity. 67 177 280 324 757
Puttenham, George. 341
puzzle. 219
Pyrocles. 337 538 566

quartos.
    The Quarto (Q1 1609). 59 348 353-54 394 400 407-08 410
        413 415 518 420 430 445-46 449 451 453 461 463-64
        467-68 470-71 488-89 498 500-02 512-13 516 518 528
        534 538 542 560 564-67 570 576 686
    "bad" Quarto. 63 399 401 413 416 421 476 502 508
        513 518 528 538 554 564
    "good" Quarto. 116 407 416 427 436-37 457 508 538
    Q2 (1609). 499
    Q3 (1611). 461
    Q4 (1619). 394 438 445

Q1-Q4.   486 501
Q1-Q6.   500
as prompt copies.   405
quest.   170 256

Rabkin, Norman.   113 142 298
Racine.   63
Raith, Josef.   359
Rajasekharaiah, T.R.   88
Ranald, Margaret.   227
The Rare Triumphs of Love and Fortune.   112
Rathnavali.   229
Ratsi, I.   143
Ratsky, I.   245
Raysor, Thomas Middleton.   1
realism.   27 123 161 519 533 564 576
reality.   19 65 158 183 212
rebirth.   29 179 443 676
recognition.   33 278
recognition scene.   16 19-20 28 60 67 102 111 116 118 121
     125 134 144 162 166 168 175 179 193 200 267 278 280 286
     304 318 322 367 369-70 375 383 424 426 533 542 565 576
     663 666-67 676 681-82 696 758 789 798
Red Crosse Knight.   155 362
Redman, Amanda.   644 779
Regan.   121
regeneration.   29 197 264
Regent's Park, London.   594 656 678
Reinking, Karl Franz.   521
Renton, Godfrey.   592
reporters.   118 158   353 413 426 457 467 470-72 513 528
     538 564
resurrection.   7 14 29 89 178 218
rhyme.   439
Ribner, Irving.   551 554
Richardson, Ian.   609 685-87
Richardson, Tony.   603-04 663-67 669-71 673 676 678 680
     699 754
Richer, Janette.   677
riddles.   167 193 219 238 276 304 320-21 355 367 372 519
Ridley, M.R.   558
[Righter] Barton, Anne.   65 134
ritual.   14 23 167 219 304 309 333 370
Roberts, Alan.   747
Roberts, Jeanne Addison.   493

Roberts, Peter. 686
Roberts, Richard. 632 747 755
Robertson, Toby. 611-12 633 640 692 694-97 700 709 712-13
  731 754 757 766-67 769
Robin Hood plays. 199
Robinson, Henry Crabb. 1
Rodriquez, Robynn. 648 790
Rohrsen, Peter. 246
romance. 91 93 170 180 196 218 245 298 303 305 314-15 333
  382 409 551 564-66
  Alexandrine. 32 127
  ancient. 368
  conventions. 235
  dramatic. 9-10 21 41 94-95 108 124 154 302 308 366
  Greek. 11 156 160 170 202 220 229 346 357 370 378 538
  566
  Latin. 368
  medieval. 94 155 170 377
  Mediterranean. 249
  motifs. 71
  narrative. 302
  older. 807
  Renaissance. 170
  Shakespearean. 25 201
  Shakespeare's. 19-20 33 36 38 42 52 47-48 51 55-57 66
  72-75 83 92-93 98-100 104 110 113-15 121-23 128 132-33
  135 139 141-42 144 149 152 154 159 162 164 172 175 183
  186 192 194 202 205 210-11 218 220-22 225 231 233 236-
  37 239-40 245-46 249 251 253-56 263 265-66 270 273 278-
  79 288 292 295 298-99 315 322 325 328 331-32 340 349
  357 380 472 491 495 508-09 513 528 538 554 559 570 686
  758 800 807
  stage. 559
  theatrical. 94
Romania, Bucharest. 636 762 764
Romano, Guilio. 287
Romeo and Juliet. 19
Ronan, Clifford J. 385
Rook, Jean. 558
Rosalind. 538
Rose, Mark. 160
Rosolimos, Alexis. 630 739-41 743 748-49
Rotas, Vassilis. 549
Rothwell, Kenneth S. 759
Round, P.Z. 498-99

The Roundhouse, London.   612 695 700 754
Roux, Susan.   161
Rowley, William.   3 135 392 405 439 442 498–99 528
Rowse, A.L.   74 567
Royal Academy of Dramatic Art.   597
Royal Court, London.   603 669
Royal Shakespeare Company.   595 603–04 609 623 625 629
    744–46 750 753–54
royalty.   7 107 287
Rubin, Don.   698
Rudolf Steiner Hall, London.   596 678
Rudolstadt, Nationaltheater.   725
ruler.   152
Rush, Felix.   208
Russell, Patricia Howard.   95
Ruszt, Jozsef.   617 720
Ruth, Léon.   601 805
Rylands, George.   677

Sackler, Howard.   683
Sacks, Elizabeth.   283
Sacksteder, William.   790
Sadler's Wells, London.   582 650–53 659 672 680
Sainthill, Loudon.   664 669 671 673
saint's legend.   155
Sálgado, Gāmini.   715
Salinger, L.G.   109
Salisbury Court Theatre.   579
Sanderson, James L.   209
Sandier, Gilles.   723
Sandoe, Anne L.   610
Sandoe, James.   610 691
Satyrane.   362
Saudek, Erik Adolf.   529
savage man.   311 362
Saviour's, St.   567
Scales, Prunella.   677
scenery.   159 672 790
scenes.   105 197 564 816
Schanzer, Ernest.   247 538 555
Scheiber, V.R.   176
Schlegel, August Wilhelm.   521
Scheller, Bernhard.   724
Schiffhorst, Gerald Joseph.   189 261 434
Schotz, Myra Glazer.   284

Schrickx, Willem. 461
Schücking, L.L. 515
Schütze, Johannes. 273
Schwartz, Hans Günther. 144
Schwartz, Murray M. 280 288 294
Scofield, Paul. 595-96 684 719
Scott, William O. 369 375
sculpture. 567
sea. 29 39 73-74 80 99 121 135 173 322 429 564 567 576
    717
sea storm. 6 14 27 34 125 172 377 443 656
Seale, Douglas. 558 600 678 731
Seiler, Elisabeth. 634
Seiler, Grace Elizabeth. 415
Sejanus. 448
Sekiya, T. 228
self-consciousness. 292
Sellars, Peter. 642 770 777
semiotics. 318
Semon, Kenneth Jeffrey. 145 190-91
Senart, Philippe. 711
Seneca the Elder. 350
Sepulchre's, St. 402 447
sermon. 207
setting. 99 151 576 664 673 676 699 717 728 789
The Seven Deadly Sins, Part 2. 199
Shakespeare, Edmund. 567
Shakespeare Centre Library. 679
Shakespeare Recording Society. 684
Shakespeare's plays.
    All's Well That Ends Well. 157 194 196 211 234
    Antony and Cleopatra. 14 267 288 291 300 520 528
    As You Like It. 181 386
    The Comedy of Errors. 14 36 82 209 230 255 280 291 385
        504 647 775 780 782-84
    Coriolanus. 3 106 134 179 247 267 288 351
    Cymbeline. 7 11 14 22 31-32 41 49 51 60 63 67 70 73 83
        94-97 99 106 112-13 123-25 129 149 158 160 165 169
        174-75 182 184 186 197-98 216 222 225 231 234 254
        257 266-67 269 271 276 286 288 292-93 298 300 303
        305 308 312-13 328 331 333-34 340 349 397 403 496
        504 508 513 528 533 559 565 735 807
    Hamlet. 36 99 188 261 276 288 462
    1 and 2 Henry 4. 134 186 188 369 386
    Henry 5. 186 319 528

1-3 Henry 6. 432 441
Henry 8. 14 48-49 73 97 124 158 251 300 332 421 483
    508 807
Julius Caesar. 469 480 484 576
King Lear. 14 18 99 121 134 162 167 175-76 188 195 232
    253 258 261 276 278 284 288 300 331 364 369 405 707
Love's Labor's Lost. 96 134 564
Macbeth. 36 167 267 288 291 300 325 441 526 528
Measure for Measure. 94 157 174 196 211 230 340 364 407
The Merchant of Venice. 167 174 320 347
A Midsummer Night's Dream. 36 82 96
Much Ado About Nothing. 96 234
Othello. 288 320 386
Richard 2. 134 323
Richard 3. 135
Romeo and Juliet. 106
The Taming of the Shrew. 96 291
The Tempest. 7 14 49 63 67 70 73-74 76 83 89 93-95 97
    99 112 123-25 129 134-35 149 158 160 165 168-69 173-
    75 179 181 186 198 217 225 231 249 254-55 257-58
    266-67 271 276 280-81 286 288-89 291-93 298 300 303
    305 308 312-13 328 330-31 333-34 340 349 397 504 508
    513 533 564-65 707 735
Timon of Athens. 3 17 21 74 82 99 106 227 247 253 267
    288 351 396 403
Titus Andronicus. 106 291 385 469 480 484
Troilus and Cressida. 82 106 112 188 288
Twelfth Night. 2-3 11 14 22 141 261 280 504
The Two Gentlemen of Verona. 96
The Two Noble Kinsmen. 158 176 218 251 330 421 807
The Winter's Tale. 7 11 14 22 31 49-50 63 67-68 70 73
    76 82-83 89 92 94-97 99 112 121 123-25 129 133 149
    158 160-62 165 169 174-75 179 186 198 217 222 225
    231 234 247 253-54 257 266-67 271 276 280 284 286
    288 291-93 298 300 303 305 308 312-13 328 331-34
    340 349 364 397 504 508 513 528 533 538 559 564-65
    686 735
Shakespeare's poetry (Sonnet 73). 380
Shattuck, Charles H. 680
Shaw, Gary Howard. 334
Shaw, Steve. 647
Shelving, Paul. 558
Shih-ch'iu. 547
Shipley, Sandra. 642
Sider, John Wm. 174

Sidney, Sir Philip. 25
   Arcadia. 25 337 366 376 528 538 560 566 807
silence. 278 296
Silva, Naoe Takei da. 285
Silverman, John Michael. 114
Silvestru, Valentin. 764
Simić, Zivojin. 517 568
Simonides. 58 426 656
Simonides and daughter. 171 244
Simonides' court. 193 656 717
Simpson, Percy. 356
Simpson, Robert Ritchie. 54
sin. 63 68 70 94 111 116 124 155 193 201 238 284 290 313
   321 324 383 407 426 429 434 471 542 685
Singer, Samuel. 337 342 660
Sinnott, Bethany Strong. 175
Sir Orfeo. 377
Sisson, Charles Jasper. 405 420 512 542
Sitwell, Edith. 15
Skelton, John. 199
Sladek, J.V. 535
slap (5.1). 60 367 369-70 383 447 792
Slater, Daphne. 595-96
Słomcyzñki, Maciej. 574
Smirnov, A. 524
Smith, Craig. 633
Smith, Gordon Ross. 485
Smith, Grover. 13
Smith, Hallett. 115 162 560-61
Smith, M.W.A. 473-77 479-80 482-83
Smith College Theatre Workshop. 568 661 794
Smyth, Albert Henry. 338 342
Snodin, David. 576
society. 197 218
Solberg, Susan Riley. 146
Solomos, Alexis. 630 739-41 743 748-49
sons. 280
Sophia. 179
Sophocles. 20
   Oedipus Rex. 276 367
Sotiriadis, H. 748
sound. 153 278
Spalding Kenneth J. 31
Speaight, Robert W. 687 699
spectacle. 69 95 159 166 170 218-19 221 278 297 351 528

567 651 710-11 760 763 807
Spencer, Hazelton. 10
Spencer, Theodore. 17
Spenser, Edmund. 18 155 290 311 362 807
Spevak, Marvin. 486 492
Spiker, Sina. 400
Sprague, Arthur Colby. 690
spring. 23
Squire, William. 677
Srinivasa, K.R. Iyengar. 75 90
stage directions. 419 421 467 486 576
stage props. 317 790
stagecraft. 109 816
staging. 80 91 207 221 265 333 409 649 651 676 681 714 717
    736 746 768 771 794
Starrett, Agnes Lynch. 408
Staník, Peter. 646
Stationers' Register. 399
Stauffer, Donald A. 18
Stedman, Jane W. 712
Steevens, George. 390
Stefko, Vladimir. 785
Steinitzer, H. 515
stella maris. 38
Stephan, Erika. 725
Stephens. 581
stereotyped characters. 71
Stevens, John. 803
Stevenson, Juliet. 644
Stewart, Fiona. 647
stoic. 261
storm. 6 14 34 56 125 151 172 270 294 377 443
storm scene. 2 3 67 121 429 538
    Pentapolis. 172
    Thaisa's "death." 172 190
storytelling. 200 266 746 750 753-54
Strachey, G. Lytton. 4
Stratford East. 643 765 768 772 789
Stratford, Ontario. 694 698 701-02 704 706 710 714 718
    754
Stratford-upon-Avon. 584 654-55 657 663-68 670-71 673
    676 678 680 685-90 731
Stratton, John David. 147
Stroux, Karl Heinz. 634 758 760 763
structure. 28 32 34 42 47-49 67-68 71 96 114 124 127 136
    144 147 160-61 167 175 183 197 231 235 243 264 268 293

300 303 319 322 324 331 349 377 443 528 538 551
Stuart, Betty Kantor. 124
Stuarts. 176
Stukas, Regine. 148
Stuttgart. 635
Styan, J.L. 718
style. 167 169 204 215 333 447 560
styles, authorial. 353 456-57 470 528
stylometrics. 456 459 465-66 469 473-77 479-84
submission. 282
subtext. 296
suffering. 282
Suga, Yasuo. 289
Sumner, Mary. 587
Sweeney, Beth. 626
Swinburne, Algernon. 2 5 414
Sykes, H. Dugdale. 348 395 398-99 406
Sylvain, Alexandre. 347 350 365-66
symbolic. 34
symbolism. 48 125
symbols. 79 107 180 231
    death and birth. 34 125
    fertility. 30
    joy of life. 30
    life journey. 128
    love. 34
    old and new. 125
    pilgrimage. 34
    religious. 79 542
    resurrection. 30
    storm and calm. 125
    tempests. 34
symmetry. 93

Tachibana, Tadnae. 64
Tacitus. 448
Takahashi, Shuzo. 274
Takahashi, Yasunari. 299
Takayama, Hiroko. 275
Tanaka, Susumu. 192
Tanner, Tony. 276
Taylerson, Marilyn. 611 696-97 700
Taylor, Don. 789
Taylor, Michael. 789
teaching. 236

television. 576 644 779 789
tempest. 6 14 34 56 125 151 172 270 294 377 443
Temple Shakespeare. 503 515
tennis. 13
Tennyson, Alfred Lord. 393 414 458
testing. 201 205
text. 118 816
text-subtext. 296
Thaisa. 7 23 34 47 67-68 89 121 125 200 234 312 383 410
    426 429 656
Thaisa and Marina. 284
Tharsus. 47 358 387 656 681 717
theatre. 10 48 115 292 297 317-18
Théâtre des Amandiers, Nanterre. 619 723
Theatre in the Bowery, New York. 633
Theatre Royal, Covent Garden. 581 791
Themelis. 749
themes. 108 231 303 331
    Antiochus. 461
    appearance and reality. 36 62 197
    art. 160
    banishment. 186
    birth. 6 14
    birth-death-rebirth. 129
    court versus country. 103
    courtship. 47
    danger. 47
    death. 6 7 14 90
    degree. 68
    disharmony. 83
    disintegration. ̄197
    disorder. 6
    evil. 90
    faith. 90 363
    families. 34 197 287
    famine. 47
    fate. 812
    father and daughter. 129 175
    feasting. 291
    fertility. 211
    finding. 7
    folk. 96
    forgiveness. 74 87 94
    fortune. 170
    friendship. 129

generations. 218 283
gentleness. 60
grace. 36 38
guilt. 89
harmony. 6 72 83
heritage. 193
husband and wife. 775
immortality. 254
incest. 167 194 217
innocence. 89
jealousy. 73
journey. 6 14
judgement. 68
king. 40 194
kingship. 313 363
life and death. 123
loss and recovery. 67 75
lost. 7
love. 6 7 212 686
magical princess. 40
magnanimity. 129
man and woman. 129
marriage. 211
masculine self-hood. 280
nature. 38
nobility. 197
obedience. 150
patience. 25 90 162 209 242 287 363 528
physician's daughter. 194
providence. 38 170
purgation. 99
quest. 170
recognition. 33
reconciliation. 20 33 74 87
recovery. 264
redemption. 38 68 99
regeneration. 29 197 264
reintegration. 218
renascence. 234
repentance. 94
restoration. 76 272
resurrection. 7 14 89 218
return. 249
reunion. 34 40 72 74
royalty. 7 287

self-recognition. 20
separation. 34 40 72 186 504
sexual maturation. 237
sin. 68 94
society. 197
spring. 23
the state. 197
storm. 172
tennis. 13
time. 287 686
virginity. 211
wandering. 249
willfulness and meekness. 129
wit and balance. 129
worth. 197
youth and age. 129
theology. 115
theophany. 51 89 178 185 201 287 308
Thomas, Sidney. 478
Thorndike, Ashley H. 66 340
Thorne, William Barry. 96 149 313
Tieck, Ludwig. 521 760
Tillyard, E.M.W. 8
time. 109 163 192 196 226 266 277 287 296 322 686 735 807
Time. 271
timelessness. 816
Timon. 21 172
Tintoretto. 287
Tobias, Richard C. 185 193
Tokyo. 622 627 738
Tomita, Soko. 314
Tomkins, J.M.S. 351 367 538
tournament. 130 158 369 376 387
tragedy. 17 29 31 33 91 127 143 158 169 174 176 254 288
    300 331
tragedies. 38 42 99 105-06 192 278 296 299
tragicomedy. 11 37 47 66 92 119 127 143 146 152 158 165
    169 176 189-90 196 198 224 240 272 290 313 330 409 508
    528 559 805 807
transformations. 128
Traversi, Derek. 34 40 79 125
Trewin, J.C. 655 675 678 690 700 726 750
trial of merit. 201
Tristram, Philippa. 321
Trow, J.D. 616 716

truth. 306 816
Twine, Laurence.
   The Patterne of Painefull Adventures. 26 170 264 335
   338-39 348 351-53 360 366 369 376 388 400 407 409 411
   413 415 418 426-27 463 470-71 504 508 513 528 538 560
   564 566-67 576 736
twins. 280
types. 161
Tyre scene (1.2). 464 656

Ueno, Yoshiko. 126 210 315
Ultz, David. 643 765 768 772 789
Ulysses. 90 367 558
Una. 362
Under Thirty Group. 596
Ungerer, Gustav. 327
unity. 146 170 189 201 209 232 363 528 576
Uphaus, Robert W. 300
Ur-Pericles. 63 348 353 360 363-64 383 399 408-09 411-12
   415-16 418 426-27 430 434 461 463 467 470-71 498 508
   513 528
Urwin, George Glencairn. 808
Usherwood, Stephen. 806

Valo, Peter. 786
Van Domelen, John Emory. 97
Vaughn, Jack A. 286
Veelo, G. Van. 668
Velz, John W. 487
Venus. 68 227 252
Vere, Edward de. 35
verisimilitude. 95 155
Vermont, Champlain Shakespeare Festival. 631 759
Vianello, Gianni. 771
villains. 311 325
Vincent, Mrs. 581
Vines, Margaret. 594
viol. 122 250 327
Virginia. 111 155
vision. 19 87-88 102 129 277 377 758
Vrbka, Stanislav. 787
Vuletic, Jenny. 647
Vydrová, Monika. 788

Waage, Frederick O. 287

Wada, Yuichi. 262
Waith, Eugene. 350
Wallach, Susan Levi. 751
Ward, Peter. 752
The Warehouse, London. 625 629 744-46 750
Warnecke, Klare. 760
Warren, Michael J. 444
Warren, Roger. 753 789
Wasson, John. 435
Weimar. 316 620 724-25 733
Weinstock, Horst. 150
Weisz, Carole Lynn. 263
Wells, Henry W. 229
Wells, Stanley. 491
Welsh, Andrew. 193
West, Timothy. 814
Weston, David. 814
Wheeler, Richard P. 194 288 301
White, Howard B. 372
White, R.S. 302
White, William. 528
Whitehall. 159 176
Wickham, Glynne. 176
Wigod, Sheldon William. 151
Wilders, John. 576
Wilkins, George. 3 76 343 348 351 353 360 388 391-92 395-
   96 398 402 431 447 452 454 460 498-99 567
   The Historie of Justine. 431
   The Miseries of Inforst Marriage. 388 395 406 439-40
   442 447 460-61
   The Painfull Aduentures. 63 335 337-39 343 348 351 353
   360 363 366 379 388 395 399-400 406-09 411 413 415 418
   424 426-27 430 447 452 460 463 467 470-71 504 508-09
   513 518 528 538 559 564-67 576 686 701 731 753 789
   Three Miseries of Barbary. 406
   Travailes of the Three English Brothers. 388 391 395
   405 439-40 442 528
Williamson, Laird. 648 790
Wilson, Gary H. 810
Wilson, Snoo. 809
Willy, Margaret. 679
Wincor, Richard. 23
Winzer, Klaus-Dieter. 761
wish fulfillment. 184 333
wishes. 196

women. 227 230 241 249 251 256 266 274 296 299 447 724
wonder. 27 145 190-91 199 257 265 278 317 370 520 538 576
  816
Wood, James O. 273 375 432 436-37 441 450-51 455 464 471
Woodbridge, L.T. 386
words. 91 104 134 166 197 278 309 318 816
Wordsworth, William. 7
Worsley, T.C. 669
Wright, Louis B. 566
Wright, William Aldis. 497
Wylie, Betty Jane. 701
Wymark, Patrick. 604 664

Yamagishi, Masayuki. 277 289
Yamamoto, Hiroshi. 738
Yasuo, Tamaizumi. 285
A Yorkshire Tragedy. 395
Yoshimatsu, Sachiko. 230
Young, C.B. 513 661
Young, David. 163
youth. 129 233 504 538 737 765 790
Yugoslavia, Nitra. 646 776 781 785-88

Zacharias, Peter James. 152
Zesmer, David M. 812
Zeynek, Theodor von. 519
Zolbrod, Paul G. 185 193
Zukofsky, Celia. 801
Zürich Stadtbibliothek. 335 353